THE SOUTHERN PRESS
IN THE CIVIL WAR

THE SOUTHERN PRESS IN THE CIVIL WAR

American Wars and the Media
in Primary Documents

Debra Reddin van Tuyll

Greenwood Press
Westport, Connecticut • London

Library of Congress Cataloging-in-Publication Data is available at www.loc.gov.

British Library Cataloguing in Publication Data is available.

ISBN: 0–313–32932–X

First published in 2005

Greenwood Press, 88 Post Road West, Westport, CT 06881
An imprint of Greenwood Publishing Group, Inc.
www.greenwood.com

Printed in the United States of America

The paper used in this book complies with the
Permanent Paper Standard issued by the National
Information Standards Organization (Z39.48–1984).

P

CONTENTS

2 Reporting the War, 1861   17

ACKNOWLEDGMENTS

Any book is a collaborative effort, even those that bear only one name on the cover. One person in particular, though, deserves the first and biggest "thank you" for all her help. That person is Dar Scarff, interlibrary loan librarian at Augusta State University. Dar has tracked down obscure Confederate newspapers for me with the intrepidity of Sherlock Holmes's most skillful Baker Street irregular. Thanks also go to Dr. Lillie Johnson, my department chair at Augusta State, for funding a student worker to help with some of the early typing of the articles in this manuscript. My greatest debt, though, is to my husband, Hubert, who juggled his own teaching, research, and home improvement projects to give me the time I needed to huddle over the microfilm reader and the computer.

TIMELINE

1860

6 November	Lincoln is elected president.
20 December	South Carolina secedes from the Union.
26 December	Major Robert Anderson moves his force from Fort Moultrie in Charleston Harbor to Fort Sumter, which he believes can be more easily defended with a small force. Southerners see this as a hostile move.

1861

9 January	Mississippi secedes; South Carolina batteries commit the first act of war by firing on the *Star of the West* to prevent it from bringing reinforcements to Fort Sumter.
10 January	Florida secedes.
11 January	Alabama secedes.
19 January	Georgia secedes.
26 January	Louisiana secedes.
29 January	Kansas is admitted to the Union.
1 February	Texas secedes.
8 February	Delegates from the six seceded states form the Confederate Congress in Montgomery and begin work on a provisional Constitution for the newly formed Confederate States of America (CSA).
9 February	Mississippian Jefferson Davis is elected president of the Confederate States of America with Georgian Alexander H. Stephens as his vice president. Davis is not in Montgomery; he is at his plantation in Mississippi when he receives word of his election.

15 February	Davis appoints a peace commission to negotiate with Union leaders. They are unsuccessful.
18 February	Davis and Stephens are inaugurated in Montgomery.
4 March	Abraham Lincoln is inaugurated president of the United States.
6 March	Davis calls for 100,000 volunteers to serve for 1 year in the Confederate army. By mid-April, the South had 35,000 men in the military, about twice the existing U.S. force of 16,367.
10 April	General Pierre Gustav Toutant Beauregard receives and carries out the order to demand the surrender of Fort Sumter. Major Anderson refuses.
12–14 April	Confederate batteries begin shelling Fort Sumter, which is garrisoned by eighty-three men, seven officers, and seventy-six enlisted.
13 April	Major Anderson officially surrenders.
14 April	Federal troops evacuate Fort Sumter.
15 April	Lincoln calls for 75,000 men to volunteer for three months of military service.
17 April	Virginia secedes.
19 April	Lincoln proclaims a blockade of Southern ports. Union troops from Massachusetts are attacked by a pro-Confederate street mob, and two soldiers are killed.
20 April	Norfolk Navy Yard is captured by the Virginia militia for the Confederacy.
3 May	Lincoln calls for volunteers for three years and orders the size of the regular army increased.
6 May	Arkansas secedes.
20 May	North Carolina secedes.
24 May	Kentucky declares its neutrality. Virginia militia occupy Alexandria.
1 June	Battle of Boonville, Missouri. Union General Nathaniel F. Lyon drives pro-South militia toward Arkansas. They are reinforced by Arkansas militia and try to retake Missouri for the Confederacy. Lyon's force wins.
3 June	First skirmish of the war at Philippi, Virginia. Major General G. B. McClellan clears the town of Confederate troops.
10 June	Confederate troops defeat Union troops at Big Bethel, Virginia.
11 June	Federal troops defeat Confederate troops at Romney, Virginia.
17 June	Federal troops defeat Confederate troops at Boonville, Missouri.
3 July	Lincoln organizes the Department of the West and places General John C. Frémont in command.
5 July	Confederate troops defeat Union troops at Cartage, Missouri.

11 July	Union troops defeat Confederate troops at Rich Mountain, Virginia.
19 July	38,000 Union soldiers move out from Washington to attack Confederate forces of 20,000 near Manassas, Virginia.
21 July	First Battle of Manassas. This is the first major battle of the war. Confederates rout the Union and chase them almost all the way back to Washington, D.C.
1 August	General George B. McClellan is given command of the Army of the Potomac.
2 August	Battle of Dug Spring, Missouri, a Union victory.
6 August	Union Brigadier General Ulysses S. Grant attempts to occupy Paducah, Kentucky, but is forestalled by Confederate forces under Major General Leonidas Polk.
10 August	Skirmish at Wilson's Creek, Missouri, a Confederate victory.
20 August	Confederates capture Union garrison at Lexington, Missouri.
28–29 August	Fighting at Hattaras Inlet, North Carolina, a Union victory.
12–13 September	Battle of Cheat Mountain. Lee is repulsed by Union troops in his attempt to recover western Virginia.
21 October	Fighting at Balls Bluff, Virginia, a Confederate victory.
31 October	General Winfield Scott, a hero of the Mexican-American War of the 1850s, retires. He is succeeded by McClellan as general-in-chief of the U.S. Armies.
7 November	Port Royal, South Carolina, falls to Union forces.
8 November	The *Trent* Affair. Charles Wilkes, captain of the USS *San Jacinto*, stopped the British packet *Trent* in the Bahamas and forcibly removed two Confederate representatives who were on their way to England to negotiate for recognition. The action nearly led to war with Great Britain, but American diplomatic efforts were able to smooth out the disagreement.

1862

19 January	Battle of Mill Springs, Kentucky, a Union victory.
27 January	Lincoln issues General War Order No. 1 authorizing a unified and aggressive attack on the Confederacy.
6 February	Fort Henry in Tennessee falls to the Union army.
8 February	Roanoke Island, North Carolina, falls to the Union.
16 February	Fort Donelson in Tennessee falls to the Union army after three days of hard fighting. Nearly 15,000 Confederate troops are captured with Fort Donelson.
17 February	CSA provisional congress is terminated. Permanent Congress of the Confederate States is organized.
18 February	Davis and Stephens are inaugurated as president and vice president of the Confederate States of America. They will serve six-year terms, as specified in the Confederate Constitution.

24 February	Nashville, Tennessee, surrenders to the Union.
26 February	Union troops occupy Nashville.
7–8 March	Battle of Pea Ridge, Arkansas. This Union victory gives the United States control of Missouri.
8 March	Peninsular Campaign begins after Lincoln reorganizes the Army of Virginia and relieves McClellan of supreme command. McClellan, who has angered the president with his refusal to act against the Confederates, is given command of the Army of the Potomac and ordered to attack Richmond. Battle of Hampton Roads, Virginia, begins.
9 March	CSS *Virginia* and USS *Monitor* battle at Hampton Roads. Results were inconclusive.
14 March	Battle of New Madrid, Missouri, a Union victory.
23 March	Stonewall Jackson is defeated at Kernstown, Virginia, the first action in the Shenandoah Valley.
6–7 April	Battle of Shiloh, Union victory. Confederate General Albert Sydney Johnson is killed.
10–11 April	Fort Pulaski near Savannah is surrendered to the Union.
15 April	Battle of Peralta, New Mexico, a Union victory.
16 April	Confederate Congress approves draft for men eighteen to thirty-five, with certain exemptions that include journalists, blacksmiths, overseers, and others.
24 April	Federal fleet gets past forts near New Orleans.
25 April	Union captures New Orleans.
1 May	Union forces officially occupy New Orleans.
4 May	Union occupies Yorktown, Virginia, after Confederate withdrawal on 3 May.
5 May	Battle of Williamsburg, Virginia, a Union victory.
8 May	Battle of McDowell, Virginia, a Confederate victory.
9 May	Union advances on Richmond; Confederates abandon Norfolk; Pensacola naval yard evacuated by Confederates.
12 May	Union occupies Baton Rouge, Louisiana.
23 May	Confederates recapture Front Royal, Virginia.
25 May	Confederates run Union troops out of Winchester, Virginia.
26 May	Bombardment of Vicksburg begins; skirmish at Hanover Court House, Virginia.
27 May	Confederates evacuate Corinth, Mississippi.
31 May	Battle of Seven Pines (Fair Oaks) begins.
1 June	Robert E. Lee is appointed to command the Army of Northern Virginia after Joseph E. Johnston is wounded.
4 June	Confederates evacuate Fort Pillow in Tennessee.

6 June	Gunboat battle in front of Memphis. City surrenders and is occupied.
8–9 June	Confederates defeat Union troops at Battle of Cross Keys and Port Republic, Virginia.
25 June	Seven Days Battles begin, resulting in Union retreat. Battles continue through 1 July. On 2 July, Confederates withdraw to Richmond, ending the Peninsular Campaign. Battles fought in this period at Mechanicsville (26–27 June); Gaines's Mill (27 June); Savage's Station (29 June); Frayser's Farm (30 June); and Malvern Hill (1 July).
26 June	Battle of Mechanicsville, Virginia.
27 June	Battle of Gaines's Mill, Virginia.
29–30 June	Battles of Peach Orchard, Savage State, White Oak Swamp, Glendale-Frayser's Farm in Virginia.
1 July	Battle of Malvern Hill, Virginia.
13 July	Battle of Murfeesboro, Tennessee.
22 July	Confederate and Union government agree to a general exchange of prisoners.
24 July	Union gunboats abandon contest at Vicksburg.
9 August	Battle of Cedar Mountain, Virginia, a Confederate victory
29–30 August	Second Battle of Manassas begins and lasts until 1 September, a Confederate victory.
30 August	Battle of Richmond, Kentucky, a Confederate victory.
31 August	Battle of Chantilly, Virginia.
4 September	Army of Northern Virginia crosses the Potomac in an invasion of Maryland.
7 September	McClellan follows Lee into Maryland.
12 September	McClellan reaches Frederick, where his advance guard finds a copy of an order Lee had written that detailed Confederate troop placements and movements.
14 September	Battle of South Mountain, Maryland.
14–15 September	Harper's Ferry falls to the Confederates, along with 12,000 Union soldiers and many supplies.
17 September	Battle of Antietam Creek near Sharpsburg, Maryland. Federals and Confederates clash in the single bloodiest day of the Civil War. More than 2,000 Union soldiers died, and 9,500 were wounded. On the Confederate side, 2,700 men lost their lives, and 9,000 were wounded. The result is inconclusive, though Lee's retreat back into Virginia allowed McClellan to claim victory. The contest had a profoundly bad result for the Confederates; the French and English decided to forestall their decisions on official recognition of the Confederacy, and it gave Lincoln

the justification to announce his Preliminary Emancipation Proclamation, which announced all slaves in areas rebelling against the United States would be freed on 1 January 1863.

19 September	Confederates defeated at Iuka, Mississippi.
20 September	Battle of Shepherdstown, Virginia.
22 September	Lincoln announces the Preliminary Emancipation Proclamation.
23 September	Battle of Sabine Pass.
25 September	General Beauregard assumes command of the army on the coast near Charleston.
3–4 October	Battle of Corinth, Mississippi.
8 October	Battle of Perryville, Kentucky.
9 October	Union occupies Galveston, Texas.
10 October	Confederate cavalry commander General J.E.B. Stuart makes a raiding expedition into Pennsylvania.
7 November	General Ambrose E. Burnside is appointed commander of the Army of the Potomac, replacing McClellan.
7 December	Battle of Prairie Grove, Arkansas. Union gains control of northern Arkansas.
11 December	Burnside crosses the Rappahannock at Fredericksburg. Lee did not contest the crossing.
13 December	Battle of Fredericksburg, a Confederate victory. The Union army lost 12,000 men in this four-day battle.
29 December	Murfreesboro Stones River Campaign, a Confederate victory.
30 December	Lincoln issues the Emancipation Proclamation.
31 December	Battle of Murfreesboro (Stones River), Tennessee; concludes 2 January 1863.

1863

1 January	Emancipation Proclamation freed slaves in the rebelling states. Major General John B. Magruder recaptures Galveston.
2 January	Battle of Stones River.
14 March	Admiral Farragut steams past Port Hudson on the Mississippi.
7 April	Federal gunboats attack Fort Sumter and begin the siege of Charleston Harbor.
1 May	Union forces, led by Ulysses S. Grant, defeat Confederate forces at Port Gibson, Mississippi, in the opening move toward Vicksburg.
1–6 May	Battle of Chancellorsville.
2 May	Battle of Chancellorsville begins. It will continue through 6 May. The Confederates force Hooker to withdraw across the Rappahannock River, but the victory is costly for the South in terms of the number of men killed or wounded.
3 May	Second Battle of Fredericksburg.

10 May	Stonewall Jackson dies of pneumonia following the amputation of his arm after the Battle of Chancellorsville. Jackson had been shot accidentally by two of his men.
16 May	Battle of Champion's Hill, Mississippi.
19 May	Siege of Vicksburg begins.
3 June	Lee's Army of Northern Virginia begins its second invasion of the North.
9 June	Battle of Brandy Station.
13 June	Second Battle of Winchester. Army of Northern Virginia defeats Union forces at Winchester, Virginia, and then continue North on their march into Maryland and Pennsylvania.
15–24 June	Lee crosses the Potomac with 76,000 men.
1–3 July	Battle of Gettysburg. This Confederate defeat puts an end to Southern hopes for recognition by England and France.
4 July	Vicksburg surrenders. Pemberton turns 30,000 Confederate soldiers over to Grant after a six-week-long siege.
4–14 July	Lee's army retreats from Maryland to Virginia.
9 July	Port Hudson, Louisiana, surrenders to federal troops.
10–11 July	Fighting at Battery Wagner in Charleston Harbor.
16 July	Major General William T. Sherman leads federal troops in an attack on Jackson, Mississippi, that leaves the city devastated.
17 August	Bombardment of Fort Sumter begins and continues for 6 days. The fort's garrison holds out.
6 September	Union troops occupy Fort Wagner near Charleston.
9 September	Federals enter Chattanooga.
19–20 September	Confederates, led by General Braxton Bragg, win the Battle of Chickamauga. Federals retreat into Chattanooga.
24 November	Battle of Lookout Mountain begins. Federal forces put Confederates away from Chattanooga and deeper into Georgia. Sets the stage for Sherman's Atlanta Campaign the following spring.
25 November	Battle of Missionary Ridge.

1864

20 February	Battle of Olustee.
22 February	Battle of Okolona, Mississippi, a Confederate victory.
28 February	First day of the Kilpatrick-Dahlgren Raid, which continued until 2 March. Union Major General Judson Kilpatrick headed toward Richmond with 4,500 horsemen. Possibly forged papers regarding the plan, found on the body of Colonel Ulric Dahlgren, indicated Kilpatrick intended to burn the city and assassinate Jefferson Davis and his cabinet. Mead disavowed any knowledge of the plan.
18 April	Confederate troops recapture Fort Pillow.

4 May	Sherman begins his Atlanta Campaign that culminates in his famed March to the Sea the following fall. Grant crosses the Rapidan to begin implementation of his planned Wilderness Campaign.
5–6 May	Battle of The Wilderness in Virginia. Lee is driven back.
8–18 May	Battle of Spotsylvania, a Confederate victory.
11 May	Battle of Yellow Tavern.
13–15 May	Battle of Resaca, Georgia, a Confederate defeat.
15 May	Battles of Drewry's Bluff and New Market.
23–31 May	North Anna and Haw's Shop.
3–12 June	Cold Harbor Campaign, Virginia, a Confederate victory. Grant loses more than 7,000 men in twenty minutes on 3 June. This is Lee's last clear victory of the war.
10 June	Battle of Brice's Cross Roads, Mississippi.
11–12 June	Battle of Trevilian Station, Virginia.
15–18 June	Battle of Petersburg, Virginia.
18 June	Grant begins siege of Petersburg, Virginia.
25 June	Battle of Missionary Ridge, Tennessee.
27 June	Battle of Kennesaw Mountain, a Confederate victory.
9 July	Battle of Monocacy, Maryland.
12 July	Confederate forces are repulsed after reaching the outskirts of Washington, D.C.
14–15 July	Battle of Tupelo, Mississippi, a Confederate defeat.
20 July	Battle of Peachtree Creek, Georgia.
22–28 July	Battle of Atlanta, a Confederate defeat.
28 July	Battle of Ezra Church, a Confederate defeat.
30 July	Battle of the Crater in Virginia, a Confederate victory.
5 August	Battle of Mobile Bay, a Confederate defeat.
27–31 August	Fall of Atlanta.
1 September	Confederates evacuate Atlanta.
2 September	Sherman captures Atlanta.
4 September	Sherman orders civilians out of Atlanta.
19 September	Third Battle of Winchester, Virginia, a Confederate defeat.
22 September	Battle of Fisher's Hill, Virginia, a Confederate defeat.
23 September	Jefferson Davis travels to Macon, Georgia, to speak to the Atlanta refugees there. He reveals that two-thirds of the Confederate army are missing from the ranks. The *Macon Telegraph* reports this story, and Sherman reads it. Fort Morgan, Alabama, the last defense for Mobile Bay, falls. The port of Mobile is closed, but the city is not captured.
19 October	Battle of Cedar Creek, Virginia. Sheridan runs Confederates from the Shenandoah Valley.

23 October	Battle of Westport, Missouri, a Confederate defeat.
15 November	Sherman burns Atlanta and leaves it behind as he embarks with two columns on his infamous March to the Sea.
22 November	Battle of Griswoldville, Georgia, a Confederate defeat.
30 November	Battle of Franklin, Tennessee. Five Confederate generals killed.
4 December	Battle of Waynesboro, Georgia, a Confederate defeat.
13 December	Sherman captures Fort McAllister, exposing Savannah.
15–16 December	Battle of Nashville, a Confederate defeat.
22 December	Sherman captures Savannah.

1865

17 February	Sherman's troops burn Columbia, South Carolina.
18 February	Fort Sumter is abandoned. Federals seize Charleston.
22 February	Fall of Wilmington, North Carolina.
2 March	Battle of Waynesboro, a Confederate defeat.
13 March	Confederate Congress approves drafting slaves into the army, with the promise of freedom for good military service.
19–20 March	Battle of Bentonville, North Carolina, a Confederate defeat.
24 March	Battle of Fort Steadman in Virginia, a Confederate defeat.
29–31 March	Battle of Dinwiddie Court House in Virginia.
1 April	Battle of Five Forks, near Petersburg, Virginia.
2 April	Confederate Congress evacuates Richmond. Petersburg, Virginia, falls after a ten-month siege. Wilson's cavalry assaults earthworks near Selma, Alabama, in the Battle of Selma, a Confederate defeat.
6–7 April	Battle at Sayler's Creek, Virginia, a Confederate defeat.
9 April	Battle of Appomattox, a Confederate defeat. Lee surrenders at Appomattox Courthouse, Virginia.
14 April	John Wilkes Booth assassinates President Lincoln.
26 April	General Joseph Johnston surrenders to Sherman at Durham, North Carolina; Confederate cabinet meets for the last time at Charlotte, North Carolina. Davis intends to flee west to meet up with Kirby Smith and his troops, but he will be captured in a few days near Washington, Georgia.
10 May	Wilson captures Jefferson Davis near Washington, Georgia.
13 May	Last battle of the war is fought, the Battle of Pamito Ranch near Brownsville, Texas.
26 May	Kirby Smith surrenders his troops.
29 May	President Andrew Johnson issues his Proclamation of Amnesty, officially ending the Civil War.

INTRODUCTION

THE BEST HISTORY OF THE WAR—The best history of the present war that has been, or ever will be, written is already penned. It will be found in the newspapers of the Confederacy. Any man who has a complete file of any good newspaper that has been published uninterruptedly during the War, has the best and most complete history of the revolution that will ever be written. He owns an invaluable piece of property, which will serve to teach his children not only the great events that occurred in the progress of this unparalleled war, but to afford them a narrative more intensely interesting than any romance that was ever written. And yet how little importance is attached to a newspaper by many people. It is read and thrown away as lightly as a squeezed orange.

—*The Western Democrat*
Charlotte, North Carolina
28 March 1865

The story of the Southern press in the Civil War did not begin at 4:30 A.M. on 12 April 1861 when Virginia newspaper editor Edmund Ruffin fired the first shot at Fort Sumter.[1] Nor did it begin some two months previously when leading men of the six seceded states gathered in Montgomery to form a new government, complete with a Constitution, a Congress, and a chief executive. The story did not even really begin with the presidential election of 1860, though for the sake of convenience, that is where this work will start. In truth, the story of the Southern press in the Civil War began at least a decade prior to 1860—and perhaps as much as thirty years before.

For the better part of the period 1832 to 1860, a number of Southern newspapers did their best to foment secession sentiment. In the early part of America's national history, the country's two regions had more commonalities than differences, but this began to change in the 1820s as the debate heated up between Southern slaveholders and Northern abolitionists. Sectional tensions developed over issues such as nullification and the westward expansion of slavery. The underlying issue involved property rights. Slaves were, by law, property, and Southerners did not believe anyone should have the right to tell them where they could or could not take their belongings. Usually, the arguments were framed more in terms of protecting Southern rights, or states' rights, but there was a subtle threat of secession, should Southern rights not be protected within the Union.

Journalists were the leading spokesmen for the parties debating these issues. Most antebellum newspapermen, even in the South, were pro-union, but those few determined voices of the fire-eaters could keep the idea of secession at the forefront of public thought. Fire-eaters were men like Robert Barnwell Rhett, a prominent Charleston journalist, politician, and disciple of John C. Calhoun. Rhett and other fire-eaters worked feverishly throughout the antebellum period for Southern rights and threatened secession if their rights were not upheld. The Charleston editor, though, had an advantage other fire-eaters did not: the *Charleston Mercury*. Rhett used his well-known newspaper to pound away mercilessly with demands for states' rights and Southern independence.

The radical fire-eating perspective was not the only one represented by Southern newspapers in the antebellum period, nor was it the position of most journalists or citizens. Opposing opinions ranged from staunch unionism, that is, the idea that the states should stay together in one country, no matter what, to a perspective described as "cooperationist." The cooperationists were a group of Southerners who did not rule out secession entirely but who believed that secession should be a last resort. For example, most fire-eaters believed the election of a Republican president was sufficient justification for secession since that party supported abolition of slavery. Cooperationists did not agree. They argued that the president alone cannot affect U.S. policy or law. It would take a Republican president and a Republican Congress to outlaw slavery, so even after Lincoln was elected in 1860, cooperationists were not ready to secede. They believed secession would be justified only if Lincoln took some action against the South. Further, cooperationists believed that any steps to dissolve the Union should be taken in concert by all the cotton states rather than by separate state action.[2] Most Southern newspapers initially advocated positions that were closer to the cooperationists or unionists than the fire-eaters. Much of that initial editorial caution began to fade and eventually move toward support for secession following the confrontation over Fort Sumter and Lincoln's call for 75,000 volunteers to put down the rebellion.

A LITTLE BACKGROUND

The nineteenth-century Southern press has sometimes been treated as an anomaly in American journalism history. Some scholars have viewed it as a poor relation of mainstream American journalism, a sort of out-of-step, slightly eccentric (some have considered it extremely eccentric), red-headed third cousin twice removed. This opinion has been based on the fact that Southern newspapers were predominantly published in small towns and therefore were not as sophisticated as the North's major metropolitan newspapers like the *New York Herald* or the *New York*

Times. It is true that the antebellum Southern press served mostly rural communities with widely dispersed readers. Southern newspapers were not as quick to pick up on some journalistic innovations as the North's metropolitan press was. The first local reporter in Charleston, South Carolina, was not hired until the late 1850s, some thirty years after the rise of the "penny press" made reporters a commonality at newspapers in large cities like New York and Baltimore. Such newspapers did exist, in limited numbers, in larger Southern cities such as New Orleans and Savannah, but they were not widespread.

The antebellum Southern press also has been viewed as backward because of its support for slavery. Some have speculated the South's newspapers took a proslavery stance because they were forced to by the planter elite who would broker no criticism of the "peculiar institution," but such criticism overlooks the fact that many Southern journalists were slave owners themselves. Further, Southern newspapermen were overwhelmingly born and reared in the South. Nearly 33 percent of Southern journalists owned slaves, a higher rate of ownership than the Southern population in general.[3] They were products of a culture that did not question the "rightness" of slave owning. Perhaps some editors were prohibited from criticizing slavery by social constraints, but many others would never have even thought to question the South's peculiar institution. As the example of Elijah Lovejoy's murder illustrated, even in the North, it was not always safe for a journalist to espouse abolitionist sentiments.

In most ways, Southern newspapers were typical of those in other regions of the United States. Some were good in that they provided strong news and editorial content for their readers, and some were little more than advertising sheets. Primarily, the South's press was built on the community newspaper model with an orientation toward printing political, agricultural, and business news, supplemented by feature material including short stories and poetry. Most Southern newspapers had at least occasional content designed specifically for female and young readers. The primary exception here was commercial newspapers like the *Charleston Courier*. Such newspapers were devoted to business and politics and covered little else until the war actually began. Most Southern newspapers, as the 1860 presidential election approached, ran four pages. Pages one and four were usually devoted to advertising with some editorial content—this would change dramatically during the Civil War when news made a permanent shift to the front page—and pages two and three were reserved for editorial and new matter. A few newspapers, the *New Orleans Picayune*, for one, printed eight pages daily and even more on Sundays. Newspapers were hand-delivered in town by carriers, some of whom were black, and by mail or train in outlying areas. Newsboys would become a standard during the Civil War, but readers had to be careful of them: They tended to be extortionists who would demand a higher price for the newspaper than the 25¢ face price.

Southerners, like Northerners, had long been huge consumers of newspapers. Newspapers were the only source of information, besides letters and personal communications, of what was going on in other American communities and on the national level. When the antebellum period's many national debates finally burst into war in April 1861, demand for newspapers rose at an almost exponential rate. The *Augusta Chronicle and Sentinel* (Augusta, Ga.) received seventy-five new subscriptions each week during the spring of 1861.[4] The day after Fort Sumter fell, a bidding war errupted in the Confederate capital over a single copy of the *Charleston Mercury* that reported the battle.[5] Demand for news grew throughout the war. North Carolinian Cornelia Phillips Spencer wrote in her diary that people in her community, many of whom had never subscribed to a newspaper other than their local weekly, had come to see the Richmond dailies as indispensible. Any sort of news was welcome, according to Spencer, but most welcome of all was news about the military. There was considerable "general anxiety to have the latest news, and above all from the army," she wrote.[6] Newspapers were seen "irreplacable media for the transmission of social ideas."[7] During the Civil War, this influence redoubled. Newspaper editors were aware of their impact. The *Augusta Chronicle and Sentinel* declared in a 25 June 1861 editorial: "The CHRONICLE AND SENTINEL, we are proud to think, is considered by many people almost second in importance to meat and bread." The *Athens Southern Watchman* (Athens, Ga.) editor was also convinced of the importance of newspapers. He argued that only the Confederate army was of greater importance than newspapers in the South's struggle for independence.[8]

As the Civil War began, Southerners were moderately well supplied with newspapers, though not in the numbers available to urban residents in the North. When Frenchman Alexis de Tocqueville visited the United States in the 1830s to study the progress of democracy here, he commented, "There is scarcely a hamlet which has not its newspaper."[9] This was not as true in the South, even in 1860, as it was in the more populated North. In the South, there were still large expanses where there was not even so much as a hamlet, much less one with its own newspaper. The tiny villages in the swamplands of southern Georgia, for example, were devoid of newspapers on the eve of the Civil War. In total the United States had some 4,051 newspapers and periodicals in circulation in 1860.[10] Of those 4,051 newspapers and periodicals, fewer than a quarter (842, or 21 percent) were being published in the eleven states that would become the Confederate States of America.[11] Some newspapers and periodicals appeared weekly, some daily, some twice weekly, some three times weekly.

Newspaper readership in the South was extensive among the white population, though circulations for individual journals were typically lower than in the North. This was due to population differences between the two regions, as well as differences in Southern and Northern economic and social life and, to some extent, literacy rates. Of the 31.4 million Americans in 1860, only 9.1 million of them lived in the South. Nearly half that number were blacks, who, whether free or slave, typically would not have had the education or the economic ability to afford newspapers. Southern newspapers, then, had a potential readership of only about 5.4 million, while in the North the potential readership was greater than 25 million.[12] Population, though, was only one influence on newspaper circulation. Regional lifestyle differences also accounted for some of the disparity. The South was rural and agarian with few large cities and a small industrial base. In the North, immigration and urbanization were spurring the growth of cities and of businesses and manufacturing industries. Larger towns and greater population density meant more advertisers, more potential subscribers with greater diversity in their backgrounds, and the need for more and more diverse newspapers.

Readership would also have been accounted for, in part, by literacy rates. Some scholars have speculated that high illiteracy rates may have been part of the reason for the lower newspaper readership rate in the South. While illiteracy was higher in the South than in the North, the difference may not have been as great as has been speculated.[13]

Most studies of circulations of nineteenth-century newspapers deal with per capita circulation, that is, how many subscribers did a newspaper have compared to how many copies it printed, rather than readership. Readership is the actual number of people who see the paper, not just those who pay for a copy. As many as twenty people other than the subscriber may have read, or heard read, each individual copy of a newspaper. From the Revolutionary War period on, American men would gather in taverns and coffee houses on publication day or at post offices on mail day to read the latest newspapers aloud to whomever was in hearing distance.[14] Still, it is difficult to establish conclusively how many readers a newspaper had since, for the most part, subscriber lists have not survived. Most Southerners, as far as can be determined using 1860 census data, and if Cornelia Phillips Spencer is to be believed, would have subscribed to their local weeklies most of the time, and they would have supplemented these with an occasional daily paper.[15]

Despite the strong increase in subscriptions at the beginning of the war, many Southern newspapers, especially weeklies, closed their doors during the conflict. Usually, the cause was either that their owners decided to join the Confederate army or, in many cases, that there was just not enough business to provide sufficient advertising or people on their subscription list were not paying regularly for their newspapers. Some newspapers adopted the practice of demanding cash up front for newspapers. A few optimists braved the business difficulties inherent in news operations and started newspapers during the war, but newspaper doors were more likely to close than to open from 1861 to 1865.

THE ROLE OF THE PRESS IN CONFEDERATE SOCIETY

The Confederate press had multiple roles and responsibilities. Most of those roles and responsibilities were similar to what they had been prior to secession; however, the "mix" of those purposes changed. On the business side, Southern newspapers continued to be economic machines that either produced or—almost as often— consumed wealth. They provided jobs and produced a consumer good. They provided a place for other businesses to advertise their products or services. On the editorial side, Confederate newspapers still provided editorial commentary to help readers contextualize news and form their own opinions of the day's issues. They provided entertainment and educational content for readers, including materials mothers could use in teaching their children to read. The Southern press continued to provide news—in a more or less timely fashion—and this was by far its most important editorial function in the Civil War. This was a big change from the antebellum period when the Southern press's role as a political commentator dominated.

The news imperative won out over political commentary for several reasons. First, Confederate politicians worked hard to downplay politics in the Southern republic. Historian George Rable, for good reason, subtitled his book about the Confederacy "A Revolution against Politics." Confederates, as Rable observed, were fearful of the effects of partisan politics. Had not partisan politics already brought about disunion? To eliminate partisan bickering and related problems, Confederates early on decided to discard the party ephemera and to create a partyless political system in which voters were encouraged to select the best man for the job rather than voting by party.[16]

The change in the Southern political system from party to partyless brought changes in the role and work of the region's press. In the antebellum period, Southerners had lived and died by politics, and that was also true—literally—for the many Southern newspapers that served as party organs. Southern editors were often ranking party officials, and they used their newspapers to accomplish party goals like getting candidates elected, spreading the party's platform, or making sure other party members were carrying out their responsibilities. It was a symbiotic relationship since elected party officials would make sure supportive newspapers received government printing contracts and would often also find government jobs for party editors.

Party politics were especially important in the antebellum South because Southerners saw politics as their one means of protecting the institution of slavery. From the Nullification Crisis of 1832 on through the other sectional crises of the antebellum period, politics gave antebellum Southerners a means by which to aggitate for legislation, to enforce that legislation once passed, to debate and argue over issues, and to find compromises that would keep the hot-headed, radically conservative Southern fire-eaters from leading their region out of the Union. The 1860 election of Lincoln, a sectional candidate and one from an abolitionist party to boot, was sufficient evidence for some Southerners that American politics could no longer protect slavery. Both the region and its labor system, they believed, would be safer outside the Union in an independent nation where partisan politics would no longer be a threat.

Changing reader tastes also contributed to the altered role of the Confederate press. Even before Fort Sumter fell, Southern boys were donning Confederate gray and butternut uniforms and marching off to Virginia to fight for the independence of their new country and glory for themselves. The mothers and sweethearts left behind had only two ways of knowing how their loved ones were faring: letters home and newspapers. Southern readers wanted news. The Confederate people were no longer worried about arcane political debates. Secession, expansion of slavery to the territories, states' rights, and the other antebellum political debates were, for all intents and purposes, settled. Secession was a done deal. Slavery could expand to whatever territory the new Southern republic could acquire either through conquest or admission of other states. States' rights and slavery were protected by the new Confederate Constitution. Southerners did not want to read an editor's ideas on those issues any more. They wanted to read about what was happening to their loved ones in faraway Virginia or Mississippi or Tennessee. They wanted to know what was happening at the front and how the war was affecting their local boys.[17]

CONFEDERATE NEWS GATHERING: PRACTICES, STANDARDS, AND REGULATIONS

American journalism historians generally have looked to the elite metropolitan press in places like New York, Boston, Washington, D.C., or Chicago to identify the press standards and norms of a period, but that approach does not work for the Confederate press. At the beginning of the war, the South had only one metropolitan area that could come anywhere near to comparing with New York City, and that was New Orleans. However, New Orleans fell to the Union in April 1862, thereby depriving the South of any vestige of elite metropolitan journalism. Tennessee's major cities, Nashville and Memphis, which might have vied for a position on the list of important newspaper towns, lost out, too, because they also fell in the spring and summer of 1862. The majority of the newspapers that made up the Confederate press, even the more prominent ones, had as much in common with the community press as they did with the metropolitan press. A major community newspaper trait probably the majority of Confederate newspapers had in common with the community press was impecunity, that is, a lack of money. While a metropolitan New York newspaper like Horace Greeley's *New York Herald* could afford to field scores of correspondents to cover the war, most Confederate newspapers did not have the $5,000 per month it could cost to put a single paid correspondent in the field. That meant Southern newspapers had to be innovative and resourceful in getting the stories their readers wanted to read. Southern editors used a combination of new and old techniques, and they made good use of new communications technologies such as the telegraph and railroad to speed up the dissemination of information.

One of the tried-and-true methods of news gathering that continued to be effective during the Civil War was the exchanges. Nineteenth-century postal law allowed newspapers to send for free one copy of each edition to other newspaper editors, and the common practice was for editors who received exchange newspapers to cut stories out of them for use in their own journals. Many an amusing editorial spat resulted when a rival newspaper did not give credit to the appropriate exchange. Considerable amounts of battlefront news circulated through all kinds of Southern newspapers via exchanges, especially stories by the South's most prominent war correspondents, the *Savannah Republican*'s Peter W. Alexander and the *Charleston Courier*'s and *Columbia South Carolinian*'s Felix G. de Fontaine.

Editors who could not afford to hire full-time journalist-correspondents had other means of attaining news as well. It was very common for newspapers to arrange for local soldiers to write letters from their posts. "Notwithstanding the hard times, we shall inform our friends of what the enemy is doing, and be sure that, as a Sentinel on the walls, we shall Chronicle all the glorious deeds of our brave soldiers," wrote the editor of the *Augusta Chronicle and Sentinel* on 27 April 1861. Quite often, soldier-correspondents were journalists who had left their newspaper work to join the army. W. P. Price and C. M. McJunkin, editor and assistant editor of the *Greenville Southern Enterprise* (Greenville, S.C.), both reported for the newspaper after they joined the army, as did Hugh Wilson, an editor of the *Abbeville Press* (Abbeville, S.C.). In February 1865, when the *Anderson Intelligencer* (Anderson, S.C.) started up again after a four-year hiatus, the paper announced that Major W. W. Humphreys of the Army of Northern Virginia would be supplying war correspondence for the paper. Humphreys, along with the rest of the *Intelligencer*'s staff, had joined the Confederate army in 1861, prompting the paper's closing. However, his partner had been invalided out of the army in the winter of 1864 and decided to start the paper up again with Humphreys as his Virginia war correspondent.[18]

After its founding in 1863, the Confederate Press Association (CPA), a cooperative news service, provided war news for the South's dailies and weeklies. The Confederate Press Association had twenty-seven permanent correspondents in the field and six "occasional" reporters who would sometimes report on local news for the wire service's forty-plus members. Members received a limited amount of copy, though, only 3,500 words of news each week.[19] The Press Association was based in Atlanta, and its correspondents provided news to subscribing newspapers from 1863 until virtually the end of the war. A CPA correspondent was filing stories by telegraph almost daily as Joseph E. Johnston's Army of Tennessee did its level best to block Sherman's invasion into North Carolina. The press organization also functioned as a trade association and worked out agreements with Southern commanders for access to military information and the Southern Congress for copyrights on news stories.

The best war reporting, though, came from the paid correspondents who were on the spot on behalf of a newspaper (or the CPA) and could provide eyewitness accounts of the conflict. The *Charleston Courier* had several full-time correspondents in Virginia for much of the war and a number of others who provided them with periodic stories. The two daily Augusta, Georgia, newspapers, the *Constitutionalist* and the *Chronicle and Sentinel*, shared a Richmond correspondent, Salem Dutcher, from 1862 on. A number of journalists covered Sherman's March to the Sea in 1864, including "Personne," "Rover," and "Kentuckian" for the *Augusta Chronicle and Sentinel* and "Observer" for the *Constitutionalist*.

These glamorous correspondents wrote under romantic noms de guerre, or pseudonyms, like Hermes, Quel Qu'un, and Bohemian, or sometimes under silly names like Grape or Mint Julep.[20] Regardless of how they signed their dispatches, the South's war correspondents were widely known and respected, and readers eagerly awaited their dispatches. The two best Southern war correspondents have already been mentioned, Peter W. Alexander of the *Savannah Republican* and Felix G. de Fontaine of the *Charleston Courier*. Alexander was particularly important because of his use of advocacy journalism techniques to get shoes, clothing, and other supplies sent to the front for Georgians serving in the Army of Northern Virginia in 1862.

Alexander and de Fontaine were both extraordinary writers who had a real knack for describing the battles they witnessed in such precise terms that readers could not help but visualize the action themselves. The two men, though, came from very different backgrounds. Alexander, who wrote under his initials rather than a pseudonym, was a lawyer and a politician from Georgia who had been an editor at the *Savannah Republican* for a while before the war. De Fontaine, "Personne" to his Southern readers, was the son of a former French aristocrat who had grown up in New York and who came South just as the war was starting to cover the siege of Fort Sumter. He had come to cover the Fort Sumter story for the *New York Herald*, but he ended up staying and becoming a correspondent for the *Courier*. Both men, though, were devoted to telling the stories of the Confederate armies in the field.

A handful of women provided correspondence for Southern newspapers, though their work focused on issues other than the battles themselves. Typically, the female correspondents wrote about hospital affairs, the treatment of wounded soldiers, or the politics of the war, or they provided descriptive accounts of camp life. The longest-lived correspondence by a female writer was that provided by "Joan," a South Carolina woman whose son was serving in Virginia. When she traveled to Virginia to be near him, she wrote about her experiences for the *Charleston Courier*. Joan wrote at least one letter and often more virtually daily from mid-July 1861 to the end of August 1861. Her correspondence was far more frequent than that of the male correspondents, though in September, her stories were conspicuously absent for several days while she moved from Richmond to an army camp near Leesville, Virginia, to be nearer her son. She wrote less frequently that fall but continued on through mid-November 1861 when her last dispatch appeared in the *Courier*. Joan's dispatches almost always ran on the front page, often paired with those of Personne's or Sumter's, the *Courier's* other Virginia correspondents. The only time a Joan dispatch was consigned to an inside page was on 12 August 1861 when news of a major fire in Charleston took up the front page.

Joan wrote mostly about the politics of the war, life in the Confederate capital, and the military hospitals in Richmond. The hospitals were her particular passion. For example, Joan advocated each state setting up hospitals for its own soldiers. She wrote approvingly about Alabama, Mississippi, and Louisiana when those states did so. She was also a master at setting a scene so that a reader could imagine a place quite vividly. In October, Joan wrote from Fairfax, Virginia, about a sunny autumn day's cool winds and how lovely a seat by a fire felt on such a day when children were "busy running to the chestnut trees, which are shedding their abundant crop, and are sought for almost as eagerly by soldiers as by children; in this land where luxuries are unheard of."[21]

Occasionally, newspaper editors themselves donned the role of war correspondent. The editors of the two Savannah newspapers, William T. Thompson of the *Daily Morning News* and James R. Sneed of the *Republican*, traveled together to Charleston to cover the shelling of Fort Sumter. After 1863, "Personne," de Fontaine, was editor of his own newspaper, the *South Carolinian* of Columbia, South Carolina, but he still struck off across Georgia to cover Sherman's Georgia campaign. An advantage of having editors in the field rather than correspondents was the greater clout they carried with military officials. An editor could hobnob with higher officials and often obtain better information.[22]

Covering the war was not an easy job for either a correspondent or an editor. Correspondents traveled with or behind armies—depending on the particular commander's sentiments about journalists. If the unit they were covering moved out at 2:00 A.M. on a rainy morning, the correspondent moved with it. The Confederate government provided at least subsistence food for its army much of the time, but correspondents had to scrounge their own meals. One of the issues J. S. Thrasher, superintendent of the Confederate Press Association, undertook was to try to arrange for his correspondents to buy food from military units. Since the Confederacy was having a hard time feeding its soldiers, Thrasher's requests fell on deaf ears.[23]

Correspondents were in just as much danger of capture, disease, or injury as the soldiers they wrote about, and several Confederate correspondents did die while on the job. John Linebaugh of the *Memphis Appeal*, for example, drowned while traveling from Richmond to Tennessee to cover John Bell Hood's invasion of that state. A correspondent for the *Augusta Chronicle and Sentinel* came near to being captured by Union troops while covering Sherman's campaign through Georgia in the fall of 1864. The correspondent was on the road from Eatonton to Madison, relying on Confederate pickets to call out the alarm if Northern troops approached. About 3:00 P.M., the correspondent wrote, "A scout came dashing down the road at a Gilpin speed, crying 'to the woods,' 'to the woods,' and we wooded." The correspondent reported that he waited several hours in the rain and then decided to risk going to the road to see what was happening. "We had not traveled a hundred yards," he wrote, "before a party of cerulean clad equestrians came dashing up, and in a very polite and insinuating manner briefly requested us to halt. The request was accompanied with most significant cocking of carbines and pistols, which, brought to a horizontal attitude in one's front are very persuasive, especially to an unarmed civilian, and we halted." The Union officers questioned the correspondent about the countryside and any Confederate troops that might be nearby before letting him go.[24]

Correspondents had to deal with fatigue and illness, just like the troops did. Once battles were over, correspondents would telegraph short articles about the fighting and then stay up late at night writing a longer version of their stories that could be either mailed back to their newspapers or hand-carried by a courier. Such long days of arduous and physically demanding labor moving through rough terrain from one section of the battlefield to another left journalists susceptible to camp diseases and other illnesses. Ivy W. Duggan, a popular soldier-correspondent for the Sandersville, Georgia, *Central Georgian* was hospitalized three times in the first year of the war for camp diseases he contracted. The *Central Georgian* editor commented, "Mr. Duggan's patriotism is greater than his strength." A correspondent for the *Carolina Spartan*, "L," contracted typhoid fever and was unable to work for nearly a month.[25]

Despite the challenges of their work, Southern war correspondents were not well paid. Henry Timrod, who would become the unofficial poet laureate of the Confederacy, received $6 a day plus traveling expenses for the reporting he did from the Army of the West for the *Charleston Mercury*. This fee would have been in addition to his military pay, but still was quite meager. The Southern Associated Press, a predecessor of the Confederate Press Association, as well as the Richmond newspapers, were paying their correspondents in Fredericksburg, Virginia, $100 a month in 1863.

Despite the hardships and low pay, the South's correspondents worked with amazing dedication to gather the news and get it back to their newspapers so that eagerly awaiting readers could know what was happening at the front. Because of reader demand, Southern newspapers adopted another innovation: placing news, rather than advertising, on the front page. The use of news on the front page was a major change.

Confederate newspapers emphasized war news not only by placement but also by quantity. War news dominated most front pages. The *Savannah Daily Morning News* devoted 59 percent of its content to war news in a two-week period just before and just after the fall of Fort Sumter. During the Battle of Chancellorsville, 2 May to 14 May 1863, the *Daily Morning News* ran 106 war stories, or about 81 percent of its content during that period. As hostilities escalated, so did the paper's war coverage.[26] Greater coverage was possible in part, too, because of the decline in advertising as the war took its toll on Southern businesses. There was more room available for news.

War news, though, was not the only news Confederate newspapers offered, nor should it have been. While the war certainly dominated the short existence of the Confederate States of America and the lives of its people, everyday life continued as well. Once the war began, there were profound differences in the quality of that everyday life, especially for women who had to keep their homes, farms, and plantations running in the absence of their menfolk. Still, even after the war began, people got married, had babies, died, held benefit concerts, ran for election, gawked at two-headed calves, committed murders, visited restaurants, and earned livings.[27] These stories, too, were told by Confederate newspapers and often made for lively reading.

Another common, though perhaps unexpected, source of news for Southern newspapers was Northern newspapers. Southern and Northern newspapers had exchanges prior to secession, and some of those continued, to some degree, even during the war. Newspapers crossed the lines, both officially and unofficially, and Southern editors published the content of those from the North with great relish, often commenting negatively on the Yankee editor's interpretation of events. The exchanges of Northern newspapers were aided in large measure by the Confederate Signal Bureau, a division of the Confederate Secret Service that regularly received mail from Washington, D.C. In fact, during one six-month stretch, the Signal Bureau got Washington and Baltimore papers within a day of publication and New York papers within two days. Northern papers were so regularly received that the *Charleston Courier* was able to complain on 15 July 1862 that the Yankee papers did not have much news in them. The Confederate Press Association was another source of Northern news. At its first board meeting, members agreed to hire an agent and provide him with the funding needed to get the latest Northern newspapers through the lines. Unfortunately, the minutes of that meeting do not indicate whether the funding was for bribes or subscriptions.[28]

Transmission of their stories back to their newspapers was a perennial problem for Confederate correspondents. Shortly after telegraph service ended between Washington, D.C., and Richmond, Virginia, on 1 June 1861, Confederate President Jefferson Davis took control of the telegraph lines for military use. The Southern press responded immediately. A. D. Banks, a member of the Richmond press corps, approached Secretary of War Leroy Walker to gain permission for journalists to use the telegraph lines.[29] Eventually, the restrictions on the telegraph were eased somewhat, but local military commanders were known to block access if they believed a dispatch would be harmful to the army, and military censors would refuse to send telegraphs they believed would be harmful to the cause. There were no restrictions, though, on putting that same information in a letter and mailing it back to the newspaper, but that, of course, slowed the delivery of the news. The Confederate post office was never particularly efficient, a problem compounded when mail had to cross through or be delivered to battle areas. In fact, later in the war, Confederate mail service got so bad that some editors resorted to sending their newspapers by Southern Express, a freight company, even thought that meant they had to pay the freight services as well as postage. Early on, Confederate Postmaster General John Regan had decided that newspapers should be considered mailable matter rather than manufactured products. That meant that they had to be mailed rather than shipped by a freight service, and that meant more revenue for the Confederate post office, which was required by law to be self-supporting.

Gathering and delivering news was not the only concern Confederate editors had about their product. They also had to ensure it met certain professional standards. Those standards were perhaps rudimentary, compared to those by which later American news organizations would function. Further, nineteenth-century journalism was highly individualistic, and so although it is possible to see the earliest seeds of professional standards being planted in this period, certainly there were few moves to bring about any sort of widespread adherence to a set of standards. However, as early as 1837, editors were gathering at professional meetings and discussing how "to do" journalism and how to punish infractions, usually on a state-by-state basis. That year, a group of North Carolina editors meeting in Raleigh approved a series of resolutions that specified journalism's best practices. Those practices emphasized the public service aspects of journalism. According to these resolutions, journalists were supposed to advocate for morality, national liberty, and social order; they were supposed to promote the arts, science, and industry; and further, newspapers were supposed to be incorruptible champions of the Constitution and of American laws. According to the resolution those editors adopted in Raleigh, North Carolina, editors who did not live up to these standards faced a truly draconian punishment: banishment from the exchanges. Since exhange newspapers were one of the primary news sources available to antebellum editors, this was indeed a serious threat.[30]

Public service was high on the list of press standards beyond North Carolina, too. William King, a Charleston printer who rose to the editorial ranks at the *Charleston Courier*, discussed nineteenth-century press standards in his history of the journalism of that city. In his small book, King wrote that the press had "a high mission to perform and responsible duties to discharge." These duties precluded, for example, using personal attacks in an editorial debate with another editor. Such invective, King wrote, diverted a newspaper from its proper public service–oriented mission.[31]

During the Civil War, journalistic standards and practices continued to evolve. In the South, the evolution was spurred to some degree by rules and regulations of the Confederate Press Association. Press Association Superintendent Thrasher set certain standards for his correspondents. However, because the CPA was a mutual news-gathering service as well as a wire service and a trade association, its standards trickled down to local writers whose copy had to be suitable for adding to the news service's offerings. Thrasher's rules required that Press Association dispatches be objective and fact-based. He also required dispatches to be timely, and he added a competitive aspect to Southern news gathering by reminding his correspondents that they were not to be beaten on stories. "I shall expect from you, and the superior facilities opened to you for procuring intelligence, that you will be seldom, if ever, beaten," Thrasher wrote to a new hire, a Mr. Wagner, in a letter of instruction.[32] Local journalists were at least exposed to the ideas of objectivity, accuracy, competitiveness, use of facts, and timeliness because of their association with the wire service.

The news values promulgated by Thrasher and the Confederate Press Association fit well with what audiences wanted and expected from their newspapers. Readers wanted truthful, accurate, and timely newspaper reports, despite the problems with and breakdowns of the Southern communications infrastructure—telegraph, mail, and railroads—that developed during the Civil War. Truth telling and accuracy were enormously demanding standards for war correspondents whose view of a battle often was limited to a narrow field of action, just like that of the soldiers fighting the battles and the generals commanding them. Most of the better and more accurate stories about the military action of the Civil War were actually those "recap" stories written a few weeks after the battle was over when correspondents had a chance to walk the battlefield and to interview participants. De Fontaine, Personne of the *Charleston Courier*, described reporting the war as being caught in an Odyssian struggle between

Scylla and Charybdis—the desire to print rumor so as to get information out and prudently holding back until the rumor could be confirmed.[33] While truth telling and accuracy may have been important professional values, they were not always adhered to. Confederate journalists, like their Northern counterparts, were known to take bribes for "revising" their stories to make some particular officer's battle performance sound better than it had been. Southern newspapers also published stories of Yankee atrocities as a kind of propaganda to steel their readers' resolve to support the war. For example, the *Atlanta Intelligencer* reported on 16 October 1863 that the Union troops had found a way to poison flesh with gunshot wounds.[34]

Fairness was another important news value of which Confederate journalists also had at least a rudimentary understanding. Several newspapers, for example, would not accept unsigned letters to the editor for publication. Pen names were common in those days, both for letter writers and for regular reporters and correspondents, but editors of these newspapers wanted to know the real names of letter writers, especially those who were writing in to support or recommend political candidates. Such policies were not always adequate protection for newspapers, though. Two months after the *Augusta Chronicle and Sentinel* adopted its no-unsigned-letters policy, it was victimized by a hoax when someone sent in a wedding announcement for Mr. George C. Conner of Atlanta and a woman from Tennessee. After being informed of the error, the *Chronicle and Sentinel* ran a terse correction. The article, the paper admitted, had been "a pure fabrication of some wicked jester." The paper added its apologies for the mistake: "We regret that we should have been made a party to a transaction so dishonorable; and we make this public statement and correction."[35]

While the Civil War certainly had an influence on the evolution of journalistic standards and ethics, American journalists, both Southern and Northern, were still a long way from having a systematized system of ethics and professional practices. In the South, most editors followed their own ideas about what were the right and wrong ways to practice journalism. Dr. Robert Gibbes, a physician and former college professor who was also editor and owner of the *Columbia South Carolinian* until early 1864, had firm ideas about his editorial responsibilities and policies. Gibbes believed newspapers should be dignified, patriotic, and conservative. Like William L. King, Gibbes believed newspaper editors should take the moral high ground and avoid condescending to name-calling with their adversaries. Gibbes was not, however, averse to giving fair reply when another newspaper started a hot debate with him. For Gibbes, though, the overarching journalistic imperative was independence, that is, espousing principles that grew from the editor's own convictions—based, of course, on sound "Southern policy." Editorial independence was desirable, but not so much as to rattle the ship of state, Gibbes believed. He was not always consistent on that point, either. A few years before the Civil War began, Gibbes sued the mayor of Columbia for access to city council meetings. The mayor had given preference to the newspaper of his political party with regard to access to minutes and to meetings. Gibbes certainly rocked the Columbia ship of state when he won his lawsuit.[36]

Despite their penchants for independence, Confederate journalists were fairly consistent in determining what was newsworthy, and their news values were not that much different from those of journalists today. An article from the 27 September 1861 *Augusta Chronicle and Sentinel* provides a useful illustration:

Is there anybody around who feels like kicking up a muss and getting his name in the papers? Reader, if you see any person who conversed with another man who told him he had been reliably informed that Mr. Whatshisname had met with a severe accident from which he would probably recover—send us word. Locals are scarce as hens-teeth. A wormy chinquepin for the first item.

"Kicking up a muss," or doing something out of the ordinary, was news, and people who did unusual things made the news. Accidents, the example the *Chronicle and Sentinel* editor used, were something out of the ordinary; most people went through their days without having accidents. Of course, the editor did not want to wish an ill fate on anyone, so he specified that "Mr. Whatshisname" should not have been injured severely. Perhap a slight injury, though, would make the story just ever so much more interesting to the reader. Further, it was specifically local news the editor wanted and for which he was willing to pay a wormy chinquepin.[37] One further and final insight regarding news values can be gleaned from this example. Note that the editor has asked specifically for a source who had been "reliably informed." This harkens back to the value of accuracy and is an example of the few clues that exist to the nature of nineteenth-century press standards.

During the Civil War, journalists were not the only group to have interests in and concerns about their standards and practices. So did the Confederate government and military. Military leaders were concerned about the spread of news from battlefields and camps because of what could happen, should sensitive information fall into the hands of the enemy. If a newspaper correspondent wrote too much about a general's plans for a campaign or the location of troops, he could be giving the enemy just the intelligence they needed to foil the plans. These fears were bolstered by the fact that the speed of news transmission in the United States had increased by more than 50 percent from 1820 to 1860. By 1860, the average newspaper article would be picked up by other newspapers within one to three days of publication. Because newspapers circulated pretty freely across enemy lines for most of the war, publication of military news, especially numbers and locations of troops and generals, posed significant risks; newspapers could reach enemy generals as quickly as they could friendly ones.[38] For the most part, Confederate newspapers and correspondents tried to handle information responsibly. A number of authors have called the Confederate press's caution about publishing "self-censorship," and while that moniker applies to some extent, Southern journalists generally held back information out of a desire to aid the national cause, not fear of punishment, the usual foundation of self-censorship. Even hard-line press libertarians like *Augusta Chronicle and Sentinel* editor Nathan Morse supported caution with the publication of military secrets. Morse wrote, "A man who happens to own a printing press should not be allowed to print sentiments intended to aid the enemy." The one primary naysayer to the idea of restraining publication to benefit the military was the *Charleston Mercury*. Its editors believed the public had a complete right to know everything possible about the Confederate military and its work since the public was supplying the men and the money to fight the war.[39]

Of course, military leaders would have liked to have had greater legal control of the Confederate press, but for the most part there was virtually no government censorship of Southern newspapers. In fact, it would have been virtually impossible for the

Confederacy to sanction official censorship of the press because of the justification it had used for secession: its desire to correct the constitutional errors of the North. A country that had gone into revolution because it believed it understood the Constitution better could not then turn around and violate a key provision. In fact, the Confederate government used its lack of censorship as a point of pride to distinguish it and its firmer grasp of the ideals of liberty from the North where Lincoln was not above suppressing the Copperhead press in great numbers. After General Robert E. Lee complained to the War Department about a dispatch in the *Richmond Dispatch*, Secretary of War George W. Randolph informed the Confederate commander that his intention was to conclude the war without the suppression of a single newspaper. That is not to imply, however, that the War Department prohibited military censorship entirely, and even Randolph himself was certainly not above threatening to censor. In response to Lee's complaint, Randolph sent a copy of the general's letter to all Richmond newspapers with a notation that he hoped it would not become necessary for him to seek legislation giving him the power to censor newspapers. Randolph's reluctance to censor, despite his threat, did not mean that military authorities were without any means of controlling what information flowed from their armies. Commanding officers were empowered, for example, to restrict press access to army camps, and many took advantage of that power. They found other means as well. Confederate military leaders responded to the possible risks of newspaper publication by imposing certain restrictions, though the Southern Congress was quick to rebuke generals who went too far in their attempts to censor the press.[40]

The Civil War was the first time in American history that government had had to consider how to regulate press publication of war information. In the country's three previous major wars, the Revolutionary War, the War of 1812, and the Mexican-American War, news moved too slowly to threaten military security. By the time newspapers could get military information into print, the battlefield situation had changed, and the reportage had no impact on the outcome.[41] By the Civil War, though, news-gathering, production, and dissemination technologies were sufficiently sophisticated and fast that military or government control was sometimes warranted. The problem was compounded in the Civil War by the fact that each side's newspapers were being published in close proximity to the other. Northern generals received Southern newspapers almost as quickly as Southern generals did.[42]

The first Confederate Secretary of War Leroy Walker was the first official to broach the topic of press censorship, but he did so in the form of a request rather than a legal regulation. Scarcely had the fighting begun when Walker asked the press not to report on unit size, number of weapons, condition of the troops, or possible military movements. The most any Confederate secretary of war would do to control the press was write letters and, on occasion, make a veiled threat about what might happen to newspapers, should he have to intervene. For the most part, though, these reminders from the War Department were sufficient to keep most Southern editors in line. When self-restraint failed, military commanders, however, were often reluctant to rely on self-censorship by the press. They were quick to act against reporters.[43]

In early 1861, Confederate General Joseph Johnston expelled all the reporters from his command after Secretary of War Judah Benjamin reminded him of his power to do so. Johnston had written the secretary of war regarding the conduct of *Richmond*

Dispatch reporter William G. Shepardson, known to readers as "Bohemian." The reporter had included in one of his stories the locations of the winter headquarters for several units in Virginia. Benjamin agreed that the publication was egregious, but he wrote Johnston that he had no power to take any action against Bohemian. The war secretary accused Johnston of being too lenient with reporters covering his command and of not enforcing the powers that military law gave Johnston to control journalists. The Southern press responded at its spring 1862 convention by appointing a committee of three distinguished journalists to write and circulate to all Southern newspapers a series of articles critical of the general.[44]

Major General Earl Van Dorn, commander of the military district of Southern Mississippi and Eastern Louisiana, got the harshest reprimand from the Confederate government for interfering with press liberties. Van Dorn published an order that declared martial law in his district and ordered the arrest of any journalist who published troop movements or anything that would impair public confidence in the military or government. Under Van Dorn's order, the penalty for communicating with the enemy was death. The biggest issue regarding Van Dorn's order was the imposition of martial law, an action that only the president was authorized to take. The order provoked a lively debate in the Confederate Congress and brought the general a rebuke from the secretary of war. Congress went further and adopted a resolution to restrain military commanders from unconstitutionally exercising military powers. Van Dorn bowed to public pressure and revoked his order.[45]

The Southern government did take affirmative steps to limit use of the telegraph lines by journalists, but they were only partially successful. In May 1861, the Confederate Congress authorized Jefferson Davis to seize the lines and to appoint censors—the resolution used the word *agents*, but the proposed function of those "agents" was clear. The measure also outlawed any transmission of military information that would endanger the success of or otherwise hinder military operations. Dispatches the telegraph agents might decline to transmit could, however, still be sent back to the home office by mail or courier. And often sensitive dispatches got sent by telegraph anyway. Despite the law adopted by the Confederate Congress, telegraphic news was only sporadically subject to "the blue pencil of any censor." Whether a dispatch would be censored depended as much on the zeal of the telegraph operator on duty as anything else.

Toward the end of the war, the issue of conscription got caught up with press censorship, and the result was a huge controversy that threatened to topple the Davis presidency. Confederate editors, along with several other types of essential workers, had been exempt from the draft since the first conscription law passed in 1862. By the fall of 1864, though, the Confederate army's numbers had been ravaged by desertions, deaths, and injuries. In a September speech at Macon, Georgia, President Davis revealed that the army was desperate for manpower. To solve the manpower shortage, Davis would propose in November that Congress repeal most of the exemptions, including that of newspaper editors. The journalists, though, were suspicious of Davis's proposal. Many believed Davis did not desire to fill the ranks of the army but to get rid of those editors who were becoming increasingly critical of the way the president was running the country and the military. They were suspicious because a second aspect of the president's proposal gave him and the secretary of war the power to detail—that is, assign—any new recruits as they saw fit. Davis was aware that the country would need newspapers, and he proposed to assign some of the newly drafted editors to continue their editorial work while sending others to fight. Editors were not spread evenly throughout the Confederacy, Davis argued. If he had the power to send some to fight and some to the homefront, he could swell the ranks of the army while ensuring the Confederate press continued to operate.[46]

Editors did not accept Davis's explanation. Most believed he would keep friendly editors at home and send opposition editors to the front as a means of silencing criticism, and a handful of Confederate congressmen agreed with the editors. All over the Confederacy, journalists declared open season on the president. They raised the banner of the constitutional guarantee of free speech in defiance of Davis's proposal. A number of newspapers started running the full text of Article 9, Section 1 of the Confederate Constitution (its counterpart, the First Amendment to the U.S. Constitution, is better known, but they say exactly the same thing), and others called Davis every unpleasant name they could devise and urged opposition to the proposal. One newspaper even went so far as to proclaim that if the South had to be ruled by a despot, its editors would prefer Lincoln.[47] Tennessee Congressman Henry S. Foote introduced a resolution to express the Congress's displeasure with the president's proposal, and the resolution passed, though in slightly altered form. It read in part, "It is the sense of this House that the exemption of one editor to each newspaper under the conditions now required by law is as narrow a margin for exemption from that class as is expedient, and that the existing law on the subject of such exemption requires no amendment."[48]

In all probability, President Davis was not trying to influence press criticism with his proposal, which did also extend to other exempt classes of workers. A greater possibility was that Davis was trying to gain control of the state militias so he could incorporate those units into the Confederate armies. Some historians believe that the idea to propose changes to the conscription law did not originate with Davis at all but with his secretary of war, Judah Benjamin. They believe Benjamin's purpose was to move toward establishing a dictatorship in the Confederacy with Davis at its head.[49]

Confederate journalists retained considerable freedom to speak and publish what they saw fit during the Civil War. Some constraints were applied, but more often by the military than the Confederate government. In almost every instance when Congress considered legislation regarding freedom of the press, it voted to protect the rights of journalists. Two historians of the Georgia press, Griffith and Talmadge, wrote, "For all its mistakes and near-sightedness, it was a free press—possibly the freest that ever published during a national emergency." These historians may be overstating the case; certainly, they were writing before the Vietnam conflict that was, essentially, an uncensored war. However, a more contemporary historian, Robert A. Rutland, also believed that the Southern press was one of the freest of all times. He wrote that Southern publishers in the Civil War "retained a wartime freedom of expression that has no modern parallel." Even Civil War historian Mark Neely, who found that the Confederacy profoundly repressed the civil liberties of its individual citizens, was forced to admit in the last pages of his book on the subject that the single exception was the Southern press, which remained essentially free to publish what it would.[50] Censorship was a reality in the Confederacy, but it was not harsh, and its only objective was to protect the military as it fought the war, an objective with which even the most passionate press libertarians would be hard-pressed to disagree.

PRODUCING AND DELIVERING A CONFEDERATE NEWSPAPER

Even before the Civil War began, producing a daily or a weekly newspaper was not an easy task. To be a successful newspaper editor, according to the *Carolina Spartan* of Spartanburg, South Carolina, one needed "the constitution of a horse, obstinacy of a mule, impudence of a beggar and entire resignation to the most confounded of all earthly treadmills; he must be a moving target for everybody to shout at, and is expected to know everything, and to assist busybodies, to pry into the business of his neighbors."[51] Without the sort of gritty perseverence of which the *Spartan* spoke, an editor's chances were not great of successfully guiding his newspaper through the war period.

Early in the war, newspapermen had fewer problems with the actual manufacture of newspapers. A circulation boom kept profits up even though advertising dollars declined as Northern clients pulled their ads from Southern newspapers and Southern businesses closed when their owners and employees went off to fight. That circulation boom, though, was both good and bad. The problem of getting subscribers to pay up was perennial, and with more subscribers, the problem expanded. By the end of the first year of the Civil War, the *Charleston Mercury's* subscribers owed the newspaper $17,000 in subscription dues. Its advertisers were not doing much better; they owed the newspaper $20,000. Many newspapers, as a result, went to a cash system that required subscribers to pay in advance. Toward the end of the war, as cash became truly scarce in the South and inflation soared at unbelievably high levels, editors would accept just about anything of value in payment for subscriptions. The *Hillsborough Recorder* (Hillsborough, N.C.) announced a subscription price increase in January 1864 but added that the editor would be willing to barter subscriptions for $1 plus "wood, corn, wheat or flour, or butter, eggs, or potatoes, or any article of the kind used in a family." The *Sandersville Central Georgian* had been accepting produce for subscriptions since 1862.[52]

Once the shooting started, demands on editors and their staffs escalated. Editors faced disruptions, dislocations, shortages, and soaring labor and materials costs, printer strikes, and loss of manpower to the army.[53] One of the more vexing shortages was labor. Nearly three-quarters of the South's printers did military service. This rate of volunteerism by printers was not uncommon among white Southern men. In South Carolina, for example, 44,000 men out of a voting population of 68,000 volunteered for the army in the first eighteen months of the war. By 1864, nearly half the men who had worked as printers at Southern newspapers in 1860 were dead. Many of those who still lived were disabled by injury or disease that resulted from their military service. Given that it took about three printers to support the work of one editor, even the loss of a single printer could have a profound effect on the production capacity of a newspaper. Of course, the number of printers needed declined as the other shortages—raw materials, advertisers, subscribers, and news—forced newspapers to cut the number of pages they printed daily and as more and more newspapers went out of business.[54]

With increased demand for news, many newspapers became essentially twenty-four-hour operations as they added evening editions for their city subscribers and bi-weekly or triweekly editions for their country readers. When the *Augusta Evening Dispatch* suspended publication in June 1861, the *Chronicle and Sentinel* was quick to add an evening edition to attract the *Dispatch*'s readers. The new edition would be delivered by carrier every day for a price of 15¢ per week. The *Chronicle and Sentinel* editors promised to provide "the latest news by telegraph, express and mail" that came in as late as 1:30 P.M. The paper's morning edition had a closeout time of 1:00 A.M. so that it could make the morning departures of the mail trains on the South Carolina Railroad and the Athens and Washington Railroad. Papers that went out on those trains would be in the hands of distant subscribers that same day. The next month, the *Chronicle and Sentinel* announced plans to add a triweekly edition as soon as 100 people indicated their interest. The new paper would carry sixteen columns of news.[55]

Local distribution of newspapers was less of a problem than was dissemination to country or out-of-town subscribers. Carriers delivered newspapers to local sub-scribers, and as long as the regular carriers serviced their well-known routes, there were few problems. However, whenever a carrier was not available or one became sick, or when a new carrier was learning a new route, apologies for mistakes were common features in newspaper columns.[56]

Out-of-town deliveries were more vulnerable to the vissicitudes of war. The *Albany Patriot* (Albany, Ga.) complained in the fall of 1864 about how few copies of the *Macon Telegraph and Confederate* were reaching its town. The Albany paper wanted to know "how it is that so few copies of Tuesday's and Wednesday's editions have reached this post office when the subscription list numbers over a hundred. We have not received a copy since Sunday." The *Patriot* speculated that the problem lay in the *Telegraph and Confederate* mail room. More likely, however, the root of the problem was the destruction of the railroads and the disruption of mail service by Union General William T. Sherman's men as they marched through Georgia on their way to the sea.[57]

Production of the South's dailies, and many of the more important weeklies, was accomplished with the aid of steam presses. The *Charleston Mercury* bought a new cylinder press before the war that could print 4,000 sheets per hour. The purchase was made because the paper's existing equipment was not sufficient to keep up with increased demand for subscriptions. The paper lost that press, though, in 1865 when it was moved to Columbia for safekeeping. The staff expected Union General William T. Sherman to strike Charleston in his campaign through the Carolinas. In-stead, Sherman's forces attacked Columbia, and the *Mercury*'s press was destroyed in the conflagration there. The *Selma Reporter* (Selma, Ala.) came up with a truly in-novative printing solution when demand for its morning and evening editions out-stripped the ability of its hand press to meet demand. The paper had extended its deadline for news so as to include the latest dispatches, but that gave the press room less time to actually produce the newspaper, especially since the press run had gone up to meet reader demand for more copies. The demands on the printing staff were so great that they often could not meet them, and the paper frequently appeared too late to make the mail trains. With no press manufacturers in the South, and little money, the situation could have been hopeless had the clever staff at the *Reporter* not devised an amazing solution. The *Reporter*'s staff figured out a way to attach a steam engine to its hand press. The article about this innovation did not describe how the newspaper staff accomplished this engineering feat, but it did note, "The introduction of steam power to the printing business in Selma is an event worthy of more than passing notice." However, since the paper's staff had "neither time or disposition to blow about it," the workers decided to "let our engine do the *puffing*."[58]

Obtaining supplies and spare parts was a constant problem for Confederate newspapers. Printing equipment and other supplies came mostly from the North or from Europe, which caused problems for the blockade-bound newspapers of the Confederacy. Spare parts, new presses, and even new fonts of type had to be smuggled in on blockade runners. A type foundry did operate for a short time in Richmond, Virginia, and it supplied spare parts for printing presses, but the organization went out of business fairly quickly.[59] Obtaining an adequate supply of newsprint and ink also became a great trial. Of the more than 300 paper manufacturing plants in the United States in 1860, fewer than thirty were located in the South, and some of those were not in business during parts of the war.[60] The papermill at Bath, South Carolina, burned in April 1863 and was out of business until the fall of 1864. Other papermills were plagued by strikes and destruction by enemy armies, especially those around Atlanta.[61]

Some Southern newspapers resorted to manufacturing their own ink and decreased their number of pages from four pages daily to two to deal with the paper shortage. Others printed only enough copies for subscribers and gave up on newsstand or street sales. Still others not only went to two pages but also reduced their page size. In September 1861, the *Charleston Courier*, for example, reduced its page size from eight to seven columns, or from 30×44 inches to 18×36 inches. The paper's size would shrink even more as the war continued. Other newspapers went to smaller typefaces for body copy or even printed on other kinds of paper. The Vicksburg papers, for example, were well known for printing on wallpaper during the siege of that city in 1863, but other newspapers made that same choice. The *Augusta Chronicle and Sentinel* in the fall of 1863 noted that it was receiving other newspapers in a multitude of colors. The recent *New Orleans Delta*, for example, had come in a shade of bright orange, and a Mississippi newspaper had arrived in a brilliant vermillion, a sort of rosy red color. Other newspapers, the *Chronicle and Sentinel* noted, were clothed in "sober brown," probably brown wrapping paper. The *Chronicle and Sentinel* itself got into hot water a little later in the war when rumors began circulating around the state that it was hording newsprint in order to resell it at extortionist prices. The editor hotly denounced this claim as a lie and speculated that whoever was spreading the rumor had started it to harm his paper's reputation with the papermills so there would be more paper available for others to purchase.[62]

Southern editors showed innovative thinking and entrepreneurship when dealing with their ink shortage. Before the Civil War, ink had cost between 25¢ and 50¢ a pound. By 1863, the price had risen to anywhere from 75¢ to $2 a pound. To avoid the price increases, as well as to have a regular supply, several newspapers started manufacturing and selling printing ink. The homemade ink was made out of oil and lamp soot or even ordinary shoe-blacking. The *Charleston Mercury* and the *Augusta Chronicle and Sentinel* were among the newspapers that went into ink manufacturing. The *Mercury* opened the Charleston Printing Inks Work on 4 May 1863. The paper was proud of the quality of its ink. The copy in an ad for the new manufacturer assured readers that "The clear print of THE MERCURY, notwithstanding the disadvantages of worn type, inferior paper, &c., ought to be sufficient recommendations of the ink."[63]

THE CONFEDERATE PEOPLE AND THEIR PRESS: EFFECTS OF THE CIVIL WAR

Sometimes war is necessary, but even then, it is not good for newspapers nor for the people who make them and read them. The American Civil War took a terrible toll on Southern newspapers and the Southern people. Nearly half of the newspapers in the South folded during the war, and some 258,000 Southerners died. Yet the South's journalists kept the news coming, and the Confederate army kept up its fight far longer than it should have. Both the soldiers at the front and the people back home relied on newspapers to bring them the latest news. Those newspapers that continued to publish did the best they could, given their circumstances. The news those newspapers offered may not have always been entirely accurate—it rarely has been in any war, at least with regard to the initial accounts of battles—and the papers may not have always arrived with the freshest news, but at least some kind of news did arrive. What happened once the news did arrive is difficult to assess. What was the value for citizens of far-flung Houston, Texas, or Tampa, Florida, to find out about the fighting in Virginia two weeks after it had happened? Was some news better than no news? And what was the effect of finding out another two weeks later that earlier reports of a great Southern victory were just wild exaggeration or wishful thinking on the part of the correspondent? How did the content of Confederate newspapers influence the morale of the people back home? It is easier to raise these questions than it is to answer them.

The problems with news accuracy and diffusion were not significantly different from what they have been in most American wars. The first reports of battles are often wrong; even military leaders themselves have not always known immediately who won or who lost a particular fight. Many in both the South and the North initially thought Confederate General Robert E. Lee's troops had won at Gettysburg, but they were wrong. Without a doubt, accurate news has greater value than inaccurate news, especially when that inaccurate news has to be corrected later to indicate not a victory but a defeat. Civilian morale, an important component of all wars, can tolerate only so much tossing about before it plummets to unfathomable depths. Some historians have blamed the press for the sagging Confederate morale in 1864 and 1865. They point out that the constant editorial criticism of Jefferson Davis must have had an ill effect on public confidence in the Confederate government and its ability to bring the war to a successful conclusion. People who lived through the war implicated newspapers even earlier for lagging civilian morale. Before the war was even a year old, some Southerners were already concerned about the adverse effect of newspapers on readers. South Carolina civil servant Benjamin F. Arthur wrote in a letter:

> The time was in South Carolina when newspapers *informed* [emphasis his] and educated the public mind. They were once conducted and contributed to by the best intellects in the country—but that time has past—and they have degenerated into the

merest trash—conducted in many cases, by men of no attachments and less character. They have become a perfect nuisance and a newspaper reputation is getting to be regarded, rather an equivocal sort of fame.[64]

Those people who read newspapers like the *Charleston Mercury*, the *Augusta Chronicle and Sentinel*, and the *Raleigh Standard* would have been exposed over and over again to articles that cast doubt on Davis's leadership and wisdom. Even the newspapers that were hypercritical of the Confederate government rarely complained about the Southern military, but when they did, army commanders were quick to respond. After a reporter for the *Mobile Advertiser and Register* criticized General Lee in December 1864, Lee retorted that he had come to believe the Confederacy had made its greatest mistake at the outset of the war; it had put all its good generals to work editing newspapers and the bad ones to work commanding the armies in the field.[65]

There were other papers, though, that never lost faith, that believed up to and beyond Appomattox that the South could still pull off a victory if only the people would get behind the cause. These newspapers were culpable for raising the hopes of Confederate citizens beyond what was reasonable or realistic, given the military and economic state of the Confederacy. Newspapers were not the only factor in the waxing and waning of Confederate civilian morale. Confederate military performance on the battlefield or the preacher's sermon on Sunday or even something as common as a neighborly discussion over the fence all had their effects on civilian morale.

The wartime experience of the Southern press was not all that different from the experience of the Southern people. Some kept the faith; some lost it. Some stuggled and fought for the entire four years and were still standing when the war ended. Some died along the way. Those newspapers that were still publishing in April 1865 were shadows of what they had been in 1860, but they were still making the effort to serve their communities, using the resources they had available. Historian Phillip Knightley concluded that newspaper coverage of the Civil War was not very good and that it was particularly bad on the Southern side because of the lack of professional correspondents and other resources. Knightley was right about the lack of resources, but he was looking at the glass as half empty. The alternative view, the one this author advocates, looks at the glass as half full. That the South's journalists kept publishing at all under the circumstances they faced—no paper, no ink, few printers, invading armies—was an amazing accomplishment and a valuable lesson in how the press can function in adversity.

A NOTE ON NEWSPAPER SELECTION CRITERIA AND THE ORGANIZATION OF THIS PART

The quotation from the Charlotte, North Carolina, *Western Democrat* that begins this work is almost prescient in its observation that anyone with a complete file of Confederate newspapers has the best history of the Civil War that could ever be written, at least of events from the Southern point of view. Unfortunately, however, full runs of few Confederate newspapers exist, and in some cases, no issues remain at all. The situation is much better than it was even thirty years ago when J. Culter Andrews published the only history of the Southern press ever written. Since then, various state projects have tracked down and microfilmed many newspapers, but their diligence cannot ferret out what has been destroyed over the years by invading armies, flames, and floods. In many instances, newspapers may exist, but they have not been microfilmed, and they are held only in distant archives to which the researcher cannot travel. For the most part, the newspapers represented in this work were either available at nearby archives, could be obtained by interlibrary loan, or were purchased. Most of the newspapers come from South Carolina, North Carolina, Virginia, Georgia, Tennessee, Alabama, and Louisiana. Newspapers from Texas, Arkansas, Mississippi, and Florida were virtually impossible to obtain, or nonexistent, and so are underrepresented in this collection of articles. The contents are compiled from a range of newspapers from small-town weeklies and dailies to the South's versions of "metropolitan" newspapers to give readers a broad, cross-sectional view of the Confederate press.

Newspaper mortality rates were high in the nineteenth century even under the best circumstances. The average newspaper lasted only a few years before it folded. This trend was exacerbated in the Confederacy. Not only did Southern newspapers face the usual economic and business problems, they also faced invading hordes of enemy soldiers who relished in destroying newsrooms and presses and tossing type out in the street for horses, wagons, and people to grind down into the dirt. A good number of Southern newspapers made it through the entire war; a few others began publication during the war; but many, many others died or were forced to publish in occupied territories. Consequently, readers will note that some newspaper voices were quite loud in 1860 or 1861 but gone entirely by 1862 or later. The *New Orleans Picayune* was a good example. It was the closest thing the South had to a metropolitan newspaper in 1860, and though it continued to publish throughout the war—in fact, is still in publication today under the title *Times-Picayune*—its home city fell into Union hands in April 1862. The *Picayune* continued to publish, but it walked a narrow line proscribed by the Union military governors. At that point, it was no longer a Confederate newspaper, and thus its content fell outside the parameters of this work. Other newspapers, including the *Memphis Appeal*, the *Knoxville Register*, and the *Chattanooga Rebel*, left their home cities and took up publishing elsewhere rather than submit to Union domination. Their voices were heard throughout the war, especially the *Appeal*'s since, in 1863 and 1864, it was a major Southern newspaper publishing a day or less from the western front.

The authors of the articles were all primarily professional journalists, either newspapers editors or paid war correspondents. There are a few exceptions. For example, a common source of war news for Southern newspapers was local soldiers who would write letters for their hometown newspapers. Sometimes, the letters would have been sent to family members who shared them with the newspapers. In all instances, the original spellings, punctuation, and so on, that appeared in the newspapers have been retained.

A final word on organization: This work is organized in chronological fashion, beginning with the 1860 presidential election and the secession crisis. The chapters on the war years, with the exception of the first year of the war, have been divided into two main sections, the Western Theater and the Eastern Theater. The Western Theater, of course, covered the Trans-Mississippi, Mississippi, Tennessee, Georgia, South Carolina, and North Carolina. The Eastern Theater focuses primarily on the action in Virginia and Lee's two attempts at invading the North. The sole exception to the chronological order of this work is the final chapter, which focuses on the Confederate homefront. The Civil War brought enormous changes for women and blacks, and a work that purports to deal with the Southern experience during that conflict cannot in good conscience avoid dealing with the homefront.

NOTES

1. According to a plaque at Fort Sumter National Monument in Charleston's harbor, Ruffin's shot was actually the second one fired that morning. The first shot, though, was a signal shot and thus not aimed nor intended directly at Fort Sumter. Consequently, it is correct to give the wiley old newspaper editor credit for firing the first shot, at the fort itself.

2. Michael F. Holt, *The Political Crisis of the 1850s* (New York: W. W. Norton, 1978), 220.

3. This finding is based on a database created by the author of the Southern press manuscript of 189 newspaper owners, publishers, and editors in North Carolina, South Carolina, and Georgia. The author collected the names of the editors from the newspapers themselves and/or several reference books, then consulted the 1860 U.S. Manuscript Census (White Schedule and Slave Schedule) for entries for each newsman. Reference materials included: Winifred Gregory (Ed.), *American Newspapers, 1821–1936: A Union List of Files Available in the United States and Canada* (New York: H. W. Wilson, 1937); Rabun Lee Brantley, *Georgia Journalism of the Civil War Period* (Nashville, Tenn.: George Peabody College for Teachers, 1929); John Hammond Moore (Ed. and Comp.), *South Carolina Newspapers* (Columbia: University of South Carolina Press, 1988); Kenneth W. Rawlings, "Statistics and Cross-Sections of the Georgia Press to 1870," *Georgia Historical Quarterly* 23 (March 1939): 177–179; Mary Westcott and Allene Ramage, "A Checklist of United States Newspapers (and Weeklies before 1900) in the General Library," *Biographical Contributions of the Duke University Libraries* (1932, 1936, 1937), Part I. Alabama–Georgia, Part II. Idaho–Massachusetts, Part IV. North Carolina, Part V. North Dakota–Vermont; H. G. Jones and Julius H. Avant (Eds.), *Union List of North Carolina Newspapers, 1751–1900* (Raleigh, N.C.: State Department of Archives and History, 1963); University of North Carolina library online catalog at http://www.lib.unc.edu; World Cat online database.

4. Augusta *Chronicle and Sentinel* (Augusta, Ga.), 27 April 1861.

5. *Charleston Mercury*, 18 April 1861.

6. Cornelia Phillips Spencer, *The Last Ninety Days of the War in North Carolina* (New York: Watchman Publishing, 1866; reprint, Wilmington, N.C.: Broadfoot Publishing, 1993), 244.

7. John Nerone, *The Culture of the Press in the Early Republic: Cincinnati, 1793–1848* (New York: Garland, 1989); L. Edward Carter, "The Revolution in Journalism during the Civil War," *Lincoln Herald* 73 (Winter 1971): 238. There are historians who would argue that the press was not particularly influential, especially due to the South's lack of literacy. See Drew Gilpin Faust, *The Creation of Confederate Nationalism* (Baton Rouge: Louisiana State University Press, 1989).

8. *Athens Southern Watchman* (Athens, Ga.), 2 November 1864.

9. Alexis de Tocqueville, *Democracy in America*, ed. and abrid. Richard D. Heffner (New York: Mentor, 1956), 93.

10. Based on figures compiled from the table of Newspapers and Periodicals in the United States in 1860, *Statistics of the United States, (Including Mortality, Property, etc.,) in 1860; Compiled from the Original Returns and Being the Final Exhibit of the Eighth Census, under the direction of the Secretary of the Interior* (Washington, D.C.: Government Printing Office, 1866), 321–322.

11. The Confederate States of America consisted of Virginia, North Carolina, South Carolina, Georgia, Florida, Alabama, Tennessee, Mississippi, Louisiana, Arkansas, and Texas.

12. *Statistics of the United States, (Including Mortality, Property, etc.,) in 1860*, l. The statistics regarding Southern and slave populations are based on calculations made from state population totals on pages 8, 17, 53, 73, 194, 270, 358, 359, 451, 486, 518, and 597 of the above-referenced book.

13. Ibid., 342, 346–348, 508.

14. Nerone, *The Culture of the Press in the Early Republic*, 42–43.

15. Ibid.

16. George C. Rable, *The Confederate Republic: A Revolution against Politics* (Chapel Hill: University of North Carolina Press, 1994).

17. Thomas Cooper DeLeon, *Four Years in Rebel Capitals* (Mobile, Ala.: Gossip Press, 1890), 289; Gerald J. Baldasty, *The Commercialization of the News in the Nineteenth Century* (Madison: University of Wisconsin Press, 1992), 44; Hazel Dicken-Garcia, *Journalistic Standards in Nineteenth-Century America* (Madison: University of Wisconsin Press, 1989), 52–54; Nathan Lande, *Dispatches from the Front: News Accounts of America's Wars from 1776–1991* (New York: Henry Holt & Co., 1995), x.

18. Patricia G. McNeely, *Fighting Words: The History of Media in South Carolina* (Columbia: South Carolina Press Association, 1998), 30; *Anderson Intelligencer* (Anderson, S.C.), 2 February 1865; *Abbeville Press* (Abbeville, S.C.), 2 October 1863.

19. William E. Huntzicker, *The Popular Press, 1833–1865* (Westport, Conn.: Greenwood Press, 1994), 139; Edwin Emery, *The Press and America: An Interpretative History of the Mass Media* (Englewood Cliffs, N.J.: Prentice Hall, 1972), 251; T. Conn Bryan, *Confederate Georgia* (Athens: University of Georgia Press, 1953), 208; J. Cutler Andrews, *The South Reports the Civil War* (Princeton, N.J.: Princeton University Press, 1970), 57.

20. Andrews, *The South Reports the Civil War*, 54, 441, 445–446, 460. For a listing of many of the South's war correspondents, see 548–551.

21. *Charleston Courier*, dispatch dated 17 October 1861.

22. Joseph S. Mathews, *Reporting the Wars* (Minneapolis: The University of Minnesota Press, 1957), 93; Henry Prentice Miller, "The Life and Works of William Tappan Thompson" (Ph.D. diss., University of Chicago, 1942), 33; Andrews, *The South Reports the Civil War*, 18, 21, 516–517; J. Ford Risley, "Georgia's Civil War Newspapers: Partisan, Sanguine, Enterprising" (Ph.D. diss., University of Florida, 1996), 2.

23. *Journal of the Confederate Congress*, vol. 4 (Washington, D.C.: Government Printing Office, 1904), 207; *Proceedings of the Second Confederate Congress, First Session and Second Session in Part*, ed. Frank Vandiver (*Southern Historical Society Papers*, New Series–No. 13; Whole No. 51, 1958), 100, 136, 234.

24. *Athens Southern Banner* (Athens, Ga.), 30 November 1864.

25. Catherine Patricia Oliver, "Problems of South Carolina Editors Who Reported the War" (Master's thesis, University of South Carolina, 1970), 33–34; *Sandersville Central Georgian*, 8 January 1862.

26. Michelle F. Robertson, "The *Savannah Daily Morning News* of the Civil War Period—A Test of Siebert's Proposition II" (Master's thesis, University of Georgia, 1976), 35–37.

27. David J. Russo, "The Origins of Local News in the U.S. Country Press, 1840s–1870s," *Journalism Monographs* 65 (February 1980): 18, 35–36.

28. August Deitz, *The Confederate States Post-Office Department, Its Stamps and Stationary*, 2nd ed. (Richmond: Deitz Press, 1950), 27; Sidney Kobre, *Foundations of American Journalism* (Tallahassee: Florida State University Press, 1958), 345; Quintus Charles Wilson, "A Study and Evaluation of the Military Censorship in the Civil War" (Master's thesis, University of Minnesota, 1945), 292; *First Annual Meeting of the Press Association* (Montgomery: Memphis Appeal Job Printing Establishment, 1864); *Minutes of the Board of Directors of the Press Association, Oct. 14, 1863 and Jan. 14* (Atlanta, Ga.: Franklin Steam Publishing House, 1864).

29. A. D. Banks to Leroy P. Walker, 4 June 1861, Letters received by the Secretary of War, War Department Collection of Confederate Records Document #1265–1861, Record Group 109, National Archives and Records Administration, Washington, D.C; James M. Mathews (Ed.), *Statutes at Large of the Provisional Government of the Confederate States of America* (Richmond, Va.: A. M. Smith, Printer to Congress, 1864), 106; Andrews, *The South Reports the Civil War*, 528.

30. Dicken-Garcia, *Journalistic Standards in Nineteenth-Century America*, 5.

31. William L. King, *The Newspaper Press of Charleston, S.C.: A Chronological and Biographical History, Embracing a Period of One Hundred and Forty Years* (Charleston, S.C.: Edward Perry Book Press, 1872), 78–79, 189.

32. "Constitution of the Press Association," *The Press Association of the Confederate States*, 1863, 9; *The Press Association of the Confederate States of America* (Griffin, Ga.: Hall & Swayze's Printing House, 1863), 28.

33. Russo, "The Origins of Local News in the U.S. Country Press, 1840s–1870s," 21; Oliver, "Problems of South Carolina Editors Who Reported the War," 36.

34. Andrews, *The South Reports the Civil War*, 527.

35. *Darlington Southerner* (Darlington, S.C.), 7 November 1862; *Augusta Chronicle and Sentinel* (Augusta, Ga.), 29 April 1863 and 27 June 1863.

36. William H. Johnson, "Dr. Robert Wilson Gibbes: Southern Editor and Publisher, 1852–1864" (Master's thesis, University of South Carolina, 1969), 66–67; *Charleston Courier*, 3 March 1858; J. L. Hatch, *Rights of Corporators and Reporters* (Columbia, S.C.: Steam-Power Press of R. W. Gibbes, 1857).

37. A *chinquepin* is a dwarf chestnut tree. Its fruit is also called a chinquepin. Chestnuts are prone to getting worms in the South.

38. Donald L. Shaw, "At the Crossroads: Change and Continuity in American Press News 1820–1860," *Journalism History* 8 (1981): 44; *Augusta Chronicle and Sentinel* (Augusta, Ga.), 15 October 1863.

39. *Augusta Chronicle and Sentinel* (Augusta, Ga.), 26 August 1863; *Charleston Mercury*, 16 July 1861.

40. *Official Record of the Rebellion* (OR), Series I, Vol. 11, pt. 3, 636.

41. Richard Kielbowicz, "The Telegraph, Censorship and Politics at the Outset of the Civil War," *Civil War History* 40 (1995): 96.

42. *Augusta Chronicle and Sentinel* (Augusta, Ga.), 15 October 1863.

43. *Charleston Mercury*, 6 July 1861; OR, Series I, Vol. 11, pt. 3, 636; Wilson, "A Study and Evaluation of Military Censorship," 208.

44. OR, Series I, Vol. 5, 1021; *Army Regulations Adopted for the Use of the Army in the Confederate States (Revised from those of the United States, 1857)* (Richmond, Va.: West and Johnson, Publ., 1861), 21; Andrews, *The South Reports the Civil War*, 162.

45. OR, Series I, Vol. 15, 771–772; Donna Lee Dickerson, *The Course of Tolerance: Freedom of the Press in Nineteenth-Century America* (Westport, Conn.: Greenwood Press, 1990), 195–196; *Proceedings of the First Confederate Congress*, Second Session, Southern Historical Society Papers (New Series–No. 7; Whole No. 45, 1925), 225–227; Robert N. Mathis, "Freedom of the Press in the Confederacy," *The Historian* 37:4 (August 1975), 638; John Paul Jones, "The Confederate Press and the Government," *Americana* (January 1943), 14–15.

46. *Athens Southern Watchman* (Athens, Ga.), 6 December 1864; Debra Reddin van Tuyll, "Journalists First, Rebels Second: An Examination of Editorial Reaction to the President's Proposed Conscription of Newspapermen," in *The Civil War and the Press*, eds. David B. Sachsman, S. Kittrell Rushing, and Debra Reddin van Tuyll (New Brunswick, N.J.: Transaction Publishers, 2000), 437–450.

47. *Raleigh Progress*, quoted in the *Augusta Chronicle and Sentinel* (Augusta, Ga.), 23 November 1864.

48. *Proceedings of the Second Congress of the Confederate States of America, Second Session*, New Series–No. 13; Whole No. 51, 285–286.

49. Wilfred Buck Yearns, *The Confederate Congress* (Athens: University of Georgia Press, 1960), 90; N. W. Stephenson, "The Question of Arming the Slaves," *American Historical Review* 18 (October 1912–July 1913): 295–308.

50. Louis Turner Griffith and John Erwin Talmadge, *Georgia Journalism, 1763–1950* (Athens: University of Georgia Press, 1951), 89; Robert A. Rutland, *The Newsmongers: Journalism in the Life of the Nation, 1690–1972* (New York: Dial Press, 1973), 209; Mark Neely, *Southern Rights: Political Prisoners and the Myth of Confederate Constitutionalism* (Charlottesville: University of Virginia Press, 1999).

51. Quoted in John Calhoun Ellen, Jr., "Political Newspapers in the Piedmont Carolinas in the 1850s" (Ph.D. diss., University of South Carolina, 1958), 119.

52. Rutland, *The Newsmongers: Journalism in the Life of the Nation, 1690–1972*, 196; Andrews, *The South Reports the Civil War*, 47; Oliver, "Problems of South Carolina Editors Who Reported the War," 54, 64; Nerone, *The Culture of the Press in the Early Republic*, 47; *Sandersville Central Georgian*, 8 January 1862.

53. Cal M. Logue, Eugene F. Miller, and Christopher J. Scoll, "The Press under Pressure: How Georgia's Newspapers Responded to Civil War Constraints," *American Journalism* 15, no. 1 (Winter 1998): 14–18.

54. *Report of the Historian of the Confederate Records of the General Assembly of South Carolina* (Columbia, S.C.: The State Co., 1898), 5; Debra Reddin van Tuyll, "Rendering the Invisible, Visible: The Wartime Experiences of Confederate Printers" (paper presented at the annual conference of the American Journalism Historians Association, Billings, Mont., 2–4 October 2003); Andrews, *The South Reports the Civil War*, 43; Oliver, "Problems of South Carolina Editors Who Reported the War," 44–45.

55. *Augusta Chronicle and Sentinel* (Augusta, Ga.), 14 January 1863; 7 June 1861; 16 June 1861; 3 July 1861.

56. *Augusta Chronicle and Sentinel* (Augusta, Ga.), 14 January 1864; *Atlanta Southern Confederacy* (Atlanta, Ga.), 14 December 1864.

57. *Albany Patriot* (Albany, Ga.), 9 December 1864; Richard L. Kielbowicz, *News in the Mail: The Press, Post Office and Public Information, 1700–1860s* (Westport, Conn.: Greenwood Press, 1989), 1–2.

58. *Rome True Flag* (Rome, Ga.), 21 September 1861; *Athens Southern Banner* (Athens, Ga.), 12 February 1862; Ernest C. Hynds, *Antebellum Athens and Clark County, Georgia* (Athens: University of Georgia Press, 1974), 97; *Greensborough Patriot* (Greensborough, N.C.), 3 January 1861; *Live Giraffe* (Raleigh, N.C.), 5 February 1859; Rev. R. H. Whitaker, *Whitaker's Remininscences* (Raleigh, N.C.: Edwards and Broughton, 1905), 432; Johnson, "Dr. Robert Wilson Gibbes: Southern Editor and Publisher, 1852–1864," 115; *Charleston Mercury*, 18 February 1861; McNeely, *Fighting Words*, 31; *Selma Reporter* (Selma, Ala.), 5 December 1862.

59. *Charleston Evening News*, 20 July 1861.

60. Lyman Horace Weeks, *A History of Paper Manufacturing in the United States, 1690–1916* (New York: Lockwood Trade Journal Co., 1916); Nancy Telfair, *A History of Columbus, Ga., 1828–1928* (Columbus, Ga.: Historical Publishing Co., 1929), 119.

61. *Constitutionalist* (Augusta, Ga.), 9 November 1864; *Columbus Enquirer* (Columbus, Ga.), 15 November 1864; Arney Robinson Childs, *The Private Journal of Henry William Ravenel* (Columbia: University of South Carolina Press, 1947), 201.

62. *Charleston Courier*, 13 February 1864; Spencer, *The Last Ninety Days of the War in North*

Carolina, 245; Herbert Ravenel Sass, *Outspoken: 150 Years of the News and Courier* (Columbia: University of South Carolina Press, 1953), 32–33; Henry Malone, "Atlanta Journalism during the Confederacy," *Georgia Historical Quarterly* (September 1953): 216; *Augusta Chronicle and Sentinel* (Augusta, Ga.), 22 October 1863.

63. Andrews, *The South Reports the Civil War,* 43; Robert Neal Elliott, Jr. *The Raleigh Register, 1799–1863* (Chapel Hill: University of North Carolina Press, 1955), 107; Oliver, "Problems of South Carolina Editors Who Reported the War," 48; Earl L. Bell and Kenneth C. Crabbe, *The Augusta Chronicle: Indomitable Voice of Dixie, 1785–1960* (Athens: University of Georgia Press, 1960), 50.

64. Benjamin F. Arthur to "My Dear Sir," 23 October 1861, Benjamin F. Arthur Collection, South Caroliniana Library, University of South Carolina, Columbia.

65. *Macon Telegraph and Confederate,* 2 December 1864.

THE 1860 PRESIDENTIAL ELECTION AND SECESSION

More than 600,000 men died during the American Civil War, and the Southern region of the country was so badly devastated—both physically and psychologically—that nearly 150 years later the effects of that conflict are still apparent. There is one legacy of secession, however, that is so profound, yet so subtle, that no one even thinks about it today: the change in the form of the verb *to be* that is used to refer to the United States of America. Prior to 1860, references to the United States often took the form: "The United States *are* . . ." After the war, usage became: "The United States *is* . . ." That shift in verbs denotes in the most succinct way possible that the South's secession from the Union in 1860 did more that lead to the bloodiest war in American history. It resolved, once and for all, questions that had never truly been answered before regarding the fundamental nature of the American Union. That debate had centered on the meaning of the Tenth Amendment and what the Framers had meant when they wrote, "The powers not delegated to the United States by the Constitution, nor prohibited by it to the States, are reserved to the States respectively, or to the people." If the states had the power to choose to enter the American Union, did they or did they not have to power to leave it when they desired? That question had been particularly important during the antebellum period when the South and the North fought over nullification, expansion of slavery into the territories, and fugitive slave laws.

Slavery was at the heart of most of the antebellum period's major political debates, and it was at the heart of the growing distance between the South and the North. While only about 25 percent of Southerners could afford to own at least one slave, it was an institution that shaped the region's culture and politics. Their regular exposure to slavery made white Southerners particularly jealous of their individual liberties. One had only to look out the back door, or across the fields to their wealthier, slave-owning neighbors, to see that the price of lost liberty was subservience. One had only to listen to the speeches of political icons like South Carolina's John

C. Calhoun to learn that the American Union was dear—but not so dear as personal liberty. Indeed, for white Southerners of all social classes, individual liberty was the one common characteristic they shared, the basis of their equality. Even if you were a dirt poor farmer with less than 20 acres of land to your name, you were, in all the important ways, the equal of the planter who owned 2,000 acres and fifty slaves, because you were a free man.

Given this mind-set, it becomes easier to understand the origins of the radical conservativism of the antebellum Southerner and the Southern response to the major issues of the period, beginning with the conflict over the admission of Missouri to the Union. While the nation debated whether to allow slaves to be imported into Missouri after it achieved statehood, many Southerners saw the subtext of the debate as whether the North would be allowed to interfere with Southern property rights. The Missouri Compromise of 1820 more or less settled the issue for the next thirty years. Any new states above the 36th parallel would be admitted as free states; any new states below that latitude would come in as slave states. That did not mean, though, an end to sectional tensions. Conflict over a proposed tariff, the growing extreme states' rights stand of many Southerners, and Northerners' moral indignation over slavery kept the tensions simmering.

In 1850 and 1854, though, the issue of the westward expansion of slavery was raised again. In 1850, the issue was what to do with territory gained in the Mexican-American War. The debate was fueled by the expanding western population brought about by the California gold rush. Antislavery forces favored a proposal made in the Wilmot Proviso to exclude slavery from all the lands acquired by the treaty that ended the Mexican war. Southerners were outraged even though the Proviso never became law. Such a decision would preclude them from exercising their liberty to move their property (i.e., slaves) about the United States as they saw fit. Stephen A. Douglas, Henry Clay, and Daniel Webster were instrumental in putting together a bill that averted secession, at least temporarily, by satisfying both the North and the South on the issue. The bill called for California to be admitted as a free state and the territories of New Mexico and Utah to be left to decide the issue for themselves. The slave trade would be prohibited in Washington, D.C., but the South would get the more stringent fugitive slave law for which it had been clamoring.

In 1854, the issue was what to do about organizing territories west of Iowa and Missouri. To satisfy Southerners, Stephen A. Douglas, chair of the Senate Committee on Territories, proposed legislation to create two new territories, Kansas and Nebraska, rather than a single one. Douglas proposed in his bill to allow residents of the territories to decide whether to come into the Union as slave or free states, a direct violation of the Missouri Compromise since both Kansas and Nebraska were north of the 36th parallel. Antislavery proponents were outraged, but the bill made it through Congress, and the president signed it. The result was anything but a peaceful outcome. Because the decision on whether to allow slavery was left to the people, both pro- and antislavery advocates streamed into Kansas to help citizens "better understand" which way to vote on the issue. The most violent result was "bleeding Kansas," a mini–civil war of sorts within the newly organized territory; the most significant result was the formation of the Republican Party by those who opposed the Kansas and Nebraska Acts.

The presidential election of 1860 was the final straw for many Southerners, especially those of fire-eating bent. They believed that if the citizens of the North were willing to elect a sectional candidate who favored abolition, then the Union was so perverted that there was no saving it. Clearly, many Southerners believed, there could be no question that Yankees and Republicans were willing to crush Southern liberty. Thus, it was time to break free, declare Southern independence, and create a new country that would more closely guard individual liberties and adhere to the requirements of the Constitution.

The fire-eaters' objections to Lincoln overlooked two important facts, though. First, Lincoln did not oppose slavery himself. True enough, his party had an abolitionist plank, but he had no inclination to do anything affirmative to implement it. Further, the president had no power to pass legislation. If slavery was to be ended in the United States, it would require the election of a Republican Congress as well as a Republican president. Those Southerners who opposed secession, or who were more cautious about what it would take to justify so rash an act, made these arguments, but secession fever swept over the South, fanned by the inflammatory rhetoric of fire-eaters such as Robert B. Rhett, South Carolina politician and owner of the *Charleston Mercury*.

Lincoln was elected on 6 November, and within six weeks, South Carolina had seceded from the Union. Within only a few weeks, six other states followed South Carolina out of the Union and then on to Montgomery, Alabama, for a convention to form the Confederate States of America. Four more Southern states would follow by or just after the capitulation of Fort Sumter. The stage was set for the bloodiest conflict in American history.

GEORGE KENDALL OR FRANCIS LUMSDEN: STATES MOVING TOWARD SECESSION IF LINCOLN ELECTED

With the 6 November election virtually upon them, Southern threats of secession became widespread and more frantic. In Mississippi, Governor John J. Pettus announced that should Lincoln be elected president, he would immediately call a special legislative session to address secession. There was little question how Mississippi's legislators would vote on the issue. Alabama's governor, Andrew Barry Moore, was also preparing to call a special legislative session that would see to the protection, that is, secession, of his state. Other Southern states, including Texas and South Carolina, likewise, were moving toward secession, though the Lone Start state's governor, the venerable Sam Houston, had vowed to resist any move toward disunion. Houston would be disappointed by his constituents' decision in February to secede from the United States. After a brief and failed attempt to reestablish the Republic of Texas, Houston resigned his governorship in March. The Mr. Yancey quoted in this story was William Lowndes Yancey, an Alabama politician and avowed fire-eating secessionist.

New Orleans Picayune, 3 November 1860

STATES MOVING

The Governor of Mississippi has announced that the same wire which brings the news of the election of Lincoln to the Presidency, shall carry through the State his call of a special meeting of the Legislature to devise measures for protection, if need be, out of the Union. He avows himself for disunion, in that contingent at all hazards.

Alabama provided last winter, by an act of the Legislature, for an election by the people of delegates to a Southern convention in case a Republican candidate should be elected President of the United States. It is stated that the Governor of the State will at once issue a proclamation for the election on the receipt of the news of Lincoln's success.

Texas took the same initiatory steps by Legislative action

before the inauguration of Gov. Houston. His conservative views will stand between the people and any rash and precipitate action.

South Carolina, it is well known, is prepared to join, if not lead, any action, however radical, against the Union, should the national party of the North triumph. Gov. Gist refuses to be a candidate for Senator of the United States Senate, as he will not serve in Congress with a Republican President.

These movements are earnest and decided the danger to the South from them is imminent. In certain sections of the States the excitement has grown to be almost beyond control. Yet, strange as it may seem, the making up of such an issue on the result simply of the Presidential contest is disapproved, and by no one of them more decidedly than by Mr. Yancey himself. At Montgomery, Alabama in the month of May last, in a public speech, he said:

> I say with all deference to my colleagues that no more inferior issue could be tendered to the South upon which we should dissolve the Union than the loss of an election. If in the contest of 1860 for the Presidency Mr. Seward should receive the legal number of votes necessary to elect him according to the terms of the constitution and the law, gentlemen say that then will be the time to dissolve the Union. If that is made the cause of disunion, I say to them I will go with them, but I will feel that I am going in the wake of an inferior issue—that there was a banner over me that is not of the kind I would wish. When I am asked to raise the flag of revolution against the constitution, I am asked to do an unconstitutional thing, according to the constitution as it now exists. I am asked to put myself in the position of a rebel, of a traitor—in a position where, if the Government should succeed and put me down in the revolution, I and my friends can be arraigned before the Supreme Court of the United States, which would be the creature of Mr. Seward, as he has given notice in the Senate, and there sentenced to be hanged for violating the constitution and laws of my country. And if I should be asked why sentence should not be passed on me, I could not then, as I can now in reference to past issues, I could not say then even to the bloody judges who would sit upon the bench, my hands are guiltless of wrong against the constitution of my country, and I appeal to an enlightened posterity, to the judgment of the world, to vindicate my name and memory when, [unreadable] country shall have taken her place once more as equal among the nations of the earth.

This opinion, so strongly stated and based upon the most hopeful view of the act by those despairing of justice in the Union, is commended to all who now are so ready to join in applause of a movement that cannot fail to awake the credit, derange the business, and destroy for years the prosperity of the entire South.

GEORGE KENDALL OR FRANCIS LUMSDEN: EDITORIAL—WHAT IS THE TRUE ISSUE IN THIS ELECTION?

In this lengthy editorial, the New Orleans paper reviewed the political controversies that had paved the way to the 1860 presidential election becoming essentially a national referendum on the questions of slavery and secession. "What is the True Issue?" the paper asked. The true issue was slavery.

New Orleans Picayune, 4 November 1860

WHAT IS THE TRUE ISSUE?

We are on the eve of a most important event. The result of the election just at hand may be fraught with momentous consequences. A determination is openly proclaimed in many quarters not to abide by the decision of a majority, if it secure a sectional triumph; and a great nation, blessed beyond all others in its basket and its store, but unfortunately torn by hostile and contending factions, seems on the very verge of revolution.

The gravity of the occasion suggests the inquiry, what is the extent of the wrongs suffered, that so arouse the fears and passions of men as to obliterate the influence of patriotism, and outweigh every consideration of public and private interest? What cause have men of the South to appeal to the god of battles for justice? On what issue is the determination made up to seek safety in a disruption of the government which has only shown an almost unlimited capacity for good?

Those who now strive to excite a tempest of popular passion, declare the election of the chief of a sectional party sufficient cause for resistance; but as if conscious of the weakness of such an issue before a people reverencing constitutional forms of action, and taught the duty of yielding to the voice of a majority, they triumphantly ask, in the manner of a most positive assertion, has not the constitution been often violated? Has not outrage followed on the heels of outrage, and forbearance but encouraged aggression, until honor and manliness, and safety, are only to be maintained by resistance? Aroused to jealousy by the fact that the free States, if united in sentiment, can control the majority of members, in the House of Representatives and the Senate, and have in their power, the distribution of the spoils of office and the direction of the policy of the government—excited beyond measure by the aggressive tendency of this Northern sectional party, that even now exults in the prospect of victory, and proclaims its irreconcilable hostility to slavery, they look back on the closed issues of the past, and all the bleeding wounds, cicatrized by time, open afresh. They seem to see but one continued series of assaults and weak defenses; one perpetual chain of concessions to be followed by those still more vital to the rights of the States, and these united in one bill of complaint are presented to the people, as an irresistible argument to stir them up to immediate and concerted resistance.

But can men of the South revive the strifes of the past to render the present issue with the North more strong? Is our cause of complaint so serious? Have the slave States been constantly suffering wrong, while possessing themselves in patience, always yielding yet never satisfying the grasping demands of the free States? Let us appeal to facts for a decision.

From the adoption of the constitution to the election of Martin Van Buren—from 1789 to 1851—a period of sixty-two years, a Southern man occupied the honored post of Chief Executive of the nation, with the exception of the single term of each of the two Adams, from Massachusetts.

During the period—that of nearly two generations—two thirds of the foreign missions and the more important of the domestic offices were enjoyed by Southern men.

From 1841 to 1860, but two Presidents have been elected—Harrison and Fillmore—who were not emphatically the choice of the South, and really nominated and elected by the South. Of the six Presidents since 1841, three were Southern men.

It was the boast of Southern statesmen as late as ten years ago that the South had dictated the domestic policy of the nation. The purchase of the Louisiana Territory was at the instigation of the South.

The annexation of Texas was conceived by Southern minds and achieved by Southern votes.

The war of 1812 from which the country emerged with so much glory, was voted and sustained by the South.

The war with Mexico, which added an empire in extent to the territory of the Republic, is due to the policy of men of the South, thus extending our Southern boundaries from the western limits of Texas to the Pacific ocean. Of all this has the South reason to complain?

But our position is scarcely less improved in three series of years in regard to the question of slavery. If, under the operation of the laws of climate and production, slavery has been extinguished in that little patch of states denominated New England, in New York, Pennsylvania, and New Jersey, the purchase of the Territory of Louisiana has given us Louisiana, Arkansas and Missouri as slave States—a region of country much larger than that from which State sovereignty has eradicated human bondage.

The annexation of Texas in 1845 devoted to slavery a territory equal to all New England, New York and New Jersey, and the acquisition of New Mexico by conquest, in which slavery has been established by territorial law, carries the institution two degrees above the line of the Missouri Compromise. Can we complain that the territorial limits of slavery have been circumscribed, or go back to this history of its extension to strengthen the catalogues of our grievances?

But, it is said, the perpetual agitation of this question in and out of Congress, has driven the South to unjust concessions, every one of which should have been made the cause of resistance to the Federal Government and that each as it followed the other in the order of succession increased the intolerance and aggressions of the free North. The Missouri Compromise was the first in order. If it was wrong the South has to blame only itself; for it came from a representative of a slave State, and was supported by the almost unanimous vote of Southern delegates in both Houses of Congress. It was ratified again and again by the popular vote of the slave States until it came to be regarded to have almost as binding a character as the constitution itself.

The next great struggle on the question of slavery resulted in the compromise bill of 1850. There again the South gave birth to the act, and it was sustained not only by the Southern vote in Congress, but was ratified by the people themselves. Georgia and Mississippi and South Carolina made the issue of resistance against it, and the people with majorities unprecedented in any political contest sustained the work of the noble patriots of that gloomy day. The South is then precluded by its own action from reopening the issues then settled and making them living questions at this time. Right or wrong, they belong to the dead past. The golden era of peace and general accord followed, until the elements of essential strife were again let loose from their sealed cavern by the repeal of the Missouri Compromise and the Kansas and Nebraska bill.

Whether the South originated this act or not, it united in almost solid phalanx to sustain it, while the North was almost alone in opposition to the measure.

This reopened the agitations happily set at rest, and again plunged the country into an excitement which has resulted in the birth of a party that now stands avowedly sectional, openly aggressive, and by its doctrines, insults and defies the South. But it has to make a forward step to present a tangible issue that can be met only be a revolution. Its principles are dangerous if an attempt be made to put them in practice. No man with a Southern heart will defend its fanatical fury, or excuse its menacing attitude towards those States coequal with the free commonwealths. But can we look back upon the history of the past and find serious reason to complain, except it be of our own blindness and folly? Can we hope to strengthen the issue now proposed by accumulating with it the series of acts, or any one of them, alluded to in this brief sketch?

The very agitation of which we complain has in one respect accrued to our benefit. It has evolved the true principles on which the institution of slavery is based. It has convinced all Southern men of the moral right, the civil, social and political benefit of slavery. It has done more; it has modified the opinion of a large number of men in the free States, on this subject, and is gradually changing the opinion of the world—bringing it to regard slavery with more liberality.

The number of slaves has increased in a remarkable ration, and to-day is stronger on the whole frontier line of the free States than it was ten, nay five years ago.

These notes of history cannot be denied, and when we meet the crisis created by the ballot of the nation about to be cast, let it be remembered that we have no cause to resist, except the unconstitutional, the weak, the untenable one of having lost our choice for the President of the Republic. The movement of demagogues and politicians to make this election, if adverse to the South, an opportunity for secession—which we have previously shown is but a word to mask the idea of revolution—is full of imminent peril to the South, not to the Union as we have been supposed to have asserted. Upon an issue so weak to go into a contest which involves all the consequences of treason, the South must fail, for she can-

not hope for accord among the citizens of any one State. The time may come when disunion with all its consequences, must be chosen, but a failure now precludes future confidence in leaders or hope in resistance.

Let every Southern man feel it to be a duty he owes not simply to his country, but to his family and himself to vote in the coming election so that he shall in no manner countenance the idea that his State or his parish is in favor of resisting the decision of the ballot. The home perils which a contrary course involve are of the most terrible character. Nations die a terrible death, just in proportion to their strength and vitality. If it be the destiny of the Union now to perish, none can estimate the throes of agony, the terrible scenes of distress, which will precede it. If the fires of civil war be kindled—and kindled they must be by any formidable movement in hostility to the Federal Government—they will burn until all is consumed that is perishable, and the land become a waste over which shall brood the silence of another and hopeless desolation.

S. B. CRAFTON: EDITORIAL—LINCOLN'S ELECTION MAKES OUTLOOK GLOOMY FOR UNION

Like many other Southerners, even on the eve of the 1860 presidential election, the editor of the weekly Sandersville Central Georgian *took the position of Stephen A. Douglas in the following untitled editorial: Election of a Republican president in and of itself did not justify secession. Before secession could be justified, the editor declared, Lincoln would have to take some overt action that directly threatened the South or its "peculiar institution"—slavery. The editor realized, however, that he was likely in the minority and that the result of the previous day's election would be civil war.*

Sandersville Central Georgian, 7 November 1860

Never, since we have been attempting to publish a newspaper, have we taken up our pen with such feelings as crowd our mind this morning. Ere this shall reach many of our readers, we fear the doom of our beloved country will be sealed. We have but little hope of the success of either of the three national candidates. In an exchange paper this morning, we see a statement, said to have been made by Hon. H. V. Johnson, on his return from a northern tour, "that Pennsylvania and New York are irretrievably lost, and that the latter will give a majority for Lincoln of 50,000." If this be true, our last hope is gone. We have never before seen our people look so gloomy on the eve of an election. All seem to realize that to-morrow (we write on Monday) is to be decided the fate of the greatest nation the world has ever known, and to be anxiously looking to the result. If Lincoln be elected, and a dissolution of the Union of these United States takes place, farewell to our heretofore prosperous and happy country. We have no

idea that a peaceable secession can be effected; but the bayonet will, we very much fear, be resorted to; the beat "to arms!" so long silent in our land, will again reverberate over hill and dale. Hostile armies will be marching to and fro over the fertile fields of our beloved South, to meet an opposing force from the North. Can it be so? Can it be so? God forbid it.

While we, individually, confess that the thought of submitting to be ruled over by an executive elected upon principles directly opposed to the interests of the South, and without the assistance of southern votes, yet we are not prepared to say we are for dissolution before some overt act has been committed by that executive. This is a matter of the greatest moments to the American people, and should be well considered before any decisive steps are taken. May the God of nations guide our people right through these troubled times!

On 20 December, the telegraph wires buzzed with the news of South Carolina's secession from the Union and reaction to it. Dispatches about the South Carolina decision came in throughout the day, but by 4:00 P.M. the Picayune's correspondent in South Carolina sent the full text of the Secession Ordinance. Other correspondents quickly sent in reaction stories. Meanwhile, in Washington, D.C., political leaders worked feverishly to reach a compromise that would keep the Union intact, or at the very least, prevent civil war.

New Orleans Picayune, 21 December 1860

FURTHER FROM SOUTH CAROLINA
FORM AND MANNER OF SECESSION
Repeal of the Ordinance of 1788

CHARLESTON, Dec. 20, 4 P.M.—The following ordinance passed the convention to day without a dissenting voice, and will be ratified at twelve o'clock to morrow, with becoming solemnity:

"An ordinance to dissolve the union between the State of South Carolina and other States united with her, under a compact entitled 'Constitution of the United States of America.'

"We, the people of the State of South Carolina, in convention assembled, do declare and ordain, and it is hereby declared and ordained, that the ordinance adopted by us in the convention of the 23rd of May, in the year of our Lord 1788, whereby the constitution of the United States of America was ratified, together with all acts and parts of acts of the General Assembly of the State ratifying amendments, said constitution is hereby repealed, and the union now existing between South Carolina and other states, under the name and title of the United States of America, is hereby dissolved."

South Carolinians rejoiced at the decision of their state convention to remove the Palmetto state from the Union. The conservative revolution had begun, and finally, the South was to be safe from the tyranny of the North. At this point, no one really expected that the South's bid for independence would result in war, much less the blood of so many being spilled.

Charleston Mercury, 21 December 1860

The 20th Day of December.

Inscribed among the calenders of the world—memorable in time to come—the 20th day of December, in the year of our Lord 1860, has become an epoch in the history of the human race. A great Confederated Republic, overwrought with arrogant and tyrannous oppressions, has fallen from its high estate amongst the nations of the earth.—Conservative liberty has been vindicated. Mobocratic license has been stricken down. Order has conquered, yet liberty has survived. Right has raised his banner aloft, and bidden defiance to Might. The problem of self-government under the check-balance of slavery, has secured itself from threatened destruction.

South Carolina has resumed her entire sovereign powers, and, unshackled, has become one of the nations of the earth.

On yesterday, the 20th of December, 1860, just before one o'clock, p.m., the Ordinance of secession was presented by the Committee on Ordinance, to the Convention of the people of South Carolina. Precisely at seven minutes after one o'clock,

the vote was taken upon the Ordinance—each man's name being called in order. As name by name fell upon the ear of the silent assembly, the brief sound was echoed back, without one solitary exception in that whole grave body—Aye!

At 1:15 o'clock, p.m.—the last name was called, the Ordinance of Secession was announced to have been passed, and the last fetter had fallen from the limbs of a brave, but too long oppressed people.

The Convention sat with closed doors. But upon the announcement outside, and upon the MERCURY bulletin board, that South Carolina was no longer a member of the Federal Union, loud shouts of joy rent the air. The enthusiasm was unsurpassed. Old men went shouting down the streets. Cannon were fired, and bright triumph was depicted on every countenance.

But before the Great Seal of the State was affixed to the Ordinance of Secession, and the names of the Delegates to the Convention were signed, it was proposed that this ceremony should be postponed until 7 o'clock that evening; when the Convention should reassemble and move in procession from the St. Andrew's Hall, where they then sat, to the great Secession Hall; and that there, before the assembled citizens of the State, the Great Seal of the State should be set, and each signature made. The proposition was favorably received.

At 6½ o'clock p.m., the Convention reassembled at St. Andrew's Hall. At 6¾ o'clock p.m., they formed in procession and moved forward in silence to Secession Hall.

The building was filled to overflowing, and they were received by some three thousand people in the Hall.

The Convention was called to order. The scene was one profoundly grand and impressive. There were a people assembled through their highest representatives—men most of them upon whose heads the snows of sixty winters had been shed—patriarchs in age—the dignitaries of the land—the High Priests of the Church of Christ—reverend statesmen—and the wise judges of the law. In the midst of deep silence, an old man, with bowed form, and hair as white as snow, the Rev. Dr. BACHMAN, advanced forward, with upraised hands, in prayer to Almighty God, for His blessing and favor in this great act of his people, about to be consummated. The whole assembly at once rose to its feet, and with hats off, listened to the touching and eloquent appeal to the All Wise Dispenser of events. At the close of the prayer the President advanced with the consecrated parchment upon which was inscribed the decision of the State, with the Great Seal attached. Slowly and solemnly it was read unto the last word—when men could contain themselves no longer, and a shout that shook the very building, reverberating, long-continued, rose to Heaven, and ceased only with the loss of breath. In proud, grave silence, the Convention itself waited the end with beating hearts.

The President then requested the Delegates (by previous decision) to step forward as they were called in the alphabetical order of the Districts which they represented, and sign the Ordinance. Two hours were occupied in this solemn ceremony—the crowd waiting patiently the end. As the delegation from St. Phillip's and St. Michael's came forward, again, the hall was filled with applause. And as the Hon. R. B. RHETT advanced to the parchment, the shouts became deafening, long-continued, until he had seated himself, signed and retired. It was a proud and worthy tribute, gracefully paid, and appreciated. The same special compliment was paid to our Ex-Governor GIST, from the Union.

At the close of the signatures the President, advancing to the front of the platform, announced that the Seal of the State had been set, the signatures of the Convention put to the Ordinance, and he thereby proclaimed the State of South Carolina a separate, independent nationality.

To describe the enthusiasm with which this announcement was greeted, is beyond the power of the pen. The high, burning, bursting heart alone can realize it. A mighty voice of great thoughts and great emotions spoke from the mighty throat of one people as a unit.

The State of South Carolina has recorded herself before the universe. In reverence before God, fearless of man, unawed by power, unterrified by clamor, she has cut the Gordian knot of colonial dependence upon the North—cast her fortune upon her right, and her own right arm, and stands ready to uphold alike her independence and her dignity before the world. Prescribing to none, she will be dictated to by none willing for peace, she is ready for war. Deprecating blood, she is willing to shed it. Valuing her liberties, she will maintain them. Neither swerved by frowns of foes, nor swayed by timorous solicitations of friends, she will pursue her direct path.

JOHN HARVEY, SOUTHERN CONSTITUTIONAL ARGUMENT FOR SECESSION

Southerners believed in the strict construction of the Constitution, that is, that the original meaning of the organic law of the United States should be followed in all circumstances. To remain true to their constitutional values, Confederates had to carefully craft their legal justification for secession carefully. The Alabama Beacon *offered its readers a constitutional argument for secession that was both common and typical in the following untitled article.*

Alabama Beacon, 18 January 1861 (Greensboro, Ala.)

Has a State the right to secede? It is a very unfair way of stating the question so far as the proposed action of the States of the South at this time is concerned. The fair way would be—Has she such a right when the Government which is the creature of the States—made by them—becomes subversive of the purposes for which it was made, and instead of promoting the happiness, security and welfare of her people, becomes

destructive of them all? Her participation in the Federal Union was certainly by the free and voluntary act of her people as a State. By this act of her as a free and independent State a portion of the allegiance due to her by her citizens was transferred to the General Government. As to all the rights of a free and independent State which were not delegated to the General Government, the people, the political organization called States, it is manifest that there could not be reserved rights, if the Federal Government, to which they had not been delegated, and over which it had no control, had the rightful power to pronounce whether there was a palpable, deliberate and dangerous assumption of powers not granted, or in other words, whether it had itself become subversive of the purposes for which it was created. This would be to make its construction of its own powers or pretended powers, and not the Constitution, the law of the land. And whereas these rights not delegated were reserved to the people and the States, this doctrine would involve the absurdity of these very rights being at the same time conferred on General Government (it choosing to claim them,) if it has the right to decide if there is or is not a palpable infringement of them. The State, as to all rights not delegated, is sovereign, and being sovereign, can have no superior to pass upon the question for her, but of necessity must decide for herself, or otherwise any infringement of them is without remedy. Now, having the right to pronounce when these reserved rights are endangered by the Government, she has, as a necessary corollary, the right and duty to decide how they must be vindicated, defended and secured. Consolidation is tyranny in this, that it abstracts from the free State whose rights are infringed or endangered, the right to vindicate, secure and defend them, and places that right in the hands of the very dominant majority of the people of the United States by whose sanction their rights have been invaded. This is not the Government our fathers made. They did not obliterate the existence of the States as free and independent sovereignties over their reserved rights. There several times was the attempt made to confer by the Constitution the right to coerce a State, and every time it failed.

Our Union has intended to be cemented by fraternal regard, and its indissolubility was intended to be secured by mutual interest and reciprocal good will; but failing these, each State was a free and sovereign political community when her rights or happiness were endangered, to pronounce on the occurrence of such fact, and to decide the mode and manner of redress. The President in his late annual message to Congress has denied the right of a State to secede, because such admission would render the Government "a rope of sand."—We would most respectfully reply that the process of disintegration is more sure to follow the denial than the admission of the right of a State to secede when the Government becomes subversive of the purposes for which it was formed. Had this right been unanimously considered and admitted, instead of the doctrine that in some places obtains that a dominant majority of the whole people have the right to decide when they shall have themselves been guilty of subverting the Constitution, the present critical condition of affairs would not now exist. Legislation would necessarily be more conciliatory in its enactments, and the attempt to ride rough shod over the security, rights and sensibilities of the different States would have been less frequently made. All Governments derive their *just* powers from the consent of the Governed, and people are always slow to change the form of Government to which they are accustomed; nor need the President, or any one else, apprehend that the right of secession would be exercised for light and transient causes, any more than they need to apprehend that human life would be insecure because any one may commit a homicide when necessary to protect his own life.

TIBER: CORRESPONDENT PREDICTS THE COMING OF WAR

As the seceded states were electing delegates to send to a convention in Montgomery, the Picayune's *Washington correspondent wrote a letter to his paper that the destruction of the Union had already been accomplished. Bitter hostility was already growing between the sections, though a number of politicians, including Senator Jefferson Davis of Mississippi, were working diligently to find a compromise. Tiber, the correspondent, had picked up the prediction that, within six months, Northern and Southern armies would be meeting on the battlefield. Almost exactly six months from the date of this letter, Confederate and Union armies met in the first major battle of the war, First Manassas.*

New Orleans Picayune, 1 February 1861

LETTER FROM WASHINGTON

[Special Correspondence of the *Picayune*.]
WASHINGTON, Jan. 23, 1861.

It may be doubted whether, even at the South, the public are aware of the fact that the Union is entirely and hopelessly destroyed and the Government on the eve of dissolution. Many have gone into the secession movement without intending that it should lead to a perpetual and total separation of

the North from the South, and perhaps to several distant and separate and sovereign confederacies. Several of the Senators from Southern States who have just withdrawn from their seats, have, in their speeches, proposed reconstruction of the Government after the Southern States shall have seceded. To call a convention of all the Southern States in March, and prepare a new constitution of the government, or a reconstruction of the Union, admitting into it only preferred States, and on terms which the convention should propose, is the process relied upon for a reconstruction of the Government. The difficulties of this project are probably not estimated. Restorations are impopular and impracticable. To heal breeches once made in a government is very difficult. The Union broken by one line, would be soon broken by many lines. It would be difficult to find any one Northern State that would agree to reconstruction upon any plan which the South would present. The Southern States in convention would not, probably, themselves agree upon a plan of reconstruction.

There will arise, and in fact have already arisen, cases of bitter and deadly hostility between the two sections, that will place reconstruction out of the question. It will be thought of after the completion of the secession programme. Measures of mutual defence and offence will occupy all minds. Mr. Jefferson Davis throws out the idea in his speech that by means of a convention of the Southern States, and a simultaneous convention of the Northern States, a league, if not a reunion could be brought about. Here is another impracticable notion. What one state would agree to another would reject, and the very principle upon which the South proceeds is that no State can be bound by any compact longer than she chooses to be.

I have seen but few men, north or south, who comprehend the entire extent and meaning of the present revolution. We shall have in ninety days a fresh, vigorous and united Southern confederacy, and a grieving and jaded and feeble Northern confederacy—the remnant of the present Union.

It is annoying that scarcely a man in New York sees this.

When the New Yorkers come here they open their eyes a little, but still say that there is nothing in the Southern movement but a little bluster. I know one or two Republican members, however, who understand the whole matter, and freely declare the opinion that in six months from this time there will be two organized Governments; that real estate in the city of New York will have fallen to one-half of its present value, and that there will be hostile armies in the field of a hundred thousand men on either side, Northern and Southern.

There is no more doubt that Virginia will secede in the latter part of February than that Louisiana will secede, and all the Southern border States except Delaware, will follow the lead of Virginia. Secession is easy and it is possible. But it leads to a new state of things, the exact bearing of which cannot be well foreseen. But it never will lead to a restoration of the Union.

The prospect of Mr. Crittenden's plan of adjustment, with Mr. Bigler's amendment, is thought by some to be improving, but it may be well doubted whether Lincoln himself could, if here, persuade and considerable number of Republican members to go for it.

The committee of five members of the House, who have had under consideration the President's message concerning the revenue laws, &c., will not report in favor of blockading the ports of the seceding States. They will report a bill that will, however, effectually destroy the trade to and from ports where revenue laws cannot be enforced.

TIBER.

GEORGE KENDALL OR FRANCIS LUMSDEN: ACCOUNT OF MONTGOMERY CONVENTION

The Southern Convention met in Montgomery in early February and within days had written a Constitution for a new nation and elected a president and vice president. The biggest issue on most Southern minds at that point was not the possibility of war. Most still thought that a remote possibility at best. Rather, the issue was whether European powers, especially France and England, would recognize the Confederacy as a sovereign nation.

New Orleans Picayune, 5 February 1861

THE MONTGOMERY CONVENTION

The southern Congress, at Montgomery commences its sessions with six States represented by a number of delegates from each, corresponding to the number of its representation, for Senators and Representatives, in Congress of the old Government. The proportion was a mere matter of discretion, for we suppose that the States will vote as units, each having one vote. Inequalities in representation were matters of compromise, under the constitution of the United States, and cease when the States resume their independence, as all sovereignties are *ex vi termini*—equals. The present number of the body, forty-three, viz: from South Carolina, 8; Georgia, 10;

Florida, 3; Alabama, 9; Louisiana, 6; and Mississippi, 7.

The number is sufficiently large to supply working men on the important committees, and yet not large enough to encourage the popular vice of long speaking. The signers to the constitution of the United States were only 38 in number, but the convention which framed it was a little larger.

The number of States being even, and the number of several of the delegations also being even, the chances are multiplied for *tie* votes on questions in regard to which differences of opinion may arise. Let us hope that these occasions will be few, and that entire harmony may prevail in their deliberations and conclusion.

Before they are many days in session there will be another member present. Texas will appear there, with her four delegates, as the seventh State.

The peaceable assembling of such a body to settle the terms of a new union and a new government for a circle of equal republics is a great epoch in the history of American institutions and principles. The grand idea of the American Revolution was the right of a people to establish their own forms of government and choose their own rulers; the grand idea of the constitution of the United States was the union of political communities under one common agency for external affairs, but with the internal capacity for each to maintain its own rights, liberties and institutions against invasion from any quarter. The recent acts of the Southern people and States have rigidly conformed to both ideas. They have pronounced that the late Government of the United States was destructive of the objects for which it was established, and asserted their right to abolish the same as respects themselves, and to erect another which shall better secure their happiness and safety. They pay homage at the same time to the federative principle, and immediately propose to substitute for the old Union, which they have thrown off as an oppression, one which shall more perfectly "establish justice, insure domestic tranquility, provide for the common defence, and secure the blessings of liberty to ourselves and our posterity."

It is a hypochondriac delusion, which seems to have seized on the minds of many of our countrymen, to despond over these results, as proofs of the utter failure of American institutions, and the final condemnation of the federative principle. There is a good deal to create profound regret and serious uneasiness in the rupture of old associations, and the downfall of a government to which we had been long devoted and from which we had hoped for so much. But, when its character was radically altered, and the government itself was the bane of the most cherished rights, and to reform or abolish it the best homage to those institutions, the effective instrument for accomplishing it was sought in the independent State governments. The dignity, power and success of the movement is the highest vindication of the vigor and value of State sovereignties for the protection of liberty.

A great revolution has been effected by the power of public opinion, freely expressed through the ballot boxes, of seven organized and orderly communities, and perfected through all the legitimate forms of established authority. In what other country, in what other times or under what other form or principle of government, could such a movement have originated and been carried through, to the final solemn announcement of the common will of seven States, without tumult, disorder or blood? How triumphantly does this fact support the theory of the wisest founders of our institutions, that however necessary a common government may be for the exigencies of commerce and war, the bulwark of our liberties and of the happiness and security of every citizen, is to be looked for in the watchful care of the States.

The federative principle is going through a severe test, but its virtue has carried us thus far to the point of a total emancipation from one system, which was tried and has failed us, to the free liberty of forming another, with all the lights of experience and the advantage of a model which leaves little to the province of speculation and experiment. The old constitution was good enough for us all, if it could have been adapted to obvious changes of circumstances, and so defined as to accomplish its own clearly defined intents. We want nothing better than it can be made to be, with few new provisions and adaptations, and the capacity to include within its scope such other States as may be willing to come into a new confederation on terms of equality.

A form of government, permanent or provisional, for the seceded States, is now the matter of urgency. In the adjustments—peaceful or otherwise—with the governments from which they have been parted, a common agency is indispensable. If we are to be opposed, we must have common counsel and common measures for defence. If the separation is to be peaceful we need the machinery for joint negotiation with the North. More especially we need, as soon as possible, a common agency for intercourse with foreign governments.

We do not doubt the readiness of all the principal governments in the world to recognize a Southern Confederacy, provisional or otherwise, as soon as formed and set in motion. It is consistent with the uniform practice of modern times, and has grown into the force of public law, that governments *de facto* are acknowledged for all purposes of trade immediately, in spite of all paper proclamations of the intention to reclaim them, thrown out by the authorities they repudiate. To a regular formed Southern Confederacy, with even eight or nine States, England and France will concede at once the fact of independence.

The same promptness cannot reasonably be looked for in receiving at once seven or eight new States as sovereigns *de facto*.

The complex relations which existed between the States and the General Government of the Union are very indistinctly comprehended, even by well informed statesmen of Europe. The ordinary idea of us which obtains even in Cabinets, and has regulated public action towards us, is that the Federal Government is a consolidated one, with the same supreme authority over the States as the European central governments have over their provinces. These false notions have pervaded most of the views which have been drawn forth on the Continent, and even in England, by the news of our dissensions. Few but close students appreciate the really distinct character of our States, or the full grown organization and perfect rights which they bear with them out of the Union. It would take a long period, and many and precarious negotiations to settle the recognition of the separate independence of so many states, and arrange commercial treaties for them with all the maritime powers.

But the concurrence of seven or eight in one organic act, constituting a common executive authority for intercourse with foreign nations, would be of such significance and dignity as to require and receive immediate recognition. It would be the demonstration of a joint purpose and a completed fact, so large, comprehensive, orderly and powerful, that there is not a government in existence that could consistently decline, and few, if any, that would not cheerfully hasten to accept the new government. They would see the grand result, even if they could not understand the vitalizing federative idea, which could so speedily aggregate the assimilating parts of a dissevered confederacy into a new, vigorous and harmonious whole.

This task is in the hands of the convention at Montgomery. May they be inspired with the wisdom to do their work, so as to command the whole support of their constituents, and establish the blessings of peace and good government forever.

GEORGE KENDALL OR FRANCIS LUMSDEN: BORDER STATE CONFERENCES SEEK COMPROMISE

Many Americans, both Northern and Southern, wanted to find some way to maintain the Union and avert civil war. Peace commissioners traveled from Montgomery to Washington, and even the Border States met to see if they could find a compromise. The Border States met at the same time as the seceded states were meeting in Montgomery to arrange their new national government. The Southerners were more successful in their work than the Border States.

New Orleans Picayune, 6 February 1861

THE BORDER STATE CONFERENCES

At the same moment when the Southern seceding States are uniting in convention at Montgomery to create a new government for a new Union, the border States are holding another convention at Washington City for the purpose of restoring, if possible, the old order of things.

This convention was invited by the Legislature of Virginia, in order, as expressed in the preamble to the resolutions which contain the proposal, "to make a final effort to restore the Union and the constitution to the spirit in which they were established by the Fathers of the Republic."

The invitation has brought together a representation highly respectable in the character and public influence of the delegates appointed from the border slave States, and from a considerable number of Northern border States. Virginia, Delaware, Maryland and Kentucky are powerfully represented. Ohio and New Jersey have sent delegations, and we believe Pennsylvania and New York, North Carolina and Tennessee. Illinois refused, and so we think did Indiana. States that are not represented directly will doubtless be consulted through their leading citizens whom the alarming state of public affairs will have brought together at Washington. There will be no want of outside and inside effort to find a basis for conciliation upon which it may be hoped that a new Union, including all the States may be constructed.

The preservation of the Union, by any of the forms of the present constitution is so plainly impossible that the first and fundamental idea of any convention which looks to a further association of these thirty-four states under one government must be that the old constitution is suspended in fact as to six of the States, and that its powers can never be renewed over them but by the result of negotiations commenced and concluded with them as independent States. They have taken positions from which it is impossible to retreat if they desired it. The dissolution of the relation of each with the Federal authorities had constituted each, by her own theory of right, an integer State, no longer competent to take part in the deliberations of the adhering States on questions of charge in the government she has thrown off. If they desire to make changes to meet her views, it must be done without her, and whatever they do cannot be presented for her concurrence as one of themselves, but for her acceptance as an independent State, free to negotiate, and as free to reject as to accept. This is the position of all the seceded States, now seven in number. They have left themselves no longer the capacity to vote as States in the Union, on any proposition for amending the constitution. Whatever is done that way in the way of conciliation, must be done without them, and submitted to them afterwards, as the original constitution was submitted to the original thirteen. Each State will be competent to accede to the amended constitution as absolutely as if it were an entirely new instrument, and as absolutely free to decline it, and remain independent.

If it were otherwise, and it be conceded by the seceding States that they can vote on proffered charges, under the forms of the constitution as when they were members of the Union, the corresponding obligation would follow, to submit to the adverse decision of the tribunal to which they had consented. To amend the constitution required three-fourths of the thirty-four States—now Kansas is admitted; that is to say, twenty-six States. Nine States could defeat any amendment. It follows that if the seceding States, which have left the Government because eighteen States have pronounced against them—which eighteen has since become nineteen—on a matter of life and death to them, should consent to refer the same questions to a tribunal in which nineteen can fore-close the chance against them, by refusing to vote for the amendment, and *nine* can defeat any proposition they please, it would be equivalent to an agreement to surrender them-selves to the judgment of nine of the Abolition States, with the pledge, necessarily implied, to acquiesce in their verdict.

Acts of secession have given formal notice that seven of the States will have no part whatever in proceedings which carry their case before such a tribunal, and which give, by implication, a right to expect that they will submit to such a verdict. They are out of the reach of being outvoted by the Abolition States and there is no way of dealing with them but by negotiating with them separately or conjointly as individ-ual States, who may perhaps be willing to confer upon a fair plan for a reconstructed Union, and perhaps not.

The adhering States do not, however, agree in considering these seven States as actually out of the Union; but persist in shaping their measures—as if they were to be retained by some measure either of compulsion or concession. In the Border State Convention, a difference of opinion on this head will be developed very soon. Some of the States there will hold that a State may rightfully secede, and several, includ-ing all the Southern delegations, will be resolute in asserting that there shall be no attempt to assert Federal supremacy by force. These differences may obstruct the action of the con-vention in *limine*, and prevent them from considering any plan for conciliation at all.

But these considerations waved or overcome, the real dif-ficulties commence.

They are manifold. They may not agree on what shall be proposed. Congress may not consent to pass them by a two-thirds vote for the action of the State Legislatures. Three-fourths of the State Legislatures may not agree to them; and if they should, the seceding States may refuse to accept them as satisfactory and prefer to remain separated.

If the other form be tried, of calling a convention by the demands of three-fourths of the States to consider the border State plan, three-fourths of the Legislatures may not concur; a general convention, if called, may fail to agree; or, if agree-ing, the plan may still be rejected by the seceding States, each of whom can act for itself.

These difficulties are made insuperable by the fact that seven of the States, which were interested, while in the Union, in amending the form of government so that they could remain, are out of it, and can take no part in the delib-erations, or no action, while the theory of the adhering States, through their representatives in Congress, is that these seven States must be counted in determining the result. In all movements for amending the constitution, thirty-four States are still reckoned as parts of the Union, and for constitutional amendments, twenty-six are necessary in order to make three-fourths.

The secession of seven States leaves only twenty-seven to deliberate and to act, and of these nineteen are non-slaveholding and eight slaveholding. On the Federal theory that the Union is not and cannot be dissolved but by the as-sent of a general convention, every proposition for amend-ment must obtain the concurrence of twenty-six States, and the whole number of States which can act being but twenty-seven, it is obvious that the vote of any two of the twenty-seven will defeat any proposition whatever. Kansas and Vermont can overrule the other twenty-five and thus settle all chance for restoration of harmony among thirty-four by shut-ting out the possibility of even a submission of terms for ad-justment of any kind by the subsisting government, even to the adhering States.

A chance for settlement which depends entirely on the all but unanimous support through all its stages, of the Black Republican States, is too remote a vision of credulous hope or unsubstantial figment of the imagination to be the basis of any acts by the Southern people either compromising their rights or their powers and modes for protecting them.

Who ever has seen any where the signs that eighteen Black Republican States will accede to such terms as will be satisfactory to the eight adhering Southern States, or toler-ated by the even seceding States, must have faith in a propi-tious close of these border State propositions, within the frame of the old constitution, and he would have the further faith that the same converted majority will deal with seces-sionism as a conceded fact and submit their propositions to free negotiation. That would be to concede at last what is de-nied at the outset—the right of independent action. Why, then, should it not be acknowledged at once, and dealt with as a basis for all attempts at conciliation, that the Union is dissolved *pro tanto*, and that the adhering states should take all steps needful for their own [unreadable] acting, to negoti-ate fairly upon the grounds of re-union, or the terms for sepa-ration.

If conducted in that spirit, the border conference may re-sult in good by presenting the ultimata of concessions in re-gard to the disputed questions on both sides, and preparing the way for either a fair presentation of a basis for recon-struction, or the general abandonment of the effort as hope-less, with peaceful agreement for each section to pursue its happiness in its own way.

In any other point of view, the Border Convention will prove a total failure in its [unreadable] design, for concilia-tion, although we cannot doubt that it will be of service in preparing the public mind for acquiescing in the necessities which it shall show to be beyond the control of the wisest and most moderate men in the nation.

GEORGE KENDALL OR FRANCIS LUMSDEN: JEFFERSON DAVIS AND ALEXANDER STEPHENS CHOSEN AS PRESIDENT AND VICE PRESIDENT OF CONFEDERACY

The new Confederate nation was established within days of the convening of the delegates in Montgomery. Members wrote a provisional Constitution, and they elected a president and vice president to lead their new country. Initial thoughts were that the presidency should go to Robert Toombs of Georgia, but his fondness for strong drink led many convention delegates to reconsider. Instead of Toombs, the Southern Congress chose Jefferson Davis, a Mississippi senator in the old Union, to be their leader. For his second, they chose Alexander H. Stephens, a well-known and -respected politician from Georgia.

New Orleans Picayune, 10 February 1861

DAVIS AND STEPHENS

The Southern movement for a new Union and a new Government is going on with a quiet force that is as wonderful as it will prove to.

The Congress [*unreadable*] has done the two things necessary to [*unreadable*] organization and the [*unreadable*] cannot be disarranged. [*Unreadable*] essential things settled are the formulation of a Provisional Government and the appointment of Executive officers for the new Confederation.

The main and gratifying fact, which disperses a great chance of misrepresentation and misapprehension is that the constitution of the United States is the model for the new frame or government. It was the work of wise men and true patriots. The alterations of empire and the change of society and time, have rendered some revision necessary, to adapt it to the wants and necessities of the day and this people. We have full trust that such changes will be made in due time, and are content that, for the present, the provisional authority of the new confederacy shall rest on the basis of fundamental truths and enlightened patriotism, which were ever the foundations of that structure which folly and fanaticism have overthrown.

It is telegraphed that the new constitution is changed from the last—in that it establishes entire free trade. We apprehend there is some misapprehension in this. It may be that free trade will be the policy of the new Government and that it is favored by the convention, but it is not likely that a question so purely a matter of legislation, and which concerns so many and diverse interests, and controverted doctrines, would be definitely decided in a provisional constitution.

The convention has also selected a President and Vice President for the Provisional Government. They are Jefferson Davis of Mississippi, for President, and Alexander H. Stephens, of Georgia for Vice President.

The selections are altogether good, both in respect to personal fitness, and in regard to great questions of policy, internal and external.

Jefferson Davis is a statesman, a scholar and a soldier. He was [*unreadable*] in military life, served early in the regular army of the United States in the [*unreadable*] 1st Infantry [*unreadable*] of the Dragoons and as adjutant in the last regiment. Twenty five years ago he resigned from the army and devoted himself to civil occupations [*unreadable*].

TIBER: FATE OF FORT SUMTER AND THE COMING OF WAR

The debate over whether secession would be peaceful or whether it would result in war consumed politicians and citizens alike in both the South and the North. Southerners sent commissioners to Washington to try to persuade the Lincoln government to agree to peaceful secession. The main issue was Fort Sumter. Would Lincoln honor the Southern demand that his forces be removed from the fort in the Charleston harbor, or would he not? Lincoln hoped to find a compromise position—resupply the fort without reinforcing it with more soldiers—but Southern patience would ultimately run out.

New Orleans Picayune, 31 March 1861

LETTER FROM WASHINGTON

[Special Correspondence of the Picayune.]
WASHINGTON, March 23.

The Cabinet conference of yesterday continued from 10 o'clock till a late hour in the evening. It is believed that the subject before it was one that involved the highest issues known to civilization, to wit: those of peace or war.

Probably the subject of consideration was Mr. Seward's answer to the Montgomery commissioner, all three of whom are now here. His answer was not to be made so early as this. But circumstances may render it necessary for the administration to hasten a development of their policy.

Last evening, as I happen to know, and as I telegraphed you, Mr. Seward sent a verbal message to the Montgomery commissioners, to the effect that the Federal Executive Government contemplated a pacific solution of the present difficulties; that no reinforcements would be sent to Fort Pickens, and that Fort Sumter would be forthwith evacuated.

There was a reason for this pacific demonstration. It was in the position of the border States, and particularly of Virginia. If the administration is to be led by Seward, then Virginia must be conciliated so far as it may be in the power of the Lincoln Government to conciliate that great and influential State.

A large majority of the Virginia Convention was elected by Union men. But with the Lincoln inaugural, and with the extraordinary efforts made by radical Republicans and immediate Secessionists to induce the belief that the Lincoln government is for war, there has been a great change of opinion in the Virginia convention. It is believed that a majority in that body is now inclined to immediate secession.

Within a few days past, Mr. R. E. Scott and other prominent Union members of the convention, informed their friends here that secession could no longer be checked, unless the Lincoln administration would show their determination to pursue a pacific policy.

I have reason to believe that response was authorized to be made to those members of the convention, and that it was of a satisfactory character.

The Administration will be obliged, therefore, if it would conciliate the border States, to show their hands very soon.

Before Senator Hunter left this city for Virginia last week he expressed his belief that Virginia would secede in thirty days. Verily, the advices from Richmond look very much like it.

But if the Lincoln Government take a decided and open course in favor of pacific measures, the Virginia Convention will adopt a plan of conciliation, and will lay it before a convention of the border Southern States, by which it will be, no doubt, adopted. The Northern States will then have an opportunity to adopt or reject the proposition. Some of them will agree to it. Pennsylvania and New Jersey will lose no time to accept it. This movement will give us peace.

There is another solution which Virginia politicians contemplate, to wit: the secession of all the States not yet seceded, and their union with the Confederate States. It is not to be doubted that when a common centre shall be established, States will gravitate to it.

A strong hostility to the pacific policy of Mr. Seward and of Gen. Cameron is manifested by the radical Republicans, and especially by some of those in the Senate. I learn, too, from men whose intelligence is to be respected, and who just come from the North and West, that the minds of the people are obstinately bent upon war.

TIBER.

SPECIAL REPORT TO THE *PICAYUNE*: CONFEDERATE CABINET AWAITS WASHINGTON'S RESPONSE TO ITS PEACE COMMISSIONERS

As the following extract from the Picayune's *Montgomery correspondent indicated, the Lincoln cabinet was not the only political body consumed by the issue of war and what the response to the Southern commissioners would be. Davis's cabinet was waiting. The irony of this story is that it ran on 12 April, the day Gen. P.G.T. Beauregard received orders to begin shelling Fort Sumter. To lighten the letter a bit, the reporter included a report of a duel between a Montgomery editor and a navy clerk who believed he had been wronged by something the editor had written.*

New Orleans Picayune, 12 April 1861

LETTER FROM MONTGOMERY

[Special Correspondence of the *Picayune*.]
MONTGOMERY, April 8, 1861.

Eds. Pic.—There is evidently something serious contemplated by the Cabinet here, as it has been in session most of the day and in telegraphic communication with our Commissioners at Washington. It is supposed they have demanded a distinct answer from Mr. Lincoln, and named an hour beyond which it would not be receivable. The murmurs of the people were making themselves heard, and the warlike demonstrations at

Washington demanded instant attention from the Administration here. Still, if the Federal ships-of-war make no attempts to reinforce at Pensacola, the Confederate States will not yet begin the war.

The affair of honor referred to in a late letter has come off at Pensacola between Mr. Banks, editor of the Confederation, of this city, and Mr. T. P. Moses, a clerk in the Navy Department, who had received a month's leave of absence. The parties exchanged shots, both being unhurt, although the ball from Mr. Banks's pistol passed through the lapel of Mr. Moses's coat. The difficulty was amicably adjusted without a second fire.

FURTHER READINGS

Channing, Steven. *Crisis of Fear: Secession in South Carolina.* New York: W. W. Norton, 1970.

Davis, William C. *"A Government of Our Own": The Making of the Confederacy.* Baton Rouge: Louisiana State University Press, 1994.

Freehling, William W. *Road to Disunion.* New York: Oxford University Press, 1990.

Nevins, Allan. *Ordeal of the Union.* 2 vols. New York: Scribner, 1947.

Phillips, Ulrich Bonnel. *Course of the South to Secession.* 1939. New York: Hill and Wang, 1964.

Potter, David M. *The Impending Crisis, 1848–1861.* New York: Harper and Row, 1976.

Rable, George C. *The Confederate Republic: A Revolution against Politics.* Chapel Hill: University of North Carolina Press, 1994.

Reynolds, Donald E. *Editors Make War: Southern Newspapers in the Secession Crisis.* Nashville, Tenn.: Vanderbilt University Press, 1970.

2

REPORTING THE WAR, 1861

The Eastern Theater dominated the war-related news in most Confederate newspapers during 1861 since that was where both of the year's major engagements occurred. Like the troops in the field, the reporters who covered these two battles were green. Many had never experienced military combat, much less tried to piece together a coherent story out of chaotically violent clashes, the significance and results of which sometimes even eluded the commanding generals. Confederate war correspondents, like most Southern soldiers, had come from jobs and professions other than the military. In fact, the entire concept of war correspondence was somewhat new. Certainly, previous wars had been reported, both in America and elsewhere, but generally the reports were based on news that circulated back from the front by chance rather than on information intentionally gathered and crafted into a story by a journalist. William H. Russell of the *London Times* had served as the first modern war correspondent only a few years earlier when England had fought against Russia in the Crimea.

The lack of war reporting experience, though, did not stop reporters—both Confederate and Yankee—from flocking to Charleston in March and April 1861. If there was to be a war, and most Southerners certainly hoped secession could be accomplished peacefully, there was no question that it would begin in Charleston. Charleston became the focal point for two reasons. First, it was one of only two federal installations that had not been seized by the Southern states as they seceded from the Union. The other was Fort Pickens at Pensacola. The second reason was that South Carolinians were fiercely protective of their honor and their state's sovereignty. The presence of a federal garrison on South Carolina soil was offensive to both of those sentiments. And so all American eyes turned to the fort in Charleston Harbor, and they and their newspapers both debated whether the Union government would, and should, resupply the garrison there or yield to Southern demands for its withdrawal. Everything hinged on what newly elected President Abraham

Lincoln would do after he was inaugurated on 4 March, for it was pretty clear that current President James Buchanan would take no meaningful action before he left office. Both American presidents were in a tough spot. If they resupplied the fort, then they would be accused of provoking a civil war. If they did nothing, Northerners might lose interest in the secession debate and come to accept the idea of the South as a separate entity.

Twenty-five days after being inaugurated, and nearly that many days of debating the issue with his cabinet, Lincoln made up his mind: Fort Sumter would be resupplied with provisions, but it would not be reinforced with additional soldiers. That was as narrow a compromise as he could devise. As he had promised to do when the Confederate government sent peace commissioners earlier in March, Lincoln sent word to South Carolina that supplies were coming for the garrison at Fort Sumter.

Any newspaper that could afford to send a correspondent to Charleston wanted to have someone on the ground there when the first shot was fired. Some newspapers, including Savannah's two dailies, sent not just ordinary correspondents but their editors in chief. James R. Sneed, of the *Savannah Republican*, and William Tappan Thompson, of the *Savannah Daily Morning News*, got news early on 12 April that the fighting at Fort Sumter had begun, and they traveled together on the 1:00 Savannah-Charleston train to be on hand for whatever happened next.

Around midnight on 12 April, Confederate General Pierre Gustave Toutant Beauregard had sent emissaries to give the Sumter garrison one last opportunity to evacuate the fort. Major Robert Anderson, in command of the federal garrison, declined. At 4:30 that morning, Beauregard offered former U.S. Congressman Roger Pryor the honor of lighting the fuse that would be the first shot of the Civil War. When the politician protested that he could not start the war, Beauregard made the offer to a 67-year-old journalist-turned-Confederate-private, Edmund Ruffin. Ruffin had no qualms. He took the string, pulled the lanyard, and the fighting began. Before the bombardment ended with the garrison's surrender, more than 4,000 shots would be hurled at the fort. The American Civil War had begun.

The day after Major Anderson surrendered Fort Sumter, President Lincoln issued a proclamation that declared the seven seceded states to be in insurrection, but worse, in terms of escalating the conflict, he also called for 75,000 volunteers to put down the rebellion. Lincoln got more than he asked for: Some 100,000 men stepped forward.

From April to mid-July, the United States and the Confederate States worked to build, arm, and train their military forces. From a practical point of view, to win the war, all the South needed to do was, well, nothing—unless the federal army invaded. The South had only to fight a defensive war. From the Northern perspective, though, the issue was far more complex. To win the war, the North would have to conquer the South physically. When the Confederacy moved its capital to Richmond, it simplified the North's military strategy. The Southern capital was no more than 100 miles from the seat of federal power in Washington, D.C. The Southern move also guaranteed that the primary theater of operations for the war would be Virginia. Southern men and boys, many of whom had never been outside their home states, went marching off to war in far, far away Virginia.

Through the early summer, small units of Confederate and Union troops met from time to time in small skirmishes in Virginia, but the second major engagement of 1861 occurred in mid-July 1861. The First Battle of Manassas occurred on the banks of a creek, Bull Run, near the Virginia village from which it took its name. The largest army ever assembled on American soil, 35,000 men under General Irvin McDowell, advanced from Alexandria toward the Confederate lines at Manassas.

While First Manassas resulted in a Confederate victory, the advantage swayed back and forth throughout the day. Who would come away victorious was not a certain thing at virtually any point during the fighting. The Southern troops were just as panicky and raw as the Northern troops, so much so that even though they routed the federal army, the Confederate army was too disorganized to follow up on its victory. There has been much criticism over the years of the Confederate officers for not ordering their army to pursue the federals all the way back to Washington. That order was not issued because it could not have been carried out.

After Manassas, both armies in the East retired to their camps to nurse their wounded, bury their dead, and learn something more about being soldiers. Small skirmishes and battles punctuated the fall, but leaders on both sides were engaged in the business of building armies and planning campaigns for 1862.

In the West, operations focused on Kentucky, which at first was neutral but later declared for the Union. Both Confederate and Union armies invaded Kentucky, but neither truly capitalized on its advances.

THE BUILDUP

South Carolina had taken the first direct step toward civil war when it seceded on 20 December 1860. The Northern states parried that move on 26 December 1860 when the garrison on Sullivan Island's Fort Moultrie, commanded by Major Robert Anderson, moved to the more easily defended Fort Sumter. Anderson's force consisted of two artillery units with a total of slightly more than eighty officers and men. South Carolinians immediately looked to the defense of their most important city and considered what Anderson's move meant. The touchstone issue was whether the U.S. government would withdraw Anderson's forces from a facility the Southerners believed rightly belonged to them, or whether some attempt would be made to resupply the garrison at Sumter so that it could retain possession of the island fort. Rumors flew between Charleston and Washington. One dispatch claimed to have it on good authority that there would be no attempt to resupply, the next that resupply awaited only Lincoln's inauguration. The rhetoric war had begun, and the *Charleston Mercury* was one of the leading "generals."

ROBERT BARNWELL RHETT, JR.: MOVE OF FEDERAL TROOPS TO FORT SUMTER MAY ENCOURAGE PROGRESS OF SOUTHERN SECESSION

The sudden movement in late December of the federal garrison at Fort Moultrie to another, more easily defended coastal fortification, Fort Sumter, was hailed by the trigger-happy in South Carolina, including the fire-eating Charleston Mercury. *The* Mercury, *along with many other Southerners, predicted the unexpected move by Major Robert Anderson and his troops would shock other Southern states into seceding as well. The paper held out hope, though, for a bloodless transition to Southern independence.*

Charleston Mercury, 31 December 1860

THE PROGRESS OF SECESSION

The last week has been full of stirring incidents in the progress of that great movement, which is now working out the deliverance and liberty of the South. Our Commissioners have appeared in Washington. The Custom House, the United States Arsenal, Fort Moultrie and Castle Pinckney are in our possession. On Morris' Island, and on Sullivan's Island, our engineers are busy throwing up earth works, with a view to the Harbor and Fort Sumter. The sudden abandonment of Fort Moultrie by the United States troops, and the occupation by them of Fort Sumter, has filled our people with military enthusiasm. The threatening aspect of the Black Republican party—the resignation of his office by the Secretary of War in Washington, and the confusion and excitement which bankruptcy of the Government and the conflict between the two sections of the Union occasion at the Federal Metropolis, augers well for our cause. The Government stands paralyzed. If it dares to send the Federal troops, now in Fortress Monroe, or the Norfolk Navy Yard, to Charleston, Virginia will rise up and seize the fortresses of the United States within her territory; and before this week is out, every military post on Southern ground will be in possession of the State authorities of the Southern States. They will all see that the issue of force is made by the Federal Government; and that the fate of our Southern State must be the fate of all. The coercive power of the Federal Government, so long vaunted as adequate to suppress the secession of a State, is rapidly proving itself to be, what it has long been supposed and said to be—a wretched humbug—a scarecrow—a dirty bundle of red rags and old clothes. We said it ten years ago, and again a few months since, that secession could not and would not be put down by the Federal Government. Even General JACKSON, in all the plenitude of his popularity, felt the inadequacy of military force to perpetuate the Union; and whilst putting forth his Proclamation and Force Bill with one hand, he was under great apprehension and most busy with the other hand in getting up a Tariff in the House of Representatives, which he afterwards said was far better for the South in its concessions, than the Compromise Tariff of 1833, made by Mr. CLAY. That still greater humbug, of the eighteen millions of freemen, north of the Ohio and MASON and DIXON'S line, who are to rush down upon the South in true Tartarie style, is also rapidly changing its frowns into grimace. Before long, we fear, we will be the tender object of their distorted smiles and grim affections; and by the aid of our frontier Southern States, they will put forth their meek endeavors to win us back to their paternal embraces.

The interest in the proceedings of South Carolina in the great drama of secession, will probably end with this week. Other actors are coming upon the stage. Other States will secede from the Union. Other ports are to be blockaded; other forts are to turn their guns upon the people, or be seized. The spirit of the South is rising to meet the great emergency her safety and honor requires; and as State after State withdraws from the Union, the fixed attention which our little State drew upon herself will be turned to the grand aggregation of free and independent Southern States seeking, in a common assemblage, those new means of preserving their liberties and institutions which their separate organization renders necessary. South Carolina will lose her attractions with the return of the garrison from Fort Sumter to Fort Moultrie, and the quiet triumph of her secession, in the control of her destinies, will be a thing of course.

TIBER: REPORT ON CRITTENDEN COMPROMISE PROPOSALS

President Lincoln was inaugurated on 4 March 1860 and began immediately to form his government. A great frustration to the Washington correspondent of the New Orleans Picayune *was the fact that the U.S. president had given little attention at all to the Southern rebellion, not even, apparently, discussing the matter with his party's representatives in the Senate. The correspondent mistakenly believed, as did many Southerners, that Lincoln would let the region secede in peace. The Crittenden resolution mentioned in the following story was an attempt by U.S. Senator John J. Crittenden to find a compromise to the secession crisis. Crittenden proposed a series of constitutional amendments to address Southern concerns that gained widespread popular favor but failed to garner sufficient Republican support to make it through Congress. Only one provision that Crittenden proposed gained enough support to be approved by Congress. It was an amendment to forbid federal interference with slavery in the states.*

New Orleans Picayune, 2 April 1861

LETTER FROM WASHINGTON

[Special Correspondence of the *Picayune*.]
WASHINGTON, March 26, 1861

The President and his Cabinet have been so closely engaged in making appointments that they have given no attention as yet to the revolution, nor even expressed or formed an opinion in regard to it. They have had the Senate here three weeks and have not communicated to a single member of the body their intended policy, if they have any, in regard to the dismemberment of the Union. When the Republican Senators are questioned on the subject, they say they have no information about it. But a number of them have, in recent debates, expressed the belief that the seceded States would return to their allegiance to Federal Union! Upon this vain hope Mr. Lincoln's Administration is to depend for its success. Therefore, it is quite certain that they will be necessarily led, whether they desired it or not, to a pacific policy. I have no doubt that they will abandon Fort Pickens as they have done Fort Sumter, and resort to no such absurd measures as the Republican press proposes for the collection of revenue.

Thus they will leave the Confederated States to consolidate their power without hindrance. The States which may be inclined to secession will be certain, therefore, to be able to carry out the measure without molestation from the Federal Government.

Secretary Chase thinks that he will be able to collect revenue enough to carry on the Government till next December, and he wants no extra session. The whole Cabinet, and Mr. Lincoln himself, are averse to an extra session, because it will distract and divide the Republican party. Every step of the Republicans as a party plays into the hands of the secessionists. Coercion is not thought of, and could not be adopted without special laws of Congress, and Lincoln will not call them for that purpose. Besides this, the Republicans have adopted a protective and prohibitory tariff at the very time when the Government of the confederated States were preparing to offer the country a free trade tariff, one that ensured diversion of foreign trade from the North to the South, and generously gave up their revenue to the new Confederation of the South.

By the same measure, too, they have furnished inducements to foreign Governments speedily to recognize the Confederate States, and establish commercial treaties with them, appointing Counsels, &c. Never was mother country more indulgent than this to a revolted colony; never was any Government so liberal to those seeking its dismemberment and destruction.

The Virginia Convention will not adopt any act of secession at present. They will recommend to the Border States the holding of a national convention at Frankfort, and that body will, upon their consultation, determine upon the course to be pursued with reference to the reorganization of the Government, and their own position in it. If they remain with the North, they must have constitutional guarantees from the North for their rights, and they will be content with nothing less than the Crittenden resolutions.

The Northern people, or at least the people of most of the Northern States, will concede this or anything else to the border States if it will keep them in the Union; but there is no way in which the people can reach the question, as the State authorities will not give them an opportunity to vote upon it. This being the case, the border States, one after another, and not long after the present year, will probably secede and apply for admission into the Confederate States. Mr. Breckinridge is decidedly of the opinion that this will be the result. The North will repel them, and the South wants them. Mr. Breckinridge declared in his speech in the Senate, to-day, that even Kentucky would withdraw and go into the Southern confederation if the North did not speedily take measures for securing to the South absolute equality in the Territories.

The next question is, how many of the free States will apply for admission into the same Confederacy? Anti-slavery is not a ruling principle in Pennsylvania and New Jersey, and those two states will come in at an early day. Should peace be preserved, the free States on the Ohio will come in.

Mr. Seward will soon lay before the several States the amendment to the constitution which was submitted by Congress at the recent session to the State Legislatures for adoption. It merely provides that the Federal Government shall not in any way interfere with slavery in the States. It will be a part of the constitution when it shall be adopted by twenty six States. It will do nothing towards removing the discontents of the South.

There was a time in December last when the adoption of the Crittenden propositions would have held in the Union every State except South Carolina. It is not so now.

Though the Lincoln government will preserve peace, till the regular session of Congress next December, yet it may not be in their power to do it long after that body shall assemble. When Virginia and Maryland shall move in concert towards secession, we shall have the real crisis of peace or war. Then this Government must recognize disunion and make treaties of peace, &c., with the Confederate States, or war may ensue. In this case it will be hard to tell where the blows will fall thickest and heaviest, but it appears to me that Maryland and this District will be the Flanders of the war.

TIBER.

ROBERT BARNWELL RHETT, JR.: LINCOLN'S DECISION TO RESUPPLY FORT SUMTER IS DECLARATION OF WAR

The same day the Mercury *ran the latest telegraphic dispatches from Washington, it carried an editorial that updated speculation regarding the dispatch of a Lincoln representative to Charleston to meet with South Carolina's Governor Francis Pickens. The messenger had brought word that supplies were on the way for Fort Sumter. That, in the* Mercury's *opinion, was a declaration of war.*

Charleston Mercury, 9 April 1861

WAR DECLARED

Our authorities yesterday evening received notice from LINCOLN'S Government, through a special messenger from Washington, that an effort would be made to supply Fort Sumter with provisions, and that, if this were permitted, no attempt would be made to reinforce it with men! This message comes simultaneously with a fleet, which we understand is now off our bar waiting for daylight and tide to make the effort threatened.

We have partially submitted to the insolent military domination of a handful of men in our bay for over three months after the declaration of our independence of the United States. The object of that self-humiliation has been to avoid the effusion of blood, while such preparation was made as to render it causeless and useless. It seems we have been unable, by discretion, forbearance and preparation, to effect the desired object; and that now the issue of battle is to be forced upon us. The gage is thrown down, and we accept the challenge. We will meet the invader, and the God of Battles must decide the issue between the hostile hirelings of Abolition hate and Northern tyranny, and the people of South Carolina defending their freedom and their homes. We hope such a blow will be struck in behalf of the South, that Sumter and Charleston harbor will be remembered at the North as long as they exist as a people.

THE WAR BEGINS

Lincoln's decision to resupply Fort Sumter put the Confederate government in a tight spot. If the South allowed the resupply, it would be an implicit admission that the facilities still belonged to the American government and that the Secession movement was only hypothetical. If the South tried to stop the resupply, it would have to take the first military action, and it would be setting off a civil war. Robert Toombs, the Confederate secretary of state, tried to dissuade Davis from stopping the resupply. He feared such an action would be tantamount to suicide. Many more Southerners, though, were demanding action be taken in the Charleston Harbor, and so the order came from Montgomery for General Beauregard to demand the immediate evacuation of Fort Sumter by Major Anderson and his garrison.

Three of South Carolina's leading men, Col. James Chesnut, Capt. Stephen D. Lee, and Lt. Col. A. R. Chilsom, were appointed to carry the surrender demand to Anderson. Anderson, a Kentuckian married to a Georgian, declined to surrender. He did, though, tell the three South Carolinians that his garrison would be starved out within a few days if they were not battered into submission sooner. Anderson was hoping with those words to keep the South from taking a precipitous action that would have irreversible results. Beauregard telegraphed Confederate Secretary of War Leroy P. Walker for instructions. Should he try to wait out Anderson? The secretary instructed Beauregard to obtain a precise evacuation date from Anderson. This time, four men sailed across Charleston Harbor shortly past midnight on 12 April under a white flag of truce.

Anderson told these men that he would withdraw no later than 15 April unless he was resupplied or received other instructions from his government. Anderson was unaware that supply ships lay just outside Charleston Harbor with plans to enter the harbor the next morning. The South's representatives, led by former U.S. Congressman Roger Pryor, demanded immediate surrender and assured Anderson that firing would begin on Fort Sumter within an hour if he chose not to capitulate the fort. At 4:30 A.M. on 12 April, Beauregard readied his batteries. He offered the first shot to Pryor, a vociferous fire-eater himself, but the former congressman did not have the stomach to actually fire the shot that would begin a civil war. The second man offered the opportunity had no such qualms. Edmund Ruffin, a 67-year-old fire-eating journalist from Virginia, stepped up to the cannon and let loose the first of more than 4,000 rounds that would be slung at the fort in Charleston Harbor during the two days and nights of the bombardment. Pryor, though reluctant to fire the first shot, did preside over the surrender of Fort Sumter.

YOUR CORRESPONDENT: REPORT OF FIGHTING AT FORT SUMTER—START OF WAR LIKELY

The Picayune's *correspondent at the Confederate capital knew when he sealed the envelope on his 11 April dispatch that it would not reach his paper's readers in time to appear before the fighting began at Fort Sumter. He was right. The dispatch predicted war would begin on 12 April, but because of the lag in the mail, the article did not reach New Orleans until the 15 or 16 April. The story ran in the 16 April edition, four days after* Picayune *readers had received the first telegraphic reports of the fighting in Charleston Harbor.*

New Orleans Picayune, 16 April 1861

LETTER FROM MONTGOMERY

[Special Correspondence of the *Picayune.*]
MONTGOMERY, April 11, 1861

Eds. Picayune—I advised you to day, by telegraph that President Davis had demanded the possession of Fort Sumter, and allowed Major Anderson til 12 o'clock noon to surrender it, so that the likelihood is, ere this letter reaches you that the Confederate flag will float over that far-famed stronghold.

The Washington Artillery, of Augusta, Georgia, with six pieces, is expected to arrive this evening, *en route,* to Pensacola, their services having been accepted by the Secretary of War. The Oglethorpe Infantry, of the same place, left Montgomery this morning. They are the last of the first requisition on the State of Georgia.

I am informed on reliable authority that our Commissioners left Washington to day.

It is stated that the second Alabama Regiment, Col. Tennent Somars, have tendered their services to the Governor of Alabama to participate in the attack of Fort Pickens.

People here are delighted that the uncertainty is at an end, and that we are now entirely justified in driving the invaders from our soil. No one [*unreadable*] a particle of doubt as to the result, and the only regret is that President Lincoln does not head the expedition.

The only arrival at the hotel from the West, are Messrs. John B. Martin, L. M. Cormack and Col. Henry Wheaton, all from Mississippi, F. Blish and lady and C. W. Alexander, from Louisiana, and F. S. Randel from Texas.

YOUR CORRESPONDENT.

BY TELEGRAPH: SOUTH CAROLINIANS OPEN FIRE ON FORT SUMTER

News of the firing on Fort Sumter did not reach New Orleans in time for the morning edition of the Picayune, *but the telegraphic dispatches did arrive in time for the afternoon edition. Most of the news from Charleston would have to wait until the next day to run, but the* Picayune *editors did find space for the wire flashes and one short editorial.*

New Orleans Picayune, 12 April 1861

IMPORTANT FROM CHARLESTON
FIRE OPENED ON FORT SUMTER!

[By the American Line.]

MONTGOMERY, April 12.—The Secretary of War (L. Pope Walker) informs me that fire was opened on Fort Sumter this morning, at half past 4 o'clock, by Gen. Beauregard. [Signed]

D. G. DUNCAN.

The above dispatch was transmitted to us, as also to other journals of the city, about half past nine o'clock this morning. It was also transmitted, in the same form, to Mayor Monroe. We have assurances, moreover, from the telegraph office, that it is authentic and may be implicitly relied upon, and therefore we give it publicity.

We may, also, remark here, and to account for the absence of further information on the subject, direct from our correspondent at Charleston, that it is understood that the telegraph lines leading from that city have passed under the control of the military authorities.

We also understand that prudence in the transmission of intelligence North and West concerning the military operations of the Confederate States, has been enjoined upon the proper office in this city.

Since writing the above we have received the following from the agent of the Associated Press:

MONTGOMERY, April 12.—The Secretary of War says Gen. Beauregard opened fire on Fort Sumter this morning at half past four o'clock.

AN ANONYMOUS REPORT: FORT SUMTER SURRENDERS

The day after the bombardment of Fort Sumter began, the telegraph brought word of the garrison's surrender. Their white flag was soon replaced by the Confederate national flag, the Stars and Bars. People throughout the South received the news of the surrender with great gladness.

New Orleans Picayune, 13 April 1861

TELEGRAPHED TO THE NEW ORLEANS PICAYUNE
LATEST FROM CHARLESTON
PARTICULARS OF THE SURRENDER
THE CONFEDERATE FLAG WAVING
OVER FORT SUMTER

Blockade of the Port of Charleston

[By the American Line.]

CHARLESTON, April 13—2 P.M.—Major Anderson has hauled down the United States flag from Fort Sumter and run up the white flag.

The fort has been burning for several hours, from the effect of the bombshells. Two explosions have also been produced by the shells thrown from our batteries.

Maj. Anderson ceased his firing sometime since. The fire of all our batteries has been continued till the present time.

Upon the raising of the white flag the firing ceased, and two aids were sent by Gen. Beauregard to Fort Sumter.

[Second Dispatch.]

CHARLESTON, April 13, 4 P.M.—The flag of the Confederate States of America now floats over Fort Sumter.

The port of Charleston has been blockaded by the U.S. ships of war which recently arrived in the offing of the harbor.

Rejoicing at Montgomery

MONTGOMERY, April 13—The above dispatches were addressed to the Secretary of War, by Gov. Pickens, of South Carolina. They were read by a clerk of the War Department in front of the executive building, and in the presence of President Davis and the Cabinet.

Seven guns were fired, and one for General Beauregard, and another for the Confederate States.

There is great rejoicing among our people.

Great Rejoicing in Mobile

MOBILE, April 13—The news of the surrender of Fort Sumter to the Confederate army was received with immense cheering. Crowds congregate about the streets to discuss the important intelligence.

The Confederate and Palmetto flags are unfurled to the breeze.

Cannon are firing, bells ringing, and the enthusiasm knows no bounds.

Savannah Republican
15 April 1863

For 32 hours, Confederate ordnance bombarded Fort Sumter. Miraculously, the fifty tons of cannon balls slung at the fort, powered by eight tons of powder, killed no one.

Providence, *Savannah Republican* Editor James R. Sneed concluded, had declared that Americans should not spill the blood of their countrymen. The fight was fought. For that day.

The Battle of Charleston

(EDITORIAL CORRESPONDENCE.)
SEAT-OF-WAR
CHARLESTON, April 13th, 1861.

Greek has met Grrek [*sic*], and we have had the "tug of war." That "DIES IRÆ" so long feared and deprecated, and which all hoped would never come to pass, when Americans should meet Americans in deadly strife, has at last arrived. In all respects one of the most remarkable battles on record, has been fought in the harbor of this city; and as it was our privilege to be an eye witness to its dreadful progress, or at least by far the most interesting portion of it, we propose to briefly sketch the event, as we, in company with thousands, saw it at a distance.

Fort Sumter is an immense and powerful fortification built up in Charleston harbor, about four miles from the city and on the south side of the channel. It is entirely surrounded by water. To this stronghold, it is already well known to our readers, Maj. Anderson, accompanied by his small band of Federal troops, retired from Fort Moultrie, late in December last, and soon after the secession of South Carolina from the Union. The number of his effective men, no one, to this day, has been able to ascertain. It has been variously estimated at from 60 to 90. The work of being incompletely armed, it is said that most of his guns have been mounted by himself, on carriages constructed of boards and such other loose materials as he found in the fortification, and bits of timber which he would capture while floating down the bay. The number of guns he secured in placing the battery in this way is also unknown. His position, however, was very strong, both from the peculiar construction of the work and its isolation. His ordnance, too, was of large calibre and of the most destructive patterns. Here we have, imperfectly sketched, one of the parties to the conflict.

The opposing army was composed, almost exclusively of South Carolinians, the General in command, and a few staff volunteers, we believe, being the only exceptions. They were also posted in fortifications around the harbor, most of which are of recent construction.

Fort Moultrie, the leading work, stands on Sullivan's Island about a mile, or a little more, north, slightly east of Fort Sumter. It was originally a formidable point, but has been greatly strengthened and secured by tiers of sand bags along the whole line of parapet on the water side. It was commanded by Major S. R. Ripley, an experienced officer, formerly of the U.S. Army.

Fort Johnson is situated on the opposite side of the Bay, and about one and a quarter miles south-west of Fort Sumter. It is an old fortification and of moderate size and strength, commanded during the engagement by Capt. George S. James.

The Morris Island battery is about twelve hundred yards south-east of Sumter, on a point of land looking out toward the bar. It is a remarkable work, an impromptu one, and wholly original in its construction. It is the invention of a Mr. Stephens, of this city, and its chief peculiarity consists of slanting sides and roof built of railroad iron and in such a position that shot which strikes it glance overhead. It did wonders in the engagement, and fully met the highest expectations of the inventor. It was commanded by Maj. P. F. Stephens, commandant of the Charleston Citadel Academy. A shot or shell from its batteries never failed of its mark.

The Floating Battery, another peculiar structure, was moored in the cove at the north western end of Sullivan's Island, and commanded by Lieutenant John Randolph Hamilton. It also did effective work, and thus disappointed the expectations of croakers.

There was also a Howitzer Battery on Sullivan's Island, a little west of Moultrie, commanded by Capt. Hallonquist, and a battery east of Moultrie, looking out upon the bar, together with several other smaller works at various points on the harbor. Castle Pinckney, owing to its distance, was not in the engagement.

I have not heard the precise number of guns in these various batteries, but they were all well armed, and garrisoned by a force of some nine thousand men, all under the command of General Beauregard of the Confederate Army.

Such are the parties of the contest, and the reader, if he has followed us, will comprehend their respective positions.

On Thursday last, the 11th instant, General Beauregard despatched several members of his staff to Fort Sumter, with orders to demand the immediate evacuation of the work. The reply of Major Anderson was, that duty to his Government and to his honor as a soldier required that he should decline a compliance with the demand. At this time three U.S. vessels of war were at anchor off the bar, in full view, laden, it is understood, with troops and provisions.

Nothing now remained but to enforce the evacuation by a resort to hostilities. Soon after day light, Friday morning, the contest was opened by two guns, fired in quick succession, from the battery at Fort Johnson. The sound was caught up by the other batteries, and in a few minutes a shower of iron hail poured in upon Sumter from nearly every point of the compass. Two hours and a quarter elapsed before Major Anderson returned the fire. All things ready, he finally opened his ports and turned his guns on Fort Moultrie and the Morris' island battery, but chiefly on the former, nearly every ball taking effect. The engagement then became general, and the rapidity and accuracy with which Major Anderson returned the fire throughout the day, is highly complimented by the officers of the opposing army. Some express the greatest admiration for his gallantry. The firing was kept up with but little intermission throughout the entire day, and though a fierce storm of rain was falling during a good portion of the time, it did not cool the ardor of the combatants. Towards night the firing almost ceased, but soon after dark the battle was resumed, and kept up steadily throughout the night. Thousands were collected on the Charleston Battery to witness the display. We will not attempt to describe that which baffles description. The scene was grand almost beyond conception.

Saturday dawned a bright and lovely day, but the flags of each of the belligerent were still flying in stately defiance, and the deep mouthed cannon continued to belch forth their fiery thunder. Major Anderson's men, though, were evidently wearied by the fatigues of the past twenty-four hours, as they returned the fire on the enemy only at long intervals. About eight o'clock a smoke was seen issuing from the southern side of his fort, showing evidently that a shell or hot shot had taken effect in the woodwork of the interior. It attracted no great attention at first, but the smoke continued to rise, until in the course of some two hours an explosion of gunpowder, yet not loud enough for a magazine, proved that the fort was on fire, and Anderson was blowing up his quarters to arrest the flames. A second explosion, but all to no effect. In a few moments his entire barracks were on fire and the entire fort wrapped in flames and smoke. Thousands were collected on the Battery to witness the conflagration, and the greatest excitement was manifested in every countenance.

And now for an incident of heroism that will go down to the last syllable of recorded time.

In the midst of this disaster, when almost suffocated, it is supposed, with heat and smoke, Anderson's men were at their guns fighting with desperation, and pouring the iron instruments of death into the works of his assailants. The fact is spoken of with the greatest admiration by everybody here; and I am credibly informed that so great was the impression made by this act of intrepidity in his terrible extremity on the garrison at Morris' island, that at every report of his guns they would pull off their hats and unanimously give him three hearty cheers. They then shook their fists at the Government war vessels, four of which were now quietly at anchor in the offing, for not flying to the rescue of their gallant countrymen!

In the course of an hour Major Anderson succeeded in reducing the flames, or rather, we should say, they went out for want of fuel, it being understood that the officers' quarters are entirely destroyed. Exhausted with labor, and finding all chance of reinforcement hopeless, Major Anderson, about ten o'clock, hung out a white flag from the parapet, his flag staff having previously been felled by a ball from Fort Moultrie, and immediately was silent and the war at an end. Boats went over immediately from Moultrie and Morris' Island, and it [*missing words.*] The terms are not yet arranged, though it is believed he will be allowed to come out with his side arms, and embark for New York in one of the Government steamers now lying off the bar. Throughout the long and tiresome engagement, the South Carolina troops—to whom, with their gallant commander Beauregard, all the honor of this great victory is due—conducted themselves with perfect order, the greatest enthusiasm, and with a courage that proved they were invincible. Though the odds were on their side, considering the strength of the fortification they had to subdue, nearly everybody considering the undertaking a hopeless one, they have won golden honors, and worthy of Palmetto fame. They have proved to Lincoln that the South is invincible.

And now for the most remarkable circumstance of the most remarkable, and we may add, unnatural struggle. The battle lasted thirty-two hours with hardly an intermission, some fifty odd tons of cannon balls were exchanged between the belligerent, some eight tons of powder burnt; the weapons used the most destructive known to modern warfare and in skillful hands, and yet *on neither side was there solitary life lost*. We may almost say, in the language of Lincoln, that "nobody is hurt"! We are credibly informed that not one is seriously wounded, and but a very few slightly. The forts though, especially Sumter and Moultrie, are greatly damaged.— There is nothing like this in the annals of the world, and verily it seems that Providence had interposed and resolved that Americans *should not* shed a brother's blood.

An account of the condition of the fortifications in another letter.

S.

GEORGE KENDALL OR FRANCIS LUMSDEN: ACCOUNT OF FALL OF FORT SUMTER

The failure of the U.S. government to turn over Fort Sumter peacefully to the Confederates was something of an epiphany for the New Orleans Picayune. *The paper had been strongly Unionist in its editorial stance since before the November presidential election. After the bombardment of Fort Sumter, though, the paper, like many other Southerners, had a change of heart. If Lincoln was going to use coercion to keep the Union together, then resistance was imperative. The United States had finally completely turned its back on the concepts of self-government and political liberty. A break was not only necessary; it was the only possible principled response.*

New Orleans Picayune, 14 April 1861

FALL OF FORT SUMTER

The flag of the Confederate States floats at least over Fort Sumter. The contest was an unequal one, and ought never to have been permitted by the Federal authorities. They should openly, with proper force, and in due time, have succored the brave soldier to whom they had committed the perilous trust, or they should have withdrawn the slender garrison all together, yielding to imperious necessity, or frankly and honestly avowed a conciliatory and pacific policy. They did nothing manfully or honestly. They halted between two courses, either of which might be sustained as at least direct and open, and temporized and equivocated, protested against violence and plotted in secret for a coup-de-main.

They used honeyed words of persuasion to lull the vigilance of the South, and talked glibly of moderation and conciliation in order to gull their own partisans so as to carry them through an election and to draw out capitalists into a loan. They were all the time contriving an underground plot, through mean tools and by the most perfidious practices, upon the trusting loyalty of the Southern people for a sudden breach of all those engagements, expressed and implied, in their good faith, and the seizure, by stealth, of the advantages they had covenanted to abstain from. If the commissioners and the Government of the Confederate States, have been lulled into false security by these tricks and had been suddenly surprised in finding a Federal force entrenched impregnably in the heart of the South, they could have excused themselves in the court of honor for having confided in the truthfulness and openness of an American Executive and his Cabinet.

But there were wary soldiers, and were not to be put off their guard, even when the world might have so indulged them, for being unsuspicious of so vile a treachery as this Lincoln scheming upon the success of violated promises and broken words of honor. A sense of high duty and great responsibility saved them from the evil consequences of having put trust in Black Republican honesty. It was, therefore, with a sense of scorn for the meanness of the attempt that they turned at once upon the baffled conspirators, and struck at once a decisive blow, invigorated by the contempt of a chivalrous spirit for whatever is paltry and false.

The fall of Fort Sumter is the first incident in the conflict which Northern folly has driven on so relentlessly to overpower the rights of self-government, and the most elementary principles of political liberty in the States of the South, and it will be remembered, not so much for the achievement itself—a wide step in the march towards Southern independence—as by the illustration which it furnishes of the energy, directness and force, with which the men of the Southern States have met this issue when it came to them, and the sinuosities and peddling manœuverings, and frauds, and suspicions by which the Cabinet to whom Lincolnism has given the custody of the honor of the once glorious Union, approached their object.

We are no longer of that people, but we remember what they were in the days when it was a pride and a glory to rally under the same old flag. We are very slow to believe that they are the degenerate race which it would show them to be if they were not ashamed of the hands into which the bastion of Washington has fallen, to be so dishonored. If there be not a wide-spread disquietude so exhibited among them at the miserable figure which their Cabinet makes in its abortive practices about Fort Sumter, as to overthrow the party of its personal supporters, for some more respectable dynasty of rulers, it will give additional cause to the Southern States for having escaped from such associations. It was said in derision of a Pagan superstition, What must the people be where the monkey is a God? It is scarcely too much to paraphrase the saying by asking, what must the people be, in this day, of whom Lincoln, and Seward, and Greeley, are the leaders and prophets?

AN ANONYMOUS REPORT: WAR PROCLAMATION BY LINCOLN

Union response to the firing on Fort Sumter was swift and decisive. President Lincoln called for 75,000 men to volunteer for three months' service in the Union army. Public opinion formed just as quickly, according to the telegraphic dispatch from the New Orleans Picayune's *Washington correspondent: Throughout the North, the sentiment was to support the Lincoln government in putting down the rebellion. Men from throughout that region had begun volunteering for military service, even before Lincoln's proclamation. In the Border States like Maryland, though, feelings were more mixed.*

New Orleans Picayune, 15 April 1861

TELEGRAPHED TO THE NEW ORLEANS PICAYUNE
HIGHLY IMPORTANT FROM WASHINGTON
WAR PROCLAMATION BY LINCOLN
75,000 MEN CALLED FOR

An Extra Session of Congress Called
The City in a Blaze of Excitement

[By the Southwestern and American Lines.]

WASHINGTON, April 14.—This city of Washington is in a perfect uproar of excitement over the proclamation issued by Lincoln, calling for the militia of the several States, and convening the Federal Congress for the 4th of July. Thirty thousand men have already been tendered. The city is strongly guarded at every point. The cavalry is on the road, and the military inside. More troops have been ordered.

Lincoln's Proclamation

The following is Lincoln's proclamation:—

"*Whereas*, the laws of the United States have been and are now opposed in several States by combinations too powerful to be suppressed in the ordinary way,

"I therefore call forth the militia of the several States of the Union to the aggregate of seventy-five thousand, to suppress said combinations and execute the laws.

"I appeal to all loyal citizens to facilitate and aid this effort to maintain the laws and the integrity of the national Union, and the perpetuity of popular governments, and redress wrongs that have been long endured.

"The first service assigned to the forces will be to repossess the forts, places and property that have been seized from the Union.

"The utmost care will be taken consistent with the object to avoid devastation and destruction or interference with the property of peaceful citizens in any part of the country, and I hereby command persons composing the aforesaid combinations to disperse within twenty days from this date.

"I hereby convene both Houses of Congress for the 4th of July next to determine upon measures which the public safety and interest demand.
[Signed]

"Abraham Lincoln."

By W. H. Seward, Sec'y of State.

Reception of the War News
The Feeling in Baltimore

BALTIMORE, April 14.—The fall of Fort Sumter has caused a feeling of gladness here, inasmuch as it is looked upon as a triumph over Lincoln.

As the inauguration of civil war, it has caused feelings of sorrow.

The Union sentiment here is unchanged, but the excitement is intense.

The News in Detroit

DETROIT, April 14.—The war news has produced a profound sensation. There is a unanimous sentiment to sustain the Government.

The News in Chicago

CHICAGO, April 14.—The feeling here is similar to that in Detroit.

The News at Erie, Pa.

ERIE, PA., April 14.—The people here sympathize greatly with the Federal Government. All our volunteer companies offer their services to the Governor to-morrow.

Lincoln's Reply to the Virginia Commissioners

WASHINGTON, April 14.—President Lincoln, in replying to the Virginia Commissioners, says if, as it appears, an unprovoked assault has been made on Fort Sumter, he holds himself at liberty to repossess like seized places, and to the best of his ability, repel force by force. It will perhaps cause the mails to be withdrawn from the seceded States. He shall collect imports by armed invasion, but may land forces to relieve the forts on the border country.

The War Feeling North
Offer of Troops from Ohio

COLUMBUS, April 15.—Adjutant General Carrington has ordered the military laws to be carried into effect providing 6,000 regular militia and a reserve of not less than 35,000 men subject to immediate transfer into the regular force.

The people, irrespective of party, are offering their services.

Lincoln Demands Aid from New York

ALBANY, April 15.—It is rumored that Gov. Morgan has received dispatches from Lincoln asking aid.

Lincoln's reply to the Virginia Commissioners has dissatisfied the Republicans and Democrats.

The Seventh and Sixty-ninth regiments have volunteered their services for the defence of Washington.

Rejoicing at Richmond

RICHMOND, April 15.—The news of the surrender of Fort Sumter was received with demonstrations of joy. A Southern flag was hoisted Saturday night on the capitol, which was subsequently removed by the guard.

Excitement East

BUFFALO, April 15.—Numerous Eastern cities are intensely excited. The military are volunteering their services for the support of the Government. A general determination is manifested to support the Government.

Volunteers from Indiana

INDIANAPOLIS, April 15.—Gov. Morton possesses information from all parts of Indiana that volunteer companies are forming everywhere.

Thirty thousand men can be relied on to defend the national flag.

MADISON, Indiana, April 15.—Several military companies are in the act of being formed for immediate service.

A Union meeting was held Saturday night, at which resolutions were passed to maintain the Government.

Extra Session Illinois Legislature

CHICAGO, April 15.—The Governor of this State has convened the Legislature for the 24th inst.

One Hundred Thousand Men from Pennsylvania

PHILADELPHIA, April 15.—Gov. Curtin has gone to Washington to say that Pennsylvania can send 100,000 men to defend the National capital.

ANONYMOUS REPORT: MAJOR ANDERSON PERMITTED TO DEPART FORT SUMTER

Major Anderson and his men were allowed to surrender with dignity. Confederate Senator Louis T. Wigfall of Texas accepted Anderson's sword but returned it to him. The Union troops were permitted a fifty-gun salute to the fallen U.S. colors, a salute that resulted in the only death at the fort. An ember from one of the guns landed on a powder keg, killing Union Private Daniel Hough and wounding five others. Hough did not merit mention in the dispatch that described the surrender.

New Orleans Picayune, 16 April 1861

FURTHER FROM CHARLESTON

Major Anderson Permitted to Depart
Reception of the News of Montgomery

[By the Southwestern and American Lines.]

MONTGOMERY, April 14.—It is stated by authority of the Secretary of War, Hon. L. Pope Walker, that Major Anderson and his men are permitted to depart unmolested.

Ex-United States Senator Wigfall, of Texas, received Major Anderson's sword at Fort Sumter as aide-de-camp of Gen. Beauregard.

All the force of the Confederate Government is to concentrated at Fort Pickens.

Twenty regiments are offered by Tennessee for our service.

The Confederate Congress on assembling will declare war if the Government at Washington blockades the ports in the Confederate States.

Seven hundred National volunteers at Washington refuse to observe under Lincoln and denounce him.

An offer has been made to the Treasury Department to take the whole Confederate loan of fifteen millions at par, by parties in New Orleans.

Secretary Toombs has received a dispatch from Hon. J. C. Breckinridge and Gov. Magoffin, of Kentucky, stating that greatly excited sympathizers are entirely with the South. Seven thousand men of the Border States are under arms, and have offered to move at a moment's notice.

In reply to a message asking what was the feeling in Montgomery, President Davis says, rough and curt: "Fort Sumter is ours and nobody is hurt. With mortar, paixhan, and petard, we tender old Abe our Beauregard."

When Major Anderson's quarters were burning, Gen. Beauregard sent offers of assistance, before the white flag was run up. Hon. L. T. Wigfall, of Texas, received the sword, and returned it to Major Anderson.

The fleet was still in sight off the Charleston harbor to day.

FIRST BATTLE OF MANASSAS

At the end of the day, the Confederate army was able to claim a victory on the battleground beside Bull Run, near Manassas, Virginia, but it performed only slightly better than its Union oponents. Union General Irvin McDowell had some 35,000 men against Confederate General Pierre T. G. Beauregard's 20,000. As the battle opened, McDowell was not aware that Confederate General Joseph E. Johnston had outmaneuvered the federal force at Harper's Ferry and had arrived with about 12,000 men to reinforce Beauregard. Both commanders, though, devised such complicated attacks that their untrained armies of raw recruits had little chance of executing the plans successfully. McDowell tried unsuccessfully to turn the weaker Confederate left, but the Union attack was checked by the arrival of General Thomas J. Jackson and his Virginians. Jackson's troops moved to envelop McDowell's force, which fled from the battlefield in a panic. It was that day that Jackson earned his well-known epithet. When Jackson arrived, the Confederate units under General Barnard Bee were near to breaking and running themselves. Bee rallied his troops by pointing to Jackson and his seemingly fearless Virginians. He urged his panicky soldiers to rally behind Jackson. Bee pointed to the steely-eyed former mathematics professor and yelled to his men, "Younder stands Jackson like a stone wall; let's go to his assistance." The battle raged throughout the day, but finally around 4:30 that afternoon, McDowell saw that his best move would be a retreat. Civilians who had come out from Washington, D.C., and soldiers alike fled in panicked disorder. The Confederate troops, who were in almost as chaotic a state, were unable to pursue the fleeing federals.

AN ANONYMOUS REPORT: REPORT OF CONFEDERATE VICTORY AT MANASSAS

Two days after the first major battle of the Civil War, the Memphis Appeal *proudly announced the Confederate victory. The* Appeal *ran both the telegraphic news dispatch and an editorial about the Southern victory. As in the initial reporting of any battle, the coverage had several inaccuracies. The Union commanding General McDowell was not mortally wounded; he lived until 1885. Also, Jefferson Davis was present at the battle as a spectator, not as a military leader.*

Memphis Appeal, 23 July 1861

BY TELEGRAPH!

THE WAR NEWS!

GREAT BATTLE AT MANASSAS!

7000 FEDERALISTS KILLED!

SOUTHERN LOSS 3000!
MCDOWELL, THE FEDERAL COMMANDER REPORTED MORTALLY WOUNDED!
BEAUREGARD'S HORSE SHOT UNDER HIM!

[Special to the New Orleans Press.]

RICHMOND, July 21—9 P.M.—The battle commenced near Manassas at 4 o'clock this morning. It became general about 12 M., and continued until 7 P.M., when the federals retired, leaving us in possession of the field.

Sherman's battery was taken.

The battle was terrible with great slaughter on both sides.

NEW ORLEANS, July 22.—A private dispatch to a gentleman in this city states that seven thousand federalists and three thousand Confederates were killed.

Gen. Beauregard had his horse shot under him, and one of the commanders of the New Orleans Washington artillery was killed early in a fight.

A special to the Delta (not yet published) says Beauregard had his horse shot under him while leading Hampton's S. C. Legion, and that General Johnson seized the colors of a wavering regiment and rallied it.

Another private message says that in the Bull's run battle 990 of the enemy were killed and wounded, and 60 Confederates.

It is reported that Gen. McDowell is mortally wounded.

NEW ORLEANS, July 22.—Dispatches from Richmond to-day say, that the reports of the killed and wounded last night were so unreliable, in the confusion following the victory at Manassas, that no mention was made of them, fearful of giving causeless pain to anxious hearts.

General Beauregard and staff are safe—though Beauregard's horse was shot under him;

General Jos. E. Johnson commands the left where the enemy made their fiercest attack. The right wing was commanded by Beauregard.

President Davis reached the field at noon, and took command of the center. When the left was most severely pressed, the center disengaged a portion of the enemy's force.

No other reliable reports have been received but are hourly expected.

It is stated the enemy was commanded by Generals Scott, Patterson and McDowell, and it is reported the latter was severely wounded.

BENJAMIN F. DILL OR JOHN McCLANAHAN: GREAT VICTORY AT MANASSAS

As great battles and great victories have gone historically, First Manassas was not much of a battle. Two untrained armies, both manned with terrified though determined soldiers, met on a creek bank, fought, killed, and died, then disintegrated into such a chaotic state that one fled and the other could not capitalize on the advantages it had gained. Still, First Manassas was vitally important to the Southern cause, for it seemed to prove the boast of many Confederates that a single soldier from the South could whip three Yankees with one arm tied behind his back. The Southern press certainly treated the battle as a major victory, as the following article from the Memphis Appeal *indicated.*

Memphis Appeal, 23 July 1861

GREAT VICTORY AT MANASSAS

Our dispatches this morning, both from northern and southern sources—Washington and Richmond—give us what we deem to be a reliable account of the great battle of the present campaign, fought with terrible slaughter and desecration at Manassas on the day of the 21st instant, and resulting in the disastrous defeat of the enemy. The details, so far as received, show it to be the grandest conflict that ever transpired upon the American continent, and besides Soiferino, in which not less than 320,000 men were engaged, unequaled, perhaps, in its importance, its splendor, the desperate ferocity with which it was waged, and the probable number of killed and wounded, by any battle of the present century. Though no mention is made of the exact number of forces on each side, there could scarcely have been less, we think, than from eight to ninety thousand federalists, and from eighty to sixty thousand Southrons, who participated immediately and remotely in the contest. The presence of SCOTT and DAVIS upon the occasion, the throwing of Johnson's forces down to the scene of the engagement from Winchester for the purpose of re-enforcement, and also the withdrawal of Patterson's command from Martinsburg on the part of the enemy, together with the daring personal exposure of officers on both sides, furnish us the most unmistakable evidence of the vast importance that was attached to the result by the combatants. The victory on the part of the South is evidently complete, and the route of the enemy scarcely less overwhelming than that which lost BONAPARTE the day at Waterloo. We can scarcely estimate the probably moral effect of this success of our arms upon the North, but have every reason to believe that it will cast a damper upon their energy, which will detract somewhat from the gusto they have so far exhibited for volunteering. It would not, perhaps, be going too far to surmise that it will be the battle of the present war, and will virtually break the backbone of the Washington government. Of such fearful contests it was that Mr. WEBSTER spoke, when he, many years ago, truthfully asserted that "battles have been fought that *fixed the fate of nations.*"

JOHN R. THOMPSON: REJOICING OVER VICTORY AT MANASSAS TEMPERED BY WAIT FOR WORD ABOUT LOVED ONES

News of the Confederate victory was received with tremendous joy in the capital city. The Memphis Appeal *correspondent, Dixie, John R. Thompson, described the reaction to the news about Manassas in a pair of letters that ran together and detailed both the jubilation of the citizens and the apprehension of mothers, sisters, and wives who awaited news of loved ones who were on the battlefield.*

Memphis Appeal, 28 July 1861

FROM THE SEAT OF WAR IN VIRGINIA

[From our Special Correspondent.]
The Battle of Manassas—Reception of the News in Richmond—General Rejoicing—Meeting of the Confederate Congress—Resolutions Adopted—Meeting of Citizens—The Wounded, etc.
RICHMOND, July 22, 1861.

The excitement which pervaded our city and the appearance presented by its streets last night can be adequately communicated to your readers by no words of description of mine. The hot, weary Sabbath had drawn toward its listless close, before the crowds of anxious and expectant citizens, assembled at every corner, had received positive intelligence of a great battle raging on the border. Then ensued three hours of terrible suspense, during which the offices of the newspapers and the telegraph were besieged by thousands, in vain asking for news of the result. At last, after a full moon had risen high in the heavens, the glad announcement was made to the throng in front of the Spotswood house, in a dispatch from President Davis, that we had gained a "glorious but dear-bought victory," and that the enemy were in full flight, closely pursued by our forces. Instantly, the shouts of the multitude were taken up and re-echoed from hill to hill, giving the glad tidings to the entire population. Until long past midnight there was a continuous stream of people of both sexes, flowing through the principal thoroughfares, while at almost every turn the stroller met some well-equipped company in full ranks marching rapidly toward the depot of the Central railway. There was gratulation and rejoicing over the triumph of our arms, but it was tempered with solicitude for relatives in the fight. Here were mothers, wives, sisters, moving in every direction to learn if by chance there were any messages from the dear brother, the fond husband, the darling son; for the "victory," said the President, had been "dearly bought" and this was a presage of desolation to many hearts. And so wore away the calm, midsummer night, with the round white moon shining down upon steeple and roof, and, alas, upon heaps of dead on that Manassas plain, adding a more ghostly pallor to the stark faces of brethren slain by each other's hands.

A pouring rain ushered in the morning, and has continued to descend all day like a deluge, but this has not prevented eager crowds from gathering upon the streets at the usual news marts, to hear further from the great battle of yesterday. At an early hour another regiment (in addition to the five or six sent off last night by the Central railroad) left town in the cars on the Fredericksburg line, to be switched off to the Central at the Junction, twenty-five miles distant from Richmond. The men marched steadily to the train, through the driving storm, their oil skin caps shedding streams of water upon the pavements as they passed along. They seemed to care for little but to keep their powder dry.

Towards noon, continuous files of reekling umbrellas led through all the wet avenues of the square toward the capitol, where the Confederate Congress was to assemble punctually at that hour. The hour had scarcely sounded from the neighboring bell house when the body was called to order by the Hon. Howell Cobb. A solemn gravity was manifest throughout the hall. The galleries and privileged seats were filled with an excited but decorous audience. Directly after the usual opening exercises, a dispatch was ready from President Davis, (which you have received at the time of this writing,) announcing the total rout of the enemy, the capture of guns, prisoners and colors, and the hot pursuit of the flying columns by our dragoons. Mr. Memminger, the Secretary of the Treasury, then rose and offered appropriate and feeling resolutions, which were adopted unanimously, and congress accordingly adjourned. The third of the series had reference to a call, in the newspapers of the morning, by the mayor of the city for a meeting of the citizens, at 5 o'clock P.M., at the base of the Washington monument, in the Capital Square, to adopt measures of succor and relief to the wounded, and provide for the proper burial of the dead. The inclemency of the weather preventing a meeting in the open air, it was held at the hour appointed in the court room of the Hustings court in the city hall. The mayor, Joseph May, Esq., presided. Resolutions, expressions of the sympathy of the entire community, were passed, and efficient acting committees were named, one of twenty-five to proceed immediately to the camp of Gen. Beauregard, at Manassas, with the view of accomplishing the speedy and comfortable removal of the wounded to this city; another to provide hospital and private lodgings for their reception, and nurses to attend them, and a third to raise a proper fund to defray the expenses attending these arrangements. Gallant fellows! The fairest and tenderest hands in Virginia shall minister, with affectionate assiduity to their wants while stretched upon the bed of sickness and suffering; shall twine the [*unreadable*] for the graves of such as languish away in death, and bind the laurel, fadeless for all time, around the brows of the survivors.

The streets have been filled with rumors, during the afternoon, of the progress of the pursuing cavalry along the road to Alexandria, some alleging that Beauregard already entered the place and was pushing toward Washington. There seems to sufficient ground of confidence for this report, as the enemy had thrown up strong entrenchments near the town, commanding the road, and the day has been eminently unfavorable for military operations. Indeed, the storm with which it commenced, so far from abating, has increased in severity, and now, at nightfall, continues with a volume of water which threatens an inundation of our rivers, and a blustering east wind, which promises small comfort during the night for the blockading vessels of Abraham Lincoln, in Chesapeake bay and Hampton Roads. If the wreck of half a dozen of them were the only damage done by the blow, we should be well content and hail the east wind as a valuable ally.

DIXIE.

Return of President Davis—Arrival of the Wounded from Manassas—Funeral Honors to the Illustrious Dead—A Traitor Prisoner—The Battle of Scary Creek in Kanawha County—the dinner Party (which Didn't Come off) of Senator Wilson—Resignation of Mr. Toombs—Congressional Tributes to the Lamented Gen. Bartow

RICHMOND, July 24, 1861.

There was a scene of much interest and excitement at the depot of the Central railroad last evening. Several thousand persons had gathered there to await the arrival of the evening train from Manassas which should bring fuller intelligence of the battle than the telegraph had been able to supply. There were the committees appointed for the reception of the wounded soldiers, together with a large number of relatives and friends of these brave but unfortunate fellows; there was a special guard of honor to escort the remains of the lamented Gens. Bartow and Bee and Col. Johnson to the capitol where they should remain during the night; there was a large military guard of another kind to march off to jail the prisoners taken in the great engagement, and then there was that miscellaneous multitude, made up of all classes from the respectable citizen to the street loafer, which can be so readily assembled at the hour of dusk in any city upon an extraordinary occasion. The crowd was at length found to be so dense in and around the depot, obstructing the tracks and impeding the convenient approach of the ambulances, that it was absolutely necessary to detail sentries to clear a space and thus prevent a dangerous confusion upon the coming of the train.

At the expected hour, the whistle was heard, and a few minutes afterward the locomotive with its long line of cars, arrived at the depot. In a moment it was known that President Davis was among the passengers, on his return to the seat of government, and a wild about of welcome went up that might have been heard throughout the city. In response to the earnest call of the crowd, the President addressed them in a short speech, marked by his usual modesty and good taste, congratulating them on the victory. [At a later hour of the evening, in acknowledgment of the call of an immense throng at the Spotswood House, where the Hon. Mr. Chesnut of South Carolina, also spoke, the President made a longer address, paying an eloquent tribute to the lofty courage and high military genius of Johnston and Beauregard, and bidding his listeners render their humble thanks to heaven for the glorious success which had crowned our arms.] The enthusiasm elicited by the speech of the President from the platform of the car was succeeded by a universal feeling of sadness and sympathy, as the wounded soldiers were lifted into the ambulances. Some of the poor fellows were dreadfully mutilated and seemed to suffer greatly, but there were no murmurs, while many others, whose arms had been almost shot away or whose faces bore frightful contusions, leaped into the wagons with the *elan* of fresh triumph. I am happy to say, with reference to the wounded, that the arrangements for their treatment are already perfected—few will be taken to the hospitals, as the citizens of Richmond, on all hands, have opened their houses to them, esteeming it at once a privilege and a duty to minister to the wants of those suffering in such a cause.

About an hour after the arrival of the train with the President and the wounded, came another with six hundred and seventy-five prisoners of war, and still later the funeral train, bringing the bodies of the lamented officers, high in rank, who fell on the field.

Among the prisoners was one who has fairly earned his title to lasting infamy, a certain Captain Edward C. Carrington, at present district-attorney for the District of Columbia. This man is nearly related to some of the best families of Virginia and South Carolina, being a nephew of the Hon. John S. Preston. He was born in Virginia, educated at the expense of the Commonwealth, at the Virginia military institute, and for several years practiced law in this city. If anything could add to the heinousness of his ingratitude toward his native State—a trait of character which he shares with his illustrious companion in arms, Gen. Winfield Scott—it would be the fact that he went out to the Manassas field with the full knowledge that he should meet a uncle and two brothers, fighting on the side of Virginia. What will be done with this miscreant is a matter of doubt, though certainly his case differs widely from that of the ordinary prisoners of war.

To the solemn strains of funeral music, the bodies of the honored dead were borne from the depot to the capitol, where they remained till this afternoon, when the mournful procession was again formed, and the sad dirge again taken up, and the coffins, conveyed through crowded but silent and mournful streets to the train, which was in readiness to bear them South. All the flags upon the public buildings were at half-mast.

We have full accounts to-day of the brilliant victory, of which you have already heard, gained over the federal troops in Kanawha county by a small force, composed entirely of Virginians. The fight took place at the mouth of Scary creek, or Scary run, a small tributary of the Kanawha river. On the afternoon of the 17th instant a body of federalists, 1200 strong, under command of Col. Norton, commander-in-chief of the expedition sent out against Brigadier General Wise, attacked the Virginia troops under Capt. George S. Patton, and were routed, with the loss of 330 killed and many more wounded—not less than seven officers falling into our hands as prisoners—three colonels, one lieut. Colonel, two captains and a lieutenant. We had but 950 men in all, and not more than 400 of these were engaged at any one time, and while the enemy were well supplied with rifled cannon we had but two small smooth bore pieces. And yet they gave way before Capt. Patton's dashing charge, and signalized the place of combat by making a *scary run* of it into an entrenched camp two miles distant from the scene. Our loss in this encounter was three killed and less than a dozen wounded. Among the latter I regret to have to mention the brave Capt. Patton, who received a bullit [sic] in the right breast and shoulder. The officers taken were Col. Norton, Col. Villiers, Col. Woodruff, Lieut. Col. Neff, Captains Hard and Austin and Lieut. Brown.

The news of the defeat at Manassas carried consternation into Washington and Baltimore, as all the arrangements had been made to celebrate the splendid victory of Gen. McDowell. At Centreville, our pursuing cavalry found a large dinner table set out and supplied with twenty baskets of Moet, (green seal) where Senator Henry Wilson of Massachusetts, was to have entertained a select party of congressional friends at dinner, in honor of the triumph of "our arms" in Virginia. The senator proposed to conduct the champagne while Gen. McDowell was conducting the campaign, and found, in his hasty retreat over the hills of Fairfax, that this side of the Potomac was not a champagne country. Among the other abandoned contents of the uneaten banquet were discovered bills of fare, printed in French, for the dinner McDowell was to give in Richmond on his arrival here. There is little doubt that the sensation preachers of the north had prepared their sensation sermons to be delivered on receipt of the grateful news; the *Te Deum* had probably been rehearsed by the "antiphonal choir" of Trinity, and the star-spangled banner gracefully disposed upon the altar cloth. Let me commend to these divines, one and all, from the Rev. Henry Ward

Beecher to the Rev. Stephen H. Tyng, to preach next Sunday from this text, which they will find recorded in II Samuel, 1:25—"How are the mighty fallen in the midst of battle! Oh, Jonathan, thou was slain in thine high places!"

Mr. Toombs has resigned his seat in the cabinet, with the intention of going into the field as a brigadier-general. There is, of course, a good deal of speculation concerning his successor as Secretary of State, but the general expectation is that it will be the Hon. R.M.T. Hunter of Virginia. It is said that John M. Daniel, of the *Examiner*, was yesterday chosen public printer in executive session, and that he declined the appointment.

Congress was to-day engaged only in paying appropriate honors to the memory of a late member, the lamented General F. S. Bartow. The customary resolutions were offered by the Hon. T.R.R. Cobb, who delivered a most impressive eulogy upon the deceased, and tributes were also paid by Messrs. B. H. Hill, Chesnut and James M. Mason. The remarks of the latter were full of eloquence and pathos.

Roger A. Pryor appeared in his seat for the first time to-day.

DIXIE.

BENJAMIN F. DILL OR JOHN McCLANAHAN: CONSEQUENCES OF MANASSAS——MUCH WORK STILL TO BE DONE

Despite its jubilation over the victory at Manassas, the Memphis Appeal's *editors, at least temporarily, put on their Cassandra costume to remind Southerners that one battlefield victory did not signify an end to the war. The paper cautioned Southerners not to believe their work was over or that it would be easy. First Manassas may have been a "brilliant achievement," but there would still be consequences to pay, and they would not all be so pleasant or as sweet as celebrating a victory.*

Memphis Appeal, 30 July 1861

THE MORAL OF MANASSAS

There is a danger we fear that the Southern mind, intoxicated with its exultations over the recent great victory of our arms at Manassas, may overestimate the present advantage as well as the ultimate consequences of that brilliant achievement.

Certainly there can be no difference of opinion as to its having proved a God-send to the cause of southern independence, and true constitutional liberty. It has greatly strengthened the confidence of our people in the ability of their government to maintain itself even at the point of the bayonet, against the marauding legions of Hessian soldiery who have been precipitated by the enemy upon our sacred soil. It has impaired the energies of the "old wreck" of the federal government, and has so far annihilated the confidence of its subjects in the final success of its boasted scheme of subjugation, as to work the most serious detriment to the national credit—which, according to the recent acknowledgment of a congressman, has

already failed. It has given a *prestige* to the young republic of the South, just emerging, like Venus, in all the perfection of her beauty, from the foaming sea of political confusion, which will put to naught the vaunting assertion of northern superiority, and perhaps, decide the question of foreign recognition which now trembles in the hesitating balance held by the hands of European powers. In addition to these there may be even other, though less important results flowing from it.

But to suppose that our independence is an accomplished fact, without other like desperate struggles, is a palpable absurdity, the entertainment of which will prove a delusion and a snare. It is true that the forces of the enemy, outnumbering our own more than two to one, were utterly routed, and driven into a retreat styled by themselves both disgraceful and cowardly. But the defeat is not such as to turn the reckless politicians, who manage this movement, from the attempted execution of their direful purpose. Their pride has been sorely wounded, and their passion of revenge stimulated to the performance of new deeds of infamy. At any sacrifice of life or of the people's money, they will rally their routed forces and attempt with still greater desperation to retrieve their lost fortunes. Relying upon the brute force of mere numbers, the enemy are evidently determined to risk other engagements, perhaps of greater magnitude, if for nothing else than the gratification of their malignity, or the palliation of their disgrace now so manifest to the eyes of foreign powers. The vast preparations that are now being made, and the great caution taken in the efficient organization of the army for the future, with the unceremonious dismissal of incompetents, are but a few of the indications to foreshadow their increased, yet fruitless determination.

It may be that the half million men voted for Mr. LINCOLN by his obsequious parliament may not all be obtained, and certainly it is that the five hundred millions of money will come in very tardily, and at great sacrifices on the part of the government, if at all. But it is quite as evident that men and money will be secured for the prosecution of this atrocious war, even though the one be obtained by drafting, and the other by direct taxation and forced loans. We may expect, and must be prepared to encounter, an army of at least four hundred thousand men, who will be gathered at various points upon the borders of our Confederacy, seeking to force an entrance with the bayonet in less than ninety days. Our preparations for the vast campaign, unequalled by any of modern times, and scarcely overshadowed by BONAPARTE'S into Russia, must be commensurate with its magnitude and the importance of confronting it with successful resistance.

The population of the eleven States, comprising the Confederate Government, according to the census of 1860, is just 5,581,649. A levy of ten per cent. Of this amount, which has always been regarded as not only practicable but extremely light for military purposes, would give us an army of five hundred and fifty-eight thousand men. Leaving out the disaffected portions of the country, where recruiting might prove somewhat difficult, we may safely calculate on raising 400,000 men with the greatest facility, for it is estimated that we have more than 200,000 armed and equipped in the field. The Confederate Government should at once exercise its energies in this work. While we can readily whip the enemy in an open field and fair fight, where they do not outnumber us in a proportion greater than three to two, we must not place ourselves in such a condition as to render the result the least doubtful. To make assurance doubly sure, it is our bounden duty to meet the invaders man for man, and by the adoption of a vigorous and aggressive policy make this war a brief one. An eye for an eye and a tooth for a tooth is the maxim that should guide us through this revolution.

But to resume. The point which we most desire to impress upon the minds of the people is the necessity of being prepared yet for the worst. No delusive hope need be entertained for a solitary moment that a peace has been conquered by the result at Manassas. It is only the entering wedge to such a consummation. We may still with propriety advise with PATRICK HENRY, when he eloquently exclaimed, "WE MUST FIGHT! I REPEAT IT, SIRS, WE MUST FIGHT!"

PETER W. ALEXANDER: DESCRIPTION OF MANASSAS BATTLEFIELD

By the time the Civil War began, it had been at least half a century since any Americans had seen actual military action on their home soil. As a result, one of the jobs of war correspondents was to ensure Americans knew something of the carnage of war, to make the fighting real. In this article, Peter W. Alexander, a former Savannah lawyer and politician who would become one of the South's greatest war correspondents, painted a word picture of the horrors of the battlefield at First Manassas.

Savannah Republican, 19 August 1861

ARMY CORRESPONDENCE OF THE SAVANNAH REPUBLICAN

The Battle Field by sunlight—Burying the Dead—Singular postures after Death—The Old Woman on the Hill—Who took Sherman's Battery and reasons of discrepancies with regard to it—The Enemy's Launching Ground—What they left behind them—Manassas in History, &c., &c.
RICHMOND, VA., Aug. 12, 1861.

I promised to give you some account of the battlefield of Manassas as seen by moonlight and by sunlight. The first part

of the promise has been redeemed—the latter, much to my regret, remains to be performed. It is anything but an inviting theme. One soon becomes accustomed to the presence of the dead and the dying—to headless bodies, torn and trembling limbs, and the cries and struggles of the wounded. His blood once up, he may even become indifferent to danger—to the dread shock of battle, "the clash of resounding arms," the leaden hurricane sweeping and crashing among the broken bones and mangled bodies of the contending hosts. The battlefield is not without its sublimity as well as its terror. The long line of glittering bayonets, the roll of a thousand drums, the wheeling and rushing of squadrons, the huge columns of dust and smoke that shoot up like great pyramids from the plains below, the incessant roar of artillery and musketry, the great balls and shells that rush screaming through the air like winged devils escaped from the regions of the damned—there is something in all this to stir the blood, to inspire the heart, nerve the arm, and to make one desire to end his life amid the mighty din and uproar. But when the conflict is over and the blood has resumed its accustomed flow, there is something repulsive, at least to me, in the sight of a battle-field.

It commenced to rain early on Monday morning—the day after the battle—and continued to pour down in torrents all day and night. Tuesday the sun came out, and it was very hot, as it was on Wednesday, when I made my second visit to the field. All of our wounded that could be found, were cared for on Sunday night, though many of them were exposed to the drenching rain on Monday, their tents not having arrived. This was no disadvantage, however, as the rain served to keep down fever and prevent mortification. On Monday our dead were buried or boxed up and sent home for internment, and many of the enemy's wounded were brought in and attended to. All day Tuesday was devoted to burying the dead on the other side, and yet the work had not been half finished when I arrived on the field Wednesday morning. So intolerable was the stench arising from the dead, and especially from the horses, that our men had been compelled to suspend their humane labors. I did hear that some of the prisoners we had taken, were subsequently sent out to finish the work, which they did, though reluctantly.

It was sad sight—the battle field, that day. The enemy's dead still lay scattered in every direction, and the silent vultures had begun to circle above them. They were well clad, and were larger and stouter men than ours. Nearly all of them were lying upon their backs, some of them with their legs and arms stretched out to the utmost. Many had their feet drawn up somewhat, while their arms, from the elbows, were raised, and the hands rather closed, after the fashion of boxers. It was a singular and yet prevailing attitude. Most of them had sandy or red hair, and I have observed that this is the predominant color among our own soldiers. Those who were not killed instantly had almost invariably torn open their shirt collars and loosened their clothing about the waist. There was another mark in addition to this, by which we could tell whether their death was sudden or lingering. It was the color of the face. If the body had time to become cool and quiet before death, the corpse was pale, though not so much so as those who die from disease. Those who were killed instantly, however, and while heated and excited, were purple and black in the face. In such cases, the blood being in full circulation, there was not time for it to return to the heart before the body had ceased all its functions. At least, I suppose such is the explanation, and a physician confirms me in it.

Such of the poor wretches as had been buried were placed in long ditches or trenches, some times twenty or thirty in the same trench. Of course, it was impossible to procure coffins or boxes for them. They were laid away in the same attitude in which they were found, and in which their bodies and limbs had become stiff and rigid—one with his arms and legs stretched out—another bent nearly double—a third with his hands raised, as described above. One poor fellow had died with his arm clasped around a small tree, and others with their hands clasped tightly about their muskets, or such twigs or roots as were in their reach. One was found with his Bible open upon his breast. Some had their hands crossed and the whole body composed after the manner of a corpse. A few were found upon whom there was not the least wound or mark. Whether they had died from sun stroke, or from exhaustion, or simple fright, it were impossible to say, though probably it was from the first cause.

Thus dying and thus buried, their dust will soon commingle, and to mortal vision become one indistinguishable mass. Whether it shall be blown about this pendent globe by the winds of heaven, or scattered by the wheels of Time in its remorseless sweep to that goal to which everything is hurrying, or whether it shall continue to repose quietly where it now sleeps, it is not for us to determine. We only know that this dust shall be gathered together on the morning of the resurrection, and that the spirits which animated it in this life will be summoned before the judgment seat to give an account of the deeds done in the body, among which will be their wicked invasion of Southern homes and altars. Having performed the duty required of us by humanity, we may well leave the rest to that dreaded Judge whose protecting kindness has been around us and over us in all our troubles.

I was glad to see that most of our own dead had been buried upon the battle ground—many of them where they had fallen. In some instances, those belonging to the same company or regiment were gathered up and buried near each other, each little hillock being marked by a board or stone with the name of the hero cut upon it. What more fitting cemetery could be found for the gallant dead than the field which has been sanctified by their precious blood and rendered forever immortal by their deeds of valor! I can sympathize with the tender sentiment that would gather up the honored ashes of its loved ones and transport them for interment in the old family burying-ground in the far South; and yet I can but admire that stern patriotism—if it must be thus called—which would prefer the torn and bloody plains of Manassas to the proudest mausoleum below the sun.

And the heroes who fell upon those plains—who would exchange their lot in this life and that which is to come, for that of the beastly tyrant who would crush us beneath his heel! To me, there has always seemed to be a species of religion in the feeling which prompts a man to forsake father and mother, wife and child, and go forth in defense of the liberties of his country. He who falls in such a case, never falls too soon. The blood thus spilt, one may hope will not be an unacceptable sacrifice before the lord of hosts, the friend of the weak, the avenger of the wronged and oppressed. We may not claim that the spirits of the fallen brave are caught up in chariots of fire, and borne to realms where there shall be no more drawing of the sword and no more oppression; and yet, we may be allowed to indulge the belief that it is no sin in the sight of Heaven for a man to defend the graves of this ancestors and the sanctity of his hearth stone, even to lay down his life in so holy a cause.

You have undoubtedly seen frequent allusions to the house of an aged woman—Mrs. Judith Henry—which occupied nearly the centre of the battlefield, and which was completely riddled by the balls of the contending armies. A son and an ancient maiden daughter, some 50 years old, were with their mother, who was almost bed ridden and got about with great difficulty. It is said that they moved her to a neighboring gully but she would not remain, and that they next placed her in the cellar, and then up stairs, or wherever her fancy would dictate.—Meanwhile, balls and shells continued to tear through the house, and whistle around and above her. Disturbed and restless, like an evil spirit as she was, she insisted upon crawling and groping about amidst the iron hail "that beat upon that house," and finally placed herself upon her own bed, where she was soon shot in three different places and killed. But I do not refer to the incident so much for the purpose of describing the house or manner of her death as to correct an error which has been set afloat by some of the newspapers, as to the character of this old woman. She is represented to have been an extremely exemplary person, of great age (85) and piety. This may be so; but her neighbors, who ought to know her well, tell me that she and her household were Tories, and were in frequent communication with the enemy. If this be true, and I have no doubt of it, then she only received her just deserts, first in the fiery ordeal through which she passed, and then in the terrible doom which ended her life.

It was within a few paces of this house that Col. Bartow fell, and it was here that the great struggle occurred over Sherman's favorite battery. The fighting was furious, and the battle raged and roared around the house, and the hill upon which it stood, until the ground was literally covered with the dead and wounded. It was Sherman's battery, though it was commanded by Capt. Ricketts—Sherman being in command of a regiment—and hence the confusion in the accounts given by correspondents and letter writers. When the battery was finally taken, every horse and man about it had been killed or wounded, or had fled. No particular regiment is entitled to the exclusive credit of capturing it. Our forces, composed of the 7th and 8th Georgia Regiments, the 4th Virginia, Hampton's Legion, and, I think, the 4th Alabama Regiment, all moved upon it about the same time, and in the form of a crescent, and they all reached it about the same time. Lieut. Paxton, of Virginia, who was bearing the flag of the 7th Georgia Regiment, at the time, and Col. Gartrell and other Georgians, insist that it was only the

standard that was planted upon the battery, and that Eli W. Hoyle, of the Atlanta Confederate Volunteers, was the first man to mount the battery. While I have no doubt of the correctness of this account, I entertain as little doubt that the honor of the capture should be equally shared by all the regiments named above.

Not the least interesting part of the battlefield to me was a body of thick woods, three-fourths of a mile in the rear of this battery, and skirting the road by which the enemy had approached from Sudley's Ford. A large body of his forces had evidently halted here long enough to consult their haversacks. It was a "hasty plate of soup," however, if one may judge from the immense quantities of bread and other eatables left scattered upon the ground. Among other things, I found castors, mustard boxes, pickle jars, pieces of fine glass ware, ale and brandy bottles, several numbers of the N. Y. Tribune, various illustrated papers, political and religious tracts, and several pieces of flute music. The officers had evidently been having a good lunch, preparatory to the grand dinner they were to take at Manassas. A little further on, I saw a mosquito net, which some boastful warrior, mindful of his rest, was doubtless taking along to be used in the swamps and lagoons of the South.

In the corner of a fence, and covered over with leaves, I found two splendid Collin's axes, with leather coverings, or holsters, for the blades. A large number of axes were captured—a part, perhaps, of the 7,000 that were sent over from Washington some six weeks ago, by Gen. Scott, to hew a way to Richmond for his grand army. The fences throughout the battle field were torn down in order to enable the men and horses to move with facility. The horses of the enemy were large and fine, and our sharp shooters were very successful in picking them off. The ground around the batteries, where the horses were, for the most part, killed, was torn and rent into gullies by bursting shells and plunging balls from the Confederate guns. Some of the horses had been disemboweled, while others had their heads and limbs carried away.

But enough. When the future historian comes to the chapter devoted to the battle of Manassas,* he will say, if he tells the truth that our soldiers were well handled by the officers, and that the infantry, the cavalry, and the artillery, were manoeuvered skillfully and successfully. He will say, also, and with emphasis, that the day was carried, and the victory won, by the unflagging pluck and dogged courage of our men. Many of these men were young, and, as it were, just from the breast of their mothers, and yet, neither Caesar's legions, nor the Old Guard of Napoleon, nor the Grenadiers of Frederick the Great, ever fought better, or charged more gallantly, or retired more doggedly. All honor, then, now and hereafter, to the last syllable of recorded time, to the heroes of Manassas!

P.W.A.

*Pronounced as if spelt Manasseh.

AFTER MANASSAS

The months immediately following Manassas were spent in small skirmishes and caring for the wounded. Hospital policies and facilities and providing adequate provisions for the soldiers were the pressing issues of the day. Throughout the remainder of the summer and into the fall, Johnston, who had been given command of what would become the Army of the Potomac, was berated by Southern newspapers for inactivity. Why had the pursuit of the Union troops to Washington been stopped? Southern journalists demanded. If only Confederate commanders had followed up on the brilliant success at Manassas and moved immediately on the Northern capital, the war would be over, they argued. Their arguments, though, were not borne out by the facts. At the end of the day at Manassas, the Confederate troops were as confused and disorganized as those of the Union. True enough, Jackson had argued strongly with Davis that pursuit should occur, but given the condition of the Southern troops, it clearly was not possible. Like the North, the Southern troops needed time to pull themselves together. In the meantime, McClellan, who had been given command of the federal armies in Virginia, and Johnston were biding their time. Citizens of both nations began to realize that this was not to be a short, three-months-long war but something much longer and much bloodier. Weapons and other materials were being stockpiled throughout both the North and the South. Through the fall, the few skirmishes fought resulted in what can best be described as a military stalemate. Neither side gained any advantage over the other.

JOAN: ARMY HOSPITALS—WHAT LOUISIANA IS DOING FOR ITS WOUNDED SOLDIERS

One of the few female correspondents for a Southern newspaper during the Civil War worked for the Charleston Courier. She signed her dispatches only as Joan. One of Joan's primary interests was the military hospitals. Not only did she volunteer for nursing duties in the Richmond hospitals, but she was a keen observer of how the various states and the Confederate government were providing care for their sick and injured soldiers. In this letter, Joan described what the state of Louisiana was doing for its soldiers. Ever the intrepid reporter, Joan let her employers know that she was working on getting a passport so she could move closer to the front and report from nearer the center of action. Joan did not add that she had an ulterior motive for wanting to get to the front: a son who was serving near Fairfax, Virginia, in a South Carolina unit.

Charleston Courier, 5 September 1861

OUR VIRGINIA CORRESPONDENCE FROM RICHMOND

Correspondence of the Courier

Richmond, August 31, 1861.

My letter had scarcely left my hands on yesterday, when I heard that the Yankee invaders had dared to pollute the soil of Carolina with their foul presence, but they need not unpack their trunks, for we can tell them they will soon get orders to leave. The news of one victory in Western Virginia, in which Colonel Tyler was defeated, came almost simultaneously with the other, and causes great rejoicing, but we cannot console ourselves for having our brave men taken prisoners, that we hold five to one of the enemy in our hands; our men are worth fifty of theirs. We cannot expect our course always to be upward and onward, we must expect some reverses, and if this will teach us to keep our powder at hand, as well as dry, it may prove a salutary lesson to us.

The Committee here from Louisiana to provide a hospital for their sick, have rented for that purpose, as long as the war shall continue, the Baptist College buildings—large commodious brick buildings situated in a very healthy locality, entirely out of the city. They were built to accommodate a hundred students, and have fine buildings on the premises where two resident physicians will be located with their families. They are to be repainted and put in most beautiful order, and elegantly furnished. Louisiana is not only thoughtful of her soldiers in the field, but of their families at home. In New Orleans they have a free market for the families of volunteers. The citizens and planters supply it,—some sending flour, others sugar, meats, vegetables and supplies of every kind,—these are given out in moderate quantities to every applicant.

A friend just from Culpeper was giving me some statistics to-day of the sick in the hospitals, the provision made for their comfort, &c. He said they were using the churches, the school houses, the court house and the jail and had erected beside long ranges of temporary buildings, rudely constructed, but with plenty of windows in them and plank floors. He says the sick might be made much more comfortable than they are if the surgeons would only allow them to go to private houses, which they will not do, for reasons best known to themselves, for no one else can define them. The people come after them for miles around, but they are seldom allowed to go. One gentleman, living near a hospital in Louisa, I think he said, has opened his house to all who were convalescent to come and eat their regular meals as long as they choose. Forty-five sat down to dinner with him that day. One company, who left Manassas a few days since to go forward, had ninety-six members, and only fourteen of the number were able to march.

The proprietors of the Daily News, in New York, have put themselves under the care of the police. A force of four hundred was detailed, ready to serve at short notice. The editor, Mr. Wood, in a card to his subscribers, over his own name, with fearless independence condemns the high-handed usurpation which has suppressed his issues, and in tomes proudly defiant declares he will denounce the war at the risk of his property, personal liberty and life. Would there were more such noble spirits. The office of the Journal of Commerce, too, is guarded.

The protest of the Day Book against the tyranny which is putting down freedom of speech, is bolder and more uncompromising even that the News. He denounces the Administration in bitter terms, and openly charges it with trying to rivet the chains of slavery on millions of white people.

In locations in Pennsylvania where newspaper offices have been mobbed, the spirit of the people is aroused, and men are protesting against it in unmeasured terms. In a regiment forming in Winchester county fifty have resigned out of about a hundred and sixty names registered, in consequence of the attack on the Jeffersonian. The materials of the office were perfectly demolished, and afterwards it was closed by the Marshal. He probably feared that the sympathy of the people would furnish the editor with means to go on again. This would have shown too plainly that the mob was not the voice of the people. The excitement was so great that a collision was feared, and a large patrol called out armed with rides and muskets.

These signs of the times are fraught with the deepest interest. The leaven is working which is to overthrow the United States Government even at home, and it needs no prophet's eye to see that they are on the very brink of a precipice awful to contemplate. Thank God they cannot draw us in. They have before them the prospect, nay they have now entered upon a reign of terror, which if it is not addressed ere it culminates threatens to tell a tale of suffering which will, only find a parallel in the record of the French revolution—to engulph [*sic*] the rights of men, to darken their homes with crime. Its result will be to stain their hearthstones with blood, to quench the light of truth, to overthrow every liberty which is dear to freemen, to prostitute the pulpit to unholy ends, to enclose the whole country in moral darkness, which can only be dissipated by fire and sword, which will deluge the earth with human gore, and make it fetid with human sacrifices, and then when the end comes, as it must eventually, who can tell whether it will open under the genius of free institutions or subject to a depots way.

"My soul enter not thou into their secret." To us they are and must ever be foreigners and strangers. We may deplore their calamities as we would those of any other member of the common race, if they do not forfeit all claims to our sympathy by their inhumanity to us and ours. We may grieve over the sufferings of those who have been dear to us in the past; we may sorrow in the name of a common humanity over free institutions so trampled on and constitutional liberty so recklessly set aside, but we have otherwise than this no common interest in the result. Our future paths diverge; they may live under such rule as suits them best. We have chosen the Constitution and Government of our fathers, and under its grateful shade will ever abide. It has borne the test of many a year, and proved itself equal to many a trying test. The great charter of our rights and bulwark of our liberties, it is our nation's pride. God forbid that it should ever have to be snatched again, at the point of the sword, from a people over-riding its authority and setting aside its provisions. Let us learn a lesson from the past, and guard with jealous care the slightest encroachment upon its statutes.

I hear many an incident which leads me to think that there must soon be a loud clash of arms. I await the tidings with the deepest solicitude. It may be that they will blot out the light of my life, and leave me to find my pilgrimage in darkness and alone, yet I do not begrudge my treasures to my country. She is welcome to them, though I do not think what the future would be to me without them. Sometimes I fear that we may be repulsed and defeated in our next movement. We have had so many successes, and my heart almost forgets to beat in the intensity of its prayer that this may not be so; if it should be we must not be discouraged. We *know* that we must ultimately succeed, and should we lose ground we must, with fresh courage, try again.

I have a slight prospect of being able to get nearer to the scene of action. If the efforts now making to get a passport for me succeed I shall go forward on Monday.

JOAN

FELIX G. DE FONTAINE: MILITARY RUMORS IN RICHMOND; SOUTH CAROLINA NEEDS TO PROVIDE FOR ITS WOUNDED SOLDIERS

Personne, the nom de guerre used by Felix Gregory de Fontaine, was a correspondent for the Charleston Courier. Personne became one of the two most famous Southern war correspondents for his reporting from Virginia and, later in the war, from the Western Theater. Personne's writing was enlivened by his mischievous sense of humor, as in this piece when he comments on the frequency of weddings occurring that summer in Richmond. He might have signed his letter, "Yours, in single blessedness," but he, too, would walk down the aisle before the end of the war, and his walk would lead Personne to hang up his nineteenth-century equivalent of a flak jacket and settle into the more staid existence of newspaper editor and publisher in Columbia, the Palmetto State's capital. In this article, Personne notes the prevalence of rumors in Richmond, of the anticipation with which Confederates awaited the army's next move on Washington. Unfortunately, the Confederate army, commanded by General Joseph Johnston, was not able to capitalize on the advantage it gained as a result of the First Battle of Manassas. Personne also took up the topic of providing for South Carolina's wounded and dead soldiers. He reminds readers of the need to establish a state hospital, suggesting Richmond as the logical location, and of the need to provide for the state's soldiers as winter comes on.

Charleston Courier, 7 September 1861

OUR VIRGINIA CORRESPONDENCE FROM RICHMOND

Correspondence of the Courier

Richmond, Va., September 4, 1861.

Now up, now down; to-day before the golden gate of anticipation; to-morrow in the Slough of Despond, alternately exultant and melancholy, jubilant and bilious, hopeful and doleful, effervescent and stale, "everything by starts and nothing long"—such has been the city of Richmond for the last week or ten days. Rumor has been the ruling god and men have worshipped at the shrine of the deity, until they are no longer able to live without the daily pablum upon which they have been feasted to repletion. The slightest suspicious incident excites the acutest apprehensions. Are the cars detained over one train—a battle is in progress. Are orders received from BEAUREGARD to forward troops or munitions of war—instantly the whole town is in a *furor*. "Hostilities are certainly about to commence—Arlington is to be attacked, and Washington taken immediately; the Potomac has been crossed by JOHNSTON and he is in full march through Maryland." The street corners are therefore thronged, the innocent bulletin boards are encompassed with a cloud of witnesses; the corridors of the Hotels fairly perspire with their loquacious contents, and the telegraph is surrounded frequently until late at night by curious inquirers after the "latest news from Manassas." There is always a moral certainty that a battle is going on. Men seem to feel it in their bones, and you can no more reason them out of their obstinacy than instill into a mule a knowledge of didactic poetry.

This has been the condition of the public mind, especially since Saturday last. I am free to confess that many events have occurred which tend to foster these impressions, but there are no well defined reasons why an attack is ready to be made at this time. While it may be true that a large portion of the army have moved forward further than ever before, that the lighting of the lamps in the city of Washington may be seen from our camps, that preparations are being made on an extensive scale for an advance upon the capital, that our troops have been greatly reinforced at various points, that Johnston is quietly preparing to cross the Potomac, that several days rations have been ordered for a certain time in the future, that the greatest secrecy is manifest in regard to the various details of army operations—while all this may be true, they are but a repetition of the scenes, which, for two or three or more weeks, preceded the battle of Manassas.

For one, therefore, I am not at present prepared to cast my faith with those who believe in immediate hostilities. They may at any moment, however, be sprung upon us. The two armies are so near that, should an encounter take place between one or more of the advanced brigades, the whole force may become engaged and a general battle be precipitated. In fact, I rather imagine that such a result would be desirable, for we should then be saved the terrible sacrifice of life, which must result from the storming of Arlington Heights. We can certainly hope for no more of those disastrous stampedes, at the tail end of which we once might have marched into Washington. McClellan learned his lesson too well not to leave substantial reserves at all pregnable points, where our victorious troops are likely to enter, whether on the North of Washington or in the rear. The coming struggle, therefore, will be of a desperate character. That of Manassas will be child's play to it, and in the rich blood poured out to attain the object will be a sacrifice greater than any which the South has yet been called upon to bear. I am reasoning upon the supposition that we are to attack Arlington Heights, and carry by storm its four hundred heavy guns. Of course, should a strategic [missing text] and ask permission to lie even upon the floor, that they may receive something of the attention of a home; but nine-tenths of the houses are already occupied, and there is no room for more.

Something ought to be done for these men, and quickly. Manassas affords no accommodations; Culpeper, Orange, and other places along the route are overflowing; and Richmond, as a central place, convenient to the rail road and all the means of transportation, is properly the best location for a general South Carolina Hospital. Let there be, in addition, a committee of two or three energetic men to attend to the forwarding home of such dead as may be desired by friends. Scores of poor fellows have lain for hours in the depots, unclaimed, until sent to the Potter's Field; and I have no doubt that the end of the war will show a long list of many brothers, husbands, and parents, who, for the want of proper care on the part of friends, will go down to oblivion with graves unmarked by name or date and unwatered by a solitary sympathizing fear. Let the people of South Carolina take care of their dead, as well as their living. With some such well-organized plan, every volunteer from our State may be made to feel that in time of adversity as well as in prosperity he has friends in Richmond who will be all to him that any man can wish.

Thus far I have seen comparatively few South Carolinians in any other than comfortable circumstances, but in the event of another battle, and with the approach of winter, hundreds will require that nursing and medical attention which can only be had in a well regulated hospital. In a few days, health permitting, I shall be at Manassas, when I shall investigate this subject further, and make such other comments as my interest in it and the necessity may suggest.

In one respect at least, whatever it may be in others, Richmond is just now, by no means a profitable place for a residence. Everything of a domestic character commands the highest price. Cotton, linen, flannel, calico, and similar fabrics, are two, three and four times their usual value, and not easy to be had at that; while articles for male use, such as boots, clothing, shirting, &c., are equally beyond the reach of ordinary purses. For articles of luxury, such as fruity, ice, loaf sugar, &c., the holders make no faces at charging the most exorbitant prices.

There are a class of traders here mean enough to crack nuts for a cripple and throw him the shells. A few are Virginians—whom, I suppose, belong to the S.F.V.'s or "Second" Families of Virginia, but the majority are a hybrid kind of Yankees, whose scruples of asking any price are few and far between. One of these, the other day, charged fifty cents to a poor ague—shivering volunteer for a glass of lemonade; another charges a sick man twenty-five cents for a pound of ice; while of peaches, pears, jellies, and such articles as would be relished by convalescents, are held at figures that make patriotism blush for shame that Shylocks can be found in such a crisis to speculate over the misfortunes of those who are fighting their battles. One or two of the city papers have been bold enough to publicly condemn these miserly miscreants, but in some communities they would be walked out of their stores and into the army, neck and heels, without ado.

Many of the wealthier residents have left the city on their usual summer jaunts to the springs. Marriage and giving in marriage continue unabated, the misfortunes of this character being on a more extensive scale this year than has ever been known before. In these cases the honey moon is either very brief or postponed for a more convenient season; but, as I remarked above, the expenses of domestic life are of a character that may well deter the boldest from dotting and carrying one to the grand sum total of humanity.

Yours, in single blessedness,

PERSONNE.

PETER W. ALEXANDER: CAMP LIFE IN VIRGINIA

In another letter on 1 October, the Savannah Republican's *Virginia correspondent, Peter W. Alexander, described what life in the army camps was like for Georgia soldiers. Most of the fighting occurring in late September was skirmishing near Washington. Manassas had been fought and won two months previously, and the prevailing sentiment of Confederate military leaders was that the South's armies should be concentrated in Virginia until the spring when a new campaign could be launched. Such a strategy*

*made for monotonous life for the South's soldiers and caused many, including Alexander, to become im-
patient with so cautious a strategy. The volunteers were ready for action, he told his readers. Later in the
story, Alexander, ever a defender and always a stalwart advocate of the Confederate soldier, complained
about inefficiencies in the Commissary and the Quartermaster departments, two problems that plagued
the army in Virginia for much of the war.*

Savannah Republican, 1 October 1861

ARMY CORRESPONDENCE
OF THE SAVANNAH REPUBLICAN

Army of the Potomac

Near Fairfax, September 25th, 1861

The campaign still "drags its slow length long." In the morning we rise at the tap of the drum. Next follows breakfast, for which we have appetites sharpened by refreshing sleep and the cool morning air. Then comes the usual drill and yesterday's papers, which are read with avidity and then passed from one to another. After this comes dinner; then guard mounting and dress parade; then supper; then short social visits; then tattoo and roll-call and then to bed. Such is our daily round of life.

"Only this, and nothing more."

The monotony is varied occasionally by the receipt of a batch of papers and letters from "home, sweet home;" or by startling camp rumors that Alexandria has been burnt, or McClellan shot; or that the long-looked-for order has been issued to unleash our columns and let them on to Washington. These rumors do no harm. They occupy the mind for the time and tend to divert the thoughts of the soldier from the dull, leaden routine of camp life, so dispiriting and benumbing in its effects on the eager and enthusiastic volunteer. What a shout will rend the skies when the order is given—"forward, march!" The sick will arise with renewed health and buckle on their knapsacks. The lame and the [*unreadable*] will take up their beds and walk. The great military virtue, Patience, will then give place to Activity. The heart will swell, the eye grow brighter, and the step more elastic, and life and vigor and confidence will be diffused throughout our now moody lines.

Does not an involuntary "God bless the brave boys!" rise to your lips when you remember how much they have endured in sickness, in labor, in privations, in marching and counter-marching, *in standing still in front of the enemy*, and then with what frantic eagerness they long to go forward! Everything else will be forgotten in the wild delirium of joy with which the line of march will be taken up. The follies of petty annoyances, of the martinets set above them, the incompetence and short comings of the Commissariat and Quartermaster's departments, the stupidity and criminal ignorance of the Medical bureau—all will be forgiven and forgotten. Lovely and heroic Maryland now writhes and screams in the arms of a brutal ravisher, and they only ask permission to clear the Potomac at a bound and set her free from the despot's embrace.

One who has not been in camp cannot appreciate the effect which an inactive, hesitating policy produces upon the volunteer. His nature is active and aggressive. Any change, any duty, however laborious, is gladly welcomed, so it but vary the dull monotony of the camp. The First Regiment, Georgia Regulars, was ordered to Munson's Hill last week on five days' duty and though they were permitted to carry only their blankets and rations, and had a march of 15 miles before them, they sent up cheer after cheer as they fell into line. The Second Regiment of Georgia Volunteers, who followed a few days after, and other regiments ordered upon the same duty, made similar demonstrations. Anything for a change.

Many interesting incidents are related by those who have returned from Mason's and Munson's Hills. The enemy, they say, has displayed great industry in throwing up defensive works. These works cover a line of several miles along the Potomac in front of Alexandria and Washington. To reach the river in either direction, our troops must turn the works on the right or left, or carry them by storm. As far as the eye can reach, every hill and strategic point seems to be covered by batteries or works of some kind. Look where one may, the enemy appears to be as busy as beavers, throwing up breastworks, digging entrenchments, felling the forests, and hoisting guns into position. Gen. McClellan has made good use of the precious time which Johnston and Beauregard have given.

The picket lines are separated by a space of only three or four hundred yards. Standing on Munson's Hill, the opposing pickets may be seen for a mile or more, patiently walking their beaten rounds and watching each other. There is a growing disposition on both sides to discontinue the practice of firing upon another, and it is only when a new regiment is assigned to duty that there is a departure from the rule. The Yankees are inclined to be very courteous and sociable. They are ready at all times to respond to a white flag and meet our men half way. Sometimes the officers advance under a flag of truce (generally a white handkerchief) and spend an hour together, discussing the news or the prospects of the respective armies. They exchange tobacco or cigars during these interviews and now and then you may hear the clinking of tin-cups when there is anything to drink. The parties separate with many expressions of distinguished personal considerations, and in some instances the Yankees have invited our officers to go over and take a game of whist or a glass of wine with them—a politeness, however, which they have declined thus far. It is said that orders have been issued within the last few days, to stop this intercourse lest some leaky picket might let drop something that would be of service to the enemy.

Every morning when the weather is favorable, Professor Lowe may be seen to ascend in his balloon from Arlington Heights. It is reported, but with what truth I cannot say, that the Professor is sometimes accompanied by Federal officers, who go up to make reconnaissances of our forces and positions. The balloon ascends some seven or eight hundred feet, and remains up about forty minutes. Occasionally it descends, and then ascends again after communicating the result of the aeronaut's first observations to those below. It is believed that the enemy is fully informed in regard to our advanced positions.

Our brigade has been without sugar for some days, owing to stupid mismanagement in the Commissariat department. We procured a small supply for our mess at Fairfax, at 25 cts. per pound, but not until we had fully tested the virtues of coffee without cream or sugar. There is an abundant supply of sugar and rice in the Southern States, and with the least possible system and energy on the part of the Commissary General, the soldier need never be without either. A similar inefficiency and lack of judgment characterize the Quartermaster's department. A simple advertisement in half a dozen papers in North Carolina, Tennessee and Georgia would have secured wagons enough by this time for the transportation of 300,000 men. Every railway and wagon in the Confederacy is at the disposal of the War Office. Why then is the army still without adequate means of transportation?

I infer from an editorial paragraph in the *Republican*, that some one now in Savannah, connected with the Regiment of Georgia Regulars, has taken exception to a remark in a former letter of mine, in which I spoke of the regular service and the regulations adopted by the War Department for its gov-

ernment. I do not know who the fault-finder is—a deprivation to which I feel reconciled by his want of discrimination. You did me no more than justice, Mr. Editor, when you expressed the belief that my remark was intended to apply to the regular service as it existed in the United States previous to the dismemberment of the Union. The rules in force in the old Federal Army for the government of regular troops, have been adopted in the army of the Confederate States for the government of Volunteers; and it is against this policy I complain. The soldier in the old army enlisted for pay. The volunteers in the Confederate service enlisted to defend his hearthstone and the graves of his ancestors. The regular, if physically capable, was received, whatever his character and antecedents might have been. In our volunteer companies, however, I have known men to be rejected on account of their social position.

The Georgia Regulars are encamped within sight of my tent. I have many friends in the regiment, officers and privates, and I know them well. It is considered the best drilled regiment in the service, and will give a good account of itself on the day of battle. But I have been accustomed to regard them as regulars only in name, and as being neither better nor worse than other regiments from Georgia. The men enlisted for three years. Many other regiments enlisted for three years also, and some for the war, whether it lasted for three years, or three times three.

I can only ask the complainant in his case, to come on to Virginia. If he should lose his blanket on the way, I will share mine with him. If his shoes should be worn out, he shall have one of mine, or both if he insist upon it. We are all brothers in this struggle—a struggle in which all sensitiveness and ungenerous suspicions should be banished forever.

P.W.A.

JAMES R. SNEED: SUPPLIES FOR SOLDIERS IN VIRGINIA—OUTRAGEOUS MISMANAGEMENT

The Savannah Republican *took up the cause put forward by Peter Alexander: inefficiencies in the Quartermaster corps. Supplies and mail were not reaching military units quickly enough, the paper contended. It called for reforms in the Quartermaster corps and encouraged the Southern press as a group to editorialize on the issue until reforms had occurred.*

Savannah Republican, 16 October 1861

SUPPLIES FOR THE SOLDIERS IN VIRGINIA— OUTRAGEOUS MISMANAGEMENT

Notwithstanding an arrangement was definitely made for the Quartermaster at Richmond to pay all freights, the sending of an agent to Richmond to receive and forward, and a contract with railroad superintendents to carry all packages promptly with the above understanding, we are reliably in-

formed that not a package sent from this place to our soldiers in Virginia since the 7th September, had reached its destination on the 5th of October. This is positively shameful, and the railroad officials north of Augusta and Charleston, with whom the fault lies, should be held to a strict account for their criminal neglect. Winter clothing and supplies of every kind, intended for our brave volunteers, have thus been allowed to lie neglected by the way side, and as a consequence, our troops to suffer for the absolute comforts and necessities of life.

Now, the Government, too, is at fault in this matter. It has called these men into the field to fight its battles, and it is *its* duty to see that they are comfortably provided for. Much *more* [*emphasis his*] is it incumbent on the authorities, when the people come forward and by liberal gratuitous contributions save the Government from such expense, to at least see that they are safely conveyed to their destination. This is all the people ask, and yet it seems they are unable to obtain even that little. Our soldiers are made to suffer from the grossest negligence on their part.

We hope the Press of the South will take this matter in hand, and ring it in thunder tones in the ears of the Government at Richmond.

No longer than yesterday, we tried to forward a supply of winter clothing to Richmond and Camp Bartow, but were told there was no security whatever for its reaching its destination for a month to come, if ever. Will the country stand such treatment?

We are satisfied that parties in this city are without blame. They have promptly sent forward everything entrusted to them, with firm contracts on the part of others that they should be forwarded with promptness and despatch. If it has not been done, it is no fault of theirs.

P.S.—Since writing the foregoing, we have received the despatch from Richmond attempting to apologize for the delay. Only think of "*several hundred car loads*" of contributions for the soldiers blocked up for weeks on the various railways of the South! The "destruction of bridges" is all gammon. It has been caused by the criminal neglect and indifference of the railroad officials, and we only regret there is no legal way by which a summary punishment can be visited upon them.

JOAN: CORRESPONDENT'S LAST LETTER FROM VIRGINIA

Joan's final dispatch was a polemic of Confederate nationalism. She decried the loss on 7 November of Port Royal, South Carolina, but she took comfort in the loyalty of the slaves she encountered in Virginia. She was a true Confederate partisan. Unfortunately, there was no further word from Joan after this dispatch. It is unknown whether her son was killed and so she returned home to Charleston, or what fate befell her. With the end of her letters to the Courier, *the South lost a correspondent who had a true love of her country and a knack for writing letters that would stir the faint-hearted.*

Charleston Courier, 19 November 1861

OUR VIRGINIA CORRESPONDENCE FROM RICHMOND

Correspondence of the Courier

Richmond, November 13, 1861.

Deeply as we regret that the Yankees have seized a harbor on our coast none are surprised at it; it would have been a matter of surprise if they had not. We must congratulate ourselves that while they have with their vast armament secured a precarious foothold, they have not taken any prisoners or inflicted upon us any serious injury. It will not take them long to find out that they are in an enemy's country, and if they hold these Sea Islands it must be by keeping a large force there, which will perhaps do as little damage there as any where else. It will keep some of their fleet busy to bring them provisions and forage which will prevent their doing mischief elsewhere; for they will not be able even to steal what they want in this line. They may attempt with great peril to themselves to ravage neighboring plantations, but when they find the crops they are in search of burned, they will feel themselves poorly repaid for the dangerous venture. It is hard on those who have had to apply the torch to their own dwellings, but the negros will feel it more than the masters. Most of the proprietors have other houses to go to, but the negros are left houseless; but if they are turned out without a shelter their masters have been living this way for months. Five hundred thousand gentlemen are living in tents within our borders, sleeping on the ground, in climes many of them less genial than Carolina, and wearing coarse clothing and submitting to coarser fare. I would be glad if I could thus comfort those who I know are grieving less for themselves than their people who are driven from their homes; and as I write I have before me one valued friend, a venerable patriarch, who I know felt no such sorrow in applying the torch to his dwelling and his abundant crops on Hilton Head, perhaps to his splendid orange orchards, as he did in burning the houses of his servants.

But we are in a common struggle, and no doubt the negros will bear their share of the common suffering cheerfully. They do so here and are as eager for our success as any of us. One said to me at Manassas, an old and petted nurse, as she stood with the rest of us watching the regiment of North Carolina cavalry as they passed on up to Centreville, "Do you think the Yankees can whip us when we have so many soldiers, and all the time acoming here." She grieved very much over the sufferings of "our children," as she called her master's sons who were in the army, and thought it hard that boys who had such a luxurious home must live out of doors in tents almost within sight of it. I told her they were more favored than many of our sons, for they could come to it when drenched with rains and find dry clothing, and receive from it many a delicacy. A Mississippian was telling me of a boy of his who had runaway and joined the Yankees, and had managed to get back to him. Said he had seen all he wanted to of Yankees; one of the Generals took him to wait on him, and to use his own expression, "he expected me to work myself to death. I couldn't stand it." He was proud and happy to return to his old position of servitude. A gentleman who left Manassas yesterday morning tells me that a skirmish occurred above Fairfax Monday Morning, between three Virginia, a Maryland and, a Tennessee Regiment on our side, and eight Federal regiment, which resulted in our driving them back without any loss on our side. We took eight prisoners.

The papers of yesterday announced as telegraphed from Augusta, that the black flag had been displayed at Charleston, Savannah, and all along the coast. I have heard several speak of it who admired the spirit it displayed, but I do not share in it. It would make a useless sacrifice of human life. Our enemies have shown again and again that they are inferior to us in courage; they yield very gracefully as prisoners. Indeed many of the prisoners have not hesitated to say that they were glad when they were captured because they would have no more fighting to do. We are abundantly able to overcome them, and it is an [unreadable] to us to keep the prisoners, our privateers must seize enough of their provisions to feed them with, or our army gain it from their own granaries. They boast of their large number of prisoners; say they have three hundred in Columbus, Ohio. Is it any honor to them to secure prisoners, when the way they do it is to surround a man's house with a large body of soldiers, under the cover of darkness, and drag him from his bed and lead him, with pinioned arms, to a prison? Me thinks even a coward ought to blush to own that they took prisoners in this way; yet they have no others but the ones they took at Hatteras.

We have one comfort in giving up the sand fortifications at Port Royal, beside not having left any prisoners in the enemy's hands, there was no treachery there. Our hero soldiers made a noble defense against the fearful odds. It is a glory to them that they fired their fifteen or twenty guns against the hundreds brought against them; but if our enemy's cannon are superior to ours they know very well that they themselves are not superior to us. Let us bide our time. When they land on our shores and attempt to march against us with their muskets, we can show them, as we have repeatedly before, on which side the valor lies.

The Senator to be chosen from Oregon, to fill the vacancy occasioned by Col. BAKER's death, will, it is said, be a man with secession proclivities.

The prevailing opinion here, with regard to FREMONT, is that LINCOLN dare not depose him, lest he should get up a party in the West which would eventually take the Western States out of the Union. He is, no doubt, the ablest General they have, and if he is unprincipled and fond of filling his own pocket, and those of his friends, he cannot excel the other officers in the United States government in his peculations. He has many friends in the West, and with his talents and overweening ambition, it would be strange if he did not give them some trouble either way, whether restrained or dismissed.

JOAN.

FURTHER READINGS

Davis, William C. *Brother against Brother: The War Begins.* Alexandria, Va.: Time-Life Books, 1983.

Detzer, David. *Allegiance: Fort Sumter, Charleston and the Beginning of the Civil War.* New York: Harcourt, 2001.

Freeman, Douglas Southall. *Lee's Lieutenants: A Study in Command.* Vol. 1. New York: Scribner's Sons, 1942–1944.

Klein, Maury. *Days of Defiance: Sumter, Secession and the Coming of the Civil War.* New York: Knopf, 1997.

Reasoner, James. *Manassas.* Nashville, Tenn.: Cumberland House, 1999.

Symonds, Craig L. *Joseph E. Johnston: A Civil War Biography.* New York: Norton, 1992.

3

REPORTING THE WAR, 1862

The dawn of 1862 found the Confederate armies in winter camp, warmed by their military successes of 1861 but still somewhat tentative and green. The coming year would temper the enthusiasm for war among many and in some points even nourish an embryonic Confederate peace movement. On the homefront, a permanent president, vice president, and Congress presided over Confederate policy, and one of its major, and most controversial, actions of the year would be to adopt legislation allowing for the draft of Confederate citizens. The conscription law was unpopular, for it represented an unwarranted expansion of government power and infringed upon cherished individual liberties.

Congress had no choice, though. The enthusiastic volunteers who had stepped forward in such large numbers the previous spring had dried up, but the Southern army's need for manpower had not. While many were optimistic about the performance of the Confederate army in 1861 and the prospects for Southern independence, 1862 would be not produce an easy victory. True, there would be some battlefield success for the South, but there were many defeats as well, including Sharpsburg, the bloodiest single day of the entire war.

On the military front, 1862 can best be summarized as a year of maneuver. The Union sought victory in Virginia by outflanking Confederate defenses by sea and by advancing on Richmond from Yorktown. In the West, Union forces advanced deep into the Confederacy. The Confederacy attempted to turn the tide by invading Kentucky and outflanking the Union through an invasion of Maryland via the Shenandoah Valley. The year also saw the rise of two generals, both of whom would become legends: Ulysses S. Grant for the Union and Robert E. Lee for the Confederacy. Both generals were capable of spectacular campaigns, and both had penchants for trying to destroy their enemy through decisive battles.

In the West, by February, Grant had successfully defeated Confederate forces at two Tennessee forts that were important in the defense of the Mississippi River:

Forts Donelson and Henry. Nashville would follow later that month. In April, Confederate fortunes would change somewhat after Shiloh, yet within only a few weeks, the Confederate army would be pushed back to Chattanooga, and the Union would retain control of western Tennessee.

In the meantime, in Virginia, General George B. McClellan was conducting a sweep by sea to the Yorktown Peninsula, but his failure to advance quickly enough would give Confederate General Joseph E. Johnston time enough to move to protect the capital. Each time the Yankees advanced in the campaign, the Confederates managed to push them back, but at considerable cost in killed and wounded on both sides. The two armies fought the inconclusive Battle of Seven Pines/Fair Oaks in late May, during which Johnston was twice wounded. On 1 June, Davis named one of his military advisers to the command of the Confederate army outside Richmond: Robert E. Lee. Lee would prove to be a skilled military tactician, and he would quickly earn the devotion of both his soldiers and the Confederate citizenry.

Lee immediately launched a series of vigorous attacks that became known as the Seven Days Battles. He forced McClellan to withdraw to the James River. Lee also dispatched General Thomas J. "Stonewall" Jackson to the Shenandoah Valley with orders to distract Union forces so they could not reinforce McClellan. Jackson succeeded beyond anyone's expectations in taking pressure off the harassed Confederate capital and the army protecting it.

By late spring in the West, Union forces threatened both New Orleans and Memphis, and both cities would fall by summer. Confederate generals Braxton Bragg and Kirby Smith staged an ill-considered invasion of Kentucky in early fall, intended to "liberate" that dark and bloody land from control of the North. Though the invasion caught the Union army by surprise, it would ultimately fail. After an inconclusive engagement at Perryville, Bragg withdrew to Chattanooga. Bragg also hoped to fill the ranks of his armies with grateful Kentuckians, but few from the Blue Grass state joined up.

In the meantime, Union forces around Washington, D.C., were formed into a separate army and ordered to attack southward under John Pope. Lee, secure in his belief that McClellan would not attack again, moved north. McClellan's forces were withdrawn from the James River and shipped back to Washington; in the meantime, however, Lee decisively defeated Pope at the Second Battle of Manassas in August. The victory at Second Manassas gave Lee the advantage he needed to invade Maryland. As Lee's army began moving north, McClellan's marched to head off the Confederates. The Union force had significant advantage over Lee as a result of either carelessness or deliberate treachery among the Southern ranks. In Frederick, Maryland, McClellan's advance guard found a copy of Lee's orders that outlined Confederate plans of attack.

On 17 September, the two armies met at Antietam Creek, near Sharpsburg, Maryland. The ensuing battle was in the bloodiest one-day engagement of the entire Civil War. Though the Union carried the day, it failed either to destroy Lee or to prevent him from escaping back into Virginia, again mostly due to McClellan's slow pursuit. As a direct result of McClellan's tardiness in following Lee, Lincoln relieved him of command of the Army of the Potomac. Lincoln's choice for a new commanding general, Ambrose E. Burnside, refused the position. Burnside, a man with remarkable self-knowledge and apparent humility, realized he was not the person to command an important army. Lincoln, however, appointed Burnside to that position anyway on 7 November.

Burnside initially did well in his new position. He planned to move his army to Fredericksburg in a move that would outflank Lee, but his efforts were curtailed by a series of mishaps that forced his army to wait on the far side of the Rappahannock River for pontoon bridges to arrive. This gave Lee enough time to entrench his army before Burnside crossed the river and tried to implement his original plan. The outcome was a major victory for the Confederates; Lee's army inflicted some 12,000 casualties on the Army of the Potomac. Burnside, after a revolt by several of his officers, was relieved of command in January 1863.

The last day of 1862 was marked by renewed action in the Western Theater. Bragg had begun to move northward from Chattanooga with the intention of driving the federals out of Tennessee. Both Bragg and Rosecrans attacked near Murfreesboro, each intending to envelop the other's right flank. Initially, Bragg was successful, but he blundered in his use of his reinforcements, which allowed William S. Rosecrans to take the initiative. Bragg was forced to retreat on 2 January. The victory was important to the federals, whose morale was waning after the recent defeat at Fredericksburg.

After a year of maneuvering, when 1862 ended, the advantage lay with the Union, though who would ultimately win the war was not yet a settled matter. The war in Virginia was essentially where it had been in January; in the West, Union forces had captured the Confederacy's most important port and secured most of Tennessee. However, 1862 had brought a significant change to the nature of the war being waged. After the Battle of Sharpsburg, Lincoln had announced the Emancipation Proclamation, to become effective 1 January 1863. Confederate President Jefferson Davis was furious. Lincoln's proclamation was clever, for it only freed the slaves in the states that had seceded. Slave owners in the states still in the Union retained ownership of their property. With the stroke of his pen, Lincoln changed the cause of the war and ensured that the Confederacy could never receive recognition as a sovereign state from the European powers it was courting and from whom it hoped to receive aid. Politically, countries such as England and France could not offer recognition to a country at war to protect the institution of slavery. The conflict had escalated into one of total war. Given the Confederacy's inferior economic situation, smaller population, and smaller army, it was an open question whether the South's slave-based economy and culture would survive.

THE WESTERN THEATER

Henry-Donelson Campaign

In September 1861, Kentucky had ended its neutrality with the announcement that it intended to remain within the Union. Confederate General Leonidas Polk invaded immediately to secure the Mississippi. His troops occupied Columbus, an important transportation center on the river where steamboats and railroads met up, and a smaller river port near the Kentucky-Tennessee border, Hickman. Polk's men spent the fall busily fortifying Columbus, which would come to be known as "The Gibraltar of the West," and booby-trapping the river in a variety of ways, including stringing an anchor across the river, rigged with torpedoes that would explode on impact. Polk further fortified the area by building Fort Henry on the Tennessee and Fort Donelson on the Cumberland. Grant countered Polk's movement into Kentucky by occupying Paducah and Smithland. Paducah, situated at the confluence of the Tennessee and Ohio rivers, was the major city in western Kentucky. Smithland, though smaller, was also important since it was at the confluence of the Tennessee and Cumberland rivers. In February, Grant combined his 15,000 men with Navy Flag Officer Andrew Foote's gunboats to take on both of the Confederacy's newly constructed forts. Fort Henry fell on 6 February as the result of overwhelming fire from the Union gunboats. Next, Grant turned toward Fort Donelson, which was garrisoned by 15,000 men under Major General John B. Floyd and his lieutenants, Major Generals Gideon Pillow and Simon Bolivar Buckner. The fort was able to repulse the first gunboat attack on 14 February, and the next day, the Confederate forces almost broke through the Union troops that had encircled the fort. The garrison at Fort Donelson held out for three days against a heavy Union bombardment. Finally, the four Confederate commanders on hand at the fort, Floyd, Pillow, Buckner, and cavalry commander Nathan Bedford Forrest, met at an inn near Dover, Kentucky, to decide what to do. Neither Floyd nor Pillow were willing to surrender, and they turned the command over to the Buckner, who accepted the responsibility. Forrest, in disgust, managed to escape with his cavalry before the surrender. Floyd and Pillow also escaped, though their failure to live up to their responsibilities essentially ended both their careers. President Davis cashiered Floyd, and Pillow was suspended for a time. Even when he returned to the army, he was never again given a significant command. Union losses in the campaign were 2,832. The Confederacy's, including prisoners, were 16,623.

BENJAMIN F. DILL OR JOHN McCLANAHAN: REPORT OF FALL OF FORT HENRY

The first of the two river fortifications to fall was Fort Henry. Five Union gunboats bombarded the fort for an hour and a half, but despite returning fire at a goodly pace, the Confederates could not hold out past 2:00 P.M. Fort Henry commander, Brigadier General Lloyd Tilghman, sent most of his men to Fort Donelson before surrendering his remaining garrison of twelve officers and sixty-six men. The victory was accomplished entirely by Foote's naval forces; heavy rains had prevented Grant's land forces from reaching Fort Henry.

Memphis Appeal, 7 February 1862

FORT HENRY FALLEN!

We are forced this morning, as we seriously apprehended, to chronicle the fall of Fort Henry. The enemy attacked the position on yesterday about half past eleven o'clock A.M., with five gunboats, and after a bombardment of an hour and a half, and the disabling of one or two of their boats, compelled a surrender. They then proceeded up the Tennessee river and burned the railroad bridge over that stream.

Our dispatch states that the fate of General TILGHMAN'S command, who were stationed at the fort, is unknown, and it is possible that they may have made good their escape to Fort Donelson, which is on the west bank of the Cumberland river, only twelve miles distant.

We are enabled to state from our own knowledge that the amount of stores and ammunition taken was small. The fort was located on the East bank of the Tennessee river, twenty miles below the railroad bridge, and was purely an earthwork defense, though of considerable magnitude. It was surrounded by a deep ditch and strengthened by rifle pits in the rear.

Only a small portion of Gen. Tilghman's command (probably some 500 men) were stationed immediately in the Fort, the remainder being within supporting distance.

The armament of the fort was very inferior, consisting of fourteen guns of the following description: One 12-pounder, not properly mounted and rendered unserviceable after being fired twice last Tuesday. One 32 pounder, rifled, the only one that could compete in range with the ten inch guns of the enemy. The other were 42 and 23 pounders.

Only four of our guns were in position so as to properly range with the ascending boats.

Submarine batteries were planted below on the east side of the island, and were being laid in the west channel on the day of the enemy's approach, but our plans were disturbed before fully perfected.

BENJAMIN F. DILL OR JOHN McCLANAHAN: SERIOUS CONSEQUENCES OF LOSS OF CUMBERLAND FORTS

The Appeal *was profoundly dismayed by the fall of the forts on the Cumberland River near Nashville and correctly saw dark and gloomy portents in their capture by Union forces. For one thing, the loss of the forts brought into greater light the lack of a Confederate navy capable of contesting control of important waterways. Indeed, Confederate Secretary of the Navy Stephen R. Mallory took considerable blame for not having a navy to counter the federal gunboats.*

Memphis Appeal, 18 February 1862

THE DARK DAYS OF THE REPUBLIC

The fall of Fort Donelson on Saturday last, the evacuation at Bowling Green and the unexplained agreement to surrender Nashville on yesterday, have forcibly engendered the conviction in the public mind that Gen. SIDNEY JOHNSTON has been out generaled by BUELL in the progress of army operations in Kentucky. We have no disposition to harshly judge him in this matter, but the fact is too palpable for denial that some of his blunders have at least temporarily transferred the war from Kentucky to Tennessee soil.

In the events of the last few days we witness disasters which will arouse the spirit of our people throughout the whole Confederacy. There is nothing, it is true, in the surrender of a city or the fall of a fort, to discourage or alarm us. Such things have happened before without [*unreadable*] the harbingers of subjugation or of [*unreadable*] disaster to a nation struggling bravely for its freedom. The price of liberty is blood, and if we would obtain the boon, we must pay the price. We cannot expect to achieve our independence without undergoing at least some of the hardships and incurring some of the misfortunes and obstacles that befell our forefathers in the dark days of the American Revolution. The colonies passed through the fiery ordeal of defeat after defeat, and were baptized with continual disasters, without allowing a cowardly despair to seize upon their hearts.

When the Britains captured Charleston and Savannah, and routed the Continental forces at Camden, South Carolina, there was no thought of surrender; nor even yet when defeat overtook the American army at Bunker Hill, and General WASHINGTON was compelled to evacuate New York and make a precipitate retreat, leaving the snow stained with the blood of his bare-footed and fugitive soldiers.

These disasters only nerved a brave and invincible people to renewed determination. The dark hour of trial was upon them, but they saw the light of victory peering through the clouds in the distance. Shall we be less brave, resolute or self-sacrificing than they? Have we less hope than they? On the contrary we have more to gain by victory—more to lose by defeat. Now is the time to test the metal of the true and loyal patriots, and to expose the base treason of the hypocrite and the time server. We have not the shadow of a doubt of the final result in this conflict even yet. Defeats may protract the war, but can subjugate us never! never!! never!!!

"Rise fellow-men, our country still remains,
By that dread name we wave the sword on high,
And swear for her to live—with her to die."

Shiloh and Northern Mississippi

Grant and Foote had won a significant victory in Kentucky with their capture of Forts Henry and Donelson. Not only had they captured Nashville; they had laid open the Tennessee heartland, as well as Alabama and Mississippi, to the Union forces. Further, if the Union army could capture Corinth, it would control the railroad and essentially secure the capitulation of Memphis. If Memphis fell, the federals would control a significant portion of the Mississippi River.

Capitalizing on his advantage would require swift action by Grant, though. Grant planned to follow Johnston to Corinth, but orders from his commanding general, Henry Halleck, stopped his advance; Grant was to wait near Savannah, Tennessee, until General Don Carlos Buell could catch up with him. Grant bivouacked at Pittsburg Landing on the west bank of the Tennessee, only 20 miles from the Confederate stronghold near Corinth. Grant's headquarters were set up next to a log church, Shiloh Chapel. *Shiloh* is a Hebrew word that means "place of peace," which is what Grant expected to find there. The Union general did not expect his Confederate foes to leave Corinth, and so he was lax in putting up defenses for the camp. He dug no entrenchments, sent out no pickets, nor any cavalry patrols.

Johnston realized that his only chance of stopping Grant's army was to attack before he could be reinforced by Buell. For once, the Confederates had the superior force, though only barely: Johnston's Army of Mississippi had 44,000 men to Grant's 42,000. Those odds would change dramatically, though, once Buell's army reached Grant's.

Johnston planned a surprise attack for dawn on 6 April, over Beauregard's objections. Johnston's army was supposed to reach Pittsburg Landing in a single day, but heavy rains slowed the march so that it took three days. The army had not advanced quietly, even taking occasional shots at game to supplement army rations. Beauregard was convinced the element of surprise had been lost, and the attack would be expected. Johnston, however, refused to turn back.

Skirmishers met early on the morning of 6 April about three-quarters of a mile from Shiloh church, but somehow, even fighting that nearby, did not alert the main body of Union troops to the Confederate advance. The Confederate main body overwhelmed the federal skirmishers and crashed in on the Union encampment that was largely unaware of the advance. In some places along the battle lines, the Confederates streamed into the Union camps without any difficulty.

Confederate victory seemed certain for the first twelve hours. The inexperienced Union troops panicked, and many soldiers desperately sought hiding places rather than their weapons. The Confederate attack, though, did not work out exactly as Johnston had planned. A little-known Union general, William T. Sherman, stepped forward to rally and regroup the troops and put up a fight. Among the Confederate high command, there was confusion about whether they were to push Grant's force back to Pittsburg Landing or away from it. In the desperate fighting, Confederate units became intermingled, making control of the Southern forces almost impossible. To make matters worse, in the early afternoon, Johnston was wounded in the leg. At first, he ignored the wound but admitted it was serious when an aid noticed that his right boot was filled with blood. The bullet had severed Johnston's femoral artery, and he was forced to retire from the field. Johnston would die from a wound that would not have been fatal, had he sought care for it sooner.

Beauregard took command of the Confederate troops and pushed the attack forward. By dark, the Southerners held virtually the entire battlefield. The federals retained only the landing itself, and Beauregard chose not to follow through with an attack there. His troops were exhausted, disorganized, and out of ammunition; they could not have carried out an attack successfully. Besides, the Confederate general, unaware that Buell had arrived with 25,000 fresh troops, believed the Yankees were whipped. Beauregard telegraphed the news of a glorious Confederate victory to Richmond.

Grant proved otherwise the next morning with an attack at dawn. He pushed the Confederates back to Corinth. Casualties totaled nearly 24,000 for the two armies combined, with each side losing nearly 2,000 men killed and 8,000 wounded. Shiloh was the bloodiest battle of the war to that time. It was also the battle that made it possible for the Union to split the Confederacy in two. Actually accomplishing that would take more than a year, but the groundwork had been laid. Perhaps if Johnston's and Beauregard's forces had been able to secure that area of Tennessee, they could have retained Memphis and greater control of the Mississippi, but that was not to be.

ROBERT ETTE: REPORTS OF BATTLE OF SHILOH

A Memphis Appeal correspondent covered the Confederate victory at Shiloh, first sending back a short telegraphic account, then following up with a longer letter. The correspondent's telegraph was sent at the height of the second day's fighting, and did not make it back to Memphis in time for publication in the evening edition of 7 April. Instead, it had to wait and run the morning of 8 April, the same edition in which the longer letter about the first day's battle ran. The correspondent Ette's first telegraph, which appeared on 8 April, along with his later and more detailed letter, follow. Ette's energetic reporting resulted in a finely detailed story that laid out the events of the battle as a crowning Southern achievement, accomplished by brave troops and the most skilled generals.

Memphis Appeal, 8, 10 April 1862

BY TELEGRAPH
THE BATTLE OF SHILOAH!
THE SECOND DAY'S CONTEST!

[Special to the Memphis Appeal]

BATTLE FIELD, April 7—2 p.m.—We slept last night in the enemy's camp.

Immense spoils and two thousand prisoners in our hands.

The enemy, reinforced by a division seven thousand strong, from below, engaged us again this morning at sunrise. The battle was desperate all the morning, our center and left being engaged.

The enemy was driven back at ten o'clock, but renewed the attack with great vigor, and fresh troops probably from Buell's column.

The battle is raging now, and the fire terrific.

Loss in number very heavy.

Gens. Bowen and Clark are wounded, and Gen. Cheatham has been injured in the shoulder. Col. Blythe, of Miss., is killed.

Sanford's Mississippi battery was captured by the enemy, except one gun.

Our troops are behaving nobly.

                                                                ETTE.

THE BATTLE OF SHILOAH!

[Special Correspondence of the Memphis Appeal]
SHILOAH, April 7, 1862

The great battle is over, and the question now stands about what are the results for both peoples engaged?

On Saturday, the 5th inst., preparations were [*unreadable*] on our side to attack the enemy. It was known then that the Federals were on this side of the river with a force of not less than 40,000 men, and it was also known that Buell was coming rapidly toward the Tennessee river, with the intention of reinforcing them, and thus oppose us again with superior numbers. Every [*unreadable*] of sound policy pointed to an immediate attack on our part, in order to prevent this junction, and consequently the attack was determined upon and made by us.

To enable you to understand well the circumstances that attended the great battle of Sunday, I will give you a brief outline of the ground upon which the fighting took place, and its location as regards the Tennessee river and Corinth.

The position occupied by the enemy was at a point called Shiloah, which is composed of an old church and a farm house, distant three and a half miles from the river at Pittsburg landing. Pittsburg landing is the place where most all the Federals landed, and where they kept their reserve in men, guns, and stores of all description, under protection of their gunboats and in sight of their transports.

Their camps extended from the river out to [*unreadable*] and beyond, being almost an uninterrupted line of camps for a distance of five miles.

Our forces had been moving since last Thursday from Corinth and the neighborhood, and marched to within two miles of Shiloah, over very bad roads running through a hilly country, very thinly inhabited and frequently interrupted by streams, branches and swamp bottoms, rendering the transportation by wagon a work undertaken with the greatest difficulty.

However, on Saturday night our troops laid upon their arms almost in sight of the enemy, and about twenty miles from Corinth, confident of a victory and fully aware of the importance of their mission.

On Saturday morning at daybreak the attack commenced.

The plan of the battle, which we understood as due to the genius of Gen. Beauregard, is the strongest one known in military science. It was composed of three parallel lines having its center and two flanks. The reserve was attached to the [unreadable] line, and the artillery laced in position between the front and center. Gen. Hardee commanded the front line, Gen. Bragg the second, and Gen. Polk the third. Gens. Johnston and Beauregard remaining with the reserve. Gen. Bragg also had command of the artillery, Gen. Trudeau acting under him.

Thus, we moved on at daybreak upon the Federals, and as the artillery opened on a line of [unreadable], the firing became terrific. The Federals fought with great valor, but nothing could [unreadable] the impetuosity of our brave Southern Troops.

At a charge at half-past eight o'clock in the morning by three regiments under Brigadier Gen. Gladden, the enemy lost four batteries. The 1st Louisiana regulars took one, the 21st Alabama took two, and Col. Blythe's Mississippi regiment took one. Our loss was very heavy, very heavy indeed. Col. Blythe was there, at the head of his regiment. The Federals engaged were commanded by Gen. Prentiss, and we have it from himself since that his troops suffered terribly.

A short time afterwards, one of their camps was in our possession; and so the fight went on, [unreadable] desperate, without mercy or rest for the whole day, every inch of ground being disputed and won by superior bravery.

At half-past two o'clock P.M., Gen. Albert Sydney Johnston fell, while leading a charge, struck by a ball and a piece of shell. Gen. Cheatham was wounded by a musket shot in the shoulder. Gen. Bowen was shot in the neck and in the side.

At 4 o'clock the enemy were in full retreat towards the river, our whole force closing upon them. Gen. Prentiss was then captured by some staff officers from Polk's command, and brought to Gen. Beauregard. Flag after flag was sent to headquarters, fresh trophies from the enemy. Squads of prisoners were brought [unreadable], and presently a whole brigade, captured by Gen. Bragg's command, moved slowly to the rear. At dark the enemy was driven to the river, finding refuge on their transports under protection of the gunboats. The firing was yet [unreadable] and incessant. Darkness was fast approaching, and all that the enemy possessed on this side of the river was ours; all their camps, ammunition, stores, the best part of eighteen batteries of artillery, one of

their generals, and seven regiments captured. The enemy himself was fast disappearing and crossing over to the other side of the river. Nothing more remained to be done, and our troops came back from the pursuit weary, hungry, and worn out from the fatigue of a 11 hours fight, but victorious. We came back to the Federal encampments and prepared for a night's rest. Fine tents, fine clothing, any quantity of forage and provision were the prey of our soldiers, and added to their comfort. A storm was preparing in the clouds; claps of thunder, mixed with the distant reports of cannonade kept by the gunboats and thus closed Sunday. More anon.

ETTE.

CORINTH, APRIL 8, 1862

I arrived last night from the battle-field and although worn out with fatigue, will try to give you an account of yesterday's fight.

On Sunday night we retired to rest victorious, and never was a victory more gloriously won than the battle of Shiloah. The enemy's plans were broken, their forces slain or disabled on the battle field, and what had escaped destruction were either prisoners or disorganized. After night came, the clouds, accumulating all day by the heavy [unreadable], broke out, and rain poured out upon us in torrents. Many of our troops were then returning homeward from the pursuit, and this added no little to the fatigue and discomfort of a day's fighting. The enemy's gunboats, in the meantime, were keeping up a constant firing into the woods, and to me it became evident that, should they receive reinforcements, they would renew the attack next morning. We knew of a Federal division, 7000 strong, which was encamped eight miles below, at Cramp's Landing, and arrangements were made by our [unreadable] to capture it if possible, and any way, be ready for another fight should it be forced upon us. Early in the morning our pickets were driven in, and while a large portion of our men were yet plundering tents and loading themselves down with all kinds of Federal property, the fight commenced in front of our center. A line of battle was already adopted, and battery after battery brought to bear upon the enemy. From the manner in which the Federals fought, it became evident that fresh troops were now arriving, and it would require the greatest energy to repel them. The fight once engaged became more furious and desperate than that of the day before. The Federals had a disaster to avenge, while we had a victory to maintain. Breckinridge's division had to fall back, and lost some artillery, but shortly afterwards advanced again, and recovered the ground and guns. Driven from the center, the enemy concentrated their fire upon the left, and from there were repulsed also.

It was then 11 o'clock A.M. We had maintained our position against superior numbers and fresh troops. The battle had been most murderous, but the enemy was retreating again, and cheer after cheer went forth from the ranks of our troops as a salute to a new victory, when suddenly we came to a stop. New batteries were found erected in front of us and volley after volley fired from a new line of opponents, clearly indicating that a new enemy was upon us. Buell had arrived with 30,000 fresh troops, and another battle had to be fought. The contest was unequal, and at once steps were taken for a retreat. Train after train, with wounded, stores and ammunition, was sent to the rear; squads of soldiery set to keep the road in passable condition over miry ices; the cavalry set to destroy the Federal property remaining in their camps, yet in our possession, and the remnant of our broken down regiments brought to face the enemy to stop his advance—so the battle went on until dark.

Sanford's Mississippi battery was captured by the enemy, except one gun. They were ordered to retreat, but thought they had time to unlimber on the way and give the enemy a few rounds to check their advance, and protect the retreat of two regiments of infantry, then falling back. They did so, effected their object, but lost some horses, and finally the battery, save one gun.

Bankhead's battery, in Breckinridge's brigade, was captured by the enemy and retaken by us.

The enemy's fire was concentrated on the left.

Gens. Bragg, Hardee, Ruggles, Polk and Beauregard himself, shared all the perils of the fight, but nature, if not courage, was giving way. Broken fragments of regiments could only be found, and yet the enemy was held at bay. Stragglers were found on every road leading to Corinth loaded down with Federal plunder and anxious to save their trophies. They could have been counted by the thousands; and while enough praise cannot be bestowed upon our troops engaged during the last two memorable days, enough reprobation cannot be given to the selfish cowards that prevented us from adding a new victory to the glorious one of yesterday, by their anxiety to secure a few spoils. Yet when darkness came upon the field, then enemy retreated to what camps they had recovered on the right and we occupied their camps in the center and on the left, holding them at bay with a handful of men and a few batteries. Arrangements for a retreat were completed, the enemy too much injured to pursue. Night favoring our movements, strong batteries placed in position to protect them, and all our enemies present on the field to organize and superintend, we retraced our steps to Corinth, where we arrived last night. A short time afterward, Gen. Beauregard and staff came in also, to organize new plans and prepare new victories, and we learn since that the whole army is ordered to fall back to Corinth. It is coming in today. The men are wearied but ready to fight, and are confident of the ultimate success of our cause.

What our losses may be, is not yet known. In wounded it is very heavy; in killed very small in proportion. This is easily accounted for when it is remembered that the battle took place over a broken country, very likely wooded, and where bayonet charges are almost impossible and that for two days it was mostly a fight of artillery and musketry at long range. As to other bases, such as guns, wagons, stores, etc., it will be very trifling, as we had time to secure enough of the enemy's property to compensate for the loss of any of our own.

In a military point of view, the result is not likely to turn against us. The only thing that saved the Federal army from total destruction on Sunday, was their proximity to their gunboats and transports. Should they attempt to attack us here, twenty four miles over such a country and such roads, we could not wish for a better chance to retrieve all our past losses at que blow.

I do not send you any list of the killed and wounded, as it is impossible yet to hear correct reports, and it would be cruel, as well as foolish, to create false alarms. As to incidents, it does hardly look well to mention what few came to your correspondent's notice, while there are so many that will come to light gradually, the principal heroes of which now sleep in a soldier's grave. Yet, I will mention a few at random, with the above restriction.

When Gen. Prentiss was taken prisoner he expressed a great desire to see Gen. Beauregard, and was brought before him on the battlefield. I was there, standing near the general, and witnessed the interview. Gen. Prentiss addressed Gen. Beauregard, and told him that he considered him the best general in our army. You are mistaken, said Beauregard; I know in our army better generals than I am, and among those I will cite Sidney Johnston, whom we have unfortunately lost to-day. Prentiss was surprised to see in Gen. Beauregard a man of small stature, and so easy in manners. He admitted our victory to be as great as Manassas, and our troops to have fought desperately. His battle flag was captured by the 9th Mississippi regiment; I saw it brought this morning to headquarters. Presently three more flags were brought to Beauregard at Shiloah. One of his aids brought in a little quail that had been so frightened by the cannonade that it laid on the ground without trying to escape capture. This will be my living trophy of the battle, remarked the general.

At six o'clock General Bragg came in from the pursuit. I have swept the enemy clear into the river, said he. They are retiring on their transports under protection of the gunboats. Their shelling is furious. Then shaking hands with Gov. Harris, he remarked: Governor, your State is restored to you. Gen. Beauregard then ordered to cease the pursuit.

This morning I saw a private pass with a federal flag. It was the regiment's colors of the 15th Illinois, captured by Private John Williams of Company C, 18th Mississippi regiment, now orderly of Gen. Garner. The 1st Louisiana infantry, in the charge upon the enemy's camp, took a whole section of artillery and three regimental colors. Col. Adams was wounded, and they lost twenty-three officers, killed and wounded, including all the captains save one. A whole brigade of Federals was captured by Gen. Bragg. The prisoners in our hands must amount to over three thousand.

I have just been over the battlefield to hunt for a friend of mine. I find many lost. I met a company in the 3d Kentucky, composed of Paducah friends. How much they have suffered. Capt. Somes, slightly wounded; Geo. Allen, struck by a ball in the foot. How sad is the morrow of a battle.

A train is coming; I must close this.

ETTE.

Northern Mississippi after Shiloh

Less than a month after the Battle of Shiloh, the Confederate and Union armies prepared to meet again, this time near the northern Mississippi town of Corinth. Or so it appeared. Samuel Chester Reid, Jr., Sparta of the *Appeal*, was on hand to report on the buildup, but little did he—or anyone else—know that the Confederates were preparing for a phantom action. General Beauregard realized his troops were hugely outnumbered by the federals, and so he planned what military men would call a "strategic withdrawal." On 29 May, Beauregard withdrew to Tupelo, before the Union army had a chance to force him into battle. At about that same time, Halleck split his force, sent Buell to threaten Chattanooga, and left Grant to defend northern Mississippi in a series of smallish battles that summer as Confederate Generals Price and Van Dorn attempted to unite forces against Grant. Beauregard's speech, which was a prelude to many smaller skirmishes rather than a major battle, was so rousing that Reid himself got caught up in the martial feeling and filed this story, which had the effect of leading Confederate readers to believe a great battle was pending in northern Mississippi, at the same time the fighting in the Peninsula of Virginia was heating up and the Confederate capital came close to falling to the enemy.

HENRY TIMROD: ARMY AT CORINTH——SITUATION IN NORTHERN MISSISSIPPI

With Beauregard's army settled in at Corinth, the Charleston Mercury, *one of the South's best-known newspapers with strong fire-eating tendencies, sent a correspondent to Mississippi to find out what was going on there. Henry Timrod, a Charleston poet and journalist who would become the Confederacy's poet laureate, had no experience as a war correspondent, as he acknowledged in the following article, and even if he had, he wrote in this story, he would not have been able to say much about the military situation due to censorship regulations imposed on reporters with the Southern army. He instead tried to paint a picture for the* Mercury's *readers of what northern Mississippi was like while addressing in a very general way the military situation.*

Charleston Mercury, 7 May 1862

THE CRISIS AT CORINTH

(FROM OUR SPECIAL CORRESPONDENT.)
CORINTH, MISS., April 27.

By a long and circuitous route, and after many tedious delays, I arrived at Corinth early last Thursday morning. But for the fact that I accompanied the Tenth Regiment of South Carolina Volunteers in trains specially appropriated to them, I might have been still upon the road. Such is the deficiency of transportation, and such the crowd pressing forward to this place, that many persons, not less eager than myself to reach the great centre of attraction, have found it as yet impossible to do so. At almost every station I met individuals who had been waiting for days, in the vain hope of getting on.

Worn out with fatigue, dazed by the bustle of the camp and the novelty of my position, I have not been able up to the present date to glean any publishable information of much interest. The enemy, very strongly reinforced, is at Hamburg, on the western side of the Tennessee River. Such, however, is the state of the roads that it is thought he cannot make an advance in less than a week. That he will make an advance as soon as practical, there seems to be no reasonable doubt. But whether, in that event, Beauregard will meet him half way, or await an assault within the lines about Corinth, I have heard too many contrary opinions to justify me in predicting. Our position here is so strong a one (being so protected, it is said, to the right and left by morasses as to compel the foe to attack in front) that the latter course would seem to be the part of prudence. Still the great moral advantage of being the attacking party, may induce Beauregard to assume the offensive. This Delphic putting of the case will, I trust, prove eminently satisfactory to your readers.

Take whatever shape events may, I think I may venture to assert, without ambiguity, that the great battle which is to decide the issue in the West, is very near at hand. Somewhere between Corinth and the Tennessee River our cause, for a time is to be lost or won!

"Tell thy name, thou trembling field,
Field of Death! where'er thou be
Groan thou with our victory!"

Alas, even if I could procure, by means natural or supernatural, an answer to this invocation, I would not be permitted at present to reveal it.

Corinth is really "quite a place!" I expected to see in it an insignificant railway station, with a hut or two, and a shop and postoffice in one. I found it, on the contrary, presenting the appearance of a large village suddenly arrested on its way to become a considerable town. There is a hotel, there are churches, several streets lined with shops (where, however, there is now little to be purchased), and many good private dwellings. But the hotel and the churches have been turned into hospitals, most of the inhabitants have gone away, and the village has been converted into a busy and populous camp.

I passed the first two days after my arrival outside of the town, and thus had an opportunity of observing the nature of the country around it. Even my inexperienced judgment may venture to pronounce that country very badly adapted to the movements of armies. It is made up of a succession of low densely wooded hills and swampy bottoms; it is intersected with innumerable creeks, while the soil is a tenacious clay that retains moisture for a long time. I found the summit of the hills scarcely less muddy than the ravines between them.

Reports of skirmishing are rife. On Thursday there was severe skirmishing between our pickets and those of the enemy near Monterey. Yesterday a body of Confederate cavalry encountered a superior force in the vicinity of Tuscumbia, killed twenty, and captured forty prisoners. A vague rumor, which I have not been able to trace to any authentic source, has just reached me, that the enemy is advancing, in spite of the bad condition of the road. If this be so, you may hear of a battle very shortly indeed.

KAPPA.

SAMUEL CHESTER REID, JR.: LETTER FROM CORINTH—BEAUREGARD'S ROUSING SPEECH TO HIS TROOPS

Samuel Chester Reid, Jr., Sparta of the Appeal, *wrote a rousing review of an address Beauregard made to his troops during their occupation of Corinth. The speech clearly convinced the reporter that complete Confederate victory could not be far off if the South succeeded in the Peninsula Campaign, then ongoing in Virginia, and if Beauregard's men could defeat Grant's at Corinth.*

Memphis Appeal, 6 May 1862

LETTER FROM CORINTH

[Special Correspondence of the Memphis Appeal.]
CORINTH, Saturday, May 3, 1862.

I send you by telegraph to-day the address of General Beauregard to our combined army. It should meet an ardent response from every patriotic heart. Its bold, soldier-like declaration tells us that on the event of the coming battle hangs the fate of the valley of the Mississippi. Already have our people evinced a heroism and devotion of country, unparalleled in the history of revolutionary struggles since the world began. Nothing in the history of Greece or Rome can compare with our struggles on the battle-field, the sacrifices and offerings of our people with their life-blood and property, nor with the high-souled patriotism, toil and devotion of our women, who have shown themselves more than Spartan mothers, and who, from the commencement of the war by the abolition barbarians of the North, have exhibited an unceasing endurance without a murmur, while they have strained to make every exertion in aid of our glorious cause. History will not fail to record their noble deeds of humanity, nor their self-sacrificing martyrdom.

There can be neither retreat, defeat, or surrender in the coming great to our arms, and the glorious deeds of valor which our braves shall exhibit on the battle-field of Corinth, will live for all ages. Let every man therefore go forth to battle as if on his single arm depended the achievement of our liberty and independence. Let them think what we are to achieve by victory, and what we are to lose by—but I will not write the word, as I feel confident no other fate than a glorious success can attend our arms.

As you are told by our noble general, we shall meet the foe in this coming conflict on terms of greater equality than we have ever met the infidels before. Let our people then be strong of heart, full of hope, and not lacking in that high and moral courage which a sincere and abiding faith in the will of the omnipotent Deity cannot fail to inspire, however He may shape and direct our destiny. With the names of Price, Beauregard, Bragg, Polk, Hardee, Breckinridge, Ruggles, Vader, Cheatham, Clark, Chalmers, Manney, Jordon, Preston, and a host of heroic braves, we cannot fail of success, and if there be any truth in the oracles of old the God of battles will surely not desert us. But whatever be our fate, let our people hope on, hope ever, for there can be no despair in the hearts of our patriotic braves who have determined to be free. It is therefore but a question of time. The northern abolition infidels cannot hold out thirty days longer if victory crown our arms at Yorktown and Corinth. Their case is a thousand times more desperate than our own, with a frightful debt engulphing and sapping the very marrow of their resources for support, and still increasing at the rate of over four millions a day, it is utterly impossible for them to hold out, and defeat to them,

gives us back New Orleans, the Mississippi, Tennessee, Kentucky, Missouri, and all our conquered territory. Let us look forward, then, to the bright and cheering prospects of the future, for this summer shall see our troops in Kentucky, if not across the Ohio, and our gallant boys revelling in the halls of Porkopolis!

The weather continues fine. The enemy is repairing the roads as he advances, in order to insure a speedy and safe "back track," which he will undoubtedly have the pleasure of making. They are making every preparation, with hospital boats at Savannah and Pittsburg, for their wounded, and everything denotes the extent and anticipated slaughter of the great struggle.

A freight train has just come in and reports having run into a train coming up before them, last night at Pocahontas, killing two men and wounding two others.

No movements of the enemy to-day whatever.

SPARTA.

Fall of New Orleans

New Orleans was the South's most important city, and its capitulation in April 1862 was a crushing blow to the Confederacy's morale, transportation, and economy. The U.S. Department of the Navy chose 60-year-old David G. Farragut to command the fleet near New Orleans. Farragut was a wise choice. Not only had he been reared in New Orleans; he literally had a lifetime's worth of military experience. Farragut had served in the U.S. Navy since 1810 when, at the age of nine, he received a midshipman's commission. Farragut had seen battle action in the War of 1812 and the Mexican-American War.

The defenses of New Orleans were formidable. Just a few miles beyond the mouth of the Mississippi sat heavily armed Forts Jackson and St. Philip. Farther upstream, only a few miles from the city, were two batteries, Chalmette and McGee. Unfortunately, the Confederates had been overly optimistic about the ability of the batteries to protect the city and had removed their heaviest guns. The weapons were installed on gunboats in Lake Pontchartrain. Beyond the batteries, Confederate Commodore George N. Hollins commanded a flotilla of six vessels, nicknamed the "Mosquito Fleet."

Hollins had virtually the same lifelong military experience as Farragut, who was two years younger than the Confederate navy man. Hollins, like Farragut, entered the navy as little more than a boy. At age fifteen, he received his midshipman's commission and was placed aboard the USS *President* under naval legend Stephen Decatur. Despite his experience, Hollins's lightly armed gunboats were no match for the Union navy vessels that had slipped past the forts to the south of New Orleans.

As Farragut's ships steamed up the Mississippi, the Confederate officer in charge of the defense of the city, Major General Mansfield Lovell, decided to abandon the city rather than risk the damage that would occur, should he put up a fight. Farragut arrived at New Orleans on 25 April and demanded the surrender of the city. On 1 May, U.S. Army General Benjamin Butler took control.

The loss of New Orleans had profound consequences for the Confederacy and for the military leaders involved. The blow to Confederate morale from the capitulation of New Orleans was tremendous, and one more blow had been struck for Union control of the Mississippi.

BY TELEGRAPH: ACCOUNT OF BOMBARDMENT OF FORT JACKSON

The fall of New Orleans began when a Northern gunboat fleet slipped past Fort Jackson and proceeded up the Mississippi River toward this most important Southern port city. Heavy fighting had occurred for several days previously. The following series of telegraphed dispatches from the Memphis Appeal *described the bombardment of Fort Jackson. The first dispatch, datelined New Orleans and signed "D," may have been written by Durant Da Ponte, a correspondent for the* New Orleans Daily Delta *who had covered the 1860 convention of Southern states in Montgomery.*

Memphis Appeal, 27 April 1862

BOMBARDMENT OF FORT JACKSON!

[Special to the Memphis Appeal]

NEW ORLEANS, April 23.—General Duncan reports that the bombardment of Fort Jackson is still progressing furiously.

Several of the Federal boats have been sunk by the guns of the fort.

The casualties in the fort are few, and its defenders are gallant, hopeful and earnest.

The attacking Federal fleet consists of twenty-one mortar boats and thirty-six other vessels.

D.

Later from Fort Jackson

[Special to the Memphis Appeal]

NEW ORLEANS, April 23, P.M.—Gen. Duncan reports to-day that the bombardment of Fort Jackson was continued by the enemy all night, and is still progressing.

He has no further casualties to report, and says that Providence is protecting the garrison, who are confident of ultimate success, and regret the doubts of their fellow citizens. Their fortitude is great, and the cause in which they are engaged commendable, and not the least idea of capitulation is entertained. The best guns of the fort continue in good working order, and the discipline of the troops is excellent.

Over 20,000 shells have been thrown by the enemy, thousands of which fell in the fort. Our enemies must soon become exhausted. If not, we can continue the contest as long as they can.

The Fight at Fort Jackson

NEW ORLEANS, April 23.—The following is a copy of an official dispatch from Major-Gen. Lovell:

"To Brigadier-Gen. Duncan, commanding at Fort Jackson: Say to the officers and men of your command that their heroic fortitude in enduring one of the most terrific bombardments ever known to have occurred, and the courage and skill with which they have crushed the enemy whenever he has dared to come from under cover, attacks the admiration of all, and will be recorded in history as a splendid example for patriots and soldiers.

"Anxious by confident families and friends are watching them with firm reliance, based upon the gallant exhibition thus far made of their indomitable courage and great military skill. The enemy will try your powers of endurance, but we believe, with no better success than he has already experienced.

[Signed]

"*M. LOVELL, Maj. Gen. Com.*"

Gen Duncan's reply to Maj. Gen. Lovell is as follows:

"GENERAL: I have to report this morning the same state of things existing. The bombardment is still going on furiously. They keep it up continuously, by reliefs of their divisions.

"One of their gunboats, painted gray, came above the point this morning, but was struck and retired.

"We are hopeful, in good spirits, and very much in earnest.

"I cannot speak in too high praise of all the officers and men, nor have I any further casualties to report.

"Let the people have faith and fortitude, and we will not disgrace them.

[Signed]

J. K. Duncan,
Brigadier-General."

Bombardment of Fort Jackson

NEW ORLEANS, April 23.—The following dispatch was received from Fort Jackson to day:

"We have had a heavy and continued bombardment all night, which is still progressing. No other casualties have occurred, except two men slightly wounded. God is certainly protecting us. We are still cheerful, and have an abiding faith in our ultimate success. We are making repairs the best we can. Our best guns are still in working order. The most of them have been disabled at times. Twenty-five thousand thirteen-inch shells have been fired by the enemy, thousands of which have fallen in the fort. They must soon exhaust themselves; if not, we can stand it as long as they can."

[Signed]

J. K. Duncan.
Brigadier-General Commanding.

GEORGE KENDALL OR FRANCIS LUMSDEN: NEW ORLEANS MUST ENDURE YANKEE OCCUPATION

After many days of heavy fighting between the Union naval forces and the Confederate land forces, New Orleans finally surrendered. The Picayune *tried to offer some encouragement to demoralized city residents. The historic city had been saved but now had to endure the yoke of Union oppression.*

New Orleans Picayune, 27 April 1862

THE DUTY OF THE HOUR

We have great satisfaction in reading the several proclamations of Mayor Monroe, addressed to the people of this city, with reference to the duty devolving upon them, at the present solemn and critical exigency. Truly, as he says in that, which has also the [*unreadable*] of the Committee of Safety, through its President, one of our best and most prominent citizens, the circumstances, sad and melancholy as they are, in which we are now placed, require on our part the exercise of the utmost wisdom and forbearance.

We have devoted freely of our men, our substance, and our exertions, to the defence of our beloved city, and have nothing wherewith to reproach ourselves, in the way of dereliction or neglect of duty, to accomplish that object. We have not succeeded. A superior force, availing itself of facilities of approach we had not the power to resist, and of an arm in which we were not capable of competing with it, has accomplished its purpose, and stands before our city, dictating to us terms of surrender.

It now devolves upon us to meet the exigency with dignity—not with craven submissiveness on the one hand, nor, as the Mayor says, with indecent alacrity on the other; but with calm and reliant hope for the moment which we may confidently trust is not remote when our brethren and countrymen will achieve our deliverance.

Meantime, we have domestic interests, near and dear to us, to guard and defend. The preservation of the peace, quiet and good order of our city, is now the paramount duty of every citizen. The Mayor tells the invader that he has a gallant people, a people sensitive of all that can affect their dignity and self-respect, over which to exercise the government he now, we trust but temporarily, can assert. Let us verify, by our example, the character our Chief Magistrate has not unjustly claimed for us. He promises to discharge all the duties imposed upon him by his office, with religious fidelity. Be it ours to sustain him, and the other authorities of our city, in that good work. Let us not, by rash acts of violence, though these may be the dictates of offended pride and deep sense of injury, give the enemy warrant for aspersions he has not been backward, in time past, in throwing upon us; nor furnish him a pretext for inflicting wanton and irreparable injury upon the city.

The strict and full performance of these high and holy duties is not by any means inconsistent with those feelings which, though temporarily defeated, we have, as men and freemen, a right to entertain; nor with that dignity which the soul conscious of rectitude may maintain, even in the midst of disaster.

We have now pressing upon us, with more stringency than ever, many relative obligations, the sacredness of which every good citizen will be free to admit. "The poor ye have ever with you," said One, whose precepts were uttered for our guidance. It is ours to consider more than ever, and in every way possible, their imperative wants. Bakeries, and groceries, and markets, and provision stores, should be kept open, during the day, and thus articles necessary for subsistence be made and kept easy of access and procurement. This is no time to practice extortion, or to haggle about prices. The exorbitant profit upon the sale of articles of prime necessity, wrung from the scantily supplied purse of a fellow citizen, is now more than ever a robbery. We trust that every such instance will meet, at the hands of the community, with the execration it so justly merits.

Battle of Corinth

Northern Mississippi remained relatively free of military engagements through the summer of 1862, but that changed in the fall. In late September, Union General William S. Rosecrans met Confederate forces under General Sterling Price near Iuka, Mississippi. Rosecrans drove the Confederates southwest of Iuka, where Price later met up with his colleague, General Earl Van Dorn. The two decided to combine their forces and march north toward Pocahontas, Tennessee. They hoped to convince Rosecrans they were planning to attack Bolivar, Tennessee. Their real plan was to attack Corinth before Rosecrans could assemble his widely disbursed troops.

Rosecrans was indeed confused by the Confederates' movements, but he was certain of the fortifications he had built in and around Corinth. He doubted the Confederates would move against a city so heavily defended, and he was uncertain whether they would move against the other cities. He expected Van Dorn and Price to try to draw him out of Corinth and into battle in open country.

Van Dorn attacked Corinth on the morning of 3 October. The Confederates met with some success the first day, though their effort was slowed by intense heat and lack of water for the soldiers. Around 3:00 P.M., the Southern soldiers were poised to capture the city when the federals retreated behind their batteries. Van Dorn's instinct was to pursue, but Price knew that his men were exhausted. He persuaded Van Dorn to wait until the next morning to press the attack. That night, both Rosecrans and Van Dorn repositioned their troops.

The next morning's fighting began with an artillery duel that soon turned into hand-to-hand and house-to-house combat inside Corinth itself. The heaviest fighting took place near the Tishomingo Hotel. The Confederates were finally forced to retreat. The second day of the battle was over by 1:00 P.M. Total losses included 315 killed, 1,812 wounded, and 232 prisoners for the federals and 1,423 killed, 5,692 wounded, and 2,268 prisoners for the Confederates.

The battles at Iuka and Corinth were the last major Confederate offensives in northern Mississippi, and the Union victories in those engagements allowed Grant to focus his attention on Vicksburg. Further, the defeats at Corinth and Antietam convinced Confederate politicians that they would not be receiving recognition as an independent country and aid from Europe.

ALBERT J. STREET: ACCOUNT OF BATTLE AT CORINTH

News of the Battle of Corinth was gathered at Tupelo, Mississippi, and telegraphed back to newspapers. This story, written on 6 October with information obtained from a courier, was fairly accurate in its description of the fighting in Corinth. The one piece of information that was completely inaccurate was the estimate of the size of Rosecrans's force. Rather than the 40,000 men General Price's son estimated, Rosecrans had only about 23,000 men at Corinth, though he did receive some reinforcements from Grant. The correspondent who wrote this dispatch may have been having a little fun with the selection of his nom de guerre. N'Importe is French for "It is not important."

Mobile Advertiser and Register, 7 October 1862

NEWS BY TELEGRAPH
SPECIAL DESPATCH
THE BATTLE AT CORINTH

Force of the Enemy Forty Thousand

[FROM OUR SPECIAL CORRESPONDENT.]

TUPELO, Oct. 6, 9 P.M.—There is nothing reliable from Corinth since General Van Dorn's despatch.

A courier arrived to day says that on the 4th our troops drove the enemy from and occupied their entrenchments, but were afterwards forced to fall back from town.

Heavy cannonading was heard yesterday from points above here. A thousand contradictory rumors are afloat. The fight must have been most bloody. A courier is hourly expected from the scene of conflict.

Brig. Gen. Ed. Price, an exchanged prisoner, son of Gen. Sterling Price, arrived to-day from Memphis, which place he left on the 1st. He represents the enemy 40,000 strong, with 70 pieces of artillery, strongly posted at Corinth.

They were fully posted as to our movements, and anticipated an attack from Van Dorn and Price. Sherman, at Memphis, knew their exact whereabouts.

Late Northern papers have been received.—Two-thirds of the press are opposed to Lincoln's abolition proclamation.

N'IMPORTE.

CLINT: ACCOUNT OF RECENT FIGHTING IN MISSISSIPPI

While Lee's army in Virginia was regrouping after its retreat from Maryland, the Confederate army in the West was fighting Union forces near Corinth. Following the Battle of Corinth, on 5 October, Van Dorn's forces were ambushed at the Hatchie River, and heavy fighting followed. While the federals regrouped, the Confederate force retreated to Holly Springs. The campaign accomplished little, other than more men killed and wounded, as the Mobile *paper's correspondent hints in his letter about the aftermath of the Battle of Corinth.*

Mobile Advertiser and Register, 14 October 1862

Letter from Jackson, Miss.
THE AFFAIR AT CORINTH

From our Special Correspondent
JACKSON, Oct. 10, 1862.

The news from Corinth and North Mississippi, while in a great measure unsatisfactory, has caused much alarm and anxiety, and set our people to work with a will that means business. The failure on the part of our army to capture and secure all that it set out to accomplish, as well as its retreat upon Ripley and Holly Springs, while it caused depression, has had its effect of arousing all to action of the most determined nature. Crimination and recriminations are freely indulged in, and there is much disposition to censure our officers, and some are particularly severe upon Gens. Van Dorn, Lovell and Pillow, although the latter General was not in the battle, and Gen. Lovell acted most gallantly, all accounts agreeing that he was brave and even reckless as to personal safety, for if what is said about him is true, he courted every post of danger. Gens. Van Dorn and Price are also said to have acted with courage and gallantry. The troops are said to have behaved as well as the troops on any field, but with all this the Confederates were defeated. In plain English we have fought an important battle and lost it, and all the fault-finding, scolding and abuse that may be resorted to will not mend matters a particle. We must "prick our flints and try again." From the manner in which Gen. Baggies, Gov. Pettus, Gens. Tilghman and Tapper have gone to work, and the efficiency of their action with the means at their action with the means at their command, affords great hopes that notwithstanding the boasted force of [unreadable] in West Tennessee, they will be essentially met and repulsed, although some evacuations may have to take place.

It is said that the Federals were thoroughly posted as to the movements of our army. There is no doubt of that fact, and they will continue to be so, just so long as martial law is not in existence in the entire Valley of the Mississippi. The abolishment of martial law was most unfortunate, and the results will continue to be injurious until it is again thoroughly endorsed. The [unreadable] does not affect this section of the country only, but it affords a natural ground through which Federal spies have undisputed passage to any portion of the Confederacy. Mobile is now a menaced point and with Pensacola on the west and the Gulf on the south, but little can be done by the authorities that the Federals will not be perfectly acquainted with, and to-day they know more about the defences of Mobile than two-thirds of its citizens. Prostitutes are used by the Federals as spies, and they work with diligence and effectiveness. They fly over the roads and lurk for a day or so about the towns and cities, and then disappear. All hail from Memphis. With the dangers that now surround your city, allow me to say that you cannot be too [*unreadable*], watchful and careful.

As the army has fallen back to Holly Springs, the Mobile and Ohio road is endangered, but to what extent I am unable to say. The enemy will hardly venture so far from its base of operations as to attack Columbus. I think his first object will be to secure the Mississippi Valley and river.

CLINT.

Battle of Perryville, Kentucky

Braxton Bragg's invasion of Kentucky started off well enough. Bragg advanced from Chattanooga and his subordinate General Edmund Kirby Smith from Knoxville. The Confederate forces won easy victories at Richmond and Munfordville. Smith's army captured Lexington and Frankfort and threatened Cincinnati, Ohio. At that point, Bragg occupied most of Kentucky, but Bragg's movement to Bardstown after the Battle of Munfordville allowed Union General Don Carlos Buell to reach Louisville uncontested, where he received 25,000 reinforcements and then quickly moved against the Confederates.

As Buell advanced on Bardstown, Bragg's forces withdrew through Springfield and Perryville to a location where some water was available. That summer and fall, Kentucky had experienced a drought, and the Southern soldiers had been suffering from the heat, dust, and lack of good water.

On 7 October, a large Union force advanced toward Perryville. Bragg ordered his subordinates Major General William J. Hardee and Polk to Perryville, where they were to defeat the Union force. On 8 October, the Confederates withstood an all-day attack by 39,000 federals. Bragg had not at first been aware that he faced a force larger than a corps. When he realized the size of the Union force, he withdrew to Harrodsburg and then through the Cumberland Gap back into Tennessee. This was the largest battle fought on Kentucky soil during the Civil War, and it was the bluegrass state's last invasion.

JOHN FORSYTH: ACCOUNT OF BATTLE OF PERRYVILLE

Also in the West, General Braxton Bragg's invasion of Kentucky was halted in what was described as a "pitched battle" at Perryville, southwest of Lexington. A portion of Bragg's army met a portion of General Don Carlos Buell's force in the only major battle to occur in Kentucky. Bragg's invasion of Kentucky had started out well enough with victories in smaller battles near Richmond and Munford, followed by the capture of Lexington and Frankfort by Bragg's lieutenant, General Edmund Kirby Smith. Both Bragg and Buell misread the situation. Bragg did not realize the size of the force his army faced, and only part of Buell's troops took part in the battle. An "acoustic shadow" kept the general from hearing the sound of the engagement. He received word of the fighting late in the afternoon and sent reinforcements. The battle ended with darkness. Losses on both sides were about equal. John Forsyth, editor of the Mobile Advertiser and Register *and a staunch Bragg supporter, was with the Confederate army on its invasion of Kentucky, and he filed an eyewitness account of the Battle of Perryville. Forsyth inaccurately described the outcome of the fight at Perryville as a Confederate victory.*

Mobile Advertiser and Register, 18 October 1862

NEWS BY TELEGRAPH
SPECIAL DESPATCHES
FROM GEN. BRAGG'S HEADQUARTERS
PARTICULARS OF BATTLE OF PERRYVILLE

Battle of Frankfort

[From Our Special Correspondent.]

HARRODSBURG, Oct. 10, via KNOXVILLE, Oct. 17.–Gen. Bragg's first Kentucky pitched battle was fought on Wednesday, the 8th instant, at Perryville, ten miles from this place. The enemy had been following us in force from Bardstown, and they also threatened Frankfort. Gen. Withers' division was sent forward to support Kirby Smith, while the divisions of Cheatham, Beckner and Anderson were countermarched to give battle to the foe in the rear.

Our lines of battle on the right and left of the turnpike, and commanding the only accessible route, opened with artillery at 6 o'clock A.M.—Gen. Bragg and his staff reached the ground about 7 o'clock, and at 10 o'clock the dispositions for the fight were complete. Our right awaited the attack in force, Cheatham and Buckner being posted to meet it.

At 3 o'clock P.M. they advanced in splendid line, with Gen. Bragg's orders to push along the whole line to close quarters. For one hour and a half the enemy maintained his ground bravely in the face of a murderous fire of artillery and musketry. Our troops fought like heroes until the enemy began to falter, when with a shout our boys moved forward and drove them three or four miles, entirely off the field. Meantime an attempt on our left had been repulsed. We captured 500 or 600 prisoners and 21 pieces of artillery, but for want of horses only eight pieces were brought off. The returns of our casualties are not all in, but they are estimated at 1,500. I have opened a list of those ascertained so far.

With one more division the enemy would have been de-

stroyed. Night put an end to the pursuit. The enemy's loss is believed to be more than double our own. Among them is Gen. Jas. Jackson, certain, and Gen. Crittenden reported. Buell was present commanding, and we have prisoners from five different divisions, from which we estimate the enemy's force to have been at least 80,000. We fought only 12,000 strong. Our army is in the highest spirits.

At Frankfort the matter was soon ended. The enemy, under M'Cook, fled before Kirby Smith, and Withers cut off his rear, capturing 700 prisoners and fourteen wagons.

Another battle is at hand. Bragg's depots being menaced, he at once withdrew his army to protect them. At daylight next morning the enemy sent a flag of truce for permission to bury their dead. In the afternoon fight there was not even a Yankee surgeon on the field, and the wounded were all left. Our wounded were removed during the night after the battle.

Gen. Polk had a narrow escape. At Dusk he left his staff and rode up to stop the fire of a Confederate regiment, as he thought, upon our own troops. Seizing the Colonel by the shoulder he demanded, "Why are you firing on your friends." The Colonel said that he did not know that he was. "Who are you?" said Polk. "The Colonel of the 23d Indiana," was the reply. The General again shook him roughly and ordered him to cease firing, and before the Yankee found out who he was, he put spurs to his horse and got away.

Gen. Bragg says he has got the best troops in the world. Two thousand Kentuckians have taken up arms, and more are organizing. Gen. McCrown's army has arrived here. Among our killed are Lieut. Col. Patterson, of the 11th Tennessee regiment; Lieut.-Col. Evans, of the Texas Rangers; Major W. Pricer, Commissary; Capts. Cartwright, of Georgia, and Wm. S. May of Gen. Claiborne's staff.

J. F.

EASTERN THEATER

Peninsula Campaign

The North's first sustained attempt to capture Richmond was supposed to have begun in February. President Lincoln, frustrated with General McClellan's procrastination and failure to explain his plans for waging war against the Confederates, ordered his commander to lead the Army of the Potomac toward the Confederate capital and to begin a campaign by 22 February. Lincoln even gave the general a plan of battle: Move directly overland from a base in Washington, D.C., through Manassas and on to Richmond. McClellan offered an alternative proposal. He preferred to move his troops by water, via the Potomac and Rappahannock rivers, to Urbana, Virginia, just opposite Richmond. McClellan argued that this plan offered the shortest feasible land route to the Confederate capital. Lincoln capitulated, but multiple delays prevented the campaign from beginning immediately. Finally, in the latter half of March, though, the Union army was ready to begin its campaign for Richmond. McClellan set out from Alexandria with his army on barges—130,000 troops, 15,000 horses, 1,100 wagons, and forty-four artillery batteries sailed down the Potomac, past the mouths of the Rappahannock and York rivers, and on to the Virginia Peninsula. By 5 April, the Union army was on land and only 75 miles from Richmond.

Confederate General John B. Magruder was waiting for the Union legions with an entrenched force about a tenth the size of McClellan's. Magruder's job was to hold the Union troops at bay until reinforcements could reach him, and so the general devised one of the most brilliant deceptions of the war. If he could trick the Union forces into believing they were facing a much larger Confederate force, then perhaps they would be less aggressive in their forward movements. Magruder's plan was simple: He would march the troops he had in circles in front of a gap in the Confederate defenses. The trick worked, and the Union army became convinced that Magruder was being reinforced by thousands of troops and that a major siege would be needed to rout the Confederates. Magruder's pantomime slowed the Union advance for a month and bought time for reinforcements to arrive.

After a failed attempt to capture Yorktown on the same day his forces landed (5 April), McClellan's forces sat outside the village for a full month and built artillery batteries. Finally, on 4 May, McClellan was ready to take on Magruder. But Magruder was gone. He had given McClellan the slip and pulled his vastly inferior force out of Yorktown under cover of darkness. McClellan telegraphed Union Secretary of War Edwin Stanton of his brilliant success in capturing Yorktown. McClellan also requested more troops. He was convinced Confederate General Joseph E. Johnston stood between him and Richmond with perhaps a force even larger than his own. McClellan was overly cautious by nature, but he was also getting bad information from Pinkerton detectives who had been hired to gather intelligence for the Union. The Pinkertons were giving McClellan's estimates of a Confederate force two, three, even four times its actual size. In reality, Johnston was certainly in position to try to defend the Confederate capital, but his fighting force was only about half that of McClellan's—some 42,000 against 85,000. Still, McClellan was on the peninsula and slowly but steadily moving toward Richmond.

The Union advance on Richmond began in earnest on 8 May but immediately and literally bogged down. Spring rains had turned the roads in the region into mud holes that could swallow up men, horses, and even wagons. Still, within two weeks, McClellan was within 7 miles of Richmond. Rather than advancing and pressing his advantage, though, McClellan dug in and began arguing with Washington for reinforcements. His force at that point outnumbered the Confederates defending Richmond by some 40,000 men. The capture of Richmond seemed eminent, until the rain started up again.

Most of the time, the Chickahominy River was little more than a stream that flowed into the James River. Generally speaking, it was easily passible. When heavy rains came, though, if the river flooded even to only 2 feet above normal, it would overflow the whole area. From 20 May to 25 May, McClellan moved three corps across the river to demonstrate against Richmond. He kept three corps on the north side of the river in reserve. Then, on 27 May, it started to rain. And it continued to rain until, on 31 May, the Chickahominy was impassible.

On 31 May, Johnston attacked two of McClellan's corps outside Richmond in what would come to be known as the Battle of Seven Pines (Fair Oaks). His attack was successful early on, but the Union lines held, and Johnston was forced to withdraw. Johnston was severely wounded in the battle, so much so, in fact, that he had to be relieved of command. Johnston's hiatus from the army opened the door of command for a man who would become a legend: Robert E. Lee. The Union, though, suffered the greatest casualty of the day. After the Battle of Seven Pines, McClellan lost his nerve. He was immobilized for three weeks.

Lee realized that a prolonged siege of Richmond would result in a Union victory due to McClellan's superior numbers. He understood that he had to go on the offensive immediately and push McClellan as far back as he could, and he knew he had to do so before the Union force's large artillery could be brought up to the front. To improve the numerical odds a bit, Lee recalled Stonewall Jackson's forces from the Shenandoah Valley. On 25 June, Lee and his lieutenants agreed on a pincer movement against McClellan to begin at 3:00 A.M. the next morning.

On 25 June, Confederate forces launched the Seven Days Battles with an attack on Union forces near Mechanicsville. The day ended inconclusively, but McClellan withdrew to Gaines's Mill. Lee pursued, and the fighting was renewed there on 27 June. Lee attacked with 65,000 men and pushed McClellan back near Malvern Hill. Again, Lee pursued the retreating federals. On 1 July, the two armies met again outside Malvern Hill. Confederates smashed into the Union lines, but they held. The obvious victory at Malvern Hill was heartening, and McClellan's men were ready to fight their way back toward Richmond. One officer, Philip Kearny, argued that a retreat and the failure to take Richmond could only be explained by cowardice or treason. McClellan was not so bold. He believed his first responsibility was to ensure his army's safety, and so he ordered a retreat to Harrison's Landing and the protection offered by the Union gunboats on the James River.

The performance of the Confederate army in the Peninsula Campaign and its concluding Seven Days Battles was both brilliant and inept. Magruder's diversions bought the time needed to gather the Confederate army's strength and to build defenses around Richmond, but the offensive campaign Lee waged after taking over what he named the Army of Northern Virginia was marred by miscommunications and tardiness of some units. Still, even though each of its attacks were repulsed during the Seven Days Battles, with the single exception of Gaines's Mill, the Confederacy had secured Richmond—at least for the time being—at the cost 19,000 men. The Union's loss in men was less, 15,000, but the cost in territory and morale was considerable.

DR. GEORGE W. BAGBY: BATTLE OF SEVEN PINES

The Battle of Seven Pines occurred across two days, 31 May to 1 June. Johnston, taking advantage of the division of the Union army and the impassible Chickahominy River, attacked McClellan's left. Johnston had planned a double envelopment, but poor staff work resulted in a series of ineffective frontal attacks that were repulsed once federal reinforcements finally made it across the swollen river. Johnston was seriously wounded in this engagement in which the Union lost 5,000 men to the Confederacy's 6,100.

Charleston Mercury, 9 June 1862

BATTLE OF THE SEVEN PINES

(FROM OUR OWN CORRESPONDENT.)

RICHMOND, Friday, June 6.

McCLELLAN claims a victory at the battles of "Seven Pines." Of course, everything short of a total rout is a victory to him. Night and the delay of one corps saved him from that destruction which even he, unbounded liar as he is, would have been compelled to confess. The fighting of our men is beyond all praise. Mr. DAVIS, who loses no occasion of informing the world of his proximity to a battle, has announced his admiration of the gallantry of our men. It was never exceeded. The South Carolinians who were engaged, covered themselves with glory. Among the troops whose conduct in the battle is spoken of in the highest terms of praise, are Col. Jenkins' Regiment of Sharpshooters; the 5th South Carolina Regiment, Col. Giles, who fell in the thickest of the fight; the 6th South Carolina Regiment, Col Bratton; Mattison's Battalion, S.C.V., and the Hampton Legion. Jenkins' brigade swept steadily and gloriously over all obstacles. The Legion, in attempting to storm a strong work of the enemy, encountered a murderous fire, and was finally repulsed; but the list of casualties tells a tale of heroism. The marvel is that in such a country the men could fight at all. Had the attack been made a day or two earlier, not a live Yankee would have been left this side of the swamp. But Johnston, worried by the newspapers, the President and Gen. Lee, declared he would not fight until he got ready. Hence the article in the Enquirer, asserting, very gratuitously, that there was perfect accord among our high officials.

Another golden opportunity was lost when 20,000 Yankees advanced to Hanover C.H., and Branch was left to his small discretion to attack them with a part of a brigade, to whose assistance, when overpowered, he refused to call reinforcements, though they were within a short distance. It is strange that a flank commanding two important railroads, possessing the advantages of an easy passage across the swamp, and the only firm, dry fighting ground in the neighborhood, should have been left to the most incompetent commanders in the whole army. Doubtless the Circumlocution Office, in its hesitation about confirming A. P. Hill's appointment as Major General, is not wholly guiltless in this matter.

An intelligent negro, who, with others, assisted in burying the Yankee dead, puts down their loss in killed alone at 2000—a surprising statement, for the highest number of dead Yankees seen by any of those who have been over the field, as given to me, is 200, and all agree that our loss in wounded exceeded theirs considerably. But the negro's story may be true, for I hear that the Texan brigade took no prisoners whatever, and other brigades may have followed that example of mercy to our own people by retribution, which the brutality of Wool, Hunter and Butler fully justifies. Our own loss will not fall far short of the number given in my letter two days ago. The killed may not amount to 500, but the wounded may be estimated by the official report of the casualties in Rode's

brigade, which went in with 2500 and lost 1,092. It is true this brigade bore much of the brunt of the fight; but there were twelve or fifteen brigades engaged, and I have yet to hear of more than three or four regiments which did not suffer heavily.

The fight failed, it is said, of its legitimate results because the corps that was to have led off early in the morning did not. After waiting two hours Longstreet led off. The enemy were advertised and had full time to prepare. Whiting who was to have gone round, could just hold his own.

As it is, the only profit derived from the victory is the lesson of blood conveyed to the invader. "On to Richmond" is going to be no holiday work. The foe may reach these walls, but, if he does, he will come in ghastly plight. Could we get him out of the swamps and forests upon an open firm field, I should not fear the result. But we will have to fight him again on much the same ground, for we cannot permit him to perfect his trenches. Already he has had too much time. But our army is in better trim than before. Our artillery, cavalry, infantry, all are now in their proper position, with pickets, scouts and videttes posted and distributed as they never were before. The skies all still hang with thick clouds, but ere this letter reaches you the fateful day will, in all probability, have come and gone.

The river is said to be higher this morning than ever before, except on a single occasion—the water belongs six feet above the tops of the obstructions, to which no serious damage is yet reported. So great, indeed, is the freshet, that it is asserted that the Monitor is coming up to Richmond by way of the Petersburg Railroad. Let her come, say the people, and bombard as much as she pleases. If the city falls, our property is all confiscated. So what difference does it make? Better, a thousand-fold, destruction than Yankee possession. I am glad to see this feeling so rife among our people.

Dr. Cullen tells me that, at the time our men stormed the redoubts in the face of a terrible cannonade—the only instance of the kind that has occurred during the war—our own twenty-four pounders were up to their muzzles in mud. The Yankees were taught that, if Richmond falls at all, it will fall into the hands of those who love death most sincerely. They need their miniature bombs not against our caissons, for we had none there, but against our men. One poor fellow is now lying in Seabrook's Warehouse with his face literally blown out—the little bomb having exploded after it entered his mouth.

Capt. Elliott, of the Whig, is raising a battalion for special service in defence of the city—the Common Council offering twenty dollars a month bounty to each man who enlists for six months. Better organize a battalion, nay a brigade, for service in the hospitals. We do not need soldiers so much as nurses.

Nothing from Jackson to-day, nor from the lines around the city. Military operations are impossible in the present state of the roads, which are likely to remain as bad as they can be, judging from the watery skies which overhang us.

I take this method of answering two despatches sent me from Columbia, by Messrs. Guerry and McLees. They were handed, yesterday, by mistake, to my father, who made many enquiries in regard to L. P. Guerry and the dead of Mattison's battalion, but could learn nothing of either. The wounded from South Carolina are not all sent to the C. S. Hospital in Manchester, but are scattered among various private and public hospitals. The same may be said of the wounded of other States. Hence the difficulty of ascertaining with certainty the facts in regard to individuals in particular corps. There should be, and doubtless soon will be, a Central Depot of Information, to which persons can repair with the assurance of getting a reliable answer. Not an unreliable answer obtained after visiting twenty or more hospitals, two of which (Camp Winder and Chimborazo) are cities of sick, holding several thousand. The distance between Chimborazo and Winder is two miles in a direct line, and the Alms House Hospital, the next largest, is a mile to the right of this line, going west. Hence the difficulty of obtaining information.

HERMES.

Seven Days' Battle

No reporters were permitted to be with the Confederate army during the Seven Days' Battle, and so reporting of the fighting in front of Richmond depended on telegraphic reports sent in from the front and information obtained from wounded soldiers who were brought to hospitals in the capital city for treatment. News of the fighting filtered out in bits and pieces, and some newspapers found it necessary to piece together accounts of the battle from wire reports and stories in exchange newspapers. The *Richmond Examiner* did have a representative present during much of the fighting. Editor John M. Daniel, who was an aide to A. P. Hill. Daniel, though, was wounded during the fighting.

DR. GEORGE W. BAGBY: ACCOUNT OF FIGHTING DURING SEVEN DAYS BATTLES

The Charleston Mercury, *like most other Southern newspapers, had to find some way to cover the Seven Days Battles other than eyewitness accounts by correspondents present during the fighting. Its reliable Richmond correspondent, Hermes, better known as George W. Babgy, collected news from dispatches sent to the Confederate War Department and forwarded it to the* Mercury's *editors by telegraph and letter. In this series of telegraphs, Hermes described the Battle of Mechanicsville and the early skirmishing that was preliminary to it.*

Charleston Mercury, 27 June 1862

NEWS BY TELEGRAPH
IMPORTANT NEWS FROM RICHMOND
THE GREAT BATTLE BEGUN YESTERDAY
AFTERNOON, ON THE LEFT WING

RICHMOND, June 26.—The difficulty of obtaining information from the lines is illustrated by the indefinite accounts given by the city papers this morning, of the fight which took place on the Williamsburg road yesterday.

It now appears certain that the 1st Louisiana regiment was engaged for some time with two brigades of the enemy, who had driven in our pickets about 8 a.m. Regardless of the heavy odds brought against them, the Louisiana advanced rapidly upon the foe, shouting, as their battle-cry, "BUTLER! BUTLER!" The Yankees in front immediately gave way before the impetuous advance of our men, and would have been driven from the field, but for the support they received from a heavy crossfire directed against us by several additional regiments of the enemy, which were ambuscaded in the woods.

The 1st Louisiana was afterwards reinforced by other regiments of Gen. WRIGHT'S brigade, and the fight was continued during the day until the Yankees were dislodged from the woods and driven back to their camp.

In the afternoon RANSOM'S and MAHONE'S brigades were engaged, and aided in driving the enemy back. Col. SHIVERS and Major NELLIGAN, of the 1st Louisiana, were both wounded in the arm. Lieuts. GILMORE and MURPHY, of the Montgomery Guards (of New Orleans), were both killed. The total Confederate loss is estimated at about 200 killed and wounded. The enemy's loss was heavy.

Later

Up to one o'clock today only occasional cannonading could be heard along the lines. The general expectation of a great battle today has not been realized.

The Latest

Nine o'clock, p.m. The battle which is to decide the fate of Richmond, was begun this afternoon, on the left wing of the Confederate army. For three hours the firing in the direction of Mechanicsville has been rapid and continuous. The cannonading can be heard distinctly in the city, and crowds have gathered on the hills north of the city, whence the bursting of the shells is occasionally visible.

At eight o'clock the firing was still progressing furiously. It is not probable that any particulars will be received from the battlefield until morning.

There was no fighting of importance on the centre or right to-day. A general engagement tomorrow is considered inevitable.

CHARLESTON MERCURY: SUMMARY OF RECENT BATTLES BEFORE RICHMOND

When original stories by a newspaper's own correspondents were hard to come by, editors would turn to exchange newspapers for news. Postal laws allowed newspapers to send copies to other newspapers for free, and the custom of the time allowed journalists to borrow freely from one another, so long as proper credit was given to the paper that originated the story. The following summary story of the recent campaigning in Virginia, for example, was taken from the Charleston Mercury, *but it first appeared in the* Richmond Dispatch *some days earlier.*

Charleston Mercury, 3 July 1862

THE GREAT BATTLE OF RICHMOND
DETAILS OF THE ENGAGEMENTS
THE BATTLE OF BEAVER DAM CREEK
CAPTURE OF ELLYSON'S MILLS
THE STORMING OF GAINES' MILLS, &c., &c., &c.

Owing to the total exclusion of the practised correspondents of the press from the lines of the Army of Richmond, the details of the recent terrible battles in front of that city, as we find them in our Virginia exchanges, are exceedingly vague and unsatisfactory. As the narrative given by the *Dispatch*, of Monday, seems to be more full and connected than the accounts contained in the other papers, we transfer it to our columns, interlarding it here and there with interesting extracts from other sources:

FRIDAY MORNING
AND SATURDAY MORNING—THE FIGHT AT
BEAVER DAM CREEK

When Gen. A. P. Hill had steadily driven the enemy from Meadow Bridge, and had taken up the line of march towards Mechanicsville and the road, evening had far advanced, and it was supposed that a halt would take place. Gen. Ripley, however, with the 44th and 48th Georgia, and 2d and 3d North Carolina, made an attack upon the Yankee fortifications at Ellyson's Mills, in which the 44th Georgia and 3d North Carolina suffered extremely, and did not succeed in taking them, owing to the impracticable nature of the ground. Operations were then suspended on our side, but the enemy kept up a deafening roar of artillery till late in the night. Longstreet's forces had meanwhile crossed, and marched parallel with the Chickahominy. The brigades of Gens. Featherstone and Pryor were in advance, and proceeding some distance, halted for the night. About midnight, Featherstone received orders to change his position, and to occupy a skirt of woods near Beaver Dam Creek, and facing the Federal batteries. He did so, and the men were scarcely asleep when, twilight approaching, the enemy discovered the bivouac, and immediately commenced to shell it vigorously. The men, thus unceremoniously aroused, seized their muskets and fell in, and Gen. Featherstone, just arrived from headquarters, led them to storm the position— mounting ten guns, and supported by two or three brigades. Sharp fighting now commenced on all sides, when Gen. Pryor sent for assistance, when Wilcox soon came upon the ground. To cover the infantry attack, and draw off the artillery fire, the 3d Richmond Howitzers, some pieces of the Donaldsonville and the Thomas Artillery moved up and played upon the enemy's position magnificently. Having engaged the enemy for a long time, and finding it impossible to cross the creek without a bridge, one was constructed by some of the 19th Mississippi and 14th Louisiana, under fire, when the whole force advanced and closed up with the enemy, driving them in great confusion from the field.

The attack of our men on this position was impetuous and daring, but the loss was great, for the foe was so screened by their position it was impossible to get at them properly.

THE FIGHT AT ELLYSON'S MILLS

While Featherstone, Pryor and Wilcox were thus successfully engaging the enemy on the right of our advance, Gen. Maxcy Gregg and his brigade were also hard at work, and successfully stormed the strong position of Ellyson's Mills, and took up the line of march on the left. They did not advance on the Mills by the road, as had been done on Friday evening by Ripley, but simply made a feint in that direction, crossed the main body higher up the creek, took the redoubts and rifle pits on flank, carried them with the bayonet, pushed through the camps, and followed the road towards Gaines' Mills, whither the enemy were retiring.

AT GAINES' MILLS

From prisoners captured at both positions—who proved to be of the Valley army—it was ascertained that we might expect stout resistance at Gaines' Mills, since three or four whole divisions were strongly encamped there—McClellan commanding in person, with Major Generals McCall, Porter, Sedgewick, and others—their estimated force being not less than thirty-odd thousand men. As our three columns moved by parallel lines, we followed and conversed with prisoners, who informed us that their loss, on Friday, at Meadow Bridge, Mechanicsville and Ellyson's Mills, had been fearful, and the whole night had been occupied in burial. The Federals carry off all their dead and wounded as fast as shot, and we only discover those who fall and are left at the actual moment of retreat. This information we believe to be correct.

The heads of our three columns having reached Walker Hogan's farm, north bank of the Chickahominy, about nine miles northeast of Richmond, all came to a halt, and Gens. Lee and Longstreet took up quarters in the house and made dispositions for a further advance towards Gaines' Mills, distant about one mile through the woods. Featherstone's brigade having suffered much in the morning, Wilcox led, being followed by Pryor, and Featherstone in reserve. The composition of Wilcox's command is mostly Alabamians; Pryor has the 14th Louisiana, St. Paul's battalion, 3d Virginia, and one other regiment; Featherstone has the 19th and 12th Mississippi, and 2d Mississippi battalion.

CHARACTER OF THE GROUND

Emerging from the woods, the road leads to the left and then to the right round Gaines' house, when the whole country, for the area of some two miles, is an open, unbroken succession of undulating hills. Standing at the north door of Gaines' house, the whole country to the right, for the distance of one mile, is a gradual slope towards a creek, through which the main road runs up an open hill and then winds to the right. In front, to the left, are orchards and gullies, running gradually to a deep creek. Directly in front, for the distance of a mile, the ground is almost table land, suddenly dipping to the deep creek mentioned above, being faced by a timber covered hill fronting all the table land. Beyond this timber covered hill, the country is again open, and a perfect plateau, a farm house and outhouses occupying the centre, the main road mentioned winding to the right and through all the Federal camps. To the left and rear of the second mentioned farm, a road comes in upon the flat lands, joining the main road mentioned. Thus, to recapitulate, except the deep creek and timber covered hill beyond it, the whole country,

as seen from the north door of Gaines' house, is unbroken, open, undulating, and table land, the right forming a descent to the wood covered creek, the left being dips and gullies, with dense timber still farther to the left; the front being for the most part table land. These particulars of the position are as correct, perhaps, as can be mentioned; but, without a map it will always be difficult to understand the topography of this hard fought and victorious field of Gaines' Mills.

But to the southeast of Gaines' house is a large tract of timber, commanding all advances upon the main road, and in this McClellan and McCall had posted a strong body of skirmishers, with artillery, to annoy our flank and rear when advancing on their camps on the high grounds, if we did so by the main road or over the table lands to the north.

STORMING ENTRENCHMENTS

It is now being 3 p.m., and the head of our column in view of the Federal camps, Gen. Pryor was sent forward with his brigade to drive away the heavy mass of skirmishers posted to our rear to annoy the advance. This being accomplished with great success, and with little loss to us, Pryor returned and awaited orders. Meanwhile the Federals, from their camps and several positions on the high grounds, swept the whole face of the country with their numerous artillery, which would have annihilated our entire force if not screened in the dips of the land and in gullies to our left. Advancing cautiously but rapidly in the skirt of woods and in the dips to the left, Wilcox and Pryor deployed their men into line of battle—Featherstone being in the rear—and suddenly appearing on the plateau facing the timber-covered hill, rushed down into the wide gully, crossed it, clambered over all the felled timber, stormed the timber breastworks beyond it, and began the ascent of the hill, under a terrific fire of sharpshooters, and an incessant discharge of grape and canister, from pieces posted on the brow of the hill, and from batteries in their camps to the right on the high flat lands. Such a position was never stormed before. In descending into the deep creek, the infantry and artillery fire that assailed the three brigades was most terrific. Twenty-six pieces were thundering at them, and a perfect hailstorm of lead fell thick and fast around them. One of Wilcox's regiments wavered, down the General rushed, furiously sword in hand, and threatened to behead the first man that hesitated. Pryor steadily advanced, but slowly; and by the time that the three brigades had stormed the position, passed up the hill through timber, and over felled trees, Featherstone was far in advance. Quickly the Federals withdrew their pieces, and took up a fresh position to assail the three brigades advancing in perfect line of battle from the woods and upon the plateau. Officers had no horses, all were shot— Brigadiers marched on foot, sword in hand—regiments were commanded by Captains, and companies by Sergeants, yet onward they rushed, with yells and colors flying, and backward, still backward fell the Federals, their men tumbling every moment in scores. But what a sight met the eyes of these three gallant brigades! In front stood Federal camps, stretching to the northeast for miles! Drawn up in line of battle were more than three full divisions, commanded by McCall, Porter, Sedgewick, &c.,—banners darkened the air—artillery vomited forth incessant volleys of grape, canister and shell—heavy masses were moving on our left through the woods to flank us! Yet onward came Wilcox to the right, Pryor to the left, and Featherstone in the centre—one grand, matchless line of battle—almost consumed by exploits of the day—yet onward they advanced to the heart of the Federal position, and when the enemy had fairly succeeded in almost flanking us on the left, great commotion is heard in the woods!—volleys upon volleys are heard in rapid succession, which are recognized and cheered by our men. "It is Jackson!" they shout, "on the right and rear!" Yes, two or three brigades of Jackson's army have flanked the enemy, and are getting in the rear! Now the fighting was bitter and terrific. Worked up to madness, Wilcox, Featherstone and Pryor dash forward at a run, and drive the enemy with irresistible fury—to our left emerge Hood's Texan brigade, Whiting's comes after, and Pender follows! The line is now complete, and "forward" rings from one end of the line to the other, and the Yankees, over 30,000 strong, begin to retreat! Wheeling their artillery from the front, the Federals turn part of it to break our left, and save their retreat. The very earth shakes at the roar! Not one piece of ours has yet opened! All has been done with the bullet and bayonet, and onward press our troops through camps upon camps, capturing guns, stores, arms, clothing, &c. Yet, like bloodhounds on the trail, the six brigades sweep everything before them, presenting an unbroken, solid front, and, closing in upon the enemy, keep up an incessant succession of volleys upon their confused masses, and unerringly slaughtering them by hundreds and thousands!

"STONEWALL" AT WORK

But "where is Jackson?" ask all. He has travelled fast, and is heading the retreating foe, and as night closes in, all in anxiety for intelligence from him. 'Tis now about 7 p.m., and just as the rout of the enemy is complete—just as the last volleys are sounding in the enemy's rear, the distant and rapid discharges of cannon tell that Jackson has fallen upon the retreating column, broken it, and captured 3000 prisoners! Far in the night, his insatiable troops land upon the enemy, and for miles upon miles are dead, wounded, prisoners, wagons, cannon, &c., scattered in inextricable confusion upon the road. Thus, for four hours, did our inferior force, unaided by a single piece of artillery, withstand over thirty thousand of the enemy, assisted by twenty-six pieces of artillery!

In total, we captured many prisoners, and thirty pieces of artillery up to 5 p.m., Friday, and in the battle of Gaines' Mills, captured 26 field pieces, 15,000 stand of arms, 6 stand of colors, three Generals (Reynolds, Sanders and Rankin), and over 4000 prisoners, including dozens of officers of every grade from Colonel to Lieutenants of the line.

THE FEDERAL FORCE

Every arm of the service was well represented in the Federal line—cavalry were there in force, and, when our men emerged from the woods, attempted to charge, but the three brigades on the right, and Jackson's three brigades on the left, closed up ranks and poured such deadly volleys upon the horsemen, that they left the ground in confusion and entirely for their infantry to decide the day. McCall's, Porter's and Sedgewicke's "crack" divisions melted away before our advance, however; and, had the fight lasted one half hour longer, not one whole regiment would have survived it. McClellan, prisoners say, repeatedly was present, and directed movements, but, when the three brigades to our left emerged from the woods, such confusion and havoc ensued, that he gave orders to retreat, slipped off his horse, and escaped as best he could. Some say that he was severely wounded, and many officers (prisoners) believe the report that he was on the field is undoubtedly true; for everything had been previously prepared for a grand fight at Gaines' Mills—McClellan even promising to capture our whole force, should we attempt to storm his camps.

CHARGES AND REPULSES

Much has been said of repeated "charges" made, and "repulses." Wild imaginations have concocted many such foolish reports. There was but one "charge," and from the moment the word of command was given—"fix bayonets: forward!" our advance was never stopped despite the awful reception which met it. It is true that one or two regiments became confused in passing over the deep ditch, abattis, and timber earth work—it is also true that several slipped from the ranks and ran to the rear, but in many cases these were wounded men; but the total number of "stragglers" would not amount to more than one hundred. This is strictly true, and redounds to our immortal honor. These facts are true of Wilcox's, Pryor's, and Featherstone's brigades, who formed our right, and we are positive that from the composition of Whiting's, Hood's, and Pender's brigades, who flanked the enemy and formed our left, they never could be made to falter, for Whiting had the 11th, 16th and 2d Mississippi, and two other regiments, unknown to us—Hood had four Texan and one Georgia regiment, and the material of Pender's command was equally as good as any, and greatly distinguished itself. These were the troops mostly engaged and that suffered most. It is gross injustice in any to talk of our troops making "three charges," "repulses," &c., &c. Our troops received the command but once, and if Satan and all his host had confronted them, instead of mortal Yankees, the result would have been the same. There were no repulses.

AT GARNETT'S FARM

About eleven o'clock Saturday, Capt. Moody's battery opened fire upon the entrenchments of the enemy, located just beyond Garnett's Farm. The battery fired some ten or fifteen minutes, and meanwhile a body of infantry, consisting of the 7th and 8th Georgia regiments, moved up under cover of the fire from the field pieces. The 8th, in advance, charged across a ravine and up a hill, beyond which the Yankee entrenchments lay. They gained the first line of works and took possession of them; but, it is proper to state, this was unoccupied at the time by the Yankees. The fire of the enemy was murderous, and as soon as our men reached the brow of the hill, rapid volleys of grape, canister, and musketry were poured into them. It was found almost impossible to proceed farther, but the attempt would have been made, had not orders been received to fall back, which was done in good order, still under fire.

The loss in the 7th is reported at seventy odd men killed, wounded and missing. In the 8th, upwards of eighty. Col. Lamar, of the 8th, was severely wounded in the groin, and fell into the hands of the enemy. Lieut. Col. Towers was captured, but uninjured. The Yankees were completely hidden behind their works, and did not suffer much apparently. We took a captain, lieutenant, and some five or six privates, the Yankee picket force at the point. Later a flag of truce was granted to take away our dead and wounded, but a conference with Col. Lamar was refused. The Federal surgeons, however, did not think his wound a fatal one, and, therefore, would not allow him to be taken away.

THE YORK RIVER RAILROAD OCCUPIED

General Lee pushed his advance until 10 o'clock Saturday night, and at 11 was in occupancy of the York River Railroad, the enemy's principal line of communication. This in effect pierces the enemy's centre, and separates their forces on the north side of the Chickahominy from those on the south side. The Confederate forces occupied the enemy's position at the White House, on the Pamunkey, but all the stores of the enemy at that point were destroyed by them in their retreat.

THE EVENTS OF SUNDAY. MCCLELLAN ELUDES US AND RETREATS TOWARDS JAMES RIVER

About 1 a.m. Sunday morning, our pickets down the Nine Mile Road were fiercely attacked by the enemy, and a severe and lively fight ensued. The enemy was easily driven back with loss, many prisoners falling in our hands. Many of the Federals threw down their arms and surrendered voluntarily. Sunday morning, about six or seven o'clock, another fierce picket fight occurred. Gen. Griffith's Mississippi brigade moved down, and pursued them past their fortifications, which were found for the most part deserted. It thus became a matter of fact that the enemy were in full flight.

Pursuit was instantly made, and several fights ensued. All their camps—wagons, commissary and quartermaster camps, also—were totally destroyed. Immense piles of stores were blazing at the moment of our visit, the Mississippians pursuing over the red ashes of the camps and stores. Land explosions were heard during the afternoon, caused by the destruction of

vast quantities of ammunition. Dense columns of smoke darkened the sky. The railroad Merrimac was far in advance of our men, and was vigorously shelling the enemy at every turn.

It is supposed that McClellan's movement is to reach his gunboats, and effect his escape by the James river. Sixty transports are reported to be lying in the stream about fifteen miles below this city; but McClellan must have been a wiser and more provident commander than we are willing to believe, if he has prepared transportation in advance for this avenue of escape.

> Sunday at about noon our troops advanced in the direction of the works, which were found deserted.

THE PURSUIT

At a late hour Sunday evening our advancing columns had not come up with him and were harassing him. The enemy could not have been more than twelve hours in advance, and we are assured that the roads taken by our pursuing columns, and the disposition of our forces between him and the river, will cut off his retreat, and enable us to complete our victory by demoralizing his whole command or capturing a large portion of it. In any event, however, it is mortifying that the enemy has eluded us when we had him in a critical situation, all the advantages of which it will be impossible to renew.

It is impossible to ascertain the precise manner in which McClellan managed to elude our guard.

Six miles from Richmond, on the York River Road, the enemy were in force on Saturday night. During the night our pickets heard them busily at work hammering, sawing, &c. The rumble of cannon carriages was also constantly audible. Sunday about noon our troops advanced in the direction of the works, which were found deserted. Their entrenchments were found to be formidable and elaborate. That immediately across the railroad, at the six mile post, which had been supposed to be a light earth work, designed to sweep the railroad, turned out to be an immense embrasured fortification, extending for hundreds of yards on either side of the track, and capable of protecting ten thousand men. Within this work were found great quantities of fixed ammunition, which had apparently been prepared for removal, and then deserted. All the cannon, as at other entrenchments, had been carried off. McClellan doubtless imagines that if he can keep his guns from falling into our hands it may furnish him with grounds for a future boast. He will claim to have "retreated in good order, carrying off all his guns." These guns he will probably find it convenient to cast into the James River or the Chickahominy.

After passing this battery, our forces cautiously pushed their way down the railroad and to the right, in the direction of the Seven Pines. At three o'clock a dense column of smoke was seen to issue from the woods two miles in advance of the battery and half a mile to the right of the railroad. The smoke was found to proceed from a perfect mountain of the enemy's commissary stores, which they had fired and deserted. The pile was at least thirty feet high, with a base sixty feet in breadth, consisting of sugar, coffee and bacon, butter, prepared meat, vegetables, &c. The fire had so far enveloped the heap as to destroy the value of its contents. The field and woods around this spot was covered with every description of clothing and camp equipage. Blue greatcoats lined the earth like leaves in Valambross. No indication was wanting that the enemy had left this encampment in haste and disorder.

THE LOSSES ON BOTH SIDES

We have been at great pains to ascertain the number of our wounded in the engagements commenced last Thursday evening, and continued almost uninterruptedly since, and are glad to announce that it has fallen far short of our fears and expectations. At five o'clock yesterday evening all of our wounded had been removed from the field, either to the roadside hospitals or to this city. Two thousand have been received at the city hospitals, and gentlemen who have been on the different battlefields, engaged in the removal of the wounded since the beginning of the first fight, inform us there are at most not more than from four to five hundred in the roadside or field hospitals.

Of the number of our killed we have no means of making an estimate, but it will be seen that our wounded fall short of those of the Seven Pines by several hundred.

With regard to the enemy's losses, the estimates vary from 15,000 to 20,000 killed, wounded and missing. Five thousand prisoners had been taken up to Sunday noon, and the Yankee loss in killed and wounded, at the least calculation, was 10,000.

THE BOOTY

The cannon and arms captured in this battle were numerous and of very superior workmanship. The 26 pieces were the most beautiful we have ever seen, while immense piles of guns could be seen on every hand—many scarcely having the manufacturer's "finish" even tarnished. The enemy seemed quite willing to throw them away on the slightest pretext, dozens being found with loads still undischarged. The number of small arms captured, we understand, was not less than 15,000, of every calibre and every make. The field pieces taken are principally Napoleon, Parrot and Blakely (English) guns. We have captured large quantities of army wagons, tents, equipments, shoes.

Money was found quite abundantly among the slain. Some men, in interring the dead, often searched the pockets, etc., one man finding not less than $150 in gold; another fished out of some old clothes not less than $500; another $1000 in Federal notes. Watches, both gold and silver, were found among the spoils, one lucky individual having not less than six chronometers ticking in his pocket at one time. As a general thing, more money was found upon the dead on the field than on any other of which we have heard.

Clothing in abundance was scattered about, and immense piles of new uniforms were found untouched. Our men seemed to take great delight in assuming Federal officers' uniforms, and strutted about serio-comically, much to the amusement of dusty, powder-begrimmed youths, who sat lolling and smoking in the shade. Every conceivable article of clothing was found in these divisional camps, and came quite apropos to our needy soldiery, scores of whom took a cool bath, and changed old for new underclothing, many articles being of costly material, and quite unique.

The amount of ammunition found was considerable, and proved of very superior quality and manufacture. The exact amount captured we have not yet ascertained, but immense piles of boxes were scattered through the camps.

INCIDENTS

The Federal flag made by the Yankees to float over our Capitol was captured by Major Bloomfield, of General Magruder's staff, in the Federal camps, and was exhibited, with great applause, to our troops. It is an immense piece of work, fully twenty feet long, having thirteen stripes and thirty-two stars thereon. We understand McClellan received it as a present from the ladies of the [*unreadable*] of Boston, and promised to plant it on the [*unreadable*] "last ditch" to which the rebels should be run, and afterwards would elevate it, with all military honors, on our Capitol at Richmond.

An armistice of two days, it is reported, was asked by McClellan to bury the dead, &c., but Gen. Lee, it is said, replied, "There is no time now to think of the dead. The only proposition I can receive from Gen. McClellan is for an unconditional surrender."

All the vessels of the enemy, which have for some weeks past been anchored near Verina, six miles below Drury's Bluff, departed on Sunday. It is not known whether they went down the river for the purpose of bringing up reinforcements, or to be in convenient distance to take on the retreating army of McClellan.

The field presented the most remarkable and singular appearance, being thickly dotted with red breeched Zouaves. The water was plenty and good, and our trains following the army were put in fine condition transporting provisions to our men. The destruction of horses was terrible. One shot is said to have killed no less than sixteen in a single battery.

A large number of the quarters of the Yankee officers on the Chickahominy, which are now in possession of our brave men, were filled with the choicest edibles, brandies, whisky, wines, &c., all of which were, of course, confiscated.

The Pennsylvania Eleventh (Reserves) and the Fourth New Jersey were taken entire, every commissioned officer, colonels, majors, captains, lieutenants, surgeons and assistant surgeons falling into our hands. Beyond these two regiments the prisoners were mostly United States regulars, with a slight sprinkling of blue Connecticut Yankees. When the Eleventh Pennsylvania marched into town their rear was brought up by six negro men and a boy about fifteen. Five of the men wore Yankee uniform pants, while the boy was decked out in full Union uniform. The negros were the property of Mrs. Watts and other citizens of Hanover, who had run off from their owners.

The regiment of Bucktail Rifles, of Fremont's command, whose watchword was, "We never Surrender!" adorned the streets yesterday, with their bucktail plumes, on their way to the Confederate States prison. Nearly every one of them was either killed or captured.

The Federal wounded were collected together and formed a very large field hospital. The courtyard of a farmhouse was selected and scores could be seen reclining on the grass and expert surgeons operating with much skill and zeal. By mutual agreement surgeons are not considered prisoners of war, hence at the close of the late battle, many Federal surgeons remained behind and their services seemed very much appreciated by the men. As many as could be were conveyed to town and attended to, good conveyance being furnished, and much care manifested for their welfare.

G. B. CUTHBERT: LATEST REPORTS FROM RICHMOND——LEE DRIVES McCLELLAN FROM CITY

The Charleston paper's Richmond correspondent joyfully reported on the repulse of McClellan from Richmond. The story illustrates how difficult it was to obtain news when correspondents were not with armies. All sorts of rumors were floating around Richmond, and none could be confirmed, but the news of Lee's rout of McClellan was reported with great joy.

Charleston Mercury, 7 July 1862

**NEWS BY TELEGRAPH
THE END OF THE GREAT BATTLE—LATEST
REPORTS FROM RICHMOND**

RICHMOND, Friday, July 4.—Owing to the remoteness of the fugitive Yankee army, it is very difficult now to obtain information of the situation of affairs. Various rumors are afloat, but none of them can be traced to trustworthy sources. It is only certain that the Grand Army of McCLELLAN has been completely routed, and that, whilst a portion of his force may have escaped in their transports, a large number will be captured. Our victory is complete. Captain FRANK RAVENAL, of Gen. RIPLEY'S Staff, fell while leading a regiment in the thickest of the fight.

Second Despatch.) Night. It is not definitely known where the enemy now is. It is supposed that some have crossed the river, that some have gone down the river in transports, and that the bulk of the army is trying to fall back to Yorktown. JACKSON and LONGSTREET are hunting them up. More fighting may take place. Active movements are going forward on our part. Hopes are still entertained of capturing a large portion of McCLELLAN'S army.

RICHMOND, July 4. To the Editor of the Mercury: The following is a list of the killed and wounded of the Palmetto Guard in the battles before Richmond:

Killed: J. H. Royal. Slightly Wounded: Lt. T. S. Brownfield, M. Prendergast, E. L. Tillinghast, J. E. Dubart, M. Brailsford, R. G. Shoolbred, J. E. Millar.

G. B. CUTHBERT,
Capt. Palmetto Guard, 2d Regt. S.C.V.

Shenandoah Valley

Stonewall Jackson, General Thomas J. Jackson, was Robert E. Lee's only rival for the devotion, affection, and trust of the Confederate people. He gained that devotion in large part as a result of the campaign he conducted in the Shenandoah Valley in May and June 1862. Jackson had one job to accomplish in the Valley: He was to stop any Union advance up the Valley and joining McClellan's forces advancing up the Virginia peninsula toward Richmond. Jackson accomplished his objective beyond what anyone could have anticipated or hoped for. With fewer than 18,000 men, Jackson successfully held back some 70,000 Union soldiers and led the federal military authorities to change their whole approach to the fighting in Virginia.

On 1 May, Jackson was at Swift Run Gap. He faced two advancing armies: General Nathaniel P. Banks was coming up the Valley, and General John C. Frémont was advancing from West Virginia with about 15,000 men. Jackson divided his army, leaving about 8,000 men with Brigadier General Richard S. Ewell to meet Banks, while he took the remainder of his force and moved toward McDowell. There, on 8 May, he met Frémont's advanced guard and threw them back. Frémont halted. For the next two weeks, Jackson quickly marched his troops through the Valley. On 23 May, Jackson's men attacked and routed the federal garrison at Front Royal and began their move on Banks's rear. Banks retired to Winchester. On 25 May, Jackson's men threw Banks out of Winchester and drove his army all the way across the Potomac River. Jackson captured 2,000 Union soldiers and 10,000 stands of small arms. Banks lost 1,500 men, killed and wounded, to the Confederacy's 400. Jackson once again had caught the attention of Washington war leaders, and they, once again, readjusted their strategy and the deployment of federal troops.

Hoping to catch Jackson between Winchester and Harper's Ferry, Union armies under Frémont and James Shields tried to squeeze the Confederates from both the east and the west. Frémont's 15,000 men marched east from their position southwest of Winchester, and Shields, with 10,000 men from McDowell's command, marched west, capturing Front Royal as he came. An additional 10,000 Union soldiers followed close behind Shields. Jackson avoided the trap. He marched his 15,000 men, 2,000 prisoners, and a double column of wagons up the Valley toward Harrisonburg. On 8 June, Ewell's men repulsed an attack from Frémont at Cross Keys. A day later, Jackson's force attacked Shields at Port Republic. The double victories cleared the Shenandoah Valley of Union forces and brought the campaign to an end.

Clearing the Valley of Union forces was only one of the tangible outcomes of Jackson's campaign. He cost the Union army more than 5,000 casualties, and he captured 9,000 small arms, while losing only a few more than 3,000 of his own troops. His campaign kept thousands of federal soldiers from reinforcing McClellan's almost-successful advance on Richmond, and Union soldiers came to have a dreadful fear of having Jackson in their rear. The campaign also produced a number of less tangible, though valuable, results. For example, Jackson's troops came to see him as a military mastermind. Their morale and esprit de corps skyrocketed. To serve in Jackson's "foot cavalry," as his men referred to themselves, was to be among the elite Confederate forces.

Real-time reporting of the Shenandoah Valley Campaign was limited. Jackson, by nature rather taciturn, was not friendly with reporters, and he had none with him on this campaign. What news did trickle out of the Valley came from telegraphic operators and local newspapers who could get information from soldiers or send a reporter out to observe what was happening.

DR. GEORGE W. BAGBY: NEWS OF McCLELLAN'S ADVANCE ON RICHMOND, JACKSON'S OPERATIONS IN SHENANDOAH VALLEY

George W. Bagby, Hermes of the Charleston Mercury, *provided an update on Jackson's progress in the Shenandoah Valley, based on a telegraph the general himself had sent back to Richmond. The story went under the heading "The Siege of the Capital" because its initial paragraph also updated readers on McClellan's advance on Richmond, the advance Jackson's efforts in the Shenandoah Valley were intended to retard.*

Charleston Mercury, 29 May 1862

THE SIEGE OF THE CAPITAL

(FROM OUR OWN CORRESPONDENT.)

RICHMOND, Monday, May 26.

If Theophilus Thistle, the successful thistlesifter, in sifting a sieve full of unsifted thistles, thrust three thousand thistles into the thick of his thumb, then must Theophilus Thistle have been the Richmond correspondent of THE CHARLESTON MERCURY on Saturday last, endeavoring to sift the truth out of a city full of unsifted rumors, reports and "reliables" in regard to the skirmishes of that day. The nearest approach to the truth seems to be this: There were two engagements—one of artillery at Mechanicsville (a blacksmith's shop and a dilapidated tavern are dignified with that name), and another of infantry at the New Bridge, on the Meadow Bridge road, which crosses the Chickahominy a mile and a half or two miles above Mechanicsville. In both of these engagements we were worsted—owing to the inferiority of our forces. Gen. Johnston refused to send reinforcements, his aim being, as many to suppose, to draw the enemy over, or to gain time for the completion of certain arrangements by which troops can be rapidly concentrated upon the field of the great battle. General Johnston is too acute to suppose that McClellan, the Cautious, will cross the swamp in force. He will occupy the bridges, while he pushes his men to the head of the Swamp, in the direction of the junction of the Central and Fredericksburg Roads, and there, I feel pretty sure, the great battle will take place. Anderson has already fallen back to the Junction, some of Stuart's cavalry went forward on Saturday, and yesterday a heavy column of infantry marched after them. The rest of the army was engaged in cooking four days' provisions, and this morning the wagons are bringing all the baggage into town. The Petersburg Road is held subject to orders for the transportation exclusively of troops. It is plain, therefore, that the battle is to be no child's play, and that it will take place neither to-day nor to-morrow, as many imagine, but whenever the disposition of the scattered forces can be arranged to the satisfaction of the Generals.

A friend has just this moment come in to tell me of Jackson's despatch to Gen. Lee, about the taking of 2000 prisoners at Winchester, 2000 more at Front Royal, all the baggage, etc., and still pursuing. This may alter the programme to some extent. It sends Shields and McDowell back to Washington, unless there are forces there of which we know nothing—only 3000 were there at last accounts—but McClellan must fight all the same. It will never do for him to go back to Washington again, or even to Fortress Monroe. He must fight where he is, against men inspired by the memories of Williamsburg and the recent victories of Jackson. An acquaintance, who rode through our lines, on the Chickahominy, yesterday, says he was told by Gen. Howell Cobb that the men were much exasperated by Johnston's positive order for them to withdraw from the infantry fight of the day before—our cavalry having just come up to charge the enemy and rout him, as they would almost certainly have done. With this temper, among our soldiers, it is not unreasonable to expect excellent results from the great battle.

It seems Ewell did join Jackson last Thursday, as I stated, and both were engaged in the affair at Winchester. Some doubt was entertained about yesterday's telegram concerning the Front Royal engagement, except by those who knew that Jackson had written to Hon. Mr. Boteler to come on, that the time had come when, according to promise made a month or more ago, he would take him home to his house in Jefferson county, not far from Harper's Ferry.

Rather a strange Sunday spectacle was witnessed yesterday, to wit: a party of a dozen young men, armed with very long muskets, very small cartridge boxes and very large haversacks, going out to hunt Yankees. They returned without any game. Not a syllable from Corinth since Thursday last—strange! We are preparing to raise a balloon on Church Hill. As both armies are now bivouacing in the dense woods, this ballooning business does little good except when columns are in motion. If these are moved at night, balloons are of no use except to detect wagon trains. The Examiner has a good article against the defensive policy. The Enquirer says that Yankees are hanging guerillas, and calls for retaliation.

HERMES.

AN ANONYMOUS REPORT: ACHIEVEMENTS OF STONEWALL JACKSON IN SHENANDOAH VALLEY CAMPAIGN

The following story, copied from the Richmond Whig, *offered a summary of Jackson's Valley campaign, with particular focus on the later battles. The story only slightly exaggerated Jackson's accomplishments. Because of the lack of information about the campaign, reconstructed narratives such as this one were the most common form of reportage about Jackson's work in the Shenandoah Valley.*

Charleston Mercury, 18 June 1862

THE ACHIEVEMENTS OF STONEWALL JACKSON—THE CAMPAIGN IN THE VALLEY— BATTLES OF CROSS KEYS AND LEWISTON

In the following article, a writer in the Richmond Whig gives some interesting particulars of the glorious campaign of General Stonewall JACKSON in the Valley of Virginia.

In reviewing the operations of General Jackson for the last three months, it will be found that he has probably accomplished more, in that brief period, with the means at his command, than ever was achieved by any other General of ancient or modern times. I believe that his campaign during the Spring will compare favorably even with the almost incredible achievements of Napoleon in his celebrated campaign in Italy. With a handful of citizen soldiers, but partially drilled, and poorly armed and equipped, he has, in little more than sixty days, marched over five hundred miles, fought about twelve battles—five of which were pitched battles—defeated four Generals—routed four armies—captured millions of dollars worth of stores, &c., and killed, wounded and secured as prisoners, almost as many of the enemy as he had soldiers under his command. These are startling assertions, but they are literally true. Explore the pages of history, and see whether they afford the record of more brilliant successes.

In the latter part of March, Jackson was at Winchester, with about three or four thousand men. Being pressed by a superior force, he was compelled to fall back before the hosts of Gen. Banks. Slowly and in good order he retired up the Valley, contesting every inch of ground. At Kernstown he turned upon his pursuer, and for two successive days gave him battle. And here permit me to remark, that the recent occupation of the lower Valley by our forces has enabled us to gather facts in regard to those battles which add new lustre to the glories of those fights. It is now ascertained that Jackson's force at Kernstown was not much over 2500, whilst that of the enemy was 12,000. Of the enemy, 860 were buried in Winchester and on the battlefield, many others were sent home for interment, and 1500 were wounded, whilst our loss in killed and wounded was less than 500. The 84th Pennsylvania Regiment went into the battle with 800 men and came out with 300.

Having taught the enemy this severe lesson, Jackson continued his progress up the Valley, holding the whole army of the enemy in check until he could obtain reinforcements. Arriving at Harrisonburg, with his men wearied and exhausted by continual marching and skirmishing, Jackson left the main Valley road and turned off eastward on the Swift Run Gap road. His object was to cross the Shenandoah river, and, having placed this strong defence between him and the enemy, to lie quiet, to give his men a chance to rest—to watch the movements of the enemy, and, to wait reinforcements. Here he was joined by Gen. Ewell, but their united force was not sufficient to meet the enemy in the open field. It must be remembered, too, that at this time Staunton and the upper part of the Valley were threatened by a large force from the West, under Milroy. Gen. Johnson, with about 3500 men, was the only obstacle to the advance of Milroy. Being thus with a command of less than 20,000 men, including Johnson's, and threatened by Banks, with an estimated force of 35,000, on the one side, and Milroy, with six or eight thousand, on the other, he was obliged to accomplish by stratagem what he could not effect in the open field. To this end, he moved across the Blue Ridge, as if with the view of uniting with the forces of Gen. Jos. E. Johnston. He took care, however, to leave Ewell's forces concealed in the gorges of the mountains, near Swift Run, and Ashby's cavalry to picket the country closely, so as to cut off all information from the enemy as to his true purposes. The maneuver effectually deceived Banks, and he forthwith telegraphed to Washington that Jackson had evacuated the Valley and fled to Gordonsville! In a day or two Jackson turned up at Staunton, and, hastening to join General Ed. Johnson, he fell upon Milroy, at McDowell, and routed him, and pursued him to Franklin, in Pendleton county.

In the meantime, Banks, supposing that Jackson was east of the Ridge, weakened his force, by sending Shields with 10,000 men to join McDowell, and another detachment to reinforce Milroy. Jackson having thus cleared his left flank, by dispersing Milroy's forces, hastened by the nearest route towards Harrisonburg, where he could act in conjunction with Ewell. Ewell came out of his hiding place, and, while a portion of the conjoint forces marched down the Valley turnpike towards Strasburg, to which place the greater portion of Banks' army had fallen back, the residue crossed the Massanutten Mountain, and hurried down the banks of the Shenandoah to Front Royal, where they attacked and captured the forces stationed at that point. The sound of the cannon gave Banks the first intimation of the proximity of an enemy, and he immediately commenced his precipitate flight to Winchester. An effort was made to intercept him near Newton, but the attempt was only partially successful. The swift-footed Banks had passed the junction of the road, with a part of his army, before the wearied forces of Jackson could come up with them. He pierced Banks' column, however, and drove a portion of it southward up the road, while the main body fled towards Winchester. A running fight of eight or ten miles ensued, Banks flying and Jackson pursuing. Near Winchester the enemy made a stand, but the invincible columns of Jackson bore down upon them with irresistible power, and they broke and fled ingloriously, and were pursued through the streets of Winchester and on to Martinsburg and Harper's Ferry; where the demoralized elements of the once powerful army of Banks sought refuge in Maryland. At Winchester, and Martinsburg, and Front Royal, stores, estimated at from three to five millions of dollars, were taken and near 3000 prisoners. Encumbered with his spoil, and embarrassed by his prisoners, on the very borders of an Enemy's country, Jackson found himself in a critical position. He remained only long enough to secure the booty, which was of the highest importance to our army, and having sent that in wagons up the Valley, he followed to protect his trains and put his prisoners in a place of security.

We all recollect the sensation which these daring achievements created throughout the country. Lincoln was thrown into a paroxysm of fright, and telegrams were despatched throughout the North calling for the whole militia force of the country to protect the United States Capital, which it was feared Jackson might seize at an early day.

When the authorities at Washington recovered from their panic, they were overwhelmed with shame and confusion, and immediately set to work to avenge the wound that had been inflicted on their national honor. It was ascertained that Jackson had but a small force—that he was encumbered with immense trains and vast numbers of prisoners, and that he would have to march 120 miles before he could reach a point of safety. The whole Northern press teemed with threats and promises of the speedy annihilation of Jackson and his daring followers. Three armies—one from the North, under Dix—one from the West, under Fremont and Milroy, and one from the East, under Shields—were immediately set in motion to intercept him, and it was even said, by some of the Northern journals, that Jackson had fallen into the trap that had been set for him.

The reader will observe the position of the parties—Jackson's forces were scattered from the Potomac to Winchester, Dix came by railway from Baltimore, Fremont was west of the North Mountain, at Franklin, in Pendleton, and Shields was east of the Blue Ridge, near Warrenton. The plan was for Fremont and Shields to push forward and unite their forces at Strasburg, and cut off Jackson's retreat up the Valley, while Dix would press him in the rear. The eagle eye of Jackson saw the danger at a glance. By a forced march of over 100 miles in three days, he won the race for Strasburg but, so close was the struggle, that, as he passed the proposed point of union, his rear guard was compelled to fight the advanced columns of the enemy.

Then commenced another retreat and running fight up the Valley, Jackson contesting the advance of the enemy so as to secure his trains and prisoners. When he had accomplished this object, learning that the enemy had divided his overwhelming force into two columns, one of which, under Shields, was advancing east of the Shenandoah river, and the other, under Fremont, up the main Valley turnpike, with a view to unite in the upper part of the Valley, Jackson again turned off at Harrisonburg, having previously caused Ashby to burn the bridge over the Shenandoah, near Swift Run Gap, and went to Port Republic, a small village situated at the point where the North and South rivers come together and form the Shenandoah. There was a bridge over the North River at Port Republic, which was the only means of crossing

the stream, which was swollen by recent rains. Jackson occupied the ground near both ends of this bridge, and thus had it in his power to elect which column he would fight, as the two were separated by an impassable river. On Sunday, he determined to attacked Fremont first, and accordingly, leaving a sufficient force to guard the bridge, he marched about five miles to the Cross Keys to meet Fremont, and after a terrible conflict of many hours he succeeded in repulsing Fremont with great loss. He then returned to the bridge, and after passing over it to the Port Republic side, burnt it, so as to prevent Fremont, in case he should be reinforced and rally, from coming to the rescue of Shields. The result vindicated his sagacity, for Fremont on Monday was reinforced and did rally, and advanced with an overwhelming force to renew the conflict with Jackson. But, when he reached the bank of the river, he fount that Jackson had passed over and destroyed the bridge, and that an impassable stream was between them. Fremont was thus compelled to be an unwilling witness of the conflict between Jackson and Shields, for, as soon as the bridge had been effectually destroyed and his rear thus secured, Jackson advanced upon Shields, who was encamped at Lewiston, the estate of Gen. Samuel H. Lewis, about two miles north of Port Republic. Shields was aware of his approach, and made every preparation to receive him. The attack was made about sunrise on Monday, 9th June, and lasted until about 10 or 11 o'clock, when the forces of Shields broke and fled in utter confusion and dismay. The rout was complete. The slaughter was great, and the pursuit continued until a late hour of the day. About 1000 prisoners were taken, and six pieces of artillery. The whole road was strewed with knapsacks, arms, blankets, etc. Those who witnessed it think that the rout was as complete as that inflicted on Banks. The loss of the enemy in the two battles of Cross Keys and Lewiston, in killed, wounded and missing, is estimated at near 6000, while ours does not exceed 600. It seems almost incredible, but it is nevertheless, true.

These two battles are among the most brilliant, if not the most brilliant, of the war. They are the crowning glory of Jackson and his gallant associates. No! I recall that. Not the crowning glory, for I believe still brighter wreaths are destined to encircle their brows if this unhallowed war shall continue.

Thus it will be seen that Jackson and his army, in one month, have routed Milroy, annihilated Banks, discomfited Fremont and overthrown Shields! Was there ever such a series of victories won by an inferior force by dauntless courage and consummate generalship?

With 50,000 fresh troops under Jackson, Lincoln would be compelled to raise the siege of Richmond and look to the security of his own Capital.

Fremont still remains on the hills opposite Port Republic. He is reported to have, about 20,000 men. Shields had 9000, and Jackson encountered him with about the same number.

What the next move will be, it would be impossible for me to say, even if I knew. But Jackson keeps his own counsels. He speaks by deeds, and not by words. Suffice it to say, he will strike at the right time, and in the right place. Whatever courage, skill, industry and patriotism can accomplish, he will be sure to effect.

Second Manassas

Strategically, Lee came out of the Peninsula Campaign in a strong position. True, his smaller army had taken many more casualties than McClellan's, but the sacrifice of lives had kept the federals out of the Confederate capital. McClellan entrenched his command at Harrison's Landing and asked for reinforcements, suggesting to Lincoln's government that he faced a foe of some 200,000 or more. An exasperated Union president had enough of McClellan's procrastination. Lincoln relieved McClellan of the command of all Virginia forces, though the Union commander retained command of a portion of the army in Virginia. Lincoln appointed General John Pope to take command of a new force to be called the Army of Virginia, which had been pieced together from the commands of McDowell, Frémont, and Banks. Pope was a fairly competent commander, but he was not a nice man, and his treatment of the people of Virginia sufficiently angered Lee that the Confederate general developed a personal grudge against his opponent. Not only did Pope mistreat Southerners, whom he considered to be traitors; he was also obnoxious to his own soldiers. Lincoln made one other significant change to the Union command structure: On 11 July, he recalled Halleck from the West to become the Union's general-in-chief.

Lee found the movements of the Union army in the summer of 1862 to be disconcerting. Curious about what exactly was happening, he sent Jackson to observe Pope. On 9 August, Jackson and Pope's commands met at Cedar Mountain, near Culpeper. The engagement was small, but it would have dire consequences for Pope. By nightfall on 9 August, Jackson had driven the Union forces back to Culpeper before withdrawing across the Rapidan.

Soon Lee learned that McClellan's portion of the Union army was moving once again toward the Peninsula, and he knew he would have to try to crush Pope before McClellan could arrive. Lee realized that if McClellan's forces met up with Pope's, the Union armies together would total 150,000 against his own army of 55,000. Lee's strategy violated a basic stratagem of war: Never separate an army in the presence of the enemy, but that was exactly what Lee did. He sent half of his forces with Major General James Longstreet across the Rappahannock to occupy Pope. The other half, he sent with Stonewall Jackson to the northwest with order to make a surprise attack on the rear of Pope's army. They planned a joint strike somewhere near Manassas.

In the meantime, a quick raid by some of Pope's men on the Confederate cavalry captured J.E.B. Stuart's fancy plumed hat, his scarlet-lined cape, and his adjutant. Outraged, Stuart planned a retaliatory raid of his own. On 22 August, Stuart overran Pope's headquarters and made off with the payroll cash, Pope's personal baggage, which included the Union general's dress uniform, 300 prisoners, and important papers that outlined Union plans.

Not long afterward, Jackson's force fell on Pope's. After marching 54 miles in two days of hot August weather, Jackson's men cut Pope's rail and communications lines and looted and burned the Union supply depot at Manassas. Pope turned to follow

Jackson, but he had taken up a hidden defensive position just west of the First Manassas battlefield. On 28 August, Jackson's men clashed with Union soldiers near Groveton. The fighting was ferocious, and it alerted Pope to Jackson's location. Pope ordered his forces to concentrate near Groveton to destroy Jackson once and for all in what would be the two-day-long Second Battle of Manassas.

PETER W. ALEXANDER: ACCOUNT OF SECOND BATTLE OF MANASSAS

As Pope concentrated his forces near Groveton, Lee and Longstreet were advancing to reinforce Jackson. Pope refused to believe Longstreet's command was near, and on 30 August he attacked Jackson, only to be hit in his flank by Longstreet. Pope's army was forced back across Bull Run toward the defenses of Washington in a decisive defeat. The Union withdrawal was in good order. Lee pursued, and in the Battle of Chantilly on 31 August, during a blinding rainstorm, Jackson's assault was checked by Union General Philip Kearny, who was killed in hand-to-hand fighting. Lee made no further advances. Confederate losses in the campaign were 9,197 to the Union's more than 16,000. The Savannah Republican's *famous correspondent, Peter W. Alexander, was on hand for the fighting at Second Manassas and filed the following summary story. Three days after the battle, Pope was relieved of his command and sent to fight the Sioux in Minnesota. McClellan was again in command of the Army of the Potomac. Lee's victory had been decisive and provided a much-needed boost for Confederate morale.*

Savannah Republican, 9 September 1862

**ARMY CORRESPONDENCE
OF THE SAVANNAH REPUBLICAN**

**Battle of Manassas No. Two
Revised and Improved Edition**

Another Brilliant Victory—Enemy Routed at all Points—Heavy Loss—Bartow and Bee Avenged—McClellan and Halleck on the Field

BATTLE FIELD OF MANASSAS, Aug. 31st.

Another great battle has been fought on the bloody Plains of Manassas, and once more has Heaven crowned our banners with the laurel of victory. The conflict opened Friday afternoon, and last night not a Federal soldier remained on the south side of Bull run, except the prisoners we had taken and those who sleep the sleep that shall know no waking until the great day of Judgment. The people of the Confederate States—those at home no less than the invincible heroes in the field, and the friends of justice and the lovers of liberty everywhere—assuredly have cause for rejoicing and thanksgiving. Never since Adam was planted in the garden of Eden, did a holier cause engage the hearts and arms of any nation; and never did any people establish more clearly their right to be freemen.

I did not arrive in time to witness the battle of Friday, the 29th. Leaving Gordonsville at 9 o'clock that day, on a freight train, I reached Rapidan Station, the present terminus of the railroad, at noon. There I took horse, forded the river; struck for the Rappahannock—forded that river also—to Warrenton

at one o'clock yesterday—rested my horse, and then took the turnpike for the battle-field, fourteen miles distant, where I arrived in one hour and fifteen minutes, and just in time to witness, for the second time, the triumph of Confederate arms on these ever memorable plains.

I cannot undertake to give the number of men engaged on either side. It is not probably, however, that the enemy had more than 75,000 troops on the field. Our own forces were considerably less, a large part of the army not having arrived in time to participate in the fight. Longstreet's *corps d'armee* held the right, A. P. Hill's and Anderson's (late Huger's) division the centre, and Jackson's veterans the left. Jackson was the first to reach to plains below the Blue Ridge; Hill came next, and then Longstreet, who entered at Thoroughfare Gap. The enemy occupied the Gap with a full division, and seemed disposed to dispute the passage of our troops; but Toombs' and Anderson's Georgia brigades, which led the corps, made a bold dash and soon drove them away with but little loss. That was on Thursday, the 28th. Jackson had brought the enemy to bay between Gainesville and Groveton, two miles from the old battle field, on the Warrenton turnpike. Knowing this, Longstreet pressed forward, and succeeded in getting into position on the right of the turnpike, in time to hold that part of our lines while Jackson engaged the enemy on the left.

It should be stated that Longstreet played the enemy a clever trick before he left the south bank of the Rappahannock.

Jackson and Hill having moved around by Sperryville above, he made feints at several fords on the Rappahannock as if he would cross over, and thus drew the attention of the enemy to those points, whilst he put his forces in motion and marched rapidly to the northward and around to Gainesville. So successful was the manoeuvre that a late northern paper now before me congratulates its readers upon the brilliant victory achieved by the Federals in driving us away from the fords.

The enemy advanced to the attack on Friday. He was probably aware of Jackson's comparative weakness. He soon discovered, however, that heavy Confederate column (Longstreet's) had got into position on the right, and immediately commenced a retrograde movement. The battle, which was hotly contested for a time, in which the artillery took a prominent part, continued through the afternoon and resulted in the repulse of the enemy along the entire line. Jackson's forces were chiefly engaged and behaved with their usual gallantry. The scene of the conflict was just in front of Gainesville and on the left of the Warrenton turnpike as you look towards Washington.

The enemy were driven back to the edge of the old battle field of Manassas. The Confederates slept upon the field; and there awaited a renewal of the attack on yesterday. They were not disappointed, for the enemy again advanced against our left at 2 o'clock P.M., and engaged Jackson first. By three the engagement became general, and the battle was joined. Gen. Lee was in command, having come to the front some days ago. But a word of explanation in regard to the field and the position of the combatants.

The Warrenton and Alexandria Turnpike runs nearly eastward, and the road from Sudley ford on Bull Run to Manassas Junction north and South. These highways intersect each other in the centre of the old battle ground. Advancing down the turnpike our forces faced to the east and in the direction of Washington, while the enemy faced to the west, but not exactly towards Richmond. The line of battle, about three miles in length, extended across the turnpike almost at right angles and nearly parallel with and just west of Sudley road. The battle of Manassas was to be fought over, and the point to be decided was, whether we should advance upon Washington or the enemy upon Richmond. This was the issue, and this the battle ground.

We learn from prisoners that Halleck, McClelland and Pope were present. McClelland had brought up his old United States Regulars, eighteen regiments, under Fitz John Porter, Heintzman's division, and other corps of his James river army. It was evident that the enemy were confident of victory. They were aware of Jackson's weakness, and of the fact that not more than half of our army had come up; and by precipitating the battle, they hoped to avenge their shameful defeat on the same ground a little more than one year ago. Indeed, we hear that McDowell, the most civilized officer in the Federal service and the commander at Manassas last year,

made an urgent appeal to his troops to wipe out the disgrace which then befell their arms, and never to leave the field but as conquerors.

As I have already stated, the enemy opened the battle by an attack upon our left. A heavy column, with a full complement of artillery, was launched against Jackson's veterans, but there, as elsewhere, they encountered a "Stonewall" as immovable as the Blue Ridge. The onslaught would have been fearful to any other but Confederate troops struggling for the dearest rights known to man. The attack was repulsed, however, and the enemy forced to retire. In the meantime a heavy force was moved up against A. P. Hill and Anderson in the centre, and Longstreet's splendid corps on the right. The attack upon the centre was not characterized by much vigor, but on the right it was made by McClellan's Regulars, and was furious. After the first movement against the left was repulsed, Jackson found but little difficulty in advancing his lines. The infantry were very reluctant to engage the stern chieftain again, and their artillery alone resisted him with spirit. But on the right the conflict raged with great violence for more than an hour before we had made any impression upon the [unreadable] ranks of the Regulars. When they did yield, it was slowly and in perfect order. It could hardly be called a retreat; we pushed them, as it were, from one elevation to another gradually following them up and firmly holding the ground they had been forced to abandon.

In this way the contest continued until near sunset, the retrograde movement of the enemy growing more rapid and less orderly as the battle proceeded. Jackson pressed forward vigorously on the left; Hill and Anderson did the same in the centre; and as the foe retired faster in that part of the field than on the right, our line finally assumed somewhat the form of a crescent.

Jackson at length bent his line around to the Sudley road, near the church of that name, and about the same time the centre and right reached the old battle ground. Then followed as splendid fighting on the part of the Confederates as the world ever saw. As the fact broke upon them that they again stood upon that glorious field, and that the enemy sought a renewal of the decision rendered there one year ago, they swept on as if they were born onward by the fiat of fate. The eye grew brighter, the arm waxed stronger, and catching the inspiration of the place, and of the children of glory who sleep upon its hills, they sent up shout after shout, that rose high above the mighty din and uproar, and sounded in the ear of the already retreating foe like a sentence of judgment.

About the same time Gen. Toombs, who had been absent under orders, reached the field at the top of his horse's speed. His appearance was greeted with the cheers of ten thousand Georgians in Longstreet's corps. The shouts were caught up along the valley and over the hills as his splendid form swept across the field in the direction of his brigade. He found it at length, and led it immediately forward in the thickest of the fight. Dashing down the hill not far from where Bee and Bartow fell, he got within forty paces of a Federal brigade, which saluted him and his men with a terrific fire. The men called to him to dismount, as otherwise he would certainly be killed. His only reply, uttered in trumpeted tones was: "President Davis can create generals; God only makes the soldier—ON!"

Finally our entire line crossed the Sudley road, and swept past the stone house at the intersection of the roads, the Henry and Lews houses on the right, on towards Bull Run. But the enemy managed his artillery with great skill and judgment. His firing was superb, and I must admit, superior to our own. His batteries were posted at commanding points, and enabled him to cover the retreat of his infantry by delaying our advance. Night, too, came to his rescue, and to Nature and not his own arms, was he indebted for his escape from utter destruction. The pursuit was kept up until darkness prevented further effort, and the order to halt was given.

The enemy escaped across Bull Run during the night, and morning found him in a hurried retreat, for the second time over the same road and from the same battle field, back to Washington. Thus the issue has been decided for a second time in our favor, and the judgment of July, 1861, stands affirmed before the world. The battle of Manassas has been fought over, and a gracious God and our own right arms have given us the victory.

Gen. Stuart advanced to Centreville and beyond this morning, but saw nothing of the enemy, except stragglers who were waiting to be taken.

It is too early to enter into details, either as the part performed by individuals or the extent of the victory. Gen. Drayton was not entirely successful in bringing his excellent brigade into action in time, but otherwise, the battle was a complete success. Every officer and man from Gen. Lee down to the humblest private, with exceptions too unimportant to justify particular notice, performed his whole duty. But our triumph however, has been purchased at the cost of much precious blood. Our loss has been heavy; not less, I fear, than six or seven thousand. The casualties of the enemy, including killed, wounded, and probably fifteen hundred or two thousand prisoners, will not fall much short of ten or twelve thousand men. Among the slain on the part of the Federals, is Gen. McDowell, Col. Webster of Massachusetts, and many other officers, at least such is the report of prisoners. On our side we have to lament the death of Gen. Ewell,* who was wounded yesterday and died this morning. Gens. Mahone and Jenkins were wounded—not dangerously; whilst a number of field officers were killed, including Col. Means, (formerly Governor) of South Carolina and Col. Wilson of the Seventh Georgia. Gen. Pryor was captured, but soon effected his escape.

Among our captures, are several thousand stand of small arms, thrown away by the flying foe, some eighteen or twenty

pieces of artillery, many wagons, a large amount of stores and other valuable property. It is reported that Stuart destroyed 17,000 pairs of shoes, by a sudden descent upon Manassas Junction on Friday, and that Jackson destroyed several railway trains loaded with provisions after filling his own wagons the day before.

The strategy of the enemy was clever, and deserves attention. He had attacked Jackson on Friday, and was repulsed. He renewed the attack yesterday, and thus sought to create the belief that his chief object was to turn our left. Having, as he supposed, produced this impression upon Gen. Lee, he suddenly precipitated upon our right a very heavy force, including the old United States Regulars and other picked troops, under Fitz John Porter and Heintzleman. His object doubtless was to turn our right, throw us back against the Blue Ridge, keep open his communications by Alexandria and Orange railway, and with Fredericksburg and his gunboats to the south, and cut us off from the base of our supplies. The conception was excellent, but the execution was faulty.

Bee, Bartow, and others who fell on this field last year have been amply revenged. The shaft erected over the spot where Bartow perished has been removed by vandals, but the ground around the place is marked by the Federal dead. The Henry house, which was riddled by the artillery shot of the enemy last year, and where its aged owner, Mrs. Henry, was killed, has also been removed piecemeal by the enemy, and probably sold as relics but before its very doors, and within its demolished walls, sleep to day the miserable myrmidons of the North.

Batteries were planted and captured yesterday where they were planted and captured last year. The pine thicket where the Fourth Alabama and Eighth Georgia suffered so terribly in the first battle, is now strewn with the slain of the invader. We charged through the same woods yesterday, though from a different point, where Kirby Smith, the Blucher of the day, entered the fight before. These are remarkable coincidences; and they extend even to my own experience. In the road way where I relieved a wounded Irishman from Wisconsin late at night last year, I to-day found another Irishman crying for succor. As I rendered it to the first, so I gave it to the second.

Is not the hand of God in all this? Who but He brought us again face to face with our enemies upon these crimsoned plains, and gave us victory? When before did the same people ever fight two separate battles upon the same ground, within so short a period? For the second time the God of Battles has spoken by the mouth of our cannon and told the North to let us go unto ourselves. Will that ill starred people require Him to repeal the command after the manner of Pharaoh and the purblind Egyptians? We shall see.

P.W.A.

*In a subsequent letter, our correspondent corrects this statement and reports Gen. Ewell doing well.—Edr.

Sharpsburg Campaign

In early September 1862, Lee decided upon a movement that would change the complexion of the war. He would, with the approval of President Davis, lead his ragtag and exhausted army of 55,000 men on an invasion of the North. He would cross the Potomac near Leesburg, Virginia, and move northward into Pennsylvania. Lee and Davis hoped the invasion would bring the desperately needed recognition by England and France that would be a prelude to aid for the Southern struggle for independence. Lee and Davis also hoped that a northward invasion would win over the Border States and inflict a killing blow on Northern morale. Lee's ill-clad, ill-shod, ill-fed army massed at Frederick, Maryland. From there, he could use the Catoctin Mountains as a screen for his troops. McClellan followed from Washington.

McClellan's advanced guard reached Frederick on 12 September, only shortly after Lee's had pulled out, and in time to benefit from a devastating mistake by one of Lee's subcommanders. Confederate General Daniel Harvey Hill had received a duplicate set of Lee's orders regarding the advance into Maryland and had discarded it—scholars disagree on whether accidentally or intentionally. McClellan's force occupied the campground Lee's had abandoned, and there Union Private W. B. Mitchell of the 27th Indiana found the document wrapped around three cigars. Mitchell is said to have retained the cigars, but he passed the orders on to his superiors. McClellan had Lee's plan laid out before him. Since he knew where the Confederates were headed, he would be able to pursue them without the normal delays for reconnaissance—except, what if the supposedly lost order was some sort of elaborate Confederate trick? The Southerners were known for such tactics, after all.

Nevertheless, McClellan pursued Lee and caught up with him on South Mountain, between Frederick and a tiny Maryland village to the west called Sharpsburg. Lee fought a delaying action at the 14 September Battle of South Mountain, one that gave him time to entrench his forces outside Sharpsburg. That same day, Jackson captured the 10,000-man garrison at Harper's Ferry, which freed his force to hurry back to Sharpsburg and reinforce Lee's troops. Lee's defenses at Sharpsburg were entrenched in a bend of the Potomac River between Sharpsburg and Antietam Creek. The creek and the ridges surrounding it provided strong natural defenses for the Confederates.

McClellan planned a three-pronged attack. He intended to attack both of Lee's flanks first, then his center. The planned assault, though, degenerated into separate and disjointed attacks. By midday, the fighting had shifted to the center along a sunken road now called "Bloody Lane." Lee had no more reserves, but the federal offensive had ground to a halt, and the action shifted to Longstreet's sector. The Union corps under Major General Ambrose E. Burnside tried for two desperate hours to take the bridge Longstreet defended. When Burnside finally broke through the Confederate line, he was repulsed by a surprise counterattack from A. P. Hill's 3,000 men who had just made an exhausting 17-mile march from Harper's Ferry. Hill's men drove Burnside across the creek and ended the bloodiest single day of the entire Civil War. Casualties of the two armies together totaled more than 26,000 men, 12,400 for the Union and 13,700 for the Confederacy. Lee's men withdrew back into Virginia, unmolested. It would be nearly a month before McClellan would follow Lee back across the Potomac.

With fewer than 50,000 men, Lee had stopped the Union 70,000 troops who had taken part in the battle—McClellan's entire force numbered some 90,000, but he had held 20,000 men in reserve all day. Tactically, Sharpsburg was a Confederate victory. Strategically, since it halted Lee's northward invasion, it was a major Union victory, which Lincoln used as the opportunity to issue his Preliminary Emancipation Proclamation, the announcement that as of 1 January 1863, all slaves in the seceded states would be emancipated.

PETER W. ALEXANDER: ACCOUNT OF LEE'S RETREAT FROM SHARPSBURG (ANTIETAM)

Lee led his Army of Northern Virginia across the Potomac in September 1862 to meet General McClellan's troops in one of the bloodiest battles of the Civil War. The two armies clashed in the picturesque town of Sharpsburg, just a handful of miles from the steep banks of the Potomac. The Savannah Republican's correspondent, Peter W. Alexander, was on hand for the battle and the silent, nighttime retreat, the subject of this story, which was filed once Lee's defeated army had recrossed the Potomac. Like many Confederates, Alexander had supported the move into Maryland, but that, he wrote, was before he saw the condition of Lee's army. At least a fifth of the men had no shoes. Many wore ragged clothing. None had sufficient food. In the aftermath of the bloodbath at Sharpsburg, Alexander admitted to his Confederate readers that the move had been a mistake. Not only had the army been defeated; the political costs in Maryland had been tremendous. Confederates still hoped to convince Marylanders to secede. A victory at Sharpsburg might have accomplished that. Failure did not. Alexander's dispatch of 25 September ran with another he had written on 20 September and posted from Winchester, Virginia, where he had sought medical treatment for an illness.

Savannah Republican, 1 October 1862

**ARMY CORRESPONDENCE
OF THE SAVANNAH REPUBLICAN**

SMITHFIELD, VA., Sept. 19th, 1862.

The Confederate army has returned to Virginia. Whether Gen. Lee took this step from a military necessity, or for some strategic purpose, or because he had accomplished the object of his movement into Maryland—the capture of Harper's Ferry—I am unable to say. The order was issued late last evening, and by the time it was quite dark, the wagons, artillery and troops began to move. All the wounded that were in condition to be moved, had been taken across the river. Those whose wounds were very severe [*unreadable*], unfortunately, had to be left behind and fell into the hands of the enemy. Some of the wounded had never been removed from the field, having fallen on a part of the ground still held by the enemy. Many of the dead were buried yesterday, and some were transferred to this bank of the river.

It was not quite three miles to the Potomac, and our wagon trains extended from Sharpsburg over to the Virginia side. There were only two roads by which we could proceed, one of which was taken by the troops and the other by the artillery and wagons. Our lines came up within a short distance of the enemy's yet so silently and adroitly was the movement conducted, that McClellan was not aware of it until the next morning. It had rained in the afternoon, and the roads were muddy below, while the heavens were covered with a light fog above, both of which facilitated the enterprise.

We had crossed into Maryland by the bright and early morning sun; we returned in silence and at the dead hour of night. The columns wound their way over the hills and along the valleys like some huge, indistinct monster. The trees and overhanging cliffs, and the majestic Blue Ridge loomed up in dim but enlarged and fantastic proportions, and made one feel as if he were in some strange and weird land of grotesque forms, visible only in the hour of dreams.

Whatever was the motive to the movement, it must be regarded as one of the most successful and extraordinary exploits in the history of any country, and stamps the man that ordered and executed it as one of the greatest military leaders in our time and generation. With the exception of the wounded and a few wagons that got turned over in the darkness, not a single man or wagon, nor a single piece of artillery was lost. Longstreet's corps, being nearest the ford, led the way, followed by D. H. Hill's and Jackson's in order of their names. The crossing was accomplished by half-past six this morning, and soon thereafter the enemy's artillery opened a harmless fire from the opposite heights. The bird had flown, however, and his rage was impotent.

There was formerly a splendid stone bridge at Sheperd-stown where the army crossed, but the enemy destroyed it last year. The ford was three-fourths of a mile below the bridge, and this made it necessary to pass down the river bank that distance, and then up it on the other side by a narrow road blasted out of the rocky precipice. The troops managed to work their way out from the river along some of the gorges that broke through the cliff, and a few wagons and artillery escaped in the same way. Thus, you perceive, the character of the Virginia side was almost as unfavorable as it could be to the safety of the movement. It is an exceedingly difficult undertaking at any time to transfer an army across a wide stream, but it is especially so under circumstances as surrounded Gen. Lee.

I am frank to say I was in favor of the movement into Maryland. I am equally ready to admit that, under the circumstances I now think it was a mistake. This conviction gradually forced itself upon my mind after I came up with the army and saw the miserable condition in which it was. A fifth of the troops are barefooted; half of them are in rags, and the whole of them insufficiently supplied with food. Men in this condition cannot be relied on to the same extent as when they are properly clothed and subsisted. The best soldiers, under such circumstances, will straggle both on the march and in battle. Since we crossed into Maryland, and even before, they frequently had to march all day, and far into the night for three or four days together, without food of any kind, except such apples and green corn as they could obtain along the way. Our supply of food was limited at best, and the base of our operations so distant, the intervening country so barren by reason of the spoilation perpetrated by Pope and his myrmidons, and our transportation so limited, that is was quite impossible to subsist the army as it should be. The difficulty of passing Confederate money in Maryland was another fruitful source of trouble.

The political effect upon Maryland of our retrograde movement must be highly injurious. We shall doubtless lose ground among the people, and it may be we shall have to make up our minds to loose [sic] the State itself. It should be the direst necessity, however, that would compel us to abandon Maryland. The waters of the Chesapeake are indispensable to the Confederate States as a naval power, as well as for our security and defense.

Gen. Toombs received a painful, though not serious wound in the hand last night, just as the army was about to move. He was mounted and at the head of his division, with his aids around him, when six or eight mounted men approached slowly along his line to where his horse was standing. They were asked who they were, and remaining silent, Capt. Troup commenced to draw upon them; whereupon they said, "don't shoot; we are Massachusetts men." Gen. Toombs was about drawing his pistol from the holsters when Capt. T. fired upon

them. They immediately returned fire, and then wheeling their horses, disappeared in the darkness. Lieut. Robt. Grant received a slight flesh wound in the arm also. The men were doubtless lost, and the affair may have contributed somewhat to the deception practiced upon McClellan by Gen. Lee in withdrawing his army across the river.

WINCHESTER, VA., Sept. 20th

I came on to this place for medical treatment, being quite unwell, and to be where there are some mail facilities for getting off letters.

Intelligence has just been received that Jackson engaged a brigade of the enemy last evening at the Shepherdstown ford. Concealing his own forces, he permitted the enemy's artillery to get into the river and many of his troops to reach the Virginia side, when he set his men upon them and had another Leesburg affair of it. He killed a large number of them and captured a good many, and one report says several pieces of artillery. Those who escaped our fire fled in dismay back into Maryland.

There is a report in circulation that we have re-crossed the river at Williamsport, but it is probably untrue. After Jackson's affair at the ford, he took up his position four miles this side the river. There a large number of our wounded who had been transferred to Shepherdstown, have fallen into the hands of the enemy. We hear they have been paroled. The enemy has also thrown forward scouting parties as far as Middleburg, Upperville and Paris on the eastern side of the Blue Ridge.

Nothing further has transpired in regard to the proposition reported to have been made by Gen. Lee to the Federal government, and alluded to in a former letter of mine. I am credibly informed that such a proposition as that described was certainly made, and under circumstances that encouraged the hope of its acceptance. Recent events, however, may have given a different turn to the affair.

I have just heard of an instance of gallantry in the late battle that deserves to be put on the record. The Floridians always fight well, but the Fifth Florida behaved with distinguished courage and intrepidity at Sharpsburg. The hero in this case was a private—Ben Flowers—of that regiment. He was wounded five different times and in as many different places; yet he continued to shoot away as fearlessly as ever, until he had received the fifth wound, which disabled one of his hands, so that he could not load his piece. He is doing very well; as soon as he is well enough, he says he shall be after the Yankees again.

Maj. Phillip Tracy of the 6th Georgia, wounded in the leg, has since died. He was wounded at Richmond, and only rejoined his regiment the evening before the battle. He had not quite recovered his strength, and the amputation to which his limb was necessarily subjected proved fatal.

P.W.A.

PETER W. ALEXANDER: OUR ARMY, ITS GREAT DEEDS, ITS TRIALS, ITS SUFFERINGS, AND ITS PERILS IN THE FUTURE

Alexander dropped out of the march from Maryland due to exhaustion, exposure, and hunger, but he took the opportunity to continue his campaign to bring the condition of the soldiers in Lee's army to the attention of the Confederates back home. This letter in particular would begin a campaign back home in Georgia to raise money for shoes and other necessities for the state's soldiers in Virginia. Alexander also took on those who criticized infantrymen for straggling in the retreat back into Virginia. In his view, lagging behind was perfectly understandable and justified. The story is perhaps the best example of advocacy journalism of the Confederate press.

Savannah Republican, 3 October 1862

**ARMY CORRESPONDENCE
OF THE SAVANNAH REPUBLICAN**

Our Army, Its Great Deeds, Its Trials,
Its Sufferings, and its Perils in the
Future.
WINCHESTER, VA., Sept. 26, 1862.

My condition is such as to render it impossible for me to rejoin the army at the present. I was not prepared for the hardships, exposures and fastings the army has encountered since it left the Rappahannock, and like many a seasoned campaigner, have had to "fall out by the way." Indeed, I can recall no parallel instance in history, except Napoleon's disastrous retreat from Moscow, where an army has ever done more marching and fighting, under such great disadvantages, than Gen. Lee's has done since it left the banks of the James river. It proceeded directly to the line of the Rappahannock, and moving out from that river, it fought its way to the Potomac, crossed that stream and moved on to Fredericktown and Hagerstown, had a heavy engagement at Boonsboro' Gap, and another at Crampton Gap below, fought the greatest pitched battle of the war at Sharpsburg, and then recrossed the Potomac back into Virginia. During all this time, covering the full space of a month, the troops rested but four days! And let it always be remembered to their honor, that of the men who performed this wonderful feat, one-fifth of them were barefooted, one-half of them in rags, and the whole of them famished. The country from the Rappahannock to the Potomac had been visited by the enemy with fire and sword, and our transportation was insufficient to keep the army supplied from so distant a base as Gordonsville; and when the provision trains would overtake the army, so pressing were the exigencies of their position, the men seldom had time to cook. Their difficulties were increased by the fact that their cooking utensils, in many cases, had been left behind, as well as everything else that would impede their movements. It was not unusual to see a company of starving men have a barrel of flower distributed to them, which it was utterly impossible for them to convert into bread with the means and the time

allowed to them. They could not procure even a piece of plank or a corn or flour sack, upon which to work up their dough.

Do you wonder, then, that there should have been stragglers from the army. That brave and true men should have fallen out of line from sheer exhaustion, or in their efforts to obtain a mouthful to eat along the roadside? Or that many seasoned veterans, the conquerors in the valley, at Richmond and Manassas, should have succumbed to disease and been forced back to the hospital? I look to hear a great outcry raised against the stragglers. Already lazy cavalry men and dainty staff officers and quartermasters, who are mounted and can forage the country for something to eat, are condemning the weary private, who, notwithstanding his body may be covered with dust and perspiration, and his feet with stone bruises, is expected to trudge along under his knapsack and cartridge box, on an empty stomach, and never to turn aside for a morsel of food to sustain his sinking limbs. Out upon such monstrous injustice! That there has been unnecessary stragglers, is readily admitted; but in a large majority of cases, the men have only to point to their bleeding feet, tattered garments and gaunt frames for an answer to the unjust charge.

No army on this continent has ever accomplished as much or suffered as much as the army of Northern Virginia within the last three months. At no period during the first Revolutionary war—not even at Valley Forge—did our forefathers in arms encounter greater hardships, or endure them more uncomplainingly.

But great as have been the trials to which the army has been subjected, they are hardly worthy to be named in comparison with the sufferings in store for this winter, unless the people of the Confederate States, everywhere and in whatever circumstances, come to its immediate relief.

The men must have clothing and shoes this winter. They must have something to cover themselves with when sleeping, and to protect themselves from the driving sleet and snow storms when on duty. This must be done, though our friends at home should have to wear cotton and sit by the fire. The army in Virginia stands guard this day, as it will stand guard this winter, over every hearthstone throughout the South. The ragged sentinel who may pace his weary rounds this winter on the bleak spurs of the Blue Ridge, or along the frozen valleys of the Shenandoah and Rappahannock, will also be your sentinels, my friend, at home. It will be for you and your household that he encounters the wrath of the tempest and the dangers of the night. He suffers and toils and fights for you, too, brave, true hearted women of the South.—Will you not clothe his nakedness then? Will you not put shoes and stockings on his feet? Is it not enough that he has written down his patriotism in crimson characters along that battle road from the Rappahannock to the Potomac? And must his bleeding feet also impress their mark of fidelity upon the snows of the coming winter? I know what your answer will be. God has spoken through the women of the South, and they are his bold oracles in this day of trial and tribulation.

It is not necessary to counsel violent measures; but it is not expected that any person will be permitted to accumulate leather and cloth for purposes of speculation. The necessities of the army rise up like a mountain and cannon, and will not be overlooked. It was hoped at one time, that we might obtain winter supplies in Maryland. This hope was born after the army left Richmond, and has now miserably perished. The Government is unable to furnish the supplies; for they are not to be had in the country. If it had exercised a little foresight last spring and summer, when vessels were running the blockade, and cargoes of calico, linen and other articles of like importance, a partial supply at least of hats, blankets, shoes and woolen goods might have been obtained from England. But foresight is a quality of mind that is seldom put in practice in these days.

But whatever may be done by the people, *should be done immediately*. Not one moment can be lost that will not be marked, as by the second hand of a watch, with the pangs of a sufferer. Already the hills and valleys in this high latitude have been visited by frost, and the nights are uncomfortably cool to the man who sleeps upon the ground. Come up, then, men and women of the South, to this sacred duty. Let nothing stand between you and the performance of it. Neither pride, nor pleasure, nor personal ease and comfort, should withhold your hands from the holy work. The supply of leather and wool, we all know, is limited; but do what you can, and all you

can, and as soon as you can. If you cannot send woolen socks, send half woolen or cotton socks; and so with under clothing, coats and pants. And if blankets are not to be had, then substitute comforts made of dyed ossaburgs stuffed with cotton. Anything that will keep off the cold will be acceptable. Even the speculator and extortioner might forego their gains for a season and unite in this religious duty. If they neither clothe the naked, nor feed the hungry, who are fighting for *their* freedom and for *their* houses and property, what right have they to expect anything but eternal damnation, both from god and man?

If the Army of Virginia could march through the South just as it is—ragged and almost barefooted and hatless—many of the men limping along and not quite well of their wounds or sickness, yet cheerful and not willing to abandon their places in the ranks—their clothes riddled with balls and their banners covered with the smoke and dust of battle, and shot into tatters, many of them inscribed with "Williamsburg," "Seven Pines," "Gaines' Mill," "Garnett's Farm," "Front Royal," "McDowel," "Cedar Run," and other victorious fields—if this army of veterans, thus clad and shod, with tattered uniforms and banners, could march from Richmond to Mississippi, it would produce a sensation that has no parallel in history since Peter the Hermit led his swelling hosts across Europe to the rescue of the Holy Sepulchre.

I do not write to create alarm, or to produce a sensation, but to arouse the people to a sense of the true condition of the army. I have yet to learn that anything is to be gained by suppressing the truth, and [unreadable].

There is nothing new from the [unreadable]. It is reported that Jackson crossed the river at Williamsport a few days ago to repair a road, which he might have occasion to use, and then returned. I see nothing, however, to change the opinion heretofore expressed, yet now the heavy work of the campaign is over, unless McClelland should seek us on the south side of the river. This, some believe, public opinion at the North will compel [unreadable]. It may be so, though I doubt it.

I had made arrangements to procure full official lists of the casualties in the Georgia, Alabama and Florida regiments as well as the account of the performances of the troops from those States, and regret that sickness should have prevented me from carrying them out.

P.W.A.

JAMES R. SNEED AND GEORGE W. RANDOLPH: CLOTHING FOR THE SOLDIERS

Savannah Republican correspondent Peter W. Alexander had marched from Virginia to Maryland with Lee's Army of Northern Virginia. He was as familiar with the condition of the men as he would have been had he been a soldier himself. Alexander was also a much respected and beloved war correspondent—the Walter Cronkite or Dan Rather of his day—whose stories were picked up through newspaper exchanges and run in papers throughout the Confederacy. For that reason, when Alexander wrote a series of passionate articles about the needs of Georgia soldiers for the coming winter, the people of the South responded generously. Alexander's stories were among the first, though not the last, examples of advocacy journalism in the Confederate press.

Alexander's claims in stories published on 1 and 3 October that Georgia soldiers were shoeless and in rags apparently evoked considerable disbelief among Savannah residents. Surely the Confederate government would not let its valiant soldiers be reduced to such a state with the onset of winter only weeks away. To answer the questions definitively, the editor of the Republican *wrote to the Confederate secretary of war, and he published the answer he received so as to dispel the public disbelief and to restore the credibility of his Virginia correspondent.*

Savannah Republican, 22 October 1862

CLOTHING FOR THE SOLDIERS—DESPATCH FROM THE SECRETARY OF WAR

As our correspondent's testimony regarding the suffering in the army had been questioned, and a statement given to the public, on the assurance of army officers, that the government was abundantly supplied with shoes, clothing, and other necessaries and comforts for the army, which would be distributed at the proper time, and that private individuals were making unnecessary sacrifices under a mistaken view of the case, we determined, if possible, to satisfy both the public and ourselves on the subject. We, accordingly, addressed a note of enquiry to the Secretary of War, who promptly replied by telegraph as follows:

RICHMOND, Oct. 21.

J. R. Sneed:

We desire all the assistance in supplying shoes, blankets and clothing that can be furnished.

GEO. W. RANDOLPH,
Secretary of War

That settles the question; and now let all the people go to work. Shoes, socks, drawers, vests, neck ties, indeed clothing of every description should be made up as fast as possible and forwarded to the army.

Parties in the state can entrust all packages to the Georgia Hospital and Relief Association, at Augusta.

PETER W. ALEXANDER: WHAT THE GOVERNMENT HAS DONE AND IS DOING FOR SICK, WOUNDED AND DESTITUTE SOLDIERS

Alexander continued his advocacy on behalf of Georgia's soldiers by critiquing the hospital facilities for the state's soldiers in Virginia. Several states set up their own hospitals in Virginia to care for their own soldiers, but even so, medical care was at best rudimentary and haphazard.

Savannah Republican, 22 October 1862

ARMY CORRESPONDENCE OF THE SAVANNAH REPUBLICAN

What the Government has done and is doing
for the Sick, Wounded, and
destitute Soldiers.
WINCHESTER, VA., Oct. 12th, 1862

In my letter of yesterday, I endeavored to anew what may be accomplished by the intelligent and well-directed effort of one State in the matter of providing for its wounded soldiers and relieving its sick and destitute. The State referred to was Georgia, and the agency through which its charity and benefactions distributed was the Georgia Relief and Hospital Association. It was shown that the State, in addition to large individual contributions of money, clothing, medicines and stores, had appropriated the sum of $200,000 for the relief of

the sick and wounded; that the Association had established four large hospitals in Richmond, that these hospitals were provided with surgeons, matrons, nurses and chaplains; that an ample supply of furniture, bed-sacks, sheets, towels, bandages, splints and medicines had been procured; that a large store room had been rented, where clothing was kept for gratuitous distribution among the troops from Georgia and the very needy from other States, where extra baggage and express freight might be stored free of charge; and that the Association had in its employ a number of agents, active and zealous agents, who, upon the occurrence of a battle, repaired immediately to the scene of action, carrying with them a supply of medicine, bed sacks, sheets, towels, bandages, clothing &c., collected up the wounded from their State, and rendered every assistance, moral and physical, it was in their

power to bestow. It was shown also, that these agents were in-
dustrious and energetic men, full of sympathy and good feeling, who did not wait for the sick and destitute to come to
them, but went out in search of the sufferers, got them into as
comfortable quarters as possible, put beds of straw under
their weary limbs, furnished them with a change of clothing,
and nursed them like brothers—as they are.

To-day I proposed to show what the Government is doing
for the sick and wounded under the same circumstances—not
with a view of finding fault, but to indicate the defects in the
system it has adopted, to the end that they may be corrected.

It is customary after a battle has been fought, to collected
the wounded together in temporary hospitals or send them to
the rear. At Richmond, they were placed in the hospitals
in that city; after the second battle of Manassas they were
sent back to Warrenton and other towns in the vicinity, and at
Sharpsburg they were sent across the river to Sheperdstown
and thence to this place and Staunton. The regimental surgeons dress the wound, and set or amputate the limb, as the
case may be, before the patient passes from their hands to the
rear. Some of these operators perform their work skillfully
and conscientiously; others do it hurriedly or ignorantly;
whilst a few do it in a manner that can only be properly characterized as brutal. I have known cases of amputations when
the lapping part of the flesh was sewed together over the bone
so stupidly that the thread would disengage itself and the
bone be exposed in less than twenty-four hours. The object of
many of the field surgeons seems to be to get through their
work, in some sort of fashion, as soon as possible, and turn
their subjects over to the hospital surgeons. While engaged
at the amputation table, many of them feel it to be their duty,
every time they administer brandy to the patient, to take a
drink themselves. This part of their work is performed with
great unction and conscientiousness. In a majority of instances, however, I am glad to say the field surgeons do quite
as well as could be expected of young men who have had but
little practical experience in the art of surgery. In cases of ordinary sickness they have but little to do, inasmuch as the
Government has been able to furnish them with but few medicines, and they have consequently but little to administer.

But it is when the wounded man falls into the hands of the
hospital surgeons that his greatest sufferings begin. I do not
mean such surgeons as those in the Richmond hospitals,
which are located in a large city under the eye of the Government, and are provided for with careful matrons and nurses
and an ample supply of hospital stores; the circumstances
surrounding these officers, if nothing else, would constrain
them to perform their duties. But I allude to the surgeons in
those hospitals which are improvised in the rear of the army,
as at this place and Warrenton, and who being of but little
value at Richmond and other central points, are sent to the
country. Shall I daguerreotype two of these surgeons for you?
Sam Weller would call them "Sawbones," and perhaps that is
a more appropriate term for them than surgeons.

Nearly two weeks after the battle of Sharpsburg, two young
gentlemen, or irreproachable moustaches, were introduced
into my room at a hotel in this place by the landlady, who informed me that they would be my room-mates for the present.
It appeared from their conversation that they had just arrived
from Richmond—that they had been acting in the capacity of
assistant surgeons there for nearly a year, and that they had
been despatched to Winchester to assist in taking care of the
wounded in the battle of Sharpsburg. Two questions of much
magnitude occupied their attention for half an hour or
more—to wit: 1st, whether they should report to the surgeon of the post in person or by note; 2d, whether, in the
event they reported in person, they should "dress up" or go
as they were. They finally decided to dress first and then
send up their report in writing. The consideration which
brought them to this conclusion arose from the fact that
they were without paper, and the idea of going into the
street to purchase a supply in their present plight, could not
be entertained for a moment. Nearly two hours were devoted to their toilet. After washing and scrubbing ever so
long, their hair and moustaches had to be carefully cleaned
and oiled, their uniforms, covered all over with gold lace,
neatly dusted, and their boots duly polished. One of them
put on a ruffled calico shirt with a large diamond pin and
immense gold studs, a pair of white linen pantaloons, and a
handsome black cloth coat made up in the extreme military
style. He first thought he would wear a pair of gaiter shoes,
but on consulting "Jim" (his companion) it was finally
agreed that boots would become the set of his pants better.
So he put on the boots.

Having finished their elaborate toilets and started out of
the room, the following laconic dialogue ensued.

Boots.—I say, Jim, don't you think we had better take a
drop before going out?

Jim.—Yes, I *do* think we had. I feel rather shaky after last
night's affair.

They courteously inquired after a moment's hesitation,
whether I would not join them; but I was suffering at the time
from fever consequent upon a chill, and a still fiercer lever of
indignation that such stupid creatures should be sent here to
attend the wounded, and I declined to participate. They returned to the room after an hour's absence, complained that
they had to walk so far through the heat and dust to get a little
paper, prepared their note to the Chief Surgeon of the post,
and sent it up to him in due form. The Chief Surgeon, who is
represented to be a man of industry and energy, replied
promptly, ordering them to a certain hospital, which they proceeded to take charge of the next morning—nearly twenty-
four hours after their arrival in town!

You are ready to inquire, of what use can such dainty gen-
try be in a dirty hospital filled with stern sufferers—men with
broken bones and ghastly wounds, whose bodies are covered
with filthy rags and alive with vermin—with nothing to lie
upon but a little straw, and the air they breathe poisoned by

exhalations from the festering wounds and feverish bodies around them? The answer is, they are of no use whatever. If ever so skilled in their profession, the neatness of their toilet and the delicacy of their noses would totally disqualify them for such work as this. A hospital at best is not a desirable place to abide in; but when filthy and filled with vermin, and crammed with sick and wounded men, whose wounds are seldom dressed and whose necessities require them to submit to the most disgusting practices, they fall but little, if any, short of purgatory. The buildings selected for hospitals, instead of being in a quiet, pleasant locality, are almost invariably located in the most noisy, dusty and dirty part of town. It was so at Corinth, and it is so in Winchester. In the former place, they were located immediately around the depot, where the cars were running day and night, and where the wagons from the camps were constantly arriving and departing, whilst the houses in the rest of the town, which the owners had been required to vacate, were occupied by Generals and their [unreadable] staff officers.

There are several hundred sick and wounded men here; and yet, if I am correctly informed, the Surgeons did not bring with them a single cot, bedsack, sheet, or towel, or solitary change of clothing for the wounded! Some of the men are now lying on a scant supply of straw, with a foul blanket over them, who are otherwise as naked as when they first came into the world! The little clothing they had was torn off when their wounds were dressed, and it was impossible to recover their knapsacks after they were wounded. But for a few cots in the York hospital, (which is very well kept,) said to have been left there by our enemy, the condition of such of the wounded who could not get into private houses is as deplorable as it can be.

The Surgeons were late in arriving here, and were equally slow, as you have seen, in reporting after they had arrived. The agents of the Georgia Relief and Hospital Association reached Warrenton with their supplies nearly a week in advance of the Surgeons sent up from Richmond. The same is true as to this place. In less than twenty-four hours after their arrival here (the time required for some of the government surgeons to arrange their toilets and report for duty) they have visited every hospital in the town, gathered up many of the wounded from their State, dressed their wounds, furnished them with a change of clothing, and gone to work to secure separate hospital buildings for their accommodation. Why cannot the government Surgeons show equal activity and humanity?

One thing has impressed me more painfully than all others connected with the army. It is the little concern which the government, its officers and surgeons show for the preservation of the lives of their troops. A great parade is made over a single piece of artillery captured from the enemy; and yet what is such a trophy compared with the life of an able-bodied man, even when considered as to its military value! We have none too many men in the South that we should adopt a system so disregardful of life. The whole country is interested in the life and health of every man in it, and if some of the energy displayed in forcing feeble and unhealthy conscripts into the service, were shown in taking care of the sick and wounded, the army would be all the better for it. A planter who would take as little care of the health of his slaves as the government does of its soldiers, would soon have none to care for, while he would be driven out of the community by his indignant neighbors.

P.W.A.

Fredericksburg Campaign

Lee's men withdrew back into Virginia after the September campaign to Sharpsburg, but McClellan's forces did not follow until directly ordered to do so by President Lincoln in early October. McClellan moved out to Warrenton, where he found himself between Longstreet's forces at Culpeper and Jackson's in the Valley. When McClellan refused to go any farther, Lincoln removed the general and gave command of the Army of the Potomac to Burnside. Burnside was not so hesitant to follow the Confederates, and he devised a plan that called for an advance toward Fredericksburg on the Rappahannock. Burnside massed his army on the northeast bank, and Lee, Longstreet, and Jackson gathered their forces on the other side of the river.

Burnside planned an attack on Richmond via Fredericksburg, but his advance was halted when the pontoons needed to build bridges across the Rappahannock failed to arrive. The delay gave Lee time to reinforce and cost Burnside the element of surprise on which he had counted. Finally, though, on 25 November, the pontoons arrived, and Burnside began building bridges.

His men began crossing the Rappahannock before dawn on 11 December. Engineers had spanned about half of the river's width when Confederates under Mississippi

General William Barksdale's men began firing on them. Burnside ordered his artillery to begin firing at Barksdale's Mississippi Brigade, but the troops were not phased by the heavy weapons. They continued to pick off Burnside's men on the bridge.

Burnside's men did get across the Rappahannock by the evening of 11 December, but it was late morning on 13 December before the battle began. Jackson's men, in combination with Stuart's artillery, threw back the Union troops. By evening, Jackson's position was intact, and the Union army held only the river line. To the north, the federals met devastating artillery and small-arms fire from Longstreet's corps on Marye's Heights. Fourteen successive Union charges were repulsed by Confederate fire. Burnside's forces withdrew on 15 December. The Union loss at the Battle of Fredericksburg was 12,653 to the Confederate loss of only 4,201. This was Lee's most lopsided victory of the war.

PETER W. ALEXANDER: ACCOUNTS OF BATTLE AT FREDERICKSBURG

The Battle of Fredericksburg was a key victory for Robert E. Lee. The Republican's *Peter W. Alexander covered the battle, at least initially, from Richmond by collecting information from the War Department and from eyewitnesses. The following two stories are his accounts, one based on an eyewitness account and the other, written the following day, from a broader array of sources. The second letter in this set was actually written on the day the battle commenced, and the first letter was written the next day. However, the mails from Virginia were so disrupted by the fighting there that the first day's letter arrived later than the second—hence the reversed publication dates.*

Savannah Republican, 24, 23 December 1862

ARMY CORRESPONDENCE
OF THE SAVANNAH REPUBLICAN

The Battle of Thursday

The irregularity of the mails has rendered very uncertain the receipt of our correspondence from the seat of war. A letter, just received, and written on the day of the great battle of Fredericksburg, contains an interesting account of the fight of Thursday when the enemy attempted to cross and immediately thereafter. We append that portion of it, omitting the commencement, which refers to the probably intentions of the enemy, which have been fully realized:—[EDS.
RICHMOND, DEC. 13th, 1862. . . .

I am indebted to an intelligent friend in the army for the following account of the fight on Thursday. He says the enemy attempted to lay pontoon bridges across the river at four places—two at Fredericksburg, one above the town, and one about a mile and a half below. The Florida brigade, in Anderson's division, repulsed them at the upper ford, and Barksdale's brigade, of McLaws' division, repulsed them three times at the town, each time with heavy loss. At the mouth of Harrison's creek below they were also driven back by the

18th Mississippi, 16th Georgia, and 15th South Carolina, Col. Dessausaure commanding. These regiments belong to McLaws' division also.

About 2 p.m. the enemy concentrated thirty-seven pieces of artillery upon the centre of the town, firing 100 shells every four minutes, and in the midst of this storm they effected a landing, but not without great loss. Barksdale's Mississippians stood manfully to their guns through this heavy bombardment, the crushing timbers and crumbling ruins of brick and mortar, for more than an hour, and stoutly contested the landing. They were finally compelled to retire, however, from their exposed position, and allow the enemy to land. They withdrew back three streets, formed anew, and again charged the heavy masses of the enemy that came pouring into the town, and drove them back across the river, inflicting a severe loss upon them. No troops could have behaved better, and they and their commander were richly entitled to the thanks which Gen. McLaws bestowed upon them for their gallant behavior.

Barksdale's loss was severe, including Capt. Clark of the 13th Miss., killed, and Capt. Green and Thurmond of the 17th and 21st Mississippi seriously wounded.

The Mississippians were relieved by Gen. T.R.R. Cobb's brigade, who held the town until night, when they were ordered to retire to the base of the hills on this side of the town.—the 16th Georgia had several wounded by shells as they lay guarding the lower bridge. Among the wounded brought down last night, I notice the names of W. J. Herring of the 14th Georgia, R. N. Robinson of the 16th Georgia, Corporal J. McCade, J. Craft, Thos. Migell, J. Fielding, J. W. Harper, W. F. Swails and H. Lewis of the 8th Florida; M. Duncan of 1st South Carolina; Lieut. T. A. Diall of the 2nd South Carolina, and W. E. Parker of the 15th South Carolina.

The city was fired in a number of places. Many of the inhabitants had been forced by the bad weather to return, and the suffering among the women and children was very great. The letter before me says "the town is a mass of ruins." The citizens are crowded into the farm houses in the vicinity of town, and in tents through the woods and fields. These tents are made of blankets, sheets, counterpanes, &c., and afford but a frail shelter to feeble women and children against the inclement weather. The enemy have not only got possession of their homes but of their furniture, provisions and clothing. The fugitives brought away but little except what they had on their backs.

Let the people of Savannah remember Fredericksburg and New Orleans, and neither remain in the city and submit to the enemy nor flee and leave all to the spoiler; but having removed the non-combatants, let them stand their ground, defend their homes, and save all—anyhow, their honor.

LATER

Eight p.m.—Heavy skirmishing continued throughout the day yesterday, resulting in a reported loss on our part of about 130 killed and wounded. The same species of warfare was kept up to-day, but with what results I am unable to say. The enemy directed their attention to the woods this side of the town, which they subjected to a heavy fire of shells. Occasionally the pickets and skirmishers took part, when a pretty sharp fire was maintained on both sides. The enemy doubtless desire to get possession of the heights on the south side with a view either to their own protection or an early advance.

The impression in unofficial circles was that the battle would be fought to-morrow, Sunday. Brig. Gen. Randolph, late Secretary at War, reported for duty after his withdrawal from the Department of War, and the President having failed to assign him to duty, he determined to throw up his commission and return to the practice of law.

P.W.A.

**ARMY CORRESPONDENCE
OF THE SAVANNAH REPUBLICAN**

RICHMOND, Dec. 14th.

A great battle was fought on the Rappahannock yesterday, and the Confederate arms were again victorious. The fight commenced at 9 o'clock in the morning and continued until six in the evening. Nothing was known of the battle here until late that night, after my letter of yesterday evening had been posted. The War Office has taken complete possession of the telegraph, and one can hardly order a bushel of salt by the wires without first getting permission from the authorities. This will explain why you have received nothing from me of late by telegraph, and why you may not in the future.

The enemy made the attack, moving first against our right wing, and as the fog lifted from the valley, it extended along the entire line to our extreme left. The conflict raged without intermission until night set in, and resulted in the complete repulse of the enemy at all points. Our success was not so decisive as to preclude the idea of renewal of the battle today. Indeed, in his description to the War Office, Gen. Lee expresses the opinion that the fighting would be resumed at daybreak this morning. If so, Burnside has greater confidence in his troops than McClellan had at Sharpsburg, where he declined to return to the attack, notwithstanding his vast superiority in numbers.

We have to mourn the loss of many brave officers—among whom are Brig. Gens. T.R.R. Cobb, of Georgia, and Maxcy Gregg, of South Carolina. Though they had not many opportunities to display their qualities for command, these gentlemen were conspicuous for skill, courage and gallantry. Bartow and Bee fell side by side at the first battle of Manassas, and now Cobb and Gregg lock arms in death. For the second time the bloody marriage of South Carolina and Georgia has been celebrated upon the field of battle and to the harsh music of artillery.

Doubtless many gallant officers of the line and hundreds of brave men in the ranks have also been slain or wounded. The enemy had decidedly the advantage in numbers, and the lists of casualties, when they come to be published, will carry grief to many a stricken home in the Confederacy. General Hampton's expedition to Dumfries may have the effect to create a diversion in favor of General Lee. He captured some twenty wagons, and fifty or sixty prisoners, whom he brought back to the Rappahannock. Whilst at Dumfries, he ascertained that Seigel's corps was expected to arrive there from Fairfax C. H. Today. Dumfries is about midway between Alexandria and Fredericksburg, or thirty miles by land from either place. In the present condition of the roads in that quarter, it would require two days' hard marching to bring Seigel to the south bank of the Rappahannock—too late to participate in the fight before Wednesday, unless he proceeded by water; and even then he could not get into position much, if any sooner. Possibly Burnside may await his arrival before renewing the attack.

The late battle at Kinston, N.C., was a glorious affair. The enemy made the attack with fifteen thousand men and nine gunboats, and was repulsed with heavy loss by Gen. Evans, whose force did not exceed one-fifth of the adversary's. There can be no impropriety in making this statement, since it will be some days before this letter can reach you, and since reinforcements have already been sent to the hero of Leesburg.

LATER

12 m.—A telegram has just been received at the War Office from Gen. Lee, dated at half-past eleven this morning, in which he says the battle had not been renewed up to that hour. It is thought here that Burnside will not return to the attack. A few hours will decide.

I hope to be able to go up to the Army tomorrow morning. A passport was granted to the correspondent of the London Times, and why should one be refused to the correspondent of the Savannah Republican? Is it because the one is an Englishman and the other a Confederate?

STILL LATER

8 p.m.—Passengers who left the Army at 1 p.m. to day, say the fighting was renewed this morning, and continued up to the time they left. Despatches to the War Office, on the contrary, speak of heavy skirmishing, especially this afternoon, but say nothing of any general engagement. I have just been to see the body of Gen. Cobb, which was brought down this evening and will be sent south by to-morrow morning's train. His brigade is posted behind a stone wall at the base of the hill, this side of Fredericksburg, and but a short distance from the town. Our batteries were placed on the elevations just behind and above the brigade, and fired over them. When the enemy charged upon Cobb's position, he reserved his fire until they got within one hundred yards, when his men poured into their ranks a fire which seemed literally to sweep them from the earth. The enemy retired, and having reformed their broken lines and been heavily reinforced,

they returned to the charge at a double quick. The Georgians again reserved their fire until they had come within easy range, when they gave them another volley like the first and with the same result. A third charge was finally made, this time in still greater force, out in this instance as in the first and second, the enemy were driven back with tremendous loss. Persons who participated in the fight say that 1,000 dead Yankees were left on the field in front of Cobb's position. Gen. Cobb himself displayed great courage and judgment. His mother was born in the town of Fredericksburg, and he acted as if he were fighting to rescue her birth place from the clutches of a hated foe. His men were protected behind the stone fence, and he and Gen. Cool, of North Carolina, were standing behind a house, from which point they could conveniently issue their orders. A shell passed through this house, and fragments of it struck both of them. Gen. Cobb was hit on the thigh, which was terribly mangled, about two o'clock and died at four. It is reported that Gen. Cook is also dead. A piece of the same shell struck Capt. Brewster, of the 24th Georgia, a most gallant officer, in the leg, and inflicted a severe, but not mortal wound.

It is feared that Capt. Lord King, son of the Hon. T. Butler King and aid to Gen. McLaws, was killed. He is missing, and a telegram to his father says his spurs had been found on the field near a pair of shoes. He had on cavalry boots, and the presumption is that he was wounded, and that some vandal relieved him of them and left his old shoes behind. Capt. K. was brave to a fault, and has always conducted himself in battle with great gallantly and fearlessness.

I hear that Lt. Col. Cook, of Phillips' Legion, was also killed. The 15th Georgia and Phillips' Legion composed a part of Cobb's brigade.

P.W.A.

AN ANONYMOUS REPORT: BATTLE OF FREDERICKSBURG—ANOTHER CONFEDERATE VICTORY

The Richmond Examiner *was able to offer its readers a report on Fredericksburg sooner than most Southern newspapers. Within two days, the paper's correspondent had supplied a summary of the fighting along the Rappahannock.*

Richmond Examiner, 15 December 1862

THE BATTLE OF FREDERICKSBURG— ANOTHER CONFEDERATE VICTORY

HAMILTON'S CROSSING,
December 14th, 1862.

Of the battle yesterday you have from other sources learned the main result, the driving in of the enemy's light batteries, and the repulse of his infantry. I will supply such particulars as came under my observation. But before doing

so, I must endeavor to give you an idea of the positions occupied by the hostile forces at the beginning of the action.

From Fredericksburg the Rappahannock flows nearly due east. The valley of the river, lying mostly on the south side, is a mile in width near the town and widening as you go down stream. At Hamilton's crossing on the railroad the valley is three miles across. From Hamilton's crossing to Fredericksburg the railroad and the old Richmond stage road, both running parallel with the river, skirt this valley. South of the railroad, beginning near the town and running to a point at Hamilton's crossing, and also parallel with the river, is a range of hills covered with dense oak forest fringed on its northern border by pine thickets.—Our forces occupied the whole length of this forest. Longstreet's corps occupied the highlands above, opposite, and for a mile below the town. Jackson's corps rested on Longstreet's right and extended away to the eastward, the extreme right under A. P. Hill crossing the railroad at Hamilton's crossing, and stretching into the valley towards the river. Our front was about six miles in length. Most of the batteries of both corps were posted in the skirts of the forest, along the line of the railroad, the seven batteries of Colonel Lindsay Walker's regiment and Stewart's horse artillery, being stationed in the valley, between the railroad at Hamilton's crossing and the river. The enemy's forces occupied the valley north of the railroad from Fredericksburg to within half a mile of our extreme right. His light batteries were posted over the southern extremity of the valley, at from a quarter of a mile to a mile from the railroad, while the hills on the northern banks of the river from Falmouth to Fitzhugh's farm, five miles below Fredericksburg, were studded at intervals of half a mile with his batteries of heavy guns.

The opinion had prevailed on the night before that the enemy was to attack our lines on yesterday morning, but when the day broke without the sound of guns being [unreadable] he had deferred his advance until this morning.

The sun rose clear, but a dim fog shrouded the valley, limiting the vision to a short half-mile. The enemy was supposed to be within a mile of the railroad at Hamilton's crossing, but there were no indications of his presence.

At half-past eight, A.M., General Lee, attended by his staff, rode slowly along the front of our lines, from west to east, and halted in the valley a mile to the east of Hamilton's crossing, and half a mile in the rear of our batteries on the extreme right. At nine o'clock a column of our troops, which proved to be Ewell's division, Gen. Early commanding, advanced up the valley from the direction of Port Royal, and defiled into the woods to the left of Hamilton's crossing.—The men were marching at a very leisurely pace, with a careless swinging gait; but there was that in the quiet dignity of their demeanor, which told that each, though undaunted, was conscious that the next hour might be one of stern battle and death.—Scarcely had the rear of this division disappeared in the woods, when directly in their front the artillery of the Old Stonewall brigade, Woodis, Braxton's and three other batteries opened a brisk fire on the enemy's batteries north of the railroad. At this time, owing to the fog, few of the enemy's infantry were visible. After events proved that they were lying close to the south bank of the river. The cannonading soon became general along the front of both armies. In ten minutes from the time of firing their first gun, the Danville battery, Captain Woodis, had lost fifteen men killed and wounded, a number of horses, and had two guns disabled.

The enemy's battery, eight hundred yards distant had the exact range from the first fire. In the beginning of the action the loss of the other batteries of Taliafero's division were also quite heavy. Our men fired with great precision, their shells bursting in front or directly above the opposing batteries. In the course of an hour the artillery fight had become so general that it was almost impossible for an observer to distinguish what particular battery of the enemy was engaging the attention of any given battery of ours, and vice versa. Scarcely a battery that had been unmasked on either side but was exposed to a direct and enfilading fire. The roar of cannon along a line of six miles was tremendous. Their air was resonant with the savage music of shells and solid shot. The white smoke wreaths of exploding shells were everywhere visible among the trees of the forest, which hid our forces in the valley and away beyond the river in Scafford.—Lines of ambulances could be seen bearing off the wounded of both armies, but there was nothing by which to judge that the advantage rested with either side.

At noon the fog had cleared away, but there was a thick haze in the atmosphere.—About this time the enemy infantry moved forward from the river towards our batteries on the hills. As they pressed forward across the Valley, Stewart's horse artillery from our extreme right opened upon them a destructive enfilading fire of round shot. This fire, which annoyed them sorely, was kept up in spite of six batteries which were directed against the horse artillery as soon as it was unmasked. By one o'clock the Yankee columns had crossed the Valley and entered the woods south of the railroad. The batteries on both sides slackened their fire, and musketry at first scattering, but quickly increasing to a crash and roar, sounded through the woods. Dense volumes of smoke rose above the trees and, as volley succeeded volley, sometimes so rapidly as to blend into a prolonged and continuous roar. A. P. Hill's division sustained the first shock of battle.—The rest of Jackson's corps were in different lines of reserves. D. H. Hill's division was drawn up in J. L. Marye's field, under a long hill, in rear of our lines of battle. Here they remained during most of the day, being moved from time to time to the right or left, as the exigencies of battle dictated. Shortly after the infantry fight began, a brigade of this division was moved at a double-quick a mile and a half to the right, and posted in a dense clump of pines in supporting distance of Stewart's horse artillery. In ten minutes they were brought back to their original position. The celerity of this movement would be incredible to anyone who had not witnessed it. To an observer the sight was singular and exciting. A long black line shoots from the position of the reserves, crosses the railroad at Hamilton's station, skims across the Valley, and in a few moments is lost in the pines nearly two miles away. After scarcely a breathing spell, the same line emerges from the pines, retraces its steps into its original position. As this brigade resumed its position in reserve, the fire of musketry directly in its front slackened. A few crackling shots were heard to our left, along Longstreet's division, and then a succession of volleys, which were kept up at intervals during the remainder of this evening. The musketry fire on our right was [*unreadable*], and the battle raged with increased fury. Our batteries along our whole front again re-opened, and Colonel Walker's artillery regiment, composed of Latham's, Letcher's, Braxton's, Pegram's, Crenshaw's, Johnson's, McIntosh's batteries, stationed in the open low grounds to the east of the railroad at Hamilton's station, moved forward several hundred yards in the direction of Fredericksburg. Hill and Early's troops had driven the enemy from the woods and across the railroad in the direction of their pontoon bridges near Deep Run. Our men pursued them a mile and a half across the bottom land, and fell back only when they had gotten under the shelter of their batteries. Our troops then retired to the mouth side of the railroad. Again the enemy rallied and returned to renew the contest, but were again, about five o'clock, P.M., driven back. All the batteries of Jackson's corps were at this time in full play, and in the approaching twilight the blaze of guns and the quick flash of shells were more distinctly visible. The move along the valley was at once splendid [*missing words*].

The result of the fight on our right wing may be summed up briefly. We drove the enemy back, killing three to one, and at night held the ground occupied by the enemy's batteries in the morning. The enemy had twenty thousand men engaged on this wing; while altogether, from first to last, we had not more than ten thousand in the line of fire.

Longstreet's victory was even more complete.

He drove the enemy into the streets of Fredericksburg, killing at least five to one. At dusk the firing ceased simultaneously on both sides.

It being as yet impossible to ascertain with accuracy the casualties on our side, I forbear to attempt a list.

Our wounded have all been removed from the field. The most severely hurt are receiving treatment in the field hospitals, whilst those slightly wounded are being sent down the railroads. The battle was renewed on our left at sunrise this morning, and soon became general. The battle field is pretty much the same as that of yesterday. No particulars have yet transpired. I hear but one of our generals having been struck yesterday, General Maxcy Gregg, of South Carolina, who is said to be mortally wounded.

FURTHER READINGS

Bannister, Don. *Long Day at Shiloh*. New York: Knopf, 1981.

Capers, Gerald Mortimer. *Occupied City: New Orleans under the Federals, 1862–1865*. Lexington: University of Kentucky Press, 1965.

Connelly, Thomas Lawrence. *Autumn of Glory: The Army of Tennessee, 1862–1865*. Baton Rouge: Louisiana State University Press, 1971.

Cozzens, Peter. *The Darkest Days of the War: The Battles of Iuka & Corinth*. Chapel Hill: University of North Carolina Press, 1997.

Daniel, Larry J. *Shiloh: The Battle That Changed the Civil War*. New York: Simon & Schuster, 1997.

Gallagher, Gary W. *The Antietam Campaign*. Chapel Hill: University of North Carolina Press, 1999.

———. *The Fredericksburg Campaign: Decision on the Rappahannock*. Chapel Hill: University of North Carolina Press, 1995.

———. *The Richmond Campaign of 1862: The Peninsula and the Seven Days*. Chapel Hill: University of North Carolina Press, 2000.

Hearn, Chester G. *When the Devil Came Down to Dixie: Ben Butler in New Orleans*. Baton Rouge: Louisiana State University Press, 1997.

Hess, Earl J. *Banners to the Breeze: The Kentucky Campaign, Corinth, and Stones River*. Lincoln: University of Nebraska Press, 2000.

Ivy, Dick. *Peninsula Campaign in York*. Yorktown, Va.: York County Historical Committee, 1992.

Martin, David G. *The Shiloh Campaign, March–April, 1862*. New York: Fairfax Press, 1987.

McDonough, James L. *War in Kentucky: From Shiloh to Perryville*. Knoxville: University of Tennessee Press, 1994.

McPherson, James M. *Crossroads of Freedom: Antietam*. Oxford: Oxford University Press, 2002.

Newton, Steven Harvey. *The Battle of Seven Pines, May 31–June 1, 1862*. Lynchburg, Va.: H. E. Howard, 1993.

O'Reilly, Francis Augustin. *The Fredericksburg Campaign: Winter War on the Rappahannock*. Baton Rouge: Louisiana State University Press, 2003.

Rable, George C. *Fredericksburg! Fredericksburg!* Chapel Hill: University of North Carolina Press, 2002.

Street, James. *The Struggle for Tennessee: Tupelo to Stones River*. Alexandria, Va.: Time-Life Books, 1985.

Tucker, Spencer. *Unconditional Surrender: The Capture of Forts Henry and Donelson*. Abilene, Tex.: McWhiney Foundation Press, 2001.

Wheeler, Richard. *Lee's Terrible Swift Sword: From Antietam to Chancellorsville: An Eyewitness History*. New York: HarperCollins, 1992.

4

REPORTING THE WAR, 1863

The war's middle year contained a contradiction of dialectical proportions. On the one hand, the Confederacy won two of its biggest battlefield victories in 1863. On the other hand, the chance that the Confederacy could win the war with decisive victories in the field was crushed. Two factors explain this apparent contradiction. First, the Confederacy's weaker economic and manpower base was beginning to undermine its military strength. Although the Southerners were still managing by 1863 to produce all the material they basically needed to wage war, they could not overcome the disabilities imposed by their much smaller industrial economy, weaker currency, and smaller free population, which was a quarter of the North's. Further, desertion rates were increasing, and the Confederate peace movement was gaining strength at an alarming rate in places like Georgia and, in particular, North Carolina.

There was another, more subtle reason why the Confederacy's battlefield victories had not spelled victory in the war; winning Civil War battles did not lead to destruction of the enemy force. Certainly on more than one occasion an army had left the battlefield in complete disorder, First Manassas (Bull Run) being the most famous example, but rarely did the attackers gain a permanent advantage from this. Victory without pursuit has limited results, and pursuit was rare. The victors were often as exhausted and disorganized as the defeated, and the armies were not hardened professional soldiers. They were citizen armies composed mostly of volunteers who had not known what they were getting into or conscriptees who did not necessarily want to be on the battlefield. This was one of the reasons why Emory Upton advocated professional soldiering after the war, arguing that the inefficiencies of amateur armies led to longer wars and greater bloodshed. And there were certain limitations to pursuit. For example, the increasing range of muskets and cannon made closing in on an enemy a hazardous occupation. The artillery of a retreating army could punish careless pursuers. The terrain in North America, especially the ubiquitousness of trees, complicated large-scale maneuvers, nor could armies carelessly rush away from their rail lines. It is not for nothing that the most famous Confederate campaign of maneuver, the Shenandoah Valley Campaign of 1862, had been conducted by exceedingly small forces that did not need the support of long supply lines.

The net result of the war's middle year was that the Confederacy could only win the war if it could exhaust the Union army, but earlier in the year, the situation appeared quite different. The year had opened in the West with the end of the Battle of Murfreesboro (Stones River), where Braxton Bragg had attempted to destroy William T. Rosecrans's Union force. The Union victory was rather narrow but significant since it sealed the doom of Confederate Tennessee. The Eastern Theater was more promising. Ambrose E. Burnside, considered the least competent of the Army of the Potomac's commanders, decided to make a January attack across the Rappahannock but failed when torrential downpours mired his army in the muck—hence the famous nickname "Mud March." The march was such a disaster that it cost Burnside his command. He was succeeded by Joseph T. Hooker, who energetically reorganized and reinvigorated the crestfallen army and in April launched an attack across the Rappahannock near Chancellorsville. Hooker caught Lee completely by surprise and was in position to block the Confederates from Richmond. He hesitated, however, and gave Lee the opportunity to take the initiative and counterattack. After several days of fighting, the Yankees retreated, having lost about 17,000 soldiers. Lee had lost 13,000 men, including the famed Thomas "Stonewall" Jackson, a devastating blow to the Confederate army.

Yet this victory could not compensate for the Confederacy's deteriorating position in the West. Union forces had advanced north and south through the Mississippi delta until Vicksburg remained the sole Confederate fortress on the river. If lost, the trans-Mississippi Confederacy, Louisiana, Texas, Missouri, and Arkansas, would be completely isolated. Grant's first attempts to capture the city were unsuccessful. He then crossed the river south of Vicksburg, abandoning his supply lines and working only with what his army could carry. This confused John C. Pemberton, the commander at Vicksburg. At this point, fate, in the person of Jefferson Davis, intervened on the side of the Union. Davis bypassed theater commander Joseph E. Johnston and ordered Pemberton to hold Vicksburg. Johnston ordered Pemberton to avoid being trapped in Vicksburg, but confused by contradicting orders, the commander chose to make his stand in the city's substantial fortifications. Grant moved north, trapped Pemberton in Vicksburg, and sent William T. Sherman to block all potential relief efforts by Johnston.

The disaster at Vicksburg may have helped Lee make a decision. Lee knew that the Confederacy could only prevail if it inflicted a decisive defeat on the Union, and the Confederate commander decided to go on the offensive—for the second and last time. His Army of Northern Virginia moved through Maryland into southeastern Pennsylvania. Many things were in his favor. The Confederate army had never been stronger, morale was high, he had the advantage of surprise, and the Union had yet another command crisis. George Gordon Meade replaced Hooker as commander of the Army of the Potomac only 48 hours before the two armies collided at Gettysburg. On 1 July 1863, one of Lee's three corps overran the town but failed to dislodge arriving Union divisions from the high ground to the south. On 2 July, Lee attempted to turn Meade's left flank and nearly succeeded. On 3 July, Lee made a desperate attempt ("Pickett's Charge") to break the Union center. Its failure ended the battle; and the day after, Lee began his withdrawal. Losses were immense; Confederate casualties totaled 28,000, Union casualties, 23,000. Meade followed cautiously.

The Confederate war effort in the Western Theater was collapsing. The same day Lee began his withdrawal from Maryland, 4 July, Vicksburg surrendered to Grant. Before too much longer in Tennessee, Rosecrans would outmaneuver Bragg and force the Confederate commander to yield Chattanooga. Confederate hopes would be revived briefly, though, when Rosecrans committed a near-fatal error. Believing that Bragg was defeated, Rosecrans advanced carelessly into northern Georgia and was surprised and defeated at Chickamauga. The Union army came close to destruction. Bragg's failure to maintain reserves deprived the Confederacy of a major chance to turn the tide. The Union army was forced to withdraw to Chattanooga, but in November, Union troops swept the Confederates off the mountains, and the road into the Deep South now lay open.

The campaigning in the closing months of 1863 in the East was indecisive. Meade approached Lee's defenses cautiously. Lee, who had sent part of his army to help Bragg, twice moved north to attack Meade but was easily parried and forced to withdraw behind the Rapidan River.

WESTERN THEATER

Battle of Murfreesboro/Stones River

The first battle of 1863 was actually the last battle of 1862. The fighting started on 31 December 1862 but did not conclude until 2 January 1863. Of all the battles fought during the Civil War, this one had the most poignant beginning, a beginning that reiterated the heartrending nature of a civil war.

The night before the battle began, soldiers in the two armies huddled around fires, trying to stay warm. Everyone in both camps knew what the icy dawn would bring: more bloody fighting. Both Confederate General Braxton Bragg and Union Major General William S. Rosecrans were intending to attack on New Year's Eve morning. To cheer the men and hearten them for the impending battle, a military band fired the first salvos of the Battle of Murfreesboro. The musicians began to play songs from back home, songs from better times. The band from the other camp quickly returned fire with its own musical contribution. Through the evening, the Confederate and Union bands competed with favorites like "Dixie" or "The Bonnie Blue Flag" or "Hail Columbia." Then something truly remarkable happened. One of the bands began to play "Home Sweet Home," a song well known and loved in both the North and the South. The men in both camps began to sing. When the singing was over, the men settled down for what sleep they could get on that cold winter eve of what would be one of the bloodiest battles of the war.[1]

Rosecrans and Bragg had been skirmishing since the end of October, but now both were ready to take the offensive. Rosecrans never got the chance, though. He was concentrating on pulling his own offensive together when he was caught unaware by Bragg's attack. Confederate soldiers streamed out from among the black cedars and smashed into the Union right, where Major General Alexander McCook's soldiers were still at breakfast. The attack was devastating; McCook could only watch as his men were driven back nearly 3 miles.

Bragg's advantage did not last long, however. Rosecrans immediately began establishing lines along the Nashville turnpike and a nearby rail line so as to protect his sources of supplies. The Confederates concentrated on the federal center where Major General George H. Thomas was in command. This was a miscalculation by Bragg. Had he concentrated instead on the Union left flank, there was every possibility that he could have cut the federal army off from its Nashville base. Confederate soldiers charged Thomas's position over and over through a dense cedar forest that came to be called "Hell's Half-Acre" for the desperate fighting there that day. Despite the repeated attacks, Thomas's men were able to hold their position and protect the vital transportation routes. Despite the success of the day, that night Rosecrans considered retreating to Nashville. Instead, he elected to say and continue the fight.

The fighting did not resume until 2 January, when Rosecrans sent a force across Stones River and occupied a position from which it could enfilade the Confederate right. *Enfilade* is a military term that means to shoot down the ranks of the enemy's lines rather than head-on. Enfilade firing is devastating to the victim; it produces many casualties. Bragg sent Breckinridge across Stones River to drive the Union force from their position, a task his men managed to accomplish but on which they could not capitalize due to heavy firing from enemy artillery. Breckinridge lost a third of his men to the relentless fire. The federals reoccupied their previous position, and on 3 January, Rosecrans received reinforcements from Nashville. Bragg was forced to retreat to Tullahoma, Tennessee. Total casualties for the battle were more than 23,000. Tactically and strategically, the battle was a victory for the North. Rosecrans's army was now in a position to threaten the Confederate rail center at Chattanooga.

JOSEPH CLISBY: SUMMARY OF VICTORY AT MURFREESBORO

The Macon Telegraph *published a summary of the Battle of Murfreesboro that was most likely written by the editor, Joseph Clisby, and based on telegraphic accounts. It provides more details and analysis than the first telegraphic report did. As always, the lack of information limited what the newspaper could convey to its readers.*

Macon Telegraph, 2 January 1863

THE VICTORY AT MURFREESBORO'

We hope to get fuller accounts before going to press, but the facts already before us indicate a signal over throw of Rosecrans and his grand army. The fight began at nine o'clock on Tuesday, the 30th, with an artillery duel, but from 12 o'clock to night-fall there was an active engagement of infantry on our left. The fight, however, was but partial, and the enemy made the attack. On Wednesday morning, at half past five, our troops commenced a general assault, and a battle of almost unparalleled spirit and obstinacy raged between the combatants for more than eleven hours, during which the enemy's right was driven back upon Stone Run, a distance of seven miles from his original line of battle, and his left wing was only able to hold its position. At night, as we have good reason to believe, our enemy encamped four miles in advance of their line the previous morning. Four thousand prisoners, and thirty-one pieces of cannon, are among the trophies of the fight. During the night of the 30th, two million dollars worth of stores, including five days rations, were destroyed by our troops in a raid upon the enemy's rear.—The loss of such an amount of provisions, the enemy being already short and on half rations, must very seriously embarrass his retreat.

All the facts must be considered as amounting, at least, to a fatal frustration of the enemy's campaign in that direction, and completes the story along the whole frontier. In Virginia at Fredericksburg—in North Carolina at Kinston—in Tennessee at Murfreesboro—in Mississippi at Tallahatchie and Vicksburg, the enemy's advance has been severely checked and repulsed, and his little raid of 2000 cavalry a day or two ago upon the East Tennessee Railroad, is as yet the only point where he has not been terribly foiled, and the only thing he can yet show, besides death and disaster, as the fruit of his enormous preparations to crush the South. The repulse has been complete and universal. Choosing, at his leisure, his points of assault and preparing out of his abundant resources a force for each which he boasted would be overwhelming, he has been everywhere driven back, with horrible slaughter, torn, bleeding, discomfited and despondent. The movement on Murfreesboro, was an effort to pierce our centre. If he could have discomfited Bragg's army, penetrated the mountains through Chattanooga, occupied the line of railway and threatened Georgia on the North, he would have carried out his designs in that quarter. The movement upon Goldsboro' was intended to cut off the other railway line, and if both had been successful, he would have severed the Confederacy in two for all practical purposes.

Then to have secured possession of the Mississippi by the capture of Vicksburg—to penetrate the Alabama by taking possession of Mobile—to take Charleston—and lastly, if Burnside could have crossed the Rappahannock and invested Richmond on the North, while the Yankee force at Suffolk marched up and attacked it on the South—the city being in the meanwhile isolated from supplies and reinforcements by cutting off all her railway communications, he would have accomplished probably all the plans of the winter's campaign, and would perhaps have held onto fatal toils.

But so far, every link in this extensive plan of operations has [unreadable]. Every thing attempted has miscarried.

Every fold of the second [unreadable] has been cut before it could fairly be tightened. The enemy has been completely frustrated and baffled in the very flush of his strength and the fullest vigor of his enterprise.

Now, what must be the moral affect of such considerations and reflections of these upon the people of the North the reader can judge for himself. One thing is certain, there has been nothing in the annals of war like the total and sweeping frustration. We have had great success—but they have been isolated triumphs, and often shorn, to some extent, of the effect by contemporaneous defeats of something which could be represented as a defeat. But here is a grand, total, sweeping, ignominious repulse along the whole frontier of the war for a distance of two thousand miles. If this fails to satisfy our enemies that subjugation is impossible—that the war is but a waste of time and money, what will? If it does not put an estoppel upon the complaints against men, and show the North that the difficulty lies not in their Cabinet or their Generals, but in the impossibility of their enterprise, what will?

Rosecrans is perhaps their brightest and best man, and he, no doubt, fought Bragg with great advantage of numbers, but it did not avail. The miscarriage is too universal to be charged to accident of imbecility—it must be traced to the fact that they are attempting an impossible achievement.

Honor to Bragg, as well as his glorious host, for this splendid achievement. He has vindicated his reputation and won back public confidence which had been partially alienated from him by the attacks of the press, and particularly the venomous pens of army correspondents. The judgment of the President and of General Johnston, who left him at so critical a moment to marshal the grand battle, is triumphantly vindicated, and it will be some time before the complains of Bragg's weakness and inefficiency will be openly removed.

Seige of Charleston Harbor and the Assault on Fort Wagner

On 7 April, Union Rear Admiral Samuel F. du Pont attacked Charleston Harbor with nine ironclads. He was decisively repulsed in what was the prelude to a lengthy bombardment that smashed much of Charleston to little more than rubble. The bombardment would begin in earnest come July when Rear Admiral John A. Dahlgren succeeded du Pont. The seige and bombardment would continue throughout much of the remainder of the war.

The naval bombardment was supported by land troops under Major General Quincy A. Gillmore, whose primary target was Fort Wagner. Gillmore made several attempts to capture Fort Wagner with considerable losses. Capturing Fort Wagner was the key to possession of Morris Island, a 400-acre barrier island on the south side of Charleston Harbor. With possession of Morris Island, federal forces could subdue Fort Sumter, which would allow the Union fleet to compel the city's surrender. An attack on the fort in July was led by Boston abolitionist Robert Gould Shaw and his black regiment, the 54th Massachusetts, made famous by the movie Glory. The Union was denied Fort Wagner, though, until 6 September when finally the Confederates were forced to evacuate. One of the interesting aspects of the coverage by the Southern press of the attack on Fort Wagner was the failure to mention the use of black troops. The bombardment of Charleston continued on through the fall and early winter, but the city's other fortifications held out.

PETER W. ALEXANDER: UNION ATTACK ON CHARLESTON REPULSED

With no fighting expected in Virginia until May, Peter W. Alexander traveled to Charleston in March to see what would come of the naval engagement that seemed to be brewing. Alexander was on hand to witness the Union's attack on Charleston, which was repulsed by the Confederates. As soon after the battle as he could, Alexander telegraphed the following story to Savannah. He followed that initial story later with a longer letter about the initial battle in the harbor. That story also ran on 10 April.

Savannah Republican, 10 April 1863

TELEGRAPHIC
THE ATTACK ON CHARLESTON
THE KEOKUK AND IRONSIDES DISABLED
THE ENEMY RETIRE

Renewal of Fight Expected To-Day

[Special to Savannah Republican]

CHARLESTON, Apr. 7—The ball opened at 3 o'clock this afternoon. The enemy commenced the engagement with five turreted vessels and the Ironsides.—Their fire was directly chiefly against Fort Sumter.—The engagement lasted until half past five o'clock, when the enemy retired. The Keokuk, with a double turret, was disabled, and the Ironside is believed to be disabled. Steam was seen issuing from the sides of the Ironsides. The monitors were hit frequently and their smoke stacks perforated.

The first on both sides was terrific but deliberate. Fort Sumter, in the harbor, Fort Moultrie, Battery Bee, and Battery Beauregard on Sullivan's Island, and Fort Wagner and the battery at Cummings Point on Morris Island, participated on our side. One gun was dismounted in Sumter, but will be replaced to-night. One drummer boy killed and five men wounded. There were no casualties on Sullivan's Island, except for a man who broke his arm in falling from the flag staff of Fort Moultrie, which had been shot away.

The Confederates remain in high spirits.

Gen. Rieley, in command of all the works, behaved handsomely.

There were no movements on land. The fight will probably be renewed tomorrow.

P. W. A.

ARMY CORRESPONDENCE OF THE
SAVANNAH REPUBLICAN
THE BATTLE OF CHARLESTON

CHARLESTON, April 7.

The day of trial and blood to Charleston has at last arrived, and the blow so long impending over this goodly city, like the sword of Damocles, has at length fallen. It has taken no one by surprise however, and especially the military authorities. Gen. Beauregard had received information some days ago, from a source and by means which must for present be nameless, that the attack would probably be made to-day, and to-day it has been made. Having already sent you a full statement of the affair by telegraph, there is but little left me to add.

It was observed at half past two p.m. That the Federal fleet, which had been lying off the bar since Sunday afternoon, was approaching in hostile array. Eight turreted iron-clads and the famous iron covered war steamer Ironsides were put in motion and advanced to the assault by what is known as "Ship Channel." Gen. Beauregard, whose headquarters are in the city, was promptly notified of the movement by telegraph from Fort Sumter. It may be stated that there are wires running from all the Forts and batteries in and around the harbor to the city, and that the telegraph communication is frequent and expeditious between the forts and batteries, as well as with Charleston.

The Ironsides and five of the monitors participated in the engagement. Fort Moultrie was the first to open fire, at five minutes past three o'clock. The double turreted Keokuk—the most formidable vessel of the Federal armada quickly responded. Fort Sumter took up the tale, and poured a broadside into the assailing squadron, and she was followed in turn by Fort Beauregard and Battery Been, on Sullivan's Island, and Fort Wagner and Cummins' Point Battery on Morris Island. In a few minutes the battle became general and the cannonading terrific. The iron clads had entered the outer circle of fire, and from every fort and battery by which the outer harbor is girded they were assailed with great ardor and coolness. The conduct of the enemy was equally spirited, and his fire deliberate and well directed. The principal attack was directed against Sumter, though all the forts and batteries came in for a share of the enemy's attention. But one shot, so far as I could see, passed over Sumter. The Ironsides threw monster shells, which burst over and around the fort with great precision, and the wonder is that the loss of life was so little.

The Keokuk led the attack, and took the post of danger and of honor. And dearly did she pay for the distinction, as will be seen in the sequel. About forty-five minutes after the engagement commenced, a shot from Fort Wagner took effect in the stern of the Ironsides. It is believed she was also penetrated in the side, as steam could be distinctly seen issuing from her side next to the city. She soon withdrew out of range of our guns, and for the remainder of the time was a silent spectator of the conflict. This was a great triumph, as she was manifestly looked to, to test the strength of Fort Sumter. About five o'clock the Keokuk, also, withdrew, evidently badly injured. The others followed soon and by half-past five the entire fleet had retired, and when last seen was rounding Morris Island to the southward.

The practice of our gunners, after they got the range, was excellent. The enemy's vessels, (which were sunk by pumping in water until the decks were nearly level with the water,) were frequently struck, and nearly all their smoke stacks were perforated. This too, notwithstanding they kept shifting their positions. Occasionally they would steam up within 1,000 yards of Sumter, but for the greater part of the time they maintained the fight at a distance of 1,500 to 2,000 yards.—Late in the evening the Ironsides and three monitors were seen moving off slowly around Morris Island, as if they might be going to Port Royal for repairs.

The casualties on our side were slight, considering the nature of the conflict and the monster projectiles used by the enemy. In Fort Sumter, a drummer boy and five men were wounded, two of the men and the boy seriously. One 10-inch Columbiad was dismounted, and one 8-inch bursted. The former will be remounted to-night. The Fort was struck 34 times,

and the flag had a hole shot through it. No casualties occurred on Sullivan's Island, except the shooting away of the flag-staff and the accidental fall of a man who was trying to replace it, and from which he died soon afterwards. On Morris Island (at Fort Wagner,) six men were wounded by the accidental explosion of an ammunition chest, two of whom have since died. Two others are badly injured and will probably die before morning.

Gen. Ripley, said to be one of the best artillery officers in the world, was in command of all the harbor defences, and is entitled to all the honors of the occasion. Col. Butler was in command of Fort Moultrie, Col. Rhett of Fort Sumter, Lieut. Col. Simpkins of Battery Bee, Capt. Sitgraves of Fort Beauregard, Major Huger of Fort Wagner, and Lieut. Lesense, with a detachment from Sumter, of the Battery on Cummings Point—all under the superior direction of Gen. Ripley, and all of whom conducted themselves with great gallantry.

The conflict was witnessed by thousands of spectators from the Battery promenade and the house tops. Among the vast throng there assembled I did not encounter one who expressed any doubt as to the result. It was a magnificent spectacle. The white puffs of smoke issuing from the port holes of their ironclads with a tongue of fire in the centre, the solemn watch kept up by these huge monsters as they wheeled past the forts, the fantastic festoons of smoke that garlanded the heads of the forts and slowly floated off to the north, the bursting of 15 inch shells in mid-air and the deep booming the titanic guns engaged in the conflict, the appearance of the Confederate rams Chicora and Palmetto State steaming energetically up and down their chosen fighting position, the silent city, and the breathless multitude who crowded its housetops and promenade, made up a spectacle at once grand and imposing.

But it is long after midnight, and I must cease.

P.W.A.

AN ANONYMOUS REPORT: ACCOUNT OF UNSUCCESSFUL UNION ATTACK ON BATTERY WAGNER, MORRIS' ISLAND

The attack on Battery Wagner was just another skirmish on an island in the Charleston Harbor, but it is one that lives on in modern memory, thanks to the movie Glory. *As* Glory *depicted, this was a battle where black Union troops played an important combat role. While the Union attack was unsuccessful, it was important because of the use of black soldiers, a fact not mentioned in the* Savannah Republican's *story.*

Savannah Republican, 12 July 1863

FROM CHARLESTON
ATTACK ON BATTERY WAGNER, MORRIS' ISLAND

Saturday morning, about daylight, the 7th Connecticut Volunteers and the 76th Pennsylvania Volunteers, under the command of Brig. Gen. Strong, attempted to carry by storm Battery Wagner, on Morris' Island, near Charleston, S.C. The enemy were met by the 18th Battalion Georgia Volunteers, Major Wm. S. Bassinger; 12th Battalion Georgia Volunteers, Lieut. Col. Capers; a battalion of the 1st Volunteer Regiment of Georgia, Col. Chars. H. Olmstead; and several companies of South Carolina Regulars. The battle raged furiously for about four hours, the enemy being quickly repulsed in every advance.

An official despatch states that the enemy's loss in killed was 95; the beach was strewn with their dead. One hundred and thirty prisoners were taken. These advanced within a short distance of our breastworks, and knowing that retreat was impossible, a large number lay flat on their faces before the works during the fight, and when it was over the precious scoundrels drew from their pockets white flags and surrendered.

Five Yankee officers were captured and five killed.

On the third or forth round of the enemy, Capt. Claus Werner, of the German Volunteers, 1st Volunteer Regiment of Georgia, was instantly killed by a minnie ball taking effect on the left breast and passing through the body.

In the 18th Battalion Georgia Volunteers, Major W. S. Bassinger, the following are the casualties: Killed—Edward Postwell, in the 19th year of his age, a native of Savannah; Julian Alexander Santina, in the 19th year of his age, a native of Savannah; B. Mulloy and James Bryan. Wounded—Lieut. Frederick Tupper, minnie ball passing across the breast; Jessee Osmond, in the wrist; Bernard Maguire, in shoulder. All of the 18th Battalion Georgia Volunteers who were killed in the action were shot in the head.

The body of Capt. Werner, accompanied by Mr. M. Meyer, of Charleston, Capt. D. Werner, brother of deceased, and Mr. A. Seydel, of the German Volunteers, reached this city yesterday morning for interment.

We are permitted by a friend to make the following extract from a letter received by him dated Charleston July 11:

"The enemy made their lodgment on the Southern portion of Morris' Island. Our troops suffered severely yesterday, over 300 casualties occurring. We have to regret the loss of Capt. Cheves of the Engineers and Capt. Haskell. Fort Wagner is now our Southern base of operations on Morris' Island. It is situated about the middle of that island, and where it is so narrow that it is more the character of an isthmus. This point the enemy endeavored to carry at daybreak this morning, with a force of about 2,000 men under Brig. Gen. Strong. Our men allowed them to approach very close and then poured destructive volleys into them. The repulse was highly successful. Ninety five dead bodies at the close of the fight strewed the ground in the vicinity of the intrenchments. One hundred and thirty-five prisoners and many wounded were brought into the city. Gen. Ripley estimates the loss of the enemy at five hundred put *hors du combat*. Four monitors have been pegging away at Fort Wagner, but without doing much damage, Fort Wagner constantly replying to them. From the fact of one monitor having retired this afternoon, it is believed she must have been damaged."

FORT WAGNER, MORRIS' ISLAND
July 11, 1863

MR. EDITOR:—We were attacked this morning at daylight by a brigade of the enemy, which was repulsed with the loss of between fifty and two hundred killed and wounded, and about one hundred prisoners.

Our own loss is very slight. In the 1st Regiment, Capt. Werner, of Co. I, was killed and Private Hancock slightly wounded in the hand. The Guards (18th Battalion) have lost five killed and three wounded. Major Bassenger will send list. The 12th Battalion lost one killed and two wounded.

CHARLES H. OLMSTEAD.
Col. 1St Vol. Reg't Ga.

OFFICIAL DESPATCH

CHARLESTON, July 11, 9:45 a.m.—The enemy attacked, in force, Battery Wagner on Morris' Island at daylight this morning but was quickly repulsed with 95 killed, many wounded and 130 prisoners. Only 5 men killed on our side.

All quiet on James Island.

JAMES R. SNEED: ACCOUNT OF RECENT FIGHTING IN CHARLESTON HARBOR

Once the spring campaign began in Virginia, Alexander returned to his usual post. The Republican *editor, James R. Sneed, went to Charleston, reporting on the siege of the harbor. Sneed cast the fighting as having mixed results for the Confederates. He noted that the Union army had achieved a foothold on Morris Island with the capture of the lower battery, but he cast the previous day's fighting at Battery Wagner as a Southern victory with 400 enemy soldiers killed and an estimated 1,000 wounded.*

Savannah Republican, 13 July 1863

EDITORIAL CORRESPONDENCE

CHARLESTON, Sunday Night,
July 12th, 1863

I have but a few minutes to write, but will devote them to the readers of the Republican, as all eyes are now anxiously turned to this city and all hearts yearning for its safety.

The siege of Charleston has regularly begun. The enemy hope to take it by gradual approaches, and they have at least gained encouragement from their first success—the capture of the lower battery on Morris' Island, thus giving them a foothold, and enabling them to set out hopefully on their tedious work. This disaster is attributable to bad engineering, for which somebody should be held responsible. The lower battery was a shackling affair, and our men left it only when the carriages of their guns had been shattered to pieces.

The battle yesterday morning claims a place among the bloodiest and most destructive of the war, at least so far as the enemy are concerned. Our loss was trifling—only one or two killed and some half-dozen wounded. The first account gave no adequate idea of the slaughter of the Yankees, it having been on evidences immediately in front of the battery. A subsequent reconnaissance exposed over four hundred dead bodies, which were buried by our men. To this add the usual proportion of wounded—five to one—and the casualties become awful. That proportion in this case, however, is too large. The fight was at close quarters, and it is believed that a majority of those who were struck were killed. An officer of high rank gave me to-day his opinion that at least one thousand of the enemy were put hors du combat in the action. In addition to the killed on the field, the surgeon of the hospital where their wounded are now laying informs me that eight died last night, and in all probability as many more will pass to their long account before morning.

Willing to do justice to a brave foe, it may be added that a more daring and gallant assault has not been made on either side since the commencement of the war. The enemy numbered fifteen hundred, according to the best authority at hand. They landed on the lower end of the island, and double quicked it up to the very mouths of our guns, coming in along our pickets, though not surprising the garrison. The advancing column got within forty yards of Battery Wagner before a gun was fired. Gen. Stromm (who commanded the assailants, and was, by the way, Beast Butler's Adjutant at New Orleans,) then cried out in a voice distinctly heard at the fort: "Now's your time boys, go in and take them," and in they went sure enough, some twenty five of them having actually scaled our works and got inside, where they were either killed or captured. The murderous fire poured into them by our artillery and infantry literally mowed down their ranks, but on they pressed until success became hopeless and the dead were piled up under their feet, when they retired.

The whole of to-day, until sundown, has been spent in a continuous artillery duel between the ships and Battery Wagner. There were three monitors, the Atlanta among them (her maiden effort on the Yankee side) and three or four heavy mortar boats. The signal corps report no casualties on our side. From some cause unknown to me, a great battle is expected to-morrow.

A supply boat that was lying on the west side of Morris' Island had a shot put through her belly, and was otherwise injured.

Lieutenant Tupper, whom I called to see this afternoon, is severely wounded, a ball having struck him in the breast, breaking two ribs and passing out at the shoulder. He is not quite easy, and doing the best possible in the hands of a good physician, and the kindest of friends. The other wounded are doing well, most of their injuries being slight.

J.R.S.

Vicksburg

While Grant's campaign to capture Vicksburg is generally dated from May 1863, the Union general had had his eye on the important Mississippi port since the previous fall. On 13 November 1862, Grant started his campaign for Vicksburg by moving south of Grand Junction, Tennessee. Grant sent Major General William T. Sherman with 40,000 men, supported by Rear Admiral David D. Porter, in an amphibious assault on Vicksburg. Raids by the Confederate cavalry under Nathan Bedford Forrest menaced Grant's advance, and an attack on the Union supply depot at Holly Springs, Mississippi, forcing Grant to back off from his objective of capturing Vicksburg.

Meanwhile, Sherman and Porter continued with their raid on Vicksburg. Sherman attempted an assault on Chickasaw Bluffs north of Vicksburg, but after a three-day fight against nearly 14,000 of Pemberton's veteran soldiers, the Union troops were forced to withdraw. Confederates retained control of the Mississippi from Vicksburg to Baton Rouge, but Grant was determined to change that, even if he had failed on his first try.

The Confederates taught Grant a valuable lesson with their attack on Holly Springs. An overland operation supported by a long communications line was impractical. Through the winter and early spring of 1863, Grant probed Vicksburg's defenses to learn more about the best approach for capturing the city and to give the rainy season time to pass.

Naval forces worked closely with Grant's operations to reconnoiter the city. Admiral Porter assigned the *Queen of the West* and the *Indianola* to play cat and mouse with the Vicksburg batteries. The two boats were to make daring runs past the batteries, and they were also to disrupt Confederate river traffic between Vicksburg and Port Hudson. While they accomplished their objectives for awhile, the Confederates captured the *Queen of the West* and destroyed the *Indianola*. From the South, Admiral Farragut fought his way up the Mississippi, though only two of his vessels, his flagship and one other, managed to get past Confederate defenses.

While Grant was slowly tightening his grip on the city, Pemberton was busily trying to figure out what he should do. His situation was made worse by two things. First, he was essentially without intelligence-gathering capabilities. His commanding general, Joseph E. Johnston, had ordered most of his cavalry away to join the Army of Tennessee, and so Pemberton was essentially blind regarding Grant's movements. Pemberton's second problem was that he was receiving contradictory orders from his superiors. On the one hand, President Davis was telling Pemberton to hang on to Vicksburg at all costs. Johnston, who was by far more competent to make intelligent military decisions than his commander-in-chief, ordered Pemberton not to get his army trapped in Vicksburg. Pemberton chose to follow Davis's orders.

Through April, the two generals maneuvered, planned, and positioned their armies. Pemberton's were strung out along the east bank of the Mississippi for about 50 miles. Grant's men were on the west bank. Grant's army marched to Hard Times, Louisiana, south of Vicksburg and waited for Porter. At the same time, Porter's gunboats and transports had begun a series of daring night actions to get past the batteries at Vicksburg and join up with the remainder of Grant's force at Hard Times. On 30 April, Porter ferried Grant's army from Hard Times south to Bruinsburg and the east bank of the Mississippi. On 1 May, Grant's army rebuffed a small Confederate force that tried to stop the Union army's inland advance in the Battle of Port Gibson.

Grant turned to arranging his forces for their assault on Vicksburg. He divided his 41,000 men into three columns. He gave Major General John McClernand orders to advance to the left, along the river. Sherman was the take the center, and his third subcommander, Major General James B. McPherson, would move forward on the right.

On 12 May, Grant met the first Confederate resistance near Raymond, about 14 miles southwest of Jackson. Confederate Brigadier General John Gregg's 5,000 men confronted McPherson's advance guard. Gregg's men held off McPherson's superior force for six hours before being forced to retreat. This gave Grant the opportunity to separate the two Confederate forces near Jackson. He sent McPherson to destroy the railroad at Clinton, and he sent Sherman through Raymond toward Jackson. McClernand was to support the other two corps and be ready to defend an attack by Pemberton from the west. The Union forces were successful at cutting both the rail and telegraph lines, thereby slowing Confederate communications.

On 13 May, Johnston arrived in Jackson, planning to meet up with Pemberton's force and take on Grant head first, but that would not happen. With Grant's force between Vicksburg and Jackson, the plan was impossible. That same day, however, Pemberton advanced out of Vicksburg toward Jackson. He was trying to find Grant's lines of communications, but they had been abandoned. Johnston saw a chance, with Pemberton's army in the field, to strike at Grant's divided forces, and he sent three couriers—three to ensure that the message got through—to order Pemberton to attack the federal column near Clinton. Grant had sent Sherman to occupy Jackson, Mississippi's capital, after Johnston abandoned it. The remainder of Grant's force turned to take on Pemberton's 22,000 men east of the Big Black River.

Johnston's new plan to use his force in combination with Pemberton's did not work for two reasons. First, Pemberton and his subordinates had decided not to follow Johnston's orders to consolidate the two armies against Grant. Second, Johnston was the victim of treachery. The already desperate Confederate situation was made worse when one of the couriers Johnston had sent to Pemberton turned out to be a secret Northern sympathizer and carried the message to Grant. With the Confederate plans laid out in front of him, Grant immediately moved against Pemberton.

Pemberton showed great ineptitude in the battle that began on 16 May. The two forces met at Champion's Hill, and rather than choosing to defend the high bluffs that bordered the west side of the river crossing, Pemberton chose to make his stand on level ground east of the river. It may have been that Pemberton believed he could stop Grant if the Union army attacked his main positions from the level ground, but that is not what Grant did. The night before, Sherman's men had crossed the river on pontoon bridges and positioned themselves to the north of Pemberton. At dawn, the federals advanced and outflanked Pemberton. When the Confederate lines collapsed, their general had no choice but to order a general retreat back to Vicksburg.

In 19 days, Grant had marched some 200 miles while living off the land. He had defeated numerically superior detachments of the enemy in five different engagements and several skirmishes, and he had inflicted 8,000 casualties on the Confederates compared with his own 4,400. And now he had his opponent locked up tight in a fortified city with few escape routes.

Again, Johnston ordered Pemberton to consolidate forces with his. Again Pemberton met with his subordinates, and again, they all agreed to disobey their commander's order. They and their 30,000 men would make a stand at Vicksburg, which Pemberton considered to be the most important place in the Confederacy at that moment. The terrain around the city did favor its defenders. The Confederates had more than 100 artillery guns in place around the city. There was, perhaps, a chance Pemberton and his men could hold on to the city, yet the importance of Vicksburg as a stronghold had been diminished considerably by Porter's continued flaunting of his ability to get past the city's river defenses. With the Union navy both to the north and south of Vicksburg, steamboats would no longer be bringing cargo to the city's railhead. The last link to the trans-Mississippi had been immobilized.

Grant was uneasy with the idea of an extended siege of the city, and so he tried twice to take it in direct assaults on 19 and 22 May. Pemberton's men repulsed both attempts and inflicted 3,000 casualties that day. Given no choice but to lay siege to the city, Grant set his engineers to digging trenches and preparing other defenses. Foreshadowing the next year's Battle of the Crater, Grant's men also dug trenches under Confederate positions and filled them with black powder so as to blow gaps in Southern defenses. Porter's gunboats and Grant's army, though short on artillery pieces, shelled the city relentlessly from middle May until its capitulation on 4 July. Civilians and defenders alike moved into the caves of the high bluffs along the river to escape the bombardment. Newspapers continued to print through the siege, but they were forced to use wallpaper or brown wrapping paper. Food supplies ran low, and citizens and soldiers alike were reduced to eating mules and rats.

Finally, on 3 July, after a forty-six-day siege, Pemberton realized that his men could stand no more. At 10:00 A.M., he arranged to meet with Grant. To Pemberton's request for terms, Grant demanded unconditional surrender, but Pemberton outfoxed the Union general. He lied. He told Grant he would not surrender unconditionally; he said the city had enough food to hold out indefinitely. The terms agreed to allowed Pemberton's men to be paroled until they could be exchanged for Union prisoners of war. On Independence Day, Pemberton surrendered. Grant's men celebrated the national holiday in high style. The army marched into the city with its band playing and its flags flying. On the river, the gunboats fired their guns in jubilation. Citizens accepted food from the occupying Union army, but Independence Day would not be celebrated again in Vicksburg until the mid-twentieth century.

Grant had solidified his reputation as a military leader and laid the foundation for his rapid advance to the rank of lieutenant general and commander of all Union armies. Pemberton earned the undying enmity of Southerners everywhere.

AN ANONYMOUS REPORT: MILITARY SITUATION AT VICKSBURG

It all came down to numbers and supplies. Once Johnston finished building his army, he managed to have a force of more than 30,000 men, considerably larger than the Confederate officer who wrote the following letter estimated, yet much smaller than Grant's force. Then there was the matter of supplies. Grant had unharrassed, well-protected supply and communications lines. Johnston's was vunerable. It was long and getting longer with each move closer to Vicksburg. The writer, who may have been the paper's assistant editor Henry Cleveland, tried hard to find an optimistic way to tell his readers back home, but clearly he was on the edge of despair.

Augusta Constitutionalist, 8 July 1863 (Augusta, Ga.)

OUR ARMY CORRESPONDENCE

From Mississippi

The Siege of Vicksburg—Condition of the Opposing Armies—Strength of Grant's Position—Johnston's Resources for Dislodging him—Deductions

From a letter to this paper, written by an intelligent correspondent—an officer in Gen. Johnston's army we make the following extract, which will be found deeply interesting:

ED. CONSTI.

I wish I had some good news to give you. I have not. People away from here expect a great deal, and I am satisfied a great deal too much from Gen. Johnston. There is no room for generalship in this case. Physical obstructions, such as Johnston will have to overcome, will quell and oppress the genius of any man. Grant has entrenched himself around Vicksburg as strongly as Pemberton has in it. The hills are in many places nearly perpendicular, with but little room on their tops, and high enough to permit a very small party to prevent the ascent of as many men as can be got to them. This almost interminable succession of steep hills and deep valleys for miles and miles around Grant's camp has been fortified with all the skill that the devilish ingenuity of these rascals could secure. The hills are crowned with heavy guns, and every gorge is ready to belch forth destruction. He has devastated the country all around him, for 20 to 80 miles, leaving nothing that could contribute to the support of an army advancing on him, and has obstructed all the roads leading towards him in every possible way for many miles. You will perceive that it would be no easy job for Johnston to get to him. Besides, Grant has from 70 to 80,000 men, Johnston not half so many. (I am afraid to commit to paper the strength of this army.) Grant's communications are open, his facilities for receiving stores, supplies and reinforcements are unbounded, while Johnston has to work hard to buy every mouthful his army eats, and then is obliged to hunt it many miles—sometimes 40 or 50, and the farther he goes towards Vicksburg, the farther he must wagon his supplies.

Now with these facts before you, work out the problem. If Grant, with all the men and all the means he wants or asks for can't take Pemberton in Vicksburg, with 18 or 15,000 men, how is Johnston, with only all the men he can get, to destroy or subdue Grant in a fortified camp equally strong, with 80,000 men to defend it. This is the proposition; work it out; put "QE.D.", at the end and send it to me, for I would like mightly to see it.

In all this I do not undervalue nor underrate the elements at Gen. Johnston's command, nor his great ability. His army, (I will state *entre nous*) not as high as 80,000 fighting men, is composed of the very best fighting stock on the continent, and if Johnston could only get Grant into the field would

maul a much larger force "till they should think the very devil himself had come from hell." They are anxious to fight, and have every confidence in the General and will do what men can do—yet this is not enough to overcome the immense disadvantages under which he labors.

I do not write this to discourage you, for I know no more of Gen. Johnston's plans than you do, perhaps not so much. I hope that he will be let alone, however, and not driven by taunts and innuendoes, and abuse to sacrifice an army which is confessedly the only barrier that at present protects, in any considerable degree, the States of Mississippi, Alabama and Georgia.

AN ANONYMOUS REPORT: EDITORIAL——WHO IS RESPONSIBLE FOR FALL OF VICKSBURG?

Once the truth began to come out about the actual state of affairs in Vicksburg, journalists began asking questions about the apparent deception that had convinced Confederates that the key city on the Mississippi River could hold out. The Savannah Republican *lashed out with a vitriolic editorial that demanded in an untitled commentary that whomever was responsible be found and, the implication was, punished.*

Savannah Republican, 9 July 1863

VICKSBURG.—There is a heavy weight of responsibility resting on somebody's shoulders for the regular and systematic lying that has been put upon the public regarding the ability of this place to hold out. The western Press, in the very vicinity of the unfortunate city, has been quite as badly imposed on as anybody else. We have forty times read reports, coming from Pemberton himself, that supplies were abundant, and the garrison could "hold out indefinitely." About ten days ago the public was assured, on unquestionable authority, that Kirby Smith had driven 800 beeves across the Mississippi into Vicksburg.

This deception was kept up until the very eve of the surrender on account of starvation. The place fell on the 5th, and just think of such an assurance as the following appearing in the Jackson Mississippian of the 3d:

SUPPLIES FOR VICKSBURG.—Our people need have

no apprehension about Vicksburg's being starved out, as we are informed upon very good authority, that there is on hand an abundant supply—and long before it is exhausted our army outside will open a way for the transmission of stores. We might mention the extent of our provisions there, but for prudential reasons refrain. This much we may say, however: If Vicksburg does not fall until her heroic garrison is "starved out," it will be many a long sultry month before the Yankee thieves will realize their dreams of capture.

Within forty eight hours after this assurance was printed, Vicksburg was in the hands of the enemy and the Mississippian "packing up to leave."

Verily the road to truth is difficult in the West. Bad news is about the only true thing we have heard from them since the commencement of the war.

Tullahouma, Chickamauga, and Chattanooga Campaigns

For six months after the Battle of Murfreesboro, Bragg's army sat at Tullahouma, Tennessee. They were a hard six months for Bragg's men. They stayed busy building defensive lines, but they had become demoralized by inactivity, hunger, and infighting among their superiors. Through most of that spring, Bragg's army had never had more than a three-day's supply of rations and had been forced to scavenge the countryside to supplement the shipments they received from Atlanta. Even more devastating to morale, though, was the infighting among the Army of Tennessee's officers. Bragg's subordinates had lost confidence in the general's ability to lead the army, and they had not merely gossiped and griped among themselves. Their public grumbling became so pronounced that at the end of January President Davis sent Joseph Johnston to Tullahouma to try to resolve the situation.

Rosecrans seemingly was content to leave Bragg be through that spring, for he made no move to menace the Confederate position, even though the two armies were no more than 30 miles apart. By June the Union's supreme commander, Henry Halleck, was tired of waiting, and he threatened to fire Rosecrans if he did not do something. Rosecrans responded with the well-planned, well-conducted maneuver he had spent the last six months preparing. With an army twice the size of Bragg's and sound intelligence as to the Army of Tennessee's location, Rosecrans had little difficulty forcing Bragg to retreat to Chattanooga just two days before Pemberton surrendered Vicksburg and Lee began his "strategic withdrawal" from Gettysburg.

Rosecrans's and Bragg's armies spent a month regrouping before beginning the sly cat-and-mouse game that would culminate in Bragg's greatest victory at Chickamauga, Georgia, in mid-September. Bragg spent most of that month rebuilding his force, and by the time Rosecrans attacked on 16 August, Bragg's Army of Tennessee was as ready as it was going to be. The offensive that began that day would squeeze Bragg out of Chattanooga and into north Georgia. Through early September, the two armies fought skirmishes, but finally, on 18 September, they faced one another across West Chickamauga Creek for a major battle that would give Bragg an important victory.

On the night of 18 September, Brag received reinforcements in the form of Longstreet's Virginia veterans. Their presence brought the Army of Tennessee to a total force of 70,000. Bragg spent the night reorganizing his army into two wings and deployed them for battle. Due to a miscommunication, though, the attack did not begin when it was supposed to. Frustrated, Bragg ordered all his divisions into action, and a day of piecemeal attacks began. That night, the federals withdrew back into Chattanooga, and Bragg did not pursue. Losses in the Battle of Chickamauga were huge, each side losing more than a quarter of the men with which it stared the fight. Federal casualties were 1,657 killed, 9,756 wounded, and 4,757 missing. The Confederates lost 2,312 killed, 14,674 wounded, and 1,486 missing. Bragg had routed Rosecrans, and he followed that success up by laying siege to Chattanooga.

In the midst of the siege, on 17 October, General Ulysses S. Grant was made overall Union commander in the West. Grant immediately started out for Chattanooga, and one of his first actions along the way was to replace Rosecrans with Thomas as commander of the Army of the Cumberland. Grant arrived at Chattanooga by mule train on 23 October and immediately set about reviving the flagging morale of the troops there. On 27 October, he took a portion of Thomas's army on pontoon boats and slipped past Confederate positions on Lookout Mountain to open a gap in the line that blockaded the city. Hooker's two corps marched through the line with supplies to relieve the city. Meanwhile, Grant sent word to the newly appointed commander of the Army of the Tennessee, William T. Sherman, to bring his men to Chattanooga. A fight was brewing.

Grant had resolved the Union leadership crisis in Chattanooga when he fired Rosecrans, but the Confederate problem remained. Bickering and infighting still plagued Bragg's Army of Tennessee. Two of Bragg's subcommanders, Nathan Bedford Forrest and James Longstreet, had been allowed to leave his command after they openly and publicly questioned his abilities. The situation among the army's high command was so bad that in October Jefferson Davis himself traveled to the Chattanooga area to try to resolve the problem. The president made the incredible decision to leave Bragg in charge but reshuffled the officer corps and told the army's officers they were responsible for getting along with Bragg.

By 15 November, the Union and Confederate armies at Chattanooga were poised for a major battle. Grant was ready to fight his way out of Bragg's siege, and Bragg was so confident in his positions on the mountaintops surrounding Chattanooga that even as a battle was brewing he sent Longstreet to lay siege to Knoxville. Bragg's plan was to reclaim all of eastern Tennessee for the Confederacy, but it did not quite work out that way because of events in Chattanooga.

Grant's plan to relieve Chattanooga called for a two-prong attack on Confederate forces entrenched along Missionary Ridge and Lookout Mountain. To keep Bragg from reinforcing his flanks, Grant planned an assault by Thomas on a hill between Chattanooga and Missionary Ridge and then a feint toward the Confederate entrenchments at the impregnable center of the ridge. Sherman moved up from the north side of the ridge. Hooker was to take two corps and set out for Lookout Mountain. On 24 November, Hooker fought and won what came to be called the "battle above the clouds" because of the low cloud ceiling that day. Sherman, on the other hand, had terrible luck in the campaign. Not only did inaccurate intelligence result in his men attacking the wrong hill; but he missed the boat that was supposed to carry him to a conference with Grant. Confederate troops under Irishman Patrick Cleburne put up stiff resistance and repulsed Sherman. The Union commander was forced to go on the defensive when he was supposed to be leading the offensive.

On 25 November, Grant put Thomas and Sherman into action. Thomas was to move up to the rifle pits at the base of Missionary Ridge, or if that did not work, move to the left and aid Sherman's advance. Sherman's advance was no more successful that day than it had been the day before, but the fighting was fierce enough that Bragg had to shift reserves from the center on Missionary Ridge to the fighting going on to the north. Meanwhile, Grant and Thomas were watching Thomas's men cautiously move forward toward the rifle pits at the base of Missionary Ridge and anxiously awaiting Hooker's return from Lookout Mountain to aid in the assault on the ridge.

Meanwhile, the attack on Missionary Ridge was taking on a life of its own. Word did not spread to all Thomas's lieutenants that the troops were supposed to stop at the base of the ridge. The fighting at the base of the mountain was so hellish that some of the Union troops attacked up the steep ridge just to get away from the carnage. Others followed, and as the blue line of troops dashed up the ridge, the gray one broke and fled. While Grant was muttering that there would be hell to pay if the attack ended in ruin, Bragg was watching in disbelief as his troops broke and ran. Cleburne's troops had to fight a rear guard defense to keep the entire Confederate army from being destroyed in its retreat to Dalton, Georgia. With the Confederates forced back into north Georgia, it was time for Grant to send aid to Burnside in Knoxville. By 6 December, the Confederates had been completely swept out of Tennessee. Casualties in the Chattanooga fighting totaled just over 12,000 for the two sides. The Union lost 349 killed, 4,722 wounded, and 349 missing. The Confederates lost 361 killed, 2,160 wounded, and 4,146 missing.

ISHAM G. HARRIS AND OTHERS: ACCOUNT OF BATTLE OF CHICKAMAUGA

Telegraphic reports like this one filed by Tennessee Gov. Isham G. Harris, of the Confederate victory at Chickamauga were received and read with great rejoicing in the Confederacy. Finally, after the crushing military defeats suffered earlier in the year, there was good news from the Southern military. In the first day of fighting at the Battle of Chickamauga, Bragg had routed the enemy, driven them from the field. But the battle was not yet decisive; there was more fighting to be done. The author of several of these reports was Isham G. Harris, Confederate governor of Tennessee. With virtually his entire state in Union hands, Harris spent most of the war with the Army of Tennessee.

Memphis Appeal, 22 September 1863

TELEGRAPHIC
BATTLE OF CHICKAMAUGA

**The Enemy Driven from
His Positions
Casualties among General Officers**

Special to the Memphis Appeal.]

BATTLEFIELD OF CHICKAMAUGA., Sunday, 8 P.M., September 20—After two days' hard fighting we have succeeded in driving the enemy from his positions. The engagement is not yet decisive.

The casualties are heavy on both sides, but those of the enemy are evidently much larger than ours.

Gen. Preston Smith was killed last night, about half past seven o'clock, when gallantly leading his brigade, within a few yards of the enemy's lines. Gen. Deshler was also killed.

Gens. John C. Brown, Hood, Gregg, Dan. Adams and Helm, are wounded.

The Federal General Little was killed.

We have captured about 2500 prisoners, and about twenty-five or thirty pieces of artillery.

Troops never fought better than ours. They are in high spirits, and ready to meet the enemy again tomorrow.

ISHAM G. HARRIS.

LATER—OUR VICTORY COMPLETE!
THE ENEMY ABANDONS HIS
KILLED AND WOUNDED!
FIVE THOUSAND PRISONERS AND
FIFTY-SIX CANNON CAPTURED!

Special to the Memphis Appeal.]

CHICKAMAUGA BATTLE FIELD, September 21, 11 A.M.—The enemy retired from our front under cover of last night, leaving his killed and wounded on the field.

Our victory is complete.

We have captured a large number of small arms. Thirty-six pieces of artillery have already been brought in, and twenty additional pieces are reported. About five thousand prisoners are reported captured.

Our army is in fine spirits and eager for a vigorous pursuit.

I have no additional particulars to report. We met the whole force of Rosecrans' army.

ISHAM G. HARRIS.

FROM THE EXTREME FRONT
THE ENEMY IN FULL RETREAT—
OUR CAVALRY IN
HOT PURSUIT

Special to the Memphis Appeal.]

NEAR CHATTANOOGA, Sept. 21, via RINGGOLD. Our victory is complete. The enemy has been routed and is now in full retreat.

Gen. Forrest is now attacking their rear with great vigor, and our forces are pressing on.

The loss is not as large as at either Shiloh or Murfreesboro.

Gens. Preston Smith and Helm were killed, and Gens. Brown and Adams wounded.

Capt. Donelson, Major Richmond, Lieut. Webber, and Capt. McConica were killed. Major Davis is wounded.

M. C. GALLAWAY.

Another Report—From Our Own
Correspondent

Special to the Memphis Appeal.]

DALTON, Sept. 21—No cannonading is heard in front this morning.

Gen. Preston Smith, of Memphis, and Capt. Donelson, (son of A. J. Donelson) and Capt. King, of his staff, were killed yesterday.

The enemy fell back along his entire line, and his right was within eight miles of Chattanooga yesterday.

Our loss is estimated at about four thousand killed, wounded and missing. The enemy's loss is much heavier.

We have taken three thousand prisoners, thirty-five pieces of artillery yesterday, and twelve pieces on Saturday.

Gen. Hood lost a leg, which was amputated above the knee yesterday.

It is thought Rosecrans has crossed the river.

VERITAS.

CPA REPORTERS: REPORTS FROM CHICKAMAUGA BATTLEFIELD

The Confederate Press Association reporters provided an important service for newspapers that did not have the resources to field war correspondents or those that wanted additional stories to flesh out their coverage. This story, datelined Atlanta, was most likely pulled together at CPA headquarters in that city by the press service's superintendent, John S. Thrasher.

Memphis Appeal, 22 September 1863

FURTHER FROM THE
BATTLE-FIELD
PRESS ASSOCIATION REPORTS

ATLANTA, September 22—Advices from the battle-field come in scantily, but sufficient has been received to show that a great success has been achieved in the three days' fighting. The main, if not the entire force of Rosecrans was engaged, and not only driven back from all his positions, but is greatly demoralized and forced to destroy large quantities of stores and baggage. Their resistance is stubborn, but the fight still goes on. Our troops are flushed with victory and eager in the fray, and there is every confidence that the foe will be driven from his present stand in Mission ridge, about six or eight miles from Chattanooga.

The fight yesterday was a most spirited one. Longstreet and Hill attacked the enemy's center at daylight and, after a desperate resistance, the enemy were driven from their positions with a loss of from four to six thousand prisoners and forty two pieces of artillery.

Our latest accounts from the field are yesterday at noon, when the enemy had made a stand at Mission ridge, and the battle would probably be continued.

Our loss in general officers is very great. Brigadier Gen. Helm, of Kentucky, was killed while leading a charge. Gen. Hood's wound is reported to be a mortal one. Brigadier-Generals Adams and John C. Brown are severely wounded. Major Richmond, of Gen. Polk's staff, was killed.

The battle began about three miles west of the east Chickamauga. The enemy was soon driven across Peavine creek, and formed his main line of battle nearly at right angles with that creek and across the road from Chattanooga, whence Rosecrans received his supplies. On this line the enemy had two lines of temporary defenses formed of felled timber, but was gallantly driven from them by our troops, and

it is still asserted that we hold the road to Chattanooga. The Yankees have been driven in all, as we are led to believe from the best accounts we can obtain, about twelve miles to his present position on Mission ridge. He has been defeated on ground of his own choosing, and we are credibly informed that Rosecrans was there with the main force of his army.

No reliable accounts of the extent of our losses or of the injury inflicted on the enemy, can yet be obtained. But few of the wounded from Saturday's fight have reached here, and none of those of the two succeeding days.

Preparations have been made at Marietta and in this city to receive the wounded, and a relief committee, with supplies and hospital appliances, left here this morning for the front.

Every one who comes from the scene of action represents the spirit of the army to be of the most confident and exhilarating character, and it is confidently hoped that Rosecrans has met his utter defeat. The field of Sunday's fight was thickly wooded, like that of Chancellorsville, which Gen. Lee called the battle of the wilderness, and afforded no play or artillery, in consequence of which most of the wounds received by our men on that day were slight, and a very small proportion of our loss is killed. We learn that Hood's division, and the Yankees who fought them, both took to the trees during the engagement, and fought in Indian style, when Benning's brigade, which supported the Texas brigade of Hood's division, made a charge, and drove the Yankees from their skulking holes.

We learn that Generals Wafford and Waithall are unhurt, and that Gen. Benning was again in the saddle after his wound in the breast was dressed. There is also hope of Gen. Hood's recovery. Gen. Presdon died yesterday at 11 o'clock.

Rosecrans has been driven back to the vicinity of the West Chickamauga, an Indian name which means "The Stream of Death."

FELIX G. DE FONTAINE: NEWS OF UNION ACTIVITY AT CHATTANOOGA

In November 1863, the federal army that occupied Chattanooga began to move out. Its objective was to push Bragg's Confederates further away from the Tennessee River town and deeper into Georgia. This movement was necessary to secure supply lines that were threatened by Confederate proximity to the rail

lines. Felix Gregory de Fontaine, one of the South's two top war correspondents, had taken on corre-
spondence work for a second newspaper, the Memphis Appeal, *by this time. He wrote for that paper un-*
der the name Quel qu'un. *De Fontaine was better known as the* Charleston Courier's *Personne. Both*
names essentially translate from French as "Someone" or "A Person." Quel qu'un noted the initial
movement of the federal army that would, later in the month, culminate in the Battle of Lookout Moun-
tain and Bragg's retreat into Georgia.

Memphis Appeal, 2 November 1863

OUR ARMY CORRESPONDENCE

Special Correspondence of the Memphis Appeal.]
ARMY OF TENNESSEE,
Wednesday, October 28, 1863.

From various manifestations now in progress of develop-ment the enemy has at last aroused himself for another strug-gle. Yesterday we were treated to the first act of the drama.

You will remember that in a former letter I described the successful manner in which our sharpshooters on the other side of Lookout mountain, and some eight or nine miles dis-tant from Chattanooga had blocked up one of the important roads by which the Federals received their supplies. We have also been in the habit of picketing with a comparatively small force along the bank of Tennessee in that locality, principally to watch the movements of the enemy. Annoyed by this pres-ence of Confederate troops, the Federal commander on Mon-day night, by means of some fifty boats suddenly crossed the river, drove in our thin line, and obtained a foothold on this side. Gen. Law promptly advanced a regiment, when a brisk skirmish ensued which resulted in temporarily checking their movements. Subsequently the enemy threw over troops until according to the statement of prisoners, they numbered between five and six thousand or more than two brigades. Un-der these circumstances our little command was forced back, with a loss of some fifteen or twenty killed and wounded. The Federals therefore commenced to fortify and to day scouts re-port a line of intrenchments on the heights occupied. The ground along the back of the river for two or three miles is of an elevated character, which of course, gives an antagonist an admirable position for defense.

During the affair, Moccasin battery, at the base of Lookout Mountain, was busy with his "thunder tongues," and for three or four hours in the morning, the shelling was, at times, in-cessant. Several of our guns replied, and it is believed, not without effect. Much of the Yankee ammunition was ex-pended in firing at Craven's house on Lookout mountain and the road which runs across the height in front—a favorite mark of the battery; but only three or four of our men were wounded. Among these I may mention the names of Col. Oates, of the 15th Alabama, who received a painful flesh wound in the thigh; Capt. Hagood, of the 1st South Carolina, contusion in leg; and Corporal Rabe of the Palmetto sharp-shooters, South Carolina volunteers, flesh wound in leg, be-hind the knee.

The occupants of Craven's house are mostly female, and although the place has been persistently shelled since the

Federals opened fire, and from ten or fifteen projectiles have passed through the premises, the ladies have determined not to budge an inch; and you know the couplet:

> When a woman will, she will, depend on't,
> And when she won't, she won't, and that's the end on't.

In this case "she won't." Yesterday while the shelling was heaviest and our men were "skedaddling" across the line of fire as industriously as their locomotive apparatus would [*unreadable*], the ladies were coolly preparing for dinner. One of the surgeons who was in the house, says that while he was there a fragment penetrated one of the rooms. Without being in the least disconcerted, the Tennessee matron spoke up in a tone very much like that in which she would reprove a servant for breaking china plate, "Eliza go in there and see what's damaged this time."

Think of that, ye weak legged, faint hearted owners of cor-duroy and Confederate rags, who dodge like "dancing jimmies" every time you hear the shriek of a shell, and take pattern after this brave, undemoralized, impregnable, bomb proof western mother, and don't get "frightened before you're hurt."

On Monday morning about 2 o'clock "Moccasin" opened on our picket lines and some of the camps on the left. Only one man was slightly injured. Several, however, had narrow escapes from death. A captain in one of the Arkansas regi-ments, who had quietly lain in his blankets listening to the explosion of the shells, at last concluded to get up. As he left the tent a fragment entered and penetrating the knapsack on which his head had rested, tore it to pieces.

The principal commotion was caused among the negroes. Which way to retreat they didn't know, and making the best of their situation, they concealed themselves behind trees and stumps, but which made the most noise, the shells or the negroes, it was difficult to tell. At each diabolical missile that came screaming through the air, you would hear the exclama-tions issuing from between chattering teeth, "Heyar she comes; hear she comes—get out de way boys—look out all you tree tousand dollar negroes—aint she got a noisy tail," etc., etc. The next morning one of the venerable body servants of the old school, a genuine family mentor among the negroes, was asked what he thought of the demonstration. The old gen-tleman actually grew blue again as he answered—"Well, I tell you massa, I tink de debbil's in dem balls, and de ole he deb-bil what frows 'em ober head is wus'u all. If dats de way de Yankees make lub to do colored people, dis chile don't re-cognize 'em, shuah."

Speaking of negroes, I am told when Kershaw's fine brigade of South Carolinians was moving into the battle of Chickamauga, an old fellow came out from his hut, with eyes distended and hair almost erect in his fright at the sounds of battle, and raising both hands in the most imploring attitude exclaimed: "Gorry 'mity gemmen, gorry mity, what's de use oh shooten one anudder in dis way—why don't you step and argy awhile."

There was a world of good sense in the suggestion of the sable individual, but unfortunately the time to "argue" has past, and naked strength of arm alone must now decide the contest.

But I have branched widely off from my starting point. In addition to the demonstration of the enemy from the rear of Chattanooga, another column, consisting of infantry, artillery and cavalry, is now moving up the valley on the opposite side of Lookout mountain, and to effect a junction with the army at Chattanooga. It is understood that the force crossed at Bridgeport, but in what numbers it is not known. Their object can only be surmised; but unquestionably, it is a well defined attempt on the part of the Federals, to possess themselves of the railroad running between Bridgeport and Chattanooga. If successful, the movement will relieve their wagon trains, and enable them to obtain supplies with both regularity and abundance. To acquire full possession of the road, Lookout mountain is indispensable to the Yankees, but I doubt whether, rather than risk a battle to obtain this situation, they will not be satisfied with a railroad up to a point where the line of transportation by wagons to Chattanooga will be only ten or fifteen miles in length. You will recall the fact predicted in a former letter, that if the enemy made any demonstration, it would be on our left, and have for its object the possession of the railroad.

It is becoming more and more patent every day that the enemy cannot maintain their hold upon Chattanooga during the winter without an improvement in their commissariat, and this can only be had by dispensing with the long and troublesome route by which supplies are brought to their camps. Only yesterday a Federal officer under flag of truce admitted that they were short of forage, and every day our men along the lines are asked by the Yankees to sell them rations or exchange them for blankets. These facts are proof positive that the Federal army are in a critical strait. Hence the movement in question. Further evidence has been furnished me while writing this letter. A scout just in states that a small squad of Yankees went to a house in which there were only females, cocked their guns at the inmates and threatened to blow their brains out if they did not give them something to eat. Afterward they made one of the ladies stand guard at the garden while they killed the hogs on the premises, and stole everything of value they could lay their hands upon. On leaving, one of the wretches remarked that they "had been fighting for the Union, but *now they were fighting for something to eat.*"

It is not proper to refer to army movements within our lines or to the probabilities connected with this extraordinary venture of the enemy, but the public may rest assured that our generals are fully alive to the emergency, and our men in fine spirits for battle.

QUEL QU'UN.

P.S. Daylight, Thursday, 29th.—The body of the enemy seen passing down yesterday, consisted of two corps. A demonstration was made by Hood's division, under command of General Jenkins, of South Carolina, about two o'clock this morning, when an engagement resulted, which continued until near daylight. Jenkins' brigade of Carolinians, Col. Bratton commanding, was sent across Lookout creek, to be left for the purpose of getting among the wagon trains and stragglers, while Law, Robertson, and Benning were aligned on a crest of hills, partially commanding the approach to Bratton's rear, yet on a line occupied by several thousand of the enemy, about two miles above. Bratton, on moving to the left, and engaging, suddenly found himself confronted by an entire corps; but nevertheless, having a full brigade, one of the largest in the army—he promptly gave battle, and was driving the Federals steadily back. The enemy above, however, now moved from their position, in the neighborhood of Brown's ferry, which is in the rear of Chattanooga, and while their artillery was playing on Law, Robertson and Benning, passed around the front of the latter commands, others engaging at the same time, and endeavored to penetrate the gap between their left and Bratton. The movement was made by from five to seven thousand men; but Jenkins, at a glance, discovering the object, checkmated the attempt by ordering Bratton to fall back, and with the rest of the division, to recross the creek, which was done in good order.

Our losses are severe. Col. Kilpatrick, of the 1st South Carolina, a gallant officer, who fired the first shot at the first battle of Manassas, was killed.

This is all the news of the affair I can send you at this hour.

QUEL QU'UN.

SAMUEL CHESTER REID, JR., REPORTS OF FIGHTING AT LOOKOUT MOUNTAIN

The Battle of Lookout Mountain began on 24 November. The federals pushed the Confederates away from Chattanooga and Lookout Mountain, deeper into Georgia, just as planned. The following dispatch is reprinted from the Atlanta Intelligencer *and written by another famous war correspondent, Samuel*

Chester Reid, Jr., who signed his dispatches "290." The story details some of the fighting, including one of the preliminary skirmishes before the main battle began. The correspondent was right in surmising the enemy's objective was to take Lookout, and indeed he was also right about the federals being concerned about Longstreet's movement on Knoxville.

Memphis Appeal, 26 November 1863

[FROM THE ARMY EDITION]

The Very Latest from the Front

Special Correspondence Atlanta Intelligencer.]

CHICKAMAUGA, November 24, 5 P.M. —As the telegraph line is not working on Missionary ridge, I had to ride down to this point, in the rain, to send off my dispatch of this afternoon.

The demonstrations of the enemy in our front, yesterday was, on their first appearance, not considered serious. By one o'clock P.M. their first line was seen to move forward, they having two lines of reserves in the rear. Our pickets were soon driven in, and at two P.M. they attacked our right and center, drove our men from their rifle pits, when the firing became very heavy on our right. A. J. Vaughan's, Dois', [*unreadable*] and Anderson's brigade becoming warmly engaged, and severely punishing the enemy.

The enemy's batteries at the same time opened briskly. Our men fell back to their intrenchments, and the enemy succeeded in taking two cedar hills on our right center, one of which they last night fortified, placing a battery on it. As night closed in all further operations ceased. Our loss did not exceed 200 killed and wounded in the skirmish. Wm. H. Martin, Isaiah Sanders, 9th Mississippi battalion, sharpshooters; Charles Williamson, Wm. Rains, R. B. Stone, Henry Epps, Arnette Shields, 29th Tennessee; Jos. Lawrence, J. W. Lawrence, J. W. Hill, 11th Tennessee, of A. J. Vaughan's— late Preston's—brigade, were slightly wounded.

This morning the enemy opened at 8 o'clock from the Cedar hill, shelling us for about an hour, but doing no damage. They then opened upon Cheatham's forces in Lookout valley from the batteries over the river, and kept up a heavy cannonading for two hours, when at noon they made an assault with infantry, endeavoring to force our position in order to take Lookout. The musketry firing was very heavy for two hours. At 2 P.M. , the rain increasing, fire ceased. At 2 1/2 P.M. It was again renewed, the enemy also making an attack on our right, having crossed a column over the Tennessee, with a small steamer, at the mouth of the Chickamauga. The firing has continued very heavy up to this time. Our troops still hold their positions, but no result is known.

It is evident the enemy's design is to carry Lookout if possible, as well as to gain the railroad on the Chickamauga side, in order to cut our line to Cleveland. There is no doubt the enemy is aware of our movement on Knoxville, and it may be that he is trying to prevent us reinforcing Longstreet, in order to save Burnside.

No general engagement of all our forces has yet taken place, but there is no telling when it may. It is supposed, however, that the enemy is not in condition to make a general attack. Things wear a curious aspect, and it is as yet impossible to tell what may be the result.

In haste,

290.

AN ANONYMOUS REPORT: ROUT OF BRAGG'S FORCES

The Appeal *was particularly concerned about the news from the front when Bragg admitted to having been routed and forced to retire in disorder. As the newspaper understood, when a proud general like Bragg made such a statement, his army was in major trouble.*

Memphis Appeal, 26 November 1863

FROM THE FRONT

The news from the front is anything but encouraging. The mere falling back of our army to Chickamauga, would not in itself be greatly discouraging provided it had done so in tact, but that the left was forced by assault and pressure and retired in considerable disorder, is a strong admission to come from Gen. BRAGG, and betokens a greater disaster than is revealed in his official dispatch. Our losses will probably not be known until they reach us through Federal sources. Whatever they may be however,

let not the country be discouraged by this temporary reverse.

If the news from Knoxville be true, LONGSTREET has done his work nobly and effectually, and this success will compensate us for our failure in front.

In addition to the intelligence contained in our telegraphic column, we learn that night before last Tuner's station and the wagon train of Gen. M. J. WRIGHT, were burned up by a raiding party of the enemy, which crossed the river near the mouth of Chickamauga creek.

BENJAMIN F. DILL OR JOHN McCLANAHAN: CONSEQUENCES OF DEFEAT AT LOOKOUT MOUNTAIN

The Confederate defeat at Lookout Mountain was devastating. The Memphis Appeal *offered grudging admiration for Bragg's admission that the day was indeed lost, rather than making unseemly excuses. Nevertheless, the paper was absolutely right: Such an ignominious loss was serious beyond question. Bragg, a favorite of President Davis's, was not yet relieved of command of the Army of Tennessee, though there was much clamoring for it. The author of this editorial was correct in his assessment of the utility of Longstreet's army to Bragg.*

Memphis Appeal, 1 December 1863

THE DUTY OF THE HOUR

It is unwise to make light of a defeat, and equally unwise to overstate it. For the first time, as we have said elsewhere, a large Confederate army has been driven from a powerful position and compelled to abandon it altogether. Whether this was done by dint of bravery or by maneuvering and the sudden precipitation of large numbers upon a comparatively weak point, we are as yet without the means of knowing. The probabilities are in favor of the latter supposition, although General Bragg, with a candor which all must admire, and which other Southern generals would do well to imitate, admits that his "left center" was "carried." It will appear, we apprehend, that this center had been weakened in order to prevent the extreme left from being flanked, a danger which all generals take care to guard against, and none are more afraid of than Gen. Bragg.

To have been whipped out of a chosen and naturally strong position is a serious thing to a Southern army. It is an inadequate consolation to know that this happened when fifteen thousand State troops of Georgia had been permitted to return to their homes for agricultural purposes, and when probably as many more under Longstreet had been sent on to what will prove to be a bloodless and hazardous attempt against Knoxville. But when it became known that Sherman, with twenty thousand men, had joined Grant, ought not every man to have been called? Nay, ought they to have been sent beyond the reach of speedy recall?

What is done is done. We can bear the disaster, and another like it, but not many more. If Longstreet be cut off from Bragg, as he doubtless is, the trouble is mightily complicated, for Grant will press his advantages, and, if possible, destroy first the one and then the other. All is clear now to the dullest observation. It was quite clear to military minds from the moment it was known that Bragg has divided his army in the face of an able general who was being rapidly reinforced. Grant seized the occasion which Bragg gratuitously made for him—that is all.

However, Bragg is back upon the field of his great victory. His loss, we know not; the morale of his army, we know not. Admit that the one is heavy, the other bad; admit, too, that there is no help to come from Longstreet. Take the case in its worst aspect, and prepare for it. This is the duty of the president, the duty of Georgia, the duty of all. Georgia will surely do her duty; she has never failed to do it. Will the president do his! We trust he will, we may say we believe he will, for we have observed it ever requires the worst to come to the worst before the pressure that insures prompt action begins to tell on the firm, stern temper of the Executive.

Much has been said about General Bragg, and the hour may come when it will be proper to say much more. But there is no time for quarrelling now. First, make ready to repel Grant and Thomas, both able men; and then we may think of preferring charges. If the army cannot be made to resist the talents of Grant and Thomas without a change of commanders, in Heaven's name let it be done, and that without delay. But until it is done, let us give all possible encouragement to the gallant army at Chickamauga—back them up, support them, strengthen them, cheer them with all that busy hands and grateful voices can accomplish. By hook or by crook, we must beat back the invader. We have done it before, and, by God's help, we will surely do it again. Let us lend every energy to that end.

EASTERN THEATER

Chancellorsville and the Second Battle of Fredericksburg

Chancellorsville, Virginia, was not so much a town as a tavern and a house at a five-way crossroads in a densely wooded region north of Fredericksburg, but it would be the site of one of Robert E. Lee's and Stonewall Jackson's greatest triumphs. They faced Joe Hooker who, since his elevation to the command of the Army of the

Potomac the previous January, had been working to rebuild his force after its igno-minious rout at Fredericksburg. Hooker had ensured that his 130,000 men were well supplied with the best food, best uniforms, and best munitions that Uncle Sam's money could buy. Along with the new equipment, Hooker had drilled his men daily into what he considered to be the best fighting force in the world. Hooker showed aptitude in another vital military area as well: He was a competent spy master and gatherer of intelligence. His sound use of a variety of information sources, including Union sympathizers, Confederate deserters, and intercepted messages, had allowed Hooker to discover not only where the weaknesses lay in Lee's lines around Freder-icksburg and along the Rappahannock but the size of the Confederate force as well. Hooker used his intelligence to devise a plan that initially tricked Lee and allowed Union forces to steal a march on the Confederate left flank.

Lee faced the challenge of Hooker's well-thought-out strategy with an ill-prepared, ill-nourished, ill-deployed army. His 60,000 men spanned a 25-mile stretch of the banks on the Fredericksburg side of the Rappahannock River. The winter had been hard on the Confederate army, but by some miracle, their morale had not yet flagged. Lee's soldiers suffered from the cold as well as lack of rations and supplies. They had subsisted on a daily ration of a few ounces of cornmeal and bacon, frequently rancid. In addition to fighting with a force of emaciated, sometimes shoeless men, Lee had diminished his strength when he sent Longstreet's corps, his largest, toward Suffolk in order to gather provisions that would ease the lack of supplies and rations.

Hooker's strategy was two-pronged. Hooker planned to force 40,000 men, com-manded by Major General John Sedgwick, across the Rappahannock at Fredericks-burg while he forded the river farther to the northwest with 73,000 men. His men would march through The Wilderness to encircle Lee's left, while Major General George Stoneman's cavalry was to sweep south and cut off Lee's communications with Richmond. While Lee may not have known the details of Hooker's strategy, he was aware of the Union army's movements, thanks to the work of his own cavalry under Major General J.E.B. Stuart.

Unfortunately for Hooker, while his strategy worked, the follow-up failed. Hooker set his plan in motion in mid-April. Almost immediately, Stoneman's cavalry ran into trouble from rain and muddy roads. Stoneman did manage to get behind Lee's lines, but Stuart's cavalry effectively screened Lee's left flank. The Union cavalry-men rode through the woods for a week without having any effect on Lee at all. Fi-nally, on 29 April, Hooker was able to push through Stuart's cavalry screen. While his men were fending off cavalry attack in the dense woods of The Wilderness, Sedg-wick was building pontoon bridges across the Rappahannock in front of Jackson's position south of Fredericksburg. At first, Lee was uncertain how to proceed in his attack on Hooker, but on 30 April, the Union general stopped his force to consoli-date his position; his advance units had met stiffer resistance than expected, and he needed to revise his plan. Hooker's hesitation, though, cost him the initiative. Strong drink may also have been involved in Hooker's hesitation.

Prisoners captured by Stuart's force, as well as intelligence from the cavalry patrols themselves, helped Lee determine that Hooker was maneuvering north toward Chancellorsville and that Sedgewick's crossing at Fredericksburg was just a rouse. Lee left Major General Jubal Early with 10,000 men to defend Fredericksburg and then moved rapidly west to meet Hooker near Chancellorsville. The first contact between the two armies was on 1 May. Despite his tremendous advantage in numbers, Hooker halted and went on the defensive.

At 4:00 A.M. on 2 May, Lee sent Jackson with 26,000 men to envelop Hooker's force, while Lee, with 17,000 men, held the front. After marching his men for 20 miles through the heat of the day, Jackson's force fell on Hooker's. The Confederates were positioned along a 2-mile-long attack formation, and as the daylight began to fade, Jackson ordered his lieutenants to begin the attack. The Union force had already called it quits for the day; some of Hooker's men were preparing their suppers when a mass of screaming Rebels burst through the woods and scattered the men. Jackson's men completely demoralized the right wing of Hooker's army before their assault was through. Jackson's advance was halted by heavier Union fire and the loss of cohesion in the darkening woods. They had one final objective to accomplish, though, before they could call their day's work complete: They were to cut Hooker off from his communications line at the Rappahannock. Jackson rode ahead with his staff to reconnoiter in person.

At about 9:00 P.M., disaster struck the Confederate cause. Jackson and his party rode past a position held by troops from the 18th North Carolina. In the darkness and confusion of the postbattle period, the Confederate soldiers made a mistake. They believed the men riding past were Union cavalry. They aimed their muskets, and they fired. Jackson and several of his staff officers were wounded. The general was hit in three places, and one of the bullets had shattered his left arm. Early word was that the doctors expected a full, though lengthy, recovery. But the worst happened: Jackson developed pneumonia, and within days, he succumbed to it. The great Stonewall was dead.

The Confederate attacks resumed on 3 May with Stuart temporarily in command of Jackson's corps. Union resistance slowed the Southern assault near Chancellorsville, and in Fredericksburg, Sedgwick's force drove Early's force from Marye's Heights. Lee left Stuart to face Hooker at Chancellorsville and hurried east to meet Sedgwick on 4 May at Salem Church. That engagement produced mixed results. The next day, Hooker, against the advice of his subordinates, ordered his army to retreat across the Rappahannock. He had the numbers to carry the day, but the Union general had lost the will to fight.

Total casualties for the Union reached more than 16,700. For the South, losses totaled more than 12,750, plus one irreplaceable soldier: Stonewall Jackson.

AN ANONYMOUS REPORT: NEWS OF ADVANCE OF HOOKER'S ARMY

On 29 April, Hooker's army was crossing the Rappahannock at fords above Fredericksburg. The crossing had begun the day before and would not be completed until 1 May. As Hooker's 70,000 men completed their crossing, they moved through The Wilderness into an area with clearings near the home of the Chancellor family, a place today referred to as Chancellorsville. Lee's 47,000-man Army of Northern Virginia would move out the next day to meet the Union forces in a fight that would become known as the Battle of Chancellorsville.

Richmond Examiner, 1 May 1863

FROM FREDERICKSBURG

[FROM OUR OWN CORRESPONDENT.]

FREDERICKSBURG, April 29th, 1863, 11 P.M.—This morning about five o'clock a courier dashed into the town with the startling exciting intelligence that the enemy were crossing the Rappahannock in this vicinity. Immediately the Episcopal church bell, the ring of which had been previously agreed upon as a signal, sounded the alarm, and the streets presented a busy spectacle of military preparation, and women and children leaving the scene of danger.

Your correspondent reached the advanced line of our pickets about seven o'clock, and found at that early hour, their pontoon bridge at the mouth of Deep Run, on the Mansfield estate, completed, and several regiments of the enemy already across. The troops stationed near report that our regiment on duty at that point was surprised about three o'clock in the morning, by a party of the enemy, who effected the passage of the river in boats. One hundred of the surprised are reported to be prisoners, an exaggeration it is to be hoped. There was no contest at this bridge after sunrise, excepting an occasional cannon shot early in the morning. Four or five other bridges, however, are said to be constructed, or in course of construction, within a space of a mile and a half from that at Mansfield which, by the way, is about that distance from Fredericksburg. Desultory discharges, both of cannon and musketry, have been occurring at those points during the day.

On reaching this side of the river the enemy threw out skirmishers at once, who met no disputants of their advance to the road leading to Hamilton's Crossing, where they established their line of pickets, and retired.

The upper bridge alone, and operations there only, were visible to your correspondent. The Yankees continued to cross there until two o'clock, P.M., infantry, artillery, and wagons. They swarmed irregularly over the field and bluffs of which they had taken possession, seeming not even to have fallen into ranks. About five, P.M., a light rain commenced, when they pitched their tents, and seemed to be making themselves at home.

All throughout the day, their balloons were in the air to a great height, and the opposite banks of the river, as far as the eye could reach, was blue with their crowded columns.

Singular to say, notwithstanding the close proximity of Fredericksburg to those exciting occurrences, the batteries in direct front of the city were not manned throughout the day; the pickets have been lulling quietly on the banks of the river, within short rifle range, of each other; and, excepting a few more spectators than customary, the line has been non-pulsing [*unreadable*]. A pontoon train is stated to have [*unreadable*] opposite the lower wharf, and [*unreadable*] behind the hill. If this be true, tomorrow will be another eventful day in the experience of the [*unreadable*] town.

It is utterly impossible to estimate, with any accuracy, the number of the enemy who have crossed the river. The force encamped this evening at the upper crossing, did not exceed five thousand. The opposite bank was still covered with infantry, and an immense force of artillery. A general engagement cannot be avoided to-morrow, unless they retire to-night.

ROBERT E. LEE/AN ANONYMOUS REPORT: COMMANDING GENERAL'S REPORT ON BATTLE OF CHANCELLORSVILLE; STONEWALL JACKSON WOUNDED

Lee made his victory over Hooker at Chancellorsville and Fredericksburg sound easy in his terse telegraph to President Davis regarding the victory. This article, though, placed less emphasis on the victory and more on Stonewall Jackson's wound from which, at the point this article was written, he was expected to recover.

Richmond Examiner, 6 May 1863

FROM FREDERICKSBURG—THREE VICTORIES IN ONE DAY—THE YANKEE ARMY
DRIVEN NORTH OF THE RAPPAHANNOCK—GENERAL JACKSON SHOT BY HIS OWN
TROOPS IN THE NIGHT—HIS WOUNDS.

The following dispatch was received from Geuineas last night:

HEADQUARTERS, 10 o'clock, A.M., May 5, 1863.

To HIS EXCELLENCY PRESIDENT DAVIS:

At the close of the battle of Chancellorsville, on Sunday, the enemy was reported advancing from Fredericksburg in our rear. General McLaws was sent back to arrest his progress, and repulsed him handsomely that afternoon. Learning that this force consisted of two corps, under General Sedgewick, I determined to attack it, and marched back yesterday with General Anderson, and uniting with McLaws and Early in the afternoon, succeeded, by the blessing of Heaven, in driving General Sedgewick over the river. We have reoccupied Fredericksburg, and no enemy remains south of the Rappahannock, in its vicinity.

(Signed,)

ROBERT E. LEE, General

From this it will be seen that our armies were thrice victorious on the same day. Hooker was beaten.

In addition to the above, our information as to the particulars of the three great battles mentioned therein amounts to next to nothing. We have heard of no casualties with sufficient certainty to feel authorized to publish them.

Some pleasurable excitement was produced here yesterday by the announcement that a telegram had been received from General Lee, stating that Hooker and his staff had been captured. The only foundation for this story, it turned out, was that the operator at Guinea's informed the operator here that such a report was in circulation at the former place.

A telegram on yesterday morning announced the fact that General Jackson's arm had been amputated, and that he was doing well. Mrs. Jackson, who is at present in the city, has been informed by a letter of the melancholy circumstances under which the General received his wounds.

The following are the facts of the most unhappy affair, as detailed in that letter: At midnight on Saturday night, his men being drawn up in line of battle, a body of troops was seen a short distance in advance of our line. It being doubtful whether they were friends or enemies, General Jackson and staff rode forward to ascertain. Whilst he was engaged in reconnoitering, his men being unaware of his movement, mistook himself and staff for enemies and fired a volley into them, instantly killing one of his staff and severely wounding General Jackson and Major Crutchfield. One bullet passed through the General's right hand, whilst another stuck his left arm below the elbow and, ranging upward, shattered the bone near the shoulder. He instantly fell to the ground. His brother-in-law, who was with him, laid down beside him to ascertain the character of his wounds. In a moment the unknown troops in front, who proved to be the enemy, advanced and captured two other staff officers who were standing over the General without noticing him. Soon after, four of our men placed him on a stretcher, and were bearing him to the rear, when they were all shot down. The injury to his right hand is severe, one of the bones having been shot away, but it is believed he will ultimately recover its use.

AN ANONYMOUS REPORT: ACCOUNT OF BATTLE OF CHANCELLORSVILLE

The Battle of Chancellorsville was a bloody, terrible fight that left the Confederate army exhausted, despite its victory over a hugely superior force. Luck was on the side of the Confederates; a shell struck the house that was serving as Hooker's headquarters. The Union general was struck on the head by falling debris and temporarily disabled. The next day, though, he lost his nerve and ordered a retreat. The following Richmond Examiner *article is an overview of the three days' fighting that had taken place near Chancellorsville.*

Richmond Examiner, 11 May 1863

FROM FREDERICKSBURG

All is once again quiet along the lines of the Rappahannock. Our army has resumed the position occupied by it previous to the advance of Hooker, and is enjoying the rest made so necessary by the terrible labors and privations of the past week. The extent of the suffering of our troops during the three days battle is almost impossible to realize. From letters written at Chancellorsville, last Monday, we learn that Jackson's command were sixty hours under arms without food and without sleep, and that the first food there obtained by them was from the knapsacks thrown away by the enemy in their flight. Both the Central and Fredericksburg roads being now in full operation the army is abundantly supplied with food for man and beast.

THE BATTLE OF CHANCELLORS

Of the grand result of this memorable battle the whole country has been informed through the official dispatches of General Lee, while many of the details have found publicity through the labors of the press. Yet much remains untold. Persons who were participants in the battles are constantly arriving in the city, each of whom adds something to the general stock of information on the subject.—From their accounts we collate some items of interest. During the battle the large brick tavern on the Orange plank road which, with its out-houses, constituted Chancellorsville, and which was occupied by the Yankees as a hospital, was accidentally set on fire by our shells, and, with all its inmates, five or six hundred in number, was consumed. Among those who lost their lives by this catastrophe, was Brigadier General Seth Williams of Maine, who was Adjutant General, first to McClellan and afterwards to Burnside, and lastly to Hooker, and who is said to have been, before the war, a warm personal friend of General Lee.—Such was the exigency of the hour, the battle being at its fiercest, that none could be spared from the ranks to save the poor wounded wretches from the most horrible of deaths—being roasted alive. As the flames approached them, and they became aware of their situation, their frantic screams were distinctly heard above the roar of battle that raged around them. Subsequently to this, another conflagration, even more appalling occurred. The woods on a portion of the battle field, where laid intermingled the dead and wounded of both armies, took fire, and many, whose wounds prevented their moving, were burnt to death. It is said by some that Hooker had the woods fired to prevent our pursuit of his shattered divisions, but this story is too horrible to be believed even of a Yankee. For the credit of human nature, we are unwilling to believe that a General, even though a Yankee, would consign his own countrymen, who had been disabled in his ranks, to the most excruciating of deaths.

The number of their dead we have heard estimated by a member of General Lee's staff at five thousand. When five thousand men of an army are killed outright the wounded cannot be less than twenty-five thousand—five wounded to one killed being less than the usual proportion. But putting it at that, Hooker's loss in the battle cannot be under forty thousand.

The number of rifles and muskets on the battle field taken from the prisoners is estimated at between thirty and forty thousand. A railroad man tells us it will take the Fredericksburg road two days to haul them to Richmond.

The prisoners continue to arrive in this city daily, the officers in the (ladies') cars and the privates afoot. As these prisoners arrived at Guinea's, we are informed the army suttlers bought up their "greenbacks" with avidity, giving them three dollars Confederate money for one dollar in United States. Many of the Yankees were heard to remark that this did not look much as if we expected to be ultimately successful in our struggle for independence, else we would not, upon the heels of what we claimed to be a great victory, be so ready to give three of our dollars for one of theirs. The moral effect of this sort of traffic is certainly very bad, but there is no help for it, as Congress has refused to pass a law forbidding it.

YANKEE GENERALS KILLED

We have it upon "rumor," which we do not always believe, that six Yankee brigadiers were killed at Chancellorsville, viz: Dan Sickles, Barry, Chief of Artillery; Ruger; Birney; Seth Williams, Chief of Staff; and Howard.

A gentleman who was in the fight at Marye's Hill, speaks of it as the most desperate battle of the war. The Confederate Artillery drove the Yankees back three times, but were overpowered by numbers. The ground near their guns was literally covered with dead Yankees. On Monday when the Yankees were driven from the hill, and while retreating across the river, it is said the First Howitzers of Richmond, fired three hundred rounds into their ranks while in a crowded condition trying to get across the river, causing great slaughter.

JOHN M. DANIEL: DEATH OF STONEWALL JACKSON

Technically, Chancellorsville was a victory for the Confederates, but the Southern cause suffered one of its most devastating losses as a result of that battle: the death of Stonewall Jackson. Jackson died of pneumonia several days after being wounded in the battle. Jackson's death was lamented throughout the South, for he was truly a hero of the people. The former mathematics professor at Virginia Military Institute was known for his bravery in combat, his skill in military tactics, and his religious faith.

Richmond Examiner, 11 May 1863

DEATH OF STONEWALL JACKSON

The hero of the war, that great genius, that noble patriot, the support and hope of this country, is no more. He died yesterday at three o'clock in the afternoon. The immediate cause of his death was pneumonia, against which his constitution, shaken by the sore wounds received in the glorious victory at Chancellors, was unable to struggle. This announcement will draw many a tear in the South, and many a shout of malignant exultation in the North.—Whatever difference of opinion may have existed among the semi-intelligent, the instinct of the people was fixed in the belief, that this silent Virginian was one of the first men, living or dead. In the popular estimate we most sincerely concur. There was the stuff of CROMWELL in JACKSON. HANNIBAL might have been proud of his campaign in the Valley, and the shades of the mightiest warriors should rise to welcome his stern ghost.

Gettysburg Campaign

Lee's decisive victory at Chancellorsville emboldened him to make another attempt to invade the North. Lee spent a month after Chancellorsville reorganizing his army into three infantry corps consisting of three divisions each. Lee named three corps commanders. He retained Longstreet and elevated Ewell and Hill to new positions. Stuart commanded the cavalry. Then, on 3 June, his reorganization complete, Lee's Army of Northern Virginia pulled out from Fredericksburg and marched up the Shenandoah Valley toward western Maryland and ultimately Pennsylvania.

The first engagement of the campaign occurred on 9 June when 12,000 Union cavalry under Major General Alfred Pleasanton surprised Stuart's 10,000-man cavalry near Brandy Station, Virginia. Stuart's horsemen fought the federals to a standstill in the largest purely cavalry battle of the war. This cavalry engagement was Hooker's first warning that Lee was on the move.

Ewell's corps was the first of Lee's 76,000 cohort to make it across the Potomac. On 13 and 14 June, Ewell's men smashed through the Union garrison at Winchester, crossed the Potomac into western Maryland, and then southern Pennsylvania. By late June, though, Ewell and the remaining two corps were deployed in an arc that spanned from Chambersburg northeast toward Harrisburg, the Pennsylvania capital, and then southeast toward York. At the center of the arc was the small college town of Gettysburg.

Hooker at first had not anticipated that Lee was making a major movement, but on 13 June, he began moving his 115,000 Army of the Potomac north to stay between Lee and Washington. The Union army missed repeated opportunities to strike the stretched-out Confederates. Hooker, after reaching Frederick, Maryland, devised a plan to envelop Lee and submitted it to his superior, Halleck, on 27 June. Halleck overruled the plan, and Hooker, in a huff, offered his resignation, which was accepted before dawn on 28 June. That day, Major General George C. Meade was named commander of the Army of the Potomac, its fifth in 10 months.

Within two days, Meade's cavalry and Lee's infantry met in an unexpected clash that led to the greatest battle of the war. On 1 July, the three-day Battle of Gettysburg began when Hill's corps opposed two Union corps under Joseph I. Reynolds and Oliver O. Howard, north and northwest of Gettysburg. Hill outflanked the Union right, but Union troops rallied south of Gettysburg on Cemetery Hill and Culp's Hill, while the Confederates held Seminary Ridge and Gettysburg itself. That night, the rest of Meade's army marched into position along Cemetery Ridge.

Lee's plan for 2 July was to use Longstreet's corps to envelop the Union left. Longstreet objected. He argued instead that, given the strength of the Union position on Cemetery Hill, a flanking move to force a retreat would be a better strategy. Lee disagreed and ordered Longstreet to go on the offensive the next morning.

Longstreet's advance was delayed until the next afternoon, but it succeeded in driving one Union corps back from a peach orchard, and he almost succeeded in turning the Union left. One of Meade's engineers kept that from happening, though, by diverting an infantry brigade and artillery battery to a knob called Little Round Top. This was a key position, and it saved the Union left. The Union army ended up firmly anchored along the ridge from Round Top to Culp's Hill.

Having been repulsed on both Union flanks, Lee decided to attack the Union center on 3 July. He launched ten brigades, supported by tremendous artillery bombardment, in an assault that is now known as "Pickett's Charge." Facing heavy Union bombardment that blew huge holes in their lines, more than 15,000 men pressed forward for half a mile. The Confederates that reached Union lines broke through briefly but were thrown back by Meade's reserves. Only half the men who started out on that charge survived, and they retreated back to Seminary Ridge. Lee, fully aware of the disaster he had ordered, waited for a counterattack, but it never came. Casualties for the two sides were eerily similar. Union casualties for the three days of battle included 3,155 killed, 14,529 wounded, and 5,365 missing. Confederate losses included 3,903 killed, 18,735 wounded, and 5,425 missing.

Given that he had lost 28,000 men in the three-day battle, Lee decided to retreat. His army pulled out on 4 July. Its train of wagons carrying the wounded stretched for 19 miles. Meade followed, but cautiously. The only fighting that occurred was during several Union cavalry raids on the Confederate wagon train. The Army of Northern Virginia crossed over a flood-swollen Potomac at the little village of Williamsport, Maryland. Lee's men were back in Virginia, and there they would remain for the duration of the war. Their leader would tender his resignation out of frustration with his inability to destroy the enemy's army, but President Davis refused to let Lee quit. The well-seasoned Confederate commander spent the remainder of 1863 directing a series of thrusts and parries with Meade's army, but all in all, the Army of Northern Virginia spent the months immediately following Gettysburg essentially in stalemate with the Army of the Potomac.

JAMES R. SNEED: FIRST REPORTS OF BATTLE AT GETTYSBURG

When news of Gettysburg first circulated, Confederates believed they had won a great victory and that Lee's retreat across the Potomac back into Virginia was nothing more than a strategic withdrawal. This article is a good example of the relish with which news of the supposed Confederate victory was received, close on the heels of the capitulation of Vicksburg.

Savannah Republican, 7 July 1863

THE NEWS

We publish this afternoon the most glorious news of the war, it being little less than the total annihilation of the much boasted Yankee Army of the Potomac—"the finest army on the planet," as the vain glorious boaster triumphantly styled it. Lee, it appears, after a battle on Wednesday and desultory fighting on Thursday, collected all his forces in Pennsylvania near the town of Gettysburg, a fight ensued on Sunday, and by one of the most brilliant movements on record, the enemy were surrounded and nearly their entire army either killed, wounded or captured. *Forty thousand prisoners* are said to be now on their way to Richmond.

Such an achievement has no parallel in history, whether as regards the brilliancy of the fight, the number of prisoners taken, or the probable results of the victory. The Yankee army of the Potomac is either in our hands or *hors du combat*, and thus opens up to us the way to Washington. We hope ere this Lee's cannon have thundered at the gates of the Federal city, or, what is more likely, that he has quietly occupied it after an inglorious flight on the part of its defenders.

A late number of the New York Daily news stated that "the army of Hooker had dwindled down to 50,000 men." Make a liberal allowance for reinforcements—say 10,000—and then take out 40,000 prisoners, and how much of the famous Army of the Potomac remains?

In all this our noble army of Virginia have won a fame that belongs to none other in the history of the world. They have shed a lustre upon the Confederate name, and their services will be embalmed in the grateful memories of their countrymen. In Lee, Napoleon, Wellington, Eugene have found their peer, if not a star of still greater magnitude, before the splendor of whose rays the world shall bow in admiration and awe.

We are told that the prisoners taken at Gettysburg refused to be paroled, and are now on their way to Richmond. The object on the part of the wily Yankees is evident; they simply wish to embarrass and clog our movements in the midst of victory by throwing the great incumbrance upon us to be guarded, fed and cared for. There is a remedy for such tricks, and we hope Gen. Lee will apply it—*take no more of the miscreants!*

PETER W. ALEXANDER: ACCOUNT OF FIGHTING AT GETTYSBURG

As soon as Alexander got to a place equipped with a working telegraph, he sent word back to Savannah of the outcome at Gettysburg. The dispatch is long for a telegraph but quite brief when compared to a typical story sent via a letter. Alexander's dispatch actually sounded rather upbeat and cheerful about the outcome. Like many Confederates, he did not realize the significance of the outcome at Gettysburg.

Savannah Republican, 14 July 1863

THE GETTYSBURG FIGHT IN RELIABLE SHAPE
YANKEE LOSS 25,000

Heavy Loss in Confederate Officers

[From our Special Army Correspondence]

GETTYSBURGH, July 5, via Winchester and Staunton. The most desperate battle of the war has been fought here. It commenced on the evening of July 1st, between portions of Ewell's and Lee's commands, and heavy Federal forces under Gen. Reynolds. We drove the enemy back the first day and killed Gens. Reynolds and Paul, and captured three thousand prisoners. The Baltimore papers admit to a loss in this preliminary battle of ten thousand killed, wounded and prisoners. On the 2nd of July both armies concentrated at 4 o'clock. McLaws and Hood, of Longstreet's corps, held the right, attacked and drove the enemy a mile and a half. Hill attacked the centre and Ewell the left. Our success on the left and center was unequal to that on the right wing.

The enemy occupied a range of hills stronger than Malvern Hill.

McLaws and Hood's division took 1,000 prisoners and several [*unreadable*] and flags, inflicted a terrible loss on the foe and suffered heavily themselves.

On the [*unreadable*] the battle was resumed. In the afternoon the enemy was driven from several positions, but not dislodged entirely from his strong position when night came.

All was quiet on the 4th. We could not provoke an attack from the enemy. During the night the enemy retreated towards Washington. No pursuit was made.

The loss was heavy on both sides. The following is a list of Confederate casualties:

Killed—Gens. Gannett and Kemper, and Col. Hartman and Williams, of Virginia; Gen. Barksdale, Col. Carter, and Captain Stump, nephew of President Davis, of Mississippi; Col. Desks, of S.C.; Colonel Jack Jones, Wilson, Harris, Wich, and Warden; Lieut. Cols. Caswell, [*unreadable*], and Mounger, Major [*unreadable*]; Lieut. Wood, and Captains Hark and Redding of Georgia.

The following were wounded: Major Gens. Hood, Trimble, Pinkett, and [*unreadable*]. Brig. Gens. Hampton, Semmes, Anderson, Armistead, Robinson, Jenkins, and Jones; Cols. Griffin, Horner, Fiske and Sayers, of Miss.; Col. Kennedy, and Majors McLeod and Miller of S.C.; Cols. Forney, Pinckard and Saunders, Major Fielcher, and Captains King and Smith of Ala.; Cols. Jack Brown, Towers, Little, Anthony; Majors Davidson, Jones and Read; Capts. Frisbee, Carlen, Butler and Lieut. Cowper of Georgia.

The following are wounded and missing: Lt. Col. Harris, Major [*unreadable*], Capt. George S. Jones, Lieuts. [Unreadable], Cummings, Grannts, R. Campbell, A. A. Freeman of Georgia.

Our total loss, twelve thousand—that of the enemy, twenty-five thousand, including six thousand prisoners.

On the 5th of July, Gen. Lee moved towards Hagerstown, as the enemy had retired. The movement was made to reopen his communications and for other reasons not proper to mention, though satisfactory.

P.W.A.

PETER W. ALEXANDER: REFLECTIONS ON FIGHTING IN 1863

Chancellorsville. Vicksburg. Gettysburg. Battery Wagner. The year 1863 was marked by escalating battlefield violence. Both the North and the South had realized this was not going to be a quick and dirty little conflict. It was all-out war for the Union, if you were a Yankee, and if you were a Confederate, it was a war for independence. With this letter to the Savannah Republican, *the paper's main battlefield reporter, Peter W. Alexander, took a moment to reflect on the bloody events thus far in 1863. He also, toward the end of the article, explained a planned addition to the Confederate army: an engineering corps that was to be organized and staffed.*

Savannah Republican, 11 September 1863

ARMY CORRESPONDENCE
OF THE SAVANNAH REPUBLICAN

ARMY OF NORTHERN VIRGINIA,
September 4, 1863

Spring and Summer have come and gone, and Autumn, with her glowing fingers, is now painting the skies and fields in those gorgeous hues produced only by her skillful hand. We have entered upon the ninth month of 1863, and three acts of the bloody tragedy have passed in review. The first was played at Chancellorsville; the scenery, a sterile soil and a dark wilderness; but the light of victory, reflected back from the Southern Cross, proclaimed the conqueror. The scene shifts, and the second act is ushered in among the rugged hills of Gettysburg. Blood flows in torrents and the slain lay in heaps, but Triumph, unable to decide in favor of either party, turns to Fortune, who warns us to return to our own soil, and fight the battle there.

Form the Potomac we pass to the Father of Waters—to Vicksburg and Port Hudson—where the third act is performed, and where Fortune, less kind than she was wont to be places the crown of victory upon the standard of our enemies. From the great river we step to the sea, and, as the curtain rolls up to the lurid sky, the fourth act opens, and Charleston, and Sumter, and Wagner rise to view. When the curtain, all torn and bloody, and soiled from the terrible conflicts ascends again, it will be upon the fifth and final act of this horrid tragedy of 1863. It may be upon the Rappahannock, and it may be upon the Tennessee.—If here, then the actors are ready; they have studied their parts, they have learned them well and are ready, with the assistance of that kind Prompter who stands above the clouds, to play them through to the bitter end.

Meanwhile, the army is not idle here. The interval between the acts is not left wholly unemployed. Fresh supplies of ammunition have been obtained; newer and better arms have been distributed where any were needed; clothing and shoes have been supplied; the men are exercising and drilling; the animals are resting and improving, and the whole army is preparing for other struggles and other triumphs. Not the least important subjects which now engages the attention of the chiefs, relates to the organization of a corps of engineers. This necessary adjunct of an army should have been provided at the beginning of the war, but better late than never. The corps is intended to embrace pioneers, pontonniers, sappers and miners, as well as engineers proper.

The duties of the engineer are important, and often laborious. If it be necessary for the traveller to be informed beforehand of the roads over which he is to pass, the streams he is to cross, the mountains he is to scale, the defiles he is to thread, and the robbers he is to encounter; how much more important is it that the commander of an army and his chief officers, upon whom depend the safety of their troops, the welfare and honor of their country, and the success of the campaign, should possess the same information? This information cannot be had without the aid of engineers, a part of whose business it is to thoroughly reconnoitre and map the whole country occupied, or expected to be occupied by either army.

This duty is usually performed by a party detailed by the chief of the Engineer Bureau. It should be done early, and the maps deposited in the office of the chief of the bureau in Richmond, where copies are prepared and sent to the department, corps, and division commanders in the field. These maps are on a sufficiently large scale to show accurately the roads, streams, cleared and uncleared land, elevations and depressions of ground, fords, bridges, [*unreadable*]. Particular care is taken to show not only the direction but also the condition of roads, which are classified and each class shown by a different line or mark. It is necessary that all neighborhood and private ways, as well as private roads, should be laid down, as frequently a proper knowledge of roads will enable a General to save much marching by sending his train on one road and his troops by another, thus making the march more rapidly and with less fatigue to his troops. The maps should also go sufficiently into details to enable the General to know where he may encamp his troops on a march. Leaving out of consideration the question of attack and defence, camps on a march should always, if possible, be located convenient to wood and water.

This duty, as above stated, belongs to the party specially detailed by the chief of the bureau; but the engineer acting with the army in the field should take every opportunity of proving the accuracy of the maps, acquiring through their assistance a thorough knowledge of the country. It is his duty, after the line of battle is established, to lay out all works for the strengthening of the line; and it is the duty of the engineer troops, with the aid of such details as are necessary, to construct such works under the superintendence of the officers of the corps. It is also the duty of the engineer, when the line of battle has been established, to acquaint himself most thoroughly with every rod of ground in the neighborhood, both in rear of the line and in front as far as it is safe to reconnoitre. He should know not only where the strong and weak points of his own line are, but also those of the enemy. His knowledge should be such that he could inform his general of the country to be passed over, either in an advance or a retreat; and roads, forts, bridges, &c., should be prepared for both as far as practicable.

As has already been stated, an engineer corps for the field is now being raised. Its organization will be the same as that of the regiment, with a Colonel, Lieut. Colonel, Major, company officers and men. Perhaps it would be more proper to speak of the men as engineer troops. Officers have been detailed to go home to raise volunteers for this inviting service. Among others, Capt. John Bradford, of Florida, an excellent officer, has gone South to raise a company. I would commend him and the service in which he is engaged, to the public generally and especially to all persons within the conscriptage.

P.W.A.

NOTE

1. See the homepage of the Army of the Cumberland at http://www.atoc.net/Murfreesboro.html.

FURTHER READINGS

Burton, E. Milby. *The Siege of Charleston, 1861–1865.* Columbia: University of South Carolina Press, 1970.

Carter, Samuel. *The Final Fortress: The Campaign for Vicksburg, 1862–1863.* New York: St. Martin's Press, 1980.

Catton, Bruce. *Glory Road: The Bloody Road from Fredericksburg to Gettysburg.* Garden City, N.Y.: Doubleday, 1952.

Doubleday, Abner. *Chancellorsville and Gettysburg.* New York: C. Scribner's Sons, 1882.

Dowdey, Clifford. *Death of a Nation: The Story of Lee and His Men at Gettysburg.* New York: Knopf, 1958.

Jones, Archer. *Confederate Strategy from Shiloh to Vicksburg.* Baton Rouge: Louisiana State University Press, 1961.

Martin, David G. *The Vicksburg Campaign April 1862–July 1863.* New York: Gallery Books, 1994.

Rawley, James A. *Turning Points of the Civil War.* Lincoln: University of Nebraska Press, 1966.

Reasoner, James. *Chancellorsville.* Nashville, Tenn.: Cumberland House, 2000.

———. *Chickamauga.* Nashville, Tenn.: Cumberland House, 2002.

———. *Vicksburg.* Nashville, Tenn.: Cumberland House, 2001.

Woodworth, Steven E. *No Band of Brothers: Problems in the Rebel High Command.* Columbia: University of Missouri Press, 1999.

———. *Six Armies in Tennessee: The Chickamauga and Chattanooga Campaigns.* Lincoln: University of Nebraska Press, 1998.

———. *This Grand Spectacle: The Battle of Chattanooga.* Abilene, Tex.: McWhiney Foundation Press, 1999.

Top left: Self-promotional advertisement for the *Southern Banner* of Athens, Georgia, featuring its steam press. Most of the South's larger newspapers, dailies, and important weeklies like the *Southern Banner*, printed with steam presses. Small town or village newspapers were still likely to use the older hand presses. (*Southern Banner*)

Top right: *Charleston Mercury* owner Robert B. Rhett owned this home in Beaufort, South Carolina. Rhett was one of the leading fire-eaters who compelled secession, despite the reluctance of many Southerners to break up the Union. He became a bitter opponent of Jefferson Davis during the war because of the president's advocacy of measures that would lead to a more centralized government and fewer freedoms for Confederate citizens. (Courtesy of the Library of Congress)

Far right: Self-promotional advertisement from the *Augusta Constitutionalist*. Newspapers used self promotions to let potential readers know about their content and their politics. Note that the *Constitutionalist* advertised its commercial (i.e., business) and telegraphic news sections. A change in the Southern political system is reflected in the *Constitutionalist's* statement on its politics. Rather than claiming to support a particular political party, as most newspapers did before 1861, the *Constitutionalist* merely claims to be "thoroughly Southern" in its political stance. This was because the Confederacy had no political parties. Southern delegates meeting in Montgomery, Alabama, in February 1861, made the decision to abandon political parties in a quest for Confederate unity. (*Augusta Constitutionalist*)

Near right: Self-promotional advertisement from the *North Carolina Argus* of Raleigh. This ad addresses subscribers of the *Argus's* "country paper." Most dailies also published weekly, bi-weekly, and/or tri-weekly editions that were available by mail to people living in small villages or on farms and plantations outside the larger cities. Note that the *Argus* advertised its war news. This was a change from the antebellum period when most Southern newspapers focused mostly on political commentary. However, with the coming of the war, readers wanted news — about what was happening on the battlefields where their loved ones were fighting. (*North Carolina Argus*)

Support your COUNTY PAPER.

$1.50

For the ensuing Year, is all that is asked For the

"ARGUS"

— IN ADVANCE.

It contains

THE LATEST NEWS,

OF THE PROGRESS OF THE

WAR,

Up to the hour of going to press,

And all other matters of interest to the general Reader.

WHO WOULD BE WITHOUT THE NEWS!

We design making the Argus more of a family paper than we have been enabled to do in tofore. There is no question likely to arise to disturb the harmony existing among us. We have confidence in our President, in our Generals, in our soldiers, in our people. We have confidence in God. So long as we have *this* confidence, we are invincible. We shall give the news—the *news* first, and then fill up with matter interesting, instructive, profitable. Come and subscribe; and stop borrowing your neighbor's paper.

THE **CONSTITUTIONALIST** IS ONE OF THE BEST PAPERS PUBLISHED IN THE SOUTH.

IN ITS **COMMERCIAL & NEWS** DEPARTMENT No labor is spared to give the EARLIEST and MOST ACCURATE intelligence from ALL QUARTERS. Its

TELEGRAPH COLUMN Is filled with AMPLE and RELIABLE information of occurrences at all Political and Commercial centres. In

POLITICS,

The Constitutionalist is *THOROUGHLY SOUTHERN,* And adheres, under our new Government, to its old principles of **State Rights and Strict Construction.**

It advocates the Admission, into the Confederacy only, of those States which recognise **PROPERTY IN SLAVES AS A** part of their Social System.

TERMS:
Daily Constitutionalist...... $10 00
Tri-Weekly................... 12 00
Weekly....................... 4 00

JAS. GARDNER, Proprietor

BOOK & JOB PRINTING

NEATLY EXECUTED

AT THIS OFFICE

AUGUSTA, GA.

Major Robert Anderson's garrison occupied Fort Moultrie in 1860, but moved to Fort Sumter in early 1861 because Anderson believed it would be safer there. Southerners saw the move as a threat of war. (Courtesy of the Library of Congress)

The interior of Fort Sumter. Built to protect Charleston from foreign naval attack, it was virtually defenseless against the heavy guns of neighboring forts. (Courtesy of the Library of Congress)

Fort Marion near Saint Augustine enabled the Confederacy to defend itself (to some degree) from seaborn attacks by the Union navy. Except for the early contest for the fortifications near Pensacola, there was little Civil War action in Florida. (Courtesy of the Library of Congress)

Near right: Delegates from the seceded states formed the Confederate States of America and in February 1861 chose Jefferson Davis, the U.S. Senator from Mississippi, to become the Confederate president. (Courtesy of the Library of Congress)

Far right: Antebellum newspapers advertised their editorial endorsements within their mastheads. This endorsement is from the *Dallas Herald*, a paper that supported John C. Breckinridge, the Southern Democratic candidate in the 1860 presidential election. Four men ran for president that year: a Republican, Abraham Lincoln; two Democrats, Beckinridge, the candidate of the Southern wing of the Democratic party, and Stephen A. Douglas, the candidate of the Northern wing of the Democratic party; and John Bell, the candidate of the Constitutional Unionist party. Lincoln was not on the ballots of the Southern states. Lincoln won only a plurality among the popular vote. He received 1,866,452 votes to the 2,815,617 cast for the other three candidates. However, he did receive a substantial majority in the Electoral College where the vote was 180 for Lincoln and 123 combined for the three challengers. (*Dallas Herald*, 31 October, 1860)

Above: The first major battle of the Civil War occurred near this creek, Bull Run, in July 1861. The Union army named the engagement after the creek, calling it the Battle of Bull Run. A second battle occurred at virtually the same place the following summer. The Confederacy's practice was to name battles after the nearest town, and so in the South, the two fights became known as the First and Second Battles of Manassas. (Courtesy of the Library of Congress)

Above right: Virginia slaves used the opportunity of the Second Battle of Manassas to escape to freedom. In this picture, they are shown fording the Rappahannock. (Courtesy of the Library of Congress)

Left: Confederate winter quarters at Centreville, Virginia. While Civil War armies could and did fight in the winter months, logistical problems discouraged it. (Courtesy of the Library of Congress)

Far left: This self-promotional graphic from the *Atlanta Southern Confederacy* represented a different approach to enticing subscribers. Most newspaper self-promotions were text-based. The *Confederacy* was experimenting with something new: advertising that was more visual than verbal. (*Atlanta Southern Confederacy*)

Near left: This graphic was promoting subscriptions to the weekly edition of the *Atlanta Southern Confederacy*. Like most dailies, the paper produced a weekly edition for readers in the countryside. Many newspapers experienced growth in subscriptions during the Civil War but had trouble collecting subscription fees from their readers. (*Southern Confederacy*)

The nameplate for the *Memphis Daily Appeal*. The banner, without any ornamentation, was more modern looking.

Above left: Masthead logo for the *Selma Reporter* of Selma, Alabama. The masthead typically ran on the second page of a newspaper, just above the editorials and included the name of the editor and, often, the publisher. The *Selma Reporter* included a graphic of a partially unrolled map of Alabama.

Above middle: This is another standing headline graphic used to help readers find the telegraphic news in the *Richmond Enquirer*. The *Enquirer*'s graphic featured a representation of the Confederate Stars and Bars, the first national flag of the Confederacy. It is apparent from the number of stars on the flag — eight — that this graphic was created early in the war, before the secession of Arkansas (May 6), North Carolina (May 20), and Tennessee (June 8). (*Richmond Enquirer*)

Right: To drum up advertising to replace what was lost from the North after secession, William H. Barnes of Atlanta established the European and Confederate States Advertising Agency. The agency's intent was to acquire European advertising for Confederate newspapers and place advertisements for Confederate businesses in European papers. Today, it is unknown how successful this enterprise was, or how long it lasted. (*Atlanta Southern Confederacy*)

Top left: Confederate women at home in Virginia. Women took up many jobs during the war that were closed off to them before. They worked in factories, ran plantations, and even helped produce newspapers by working in composing rooms. At least three Southern women served as Confederate war correspondents, but their names have not been preserved for history. (Courtesy of the Library of Congress)

Top right: Captured Confederate fortifications at Manassas. This seemingly unimportant place was the site of two major battles. (Courtesy of the Library of Congress)

Bottom left: Captured Confederate soldiers in Culpeper, Virginia. Early in the war, prisoners of war were generally exchanged or paroled shortly after battles. However, after the middle of 1863, this system broke down, and both the Union and the Confederacy had to find ways to deal with long-term prisoners. (Courtesy of the Library of Congress)

Middle left: A view of Sharpsburg, Maryland. The battle fought here in 1862 was the single bloodiest day of the war. (Courtesy of the Library of Congress)

A page from the 21 May 1862 *New Orleans Picayune* shortly after the city fell to the Union. Note that the paper did not use a banner. This saved space since paper supplies were difficult to acquire. Many newspapers, including the *Picayune*, switched from a four-or-more page format to two pages and reduced the size of their pages in order to save paper.

Top left: Confederate prisoners of war at Gettysburg. Never again would the Confederacy launch a major invasion of the North. (Courtesy of the Library of Congress)

Top right: Confederate soldiers killed on July 1, 1863, at Gettysburg. Lee's Confederates were initially successful on the first day of the battle, but they could not capitalize on their early success. (Courtesy of National Archives)

Bottom right: The battlefield at Cold Harbor, Virginia. Grant lost about 7,000 men in the first hour of this battle, compounding the already staggering casualties his assault on Richmond had cost in the spring of 1864. In the month-long campaign for Richmond that began with the Battle of the Wilderness in early May, Grant lost some 55,000 men. (Courtesy of the Library of Congress)

Bottom left: Confederate prisoners of war at Chattanooga. The second loss of Chattanooga was one of the Confederacy's most embarrassing moments, and it opened the door for Sherman's assault on Atlanta and his March to the Sea. (Courtesy of the Library of Congress)

Middle left: The summit of Lookout Mountain, near Chattanooga. Because of the steep cliffs leading to the summit, Confederate guns were virtually useless to repel the Union assault; they could not be aimed at a sharp enough angle to shoot at the advancing Federal troops. (Courtesy of the Library of Congress)

Above: A view of one of Atlanta's main thoroughfares, White Hall Street. By saving Lincoln's administration, the loss of Atlanta sealed the Confederacy's doom. (Courtesy of the Library of Congress)

Top right: The front page of the *Mobile Advertiser and Register,* 8 May 1864. By this time, newspapers were running news on their front pages. This was a change from the prewar practice of putting news on the inside pages and devoting the front page to advertising.

Above: Refugees at the Atlanta train depot, fleeing Sherman's occupation. Once Sherman decided to abandon the city in the fall of 1864, he ordered the remaining civilians to evacuate the city. (Courtesy of the Library of Congress)

Bottom left: Sherman's shelling of Atlanta left the train depot in rubble. The campaign began in early May 1864. Its purpose was to reach Atlanta and stop the flow of resources from the Deep South to the Confederate troops in Virginia. Sherman understood that the Southern fight for independence would not end until the Union had won a devastating victory, and so he embarked upon a campaign of "total war," intending to break up the flow of resources and to demoralize the Southern population. After Atlanta fell in early September, Sherman's troops rested for a few weeks before moving out on his infamous March to the Sea and an even more destructive march through the Carolinas. (Courtesy of the Library of Congress)

Top left: An Atlanta slave market. According to historian Peter Kolchin, in 1860 about one-quarter of Southern slaves lived with resident masters in small holdings of between one and nine slaves. About half lived in mid-sized holdings of ten to forty nine slaves, and the final quarter lived in large holdings of fifty or more slaves. About three-quarters of the slaves in the South worked as field hands, and the other quarter were trained for a variety of jobs, including mill work, blacksmithing, cooking, and nursing the sick and injured. Sometimes slaves even worked as overseers of other slaves. (Courtesy of the Library of Congress)

Top right: The *Atlanta Intelligencer* office on White Hall Street. The *Intelligencer* office was located next to the railroad depot, which made it very easy for the newspaper to get the latest news as each train arrived in town. (Courtesy of the Library of Congress)

Middle right: View of Nashville from the steps of the Tennessee capitol building. The city's early loss was a major blow for the Confederacy and Isham Harris, leader of the Confederate faction in Tennessee. (Courtesy of the Library of Congress)

Bottom right: Fort McAllister guarded the Southern approach to Savannah and represented the last obstacle Union General William T. Sherman had to conquer to be successful in his march through Georgia. The fort's worn out guns were no match for the Union forces that assaulted it on the afternoon of 13 December 1864. The contest for the fort was reduced to hand-to-hand combat, but the bastion fell after only ten or fifteen minutes of fighting. (Courtesy of the Library of Congress)

Left: Confederate works at Petersburg. Artillery proved inadequate to destroy well-built field fortifications. (Courtesy of the Library of Congress)

Above: The siege of Petersburg was one of the most dramatic actions of the war. From June 1864 until April 1865, the Union army ringed Virginia's second largest city to keep supplies from reaching Lee's Confederates. This soldier is one of many Southerners who died in the frequent skirmishes at Petersburg during the nine-month siege. (Courtesy of the Library of Congress)

Confederate encampment at Petersburg, Virginia. The nine-month-long struggle for Virginia's second largest city, with both sides heavily dug in, resembled the trench warfare of World War I. Petersburg was strategically important because it was home to a bullet manufacturer and because it was a railroad hub that connected many different parts of the Confederacy. (Courtesy of the Library of Congress)

Top left: Many of the majestic homes along Charleston's Battery were destroyed by shelling during the siege of the city that began in April 1863. (Courtesy of the Library of Congress)

Top right: Meeting Street, a main thoroughfare in Charleston, was also destroyed by shelling during the siege that began in April 1863. (Courtesy of the Library of Congress)

Bottom right: The Circular Church was destroyed in the siege of Charleston. (Courtesy of the Library of Congress)

Top: A view of Richmond. When a city fell, first its defenders would destroy as much as possible to keep it from the enemy, then looters would help themselves, and then the invaders would destroy what they wished. (Courtesy of the Library of Congress)

Middle left: The Confederate capitol building in Richmond, Virginia. This is where the Confederate Congress met during its sessions. Because of the proximity of Richmond to Washington, D.C., its conquest became a top objective for the Union army. (Courtesy of the Library of Congress)

Above and right: Ruined papermill in Richmond, Virginia. When the Civil War began, the South had only a handful of papermills and relied on European and Northern imports to supply its needs for paper. Paper shortages bedeviled Confederate newspapers from almost the beginning of the conflict. The mill was destroyed in the final Union assault on the Confederate capital in early April 1865. (Courtesy of the Library of Congress)

Civilians gather at Appomattox following Lee's surrender. The surrender agreement was negotiated at the home of Wilmer McLean. McLean had moved to Appomattox after his home near Manassas, Virginia, was converted into a Confederate hospital and headquarters following the First Battle of Manassas. (Courtesy of the Library of Congress)

Confederate General Robert E. Lee (*right*) surrendered to Grant at the McLean house near Appomattox, Virginia (*above*). (Courtesy of the Library of Congress)

5

REPORTING THE WAR, 1864

A slight glimmer of hope remained for the Confederacy in 1864. The Union was, after all, no closer to Richmond than it had been in 1861, and Virginia geography so favored its Southern defenders that the Union had little to show for its gargantuan casualty lists. The situation in the West, though, told the rest of the story. Tennessee remained solidly in Union hands, Sherman and Grant having successfully rolled the Confederates out of the eastern part of the state the previous fall. The South's chances of destroying a Union army in a great decisive battle were shrinking as rapidly as the ranks of the Confederate army. Fewer men were available, and more were deserting. Dissent and dissatisfaction with the war effort would reach a fever pitch before 1864 was out.

The Union war effort was dominated by two generals who had spent most of the war together: Grant, now overall commander as well as effective commander in the East, and Sherman in the West. More modern in their thinking than most of their contemporaries, they sought to attack the Confederacy's capacity to make war, although in different ways. Sherman would attack rebel morale, while Grant decided to grind Lee's army down. The Confederate army, not Richmond, was his real target. In a famously terse order, Grant told his subordinate Meade: "Wherever Lee goes, there you will go also." In May, the Union soldiers set off south again.

Although Grant finally brought strategic clarity to the Union's war effort, his operational perspective was soon found wanting. Constantly underestimating Lee and overestimating Confederate losses, the series of battles Grant waged in May and June of 1864 nearly destroyed the Union army rather than its target. The Battles of The Wilderness, Spotsylvania Courthouse, the North Anna, and Cold Harbor cost him 60,000 men, about 10,000 a week, decimated his best veteran regiments, demoralized many men at a time that enlistments were about to expire, and left Lee undestroyed and Richmond uncaptured. At Cold Harbor, Grant had suffered one of the worst Union defeats of the war, yet it brought him no closer to Richmond than

McClellan had been. To be sure, Grant finally stopped his battering-ram attacks and slipped to the southeast and invested Petersburg, thereby cutting Richmond off from much of the Confederacy. But this brilliant move did little in the short run to make up for his massive casualties—and raised the specter of a Democratic victory in the fall presidential election. Lincoln's opponent, his former chief general, George McClellan, represented a party that was committed to a negotiated peace. Attacking and laying siege to Petersburg would not dissuade people from voting for the Democrats, possibly giving the Confederacy the proverbial eleventh-hour reprieve.

All hopes, both Southern and Northern, hinged on what happened in the West. If the Union could capture Atlanta, Lincoln's reelection would be assured. If the South could stop the assault on its important transportation center, Southern longing for independence had a chance of becoming reality. Northerners and Southerners alike watched the campaign in north Georgia with trepidation. Sherman's advance toward Atlanta progressed slowly at first. His opponent, the wily Johnston, severely punished the Yankees' one attempt to break through, at Kennesaw Mountain in late June. As the battle lines closed in on Atlanta, however, fate, in the person of Jefferson Davis, intervened. Worried about the future of Atlanta, and failing to get clear answers from Johnston on his plans, Davis appointed the aggressive John B. Hood in his place. Hood promptly launched several attacks from the Atlanta fortifications, all of which failed and culminated in his forced withdrawal from the city. On 2 September 1864, Sherman entered Atlanta, probably saving the Lincoln administration in the process.

Grant could now continue his lengthy siege operations at Petersburg, weakening Lee by attacks and stretching the lines to the west, forcing the Confederate front to become thinner and thinner. Although there were occasional disasters, such as the Battle of the Crater on 30 July, which cost the Union nearly 4,000 men to the Confederates' 1,200, the siege forced the Confederate army to sit still, depriving Lee of his vaunted skills at maneuvering an army. The chance for a decisive Confederate battlefield victory had disappeared, because the traditional battlefield had disappeared.

Sherman, however, was concerned that the South might continue the war indefinitely, especially through irregular operations. He resolved to convince the South that its victory was an impossibility. He would do it by waging a total war to end the conflict. In this the Union general was immensely helped by a speech Davis gave in Macon in late September. Speaking to a crowd of refugees who had come to Macon when they fled Atlanta, the president revealed the manpower problems that plagued the Confederate army. The president estimated that somewhere around a third of the soldiers were missing from their positions. Sherman realized that he had virtually no serious opposition. A handful of Confederate cavalry under the controversial General Joseph Wheeler and a few thousand Georgia militiamen and Confederate regulars were all that stood between him and the Atlantic Ocean. The majority of the Confederacy's troops were in Virginia, and the western army against which he had fought so long for possession of Atlanta was off in Tennessee. Come mid-December, Hood's ill-considered plan to draw Sherman away from Atlanta by invading Tennessee would result in the almost total destruction of the Army of Tennessee near Nashville. Thus, Sherman was emboldened to embark on his infamous March to the Sea, burning public buildings along the way and living off the land. Sherman's army captured Savannah on 22 December, prompting the general to send Lincoln the most famous telegraph of the war, the one in which he flamboyantly presented Savannah to Lincoln as a Christmas present. The vulnerability of the Southern interior lands, and the impotence of the Confederate government, had been decisively demonstrated. The plantation economy collapsed as huge numbers of slaves abandoned their bondage.

WESTERN THEATER

Atlanta Campaign

Union General William T. Sherman was reputed to be crazy, but what he truly was, was clever. After the hard fighting at Chattanooga late in 1863, Sherman had several months to survey the situation of the South and to think about his next step in winning a war that had been just as long and bloody as he had predicted it would be back in 1861. The key, he realized, was Atlanta. So long as Lee could get supplies for his Army of Northern Virginia, he could keep up at least some semblance of a fighting force. Georgia was where most of those supplies were produced, and Atlanta was the rail center from which they were shipped. That meant Atlanta had to fall. Sherman, with the blessing of his commanding officer, Ulysses S. Grant, set about building up his army. By spring, Sherman had nearly 100,000 men under his command, and he was ready to begin his campaign for Atlanta through territory with which he was imminently familiar. Early in his army career, Sherman had been stationed in Marietta, a small town to the northwest of Atlanta, and he had thoroughly reconnoitered north Georgia then.

Opposing Sherman was one of the Confederacy's most stalwart and reliable generals, Joseph E. Johnston. Johnston, who had been sent to resolve the hopeless situation at Vicksburg in the summer of 1863, once again got the job of keeping a vastly superior force from capturing a vital Southern city. Johnston had been named commander of the 60,000-man Army of Tennessee after its previous leader, Braxton Bragg, resigned in humiliation over the loss of Chattanooga. Johnston was exactly the right man for the job. He was a master of defensive strategy, almost prescient at knowing when to withdraw and where to put up the mightiest fight. But there was a bad side to Johnston's selection, too: Davis hated him. The president blamed Johnston, not Pemberton, for the loss of Vicksburg, and he was willing to listen to just about any criticism of his least favorite general.

In early May, Sherman's army moved out from Chattanooga. Through May, Johnston skillfully fought Sherman in a series of delaying positions at Dalton, Resaca, and Cassville. Sherman, equally skillfully, outmaneuvered Johnston each time the two forces met. In late May, Sherman began a drive due south and swept past Johnston's position near Allatoona. Johnston withdrew to Marietta to meet Sherman face-to-face in the Battle of Kennesaw Mountain. Through June, the two commanders toyed with one another in small engagements and maneuvers. In late June, the impatient and impetuous Sherman decided he had had enough of small probing movements that bought little ground. It was time to get serious and destroy the Army of Tennessee in one huge, decisive battle. Sherman ordered a direct assault on the Confederate entrenchments on Kennesaw Mountain. The attack began at 8:00 A.M. on 27 June with a Union artillery barrage. Sherman sent McPherson to attack the Confederate positions on the south side of the mountain, Thomas was to support McPherson, and Schofield was to create a diversion with a feint to the south. Almost immediately, Sherman's plans got derailed. The feint did not work, and McPherson's men, though initially successful, were pinned down by heavy Confederate fire. Thomas's men advanced, with bayonets only initially, to within 15 yards of the Confederate line, but after a three-hour fight, they, too, were forced to withdraw. The battle for Sherman was a disaster. He lost 3,000 men to the Confederacy's 800.

Sherman rested his demoralized men for a week before once again moving against Johnston. This time, the Union general's plan was to turn Johnston's left and sweep past him into Marietta. Informed by his scouts of Sherman's movements, Johnston chose to abandon Marietta and take up a strong entrenched position north of the Chattahoochee River.

On 9 July, Sherman's men bypassed Johnston to cross the Chattahoochee, the last natural barrier between the Union army and Atlanta. Two days later, Sherman sent McPherson east to Decatur and Stone Mountain to cut the railroad lines between Atlanta and Augusta, which eliminated the possibility of Johnston receiving reinforcements by rail from Virginia. Johnston was watching the Union army carefully and noted a gap between Thomas's and Schofield's lines. He saw an opening there for a successful attack, but Johnston was waiting for the federals to get closer before attacking. He never got the chance to go on the offensive, though. Jefferson Davis chose that precise moment to fire Johnston. It was one of the worst decisions the president made in the entire war. The ungrateful president had failed to note that his general had waged a remarkable defensive campaign through the early summer. For 2.5 months, Johnston had managed to hold Sherman's advance to an average of 1 mile per day, and the Confederate general had suffered few losses in the campaign. Nevertheless, on 17 July, Johnston was summarily relieved, and his impulsive subordinate, John B. Hood, was elevated to the rank of general and given the command of the Army of Tennessee.

Hood, who had a reputation for being a battlefield brawler, immediately went on the offensive. On 20 July, he ordered an attack intended to push entrenched Thomas's Union infantrymen away from the banks of Peachtree Creek and back toward the Chattahoochee. Hood's orders prior to the attack confused his men about where they were to advance, but he went on with the attack anyway. Hood caught Thomas by surprise but was repulsed nevertheless. Both forces in the Battle of Peachtree Creek had about 20,000 men each. Union losses were 1,600 to the Confederacy's 2,500.

Even before the fighting died down from Peachtree Creek, Sherman was pulling together his forces for an assault on the prize itself: Atlanta. Hood believed he had an opportunity to go on the offensive against McPherson. He positioned Stewart's corps and the Georgia militia in a defensive ring around Atlanta and sent Hardee's troops on an all-night forced march to the east in an attempt to get behind the Northern lines. Wheeler's cavalry also moved east to destroy federal wagons near the town of Decatur. McPherson had anticipated that the Confederates would make exactly this move and had repositioned his forces to repulse the attack. The day ended at least indecisively, if not in outright disaster, for the Confederates.

Despite consecutive successes, Sherman realized he did not have the manpower to besiege Atlanta, but his objective was not so much possession of the Gate City as destroying its function as a transportation center. He could accomplish his objective with fewer resources, in either men or supplies, by focusing on destruction of the last two open railroads into Atlanta. Sherman sent Major General Oliver O. Howard west to destroy the Macon and Western and the Atlanta and West Point lines. He sent his cavalry raiding to the south. Hood learned of Howard's movement and sent two corps to oppose him in the Battle of Ezra Church on 28 July. The Confederates were repulsed, with losses of some 4,300 men to the federal loss of 632. The cavalry raids had less success.

Sherman's 6,000 cavalry, commanded by Hugh Judson Kilpatrick, had two jobs. The first was to cut the railroad, and the second was to liberate Union prisoners at Andersonville. The cavalry worked for nearly a month to accomplish those objectives but failed and lost some 2,000 men on 4 August when Major General George Stoneman was surrounded and forced to surrender.

Sherman was becoming more frustrated with his inability to cut the rail lines and looked for other alternatives. Atlanta's defenses were far too strong for a direct attack, and he had already rejected the idea of a siege. The only option was to shell Atlanta into submission, and so on 9 August, Sherman began an intense bombardment of the city. His artillerymen responded by slinging more than 5,000 shells into the city that day alone. The bombardment continued for two weeks until, finally, on 25 August, it just stopped. The first thought was that Sherman had given up and moved off, but soon word reached Hood of a new federal advance. Sherman left one corps to guard his communications lines and took his remaining three armies forward in a wheeling movement toward the rail lines south of Atlanta. The movement was so successful that it forced Hood to abandon Atlanta.

On 1 September, Sherman's determination paid off. The last rail line into Atlanta was cut. Hardee had managed to hold his position until after nightfall on 1 September, but he could not do anything more. Hood ordered warehouses of Confederate supplies to be put to the torch rather than allow them to fall into Union hands. After midnight, a huge explosion announced the end of an ammunition train Hood had been unable to get away from the city. Sherman heard the explosion 15 miles away in Jonesboro, and he knew then that Atlanta was his.

WAVERLY: STATE OF GENERAL JOHNSTON'S ARMY

In early May, federal General William T. Sherman made the first move in a campaign that would take him through the heartland of the remaining unoccupied Confederate states. The Army of Tennessee, now under command of Joseph E. Johnston, cleverly parried each Union advance and slowed Sherman's force to a snail's pace. The effort would not be sufficient to repulse Sherman, but the Army of Tennessee made him pay dearly for each step toward Atlanta. This was one of the better covered campaigns since reporters from several newspapers were with Johnston, and the Atlanta and Augusta papers, as well as the Confederate Press Association, could easily send reporters to the front from time to time. Waverly, the Memphis Appeal's *correspondent with Johnston's army, sent a pair of dispatches that described the initial advance of Sherman's troops. The* Appeal *had been published in Atlanta since the previous summer. In his first dispatch, Waverly dealt primarily with military matters. He discussed the morale of the Confederate troops and early skirmishes but inaccurately estimated the federal army had some 60,000 men. In truth, Sherman's force at that point was closer to 100,000. Waverly's second dispatch, begun on a quiet Sunday morning, is almost lyrical in its description of Dalton that morning and his anticipation of whether he would hear church bells first or cannon fire that would signal the beginning of the day's engagement. The fight for Atlanta was long and bitter, and Waverly and the other correspondents with Johnston would do their best to tell Confederate citizens what was happening in northern Georgia, but by the end of May, strict censorship by the military would curtail—though not stop—the reporting.*

Memphis Appeal, 9 May 1864

GENERAL JOHNSTON'S ARMY
Letter No. 1
Special Correspondence of the Memphis Appeal
In the Field, May 6, 1864

To-Day

The ball opened at 8 o'clock this morning. The enemy advanced, one division in force, toward Sulcker's gap, four miles above Dalton, on our left, and were handsomely repulsed. The skirmish lay along Stewart's line. The firing was regular for several hours, but not particularly heavy. Small arms were only used by sharp-shooters. Considerable damage was done. Loss trifling on our side.

The Prospect

Every one anticipates a great battle to morrow. The outside indications certainly favor this idea. Couriers are dashing hither and thither, guns are booming now and then, and reports of the most exaggerated description go from lip to lip. I do not look for a fight quite so soon, although it is highly probable that they will attack our left to-morrow. Hitherto our right has been regarded as the point of investment, but the scene has shifted.

The Tennessee Troops

Your heart would swell with pride if you could see the noble Tennessee boys, who compose so large a part of this army. Led by the most skillful and vallant commanders, they are especially cheered by the presence of their governor. He is here, and he never fails to be, when a fight is on hand. Just out of West Tennessee, where he passed through Forrest's late campaign, Gov. Harris breathes the air of home to the troops. He appears among them constantly, delivers the most encouraging addresses, and is met with expressions of enthusiastic welcome.

The Force of the Enemy

I know that you want to know something of Sherman's force. Wiser heads estimate it at not over sixty thousand. Kilpatrick's cavalry will not exceed a tenth part of that number. As to our force it is sufficient to say that no one here is frightened.

The Result

Keep up the liveliest heart imaginable in the rear. There is no sort of danger. You never saw such pluck in all your born days. Especially do not believe the monstrous rumors in circulation among the speculators.

WAVERLY.

AFFAIRS IN FRONT
Letter No II

Special Correspondence of the Appeal.]
DALTON, Sunday Morning, May 7, 1864.
The Sabbath Day Near the Enemy—What is the Prospect?—The Struggle for Position—News from Middle Tennessee—The Guns Open, etc.

I take out my watch. The time is just five minutes to 8 o'clock, and the morning is as bright and clear as ever a Sunday in the peaceful days of yore. The birds are bob-o-linking in the leafy trees; the sunny greet, that dances in the wind, is moving with them. The troops slept on their arms last night, but Dalton has very little semblance of war. I think I shall hear the bells presently, and have once or twice oddly fancied that it was most time for Sunday school. Any one of these quiet moments, which steal around me as I write, may be broken into a thousand fragments by the loud report of cannon echoing among the hills and glens. The first gun will call me hence, and so I will hasten to jot you a few random notes before I am disturbed.

The Impending Battle

So the fight has not yet opened. As I wrote you, the wager of battle is not determined. The handkerchief, whose fall is to signal the two armies to combat, still flutters in the air. It may drop today—it may not touch the ground for a week to come. This looks like "an opinion as [*unreadable*] opinion," but it is quite logical. You see both sides are maneuvering for positions. Johnston is so apt at their species of strategy that he befogs Sherman, who shifts from right to left and from left to right, and then masses on the center, like the shuttle of a loom, with this difference, that he isn't weaving much cloth. How far the Virginia news will effect his plans I cannot say, but if there is not a battle of some sort tomorrow (Monday) I shall be very much surprised.

The Mountains of Tennessee

I have had a conversation with one of our scouts lately out of Middle Tennessee. Stokes' (Yankee) cavalry are operating in the mountains with a free hand. One of their latest atrocities was the murder of young Marchbanks, a son of the eminent jurist. Captain Marchbanks was organizing a company in White county, not many miles above his own home. He was pursued, made captive, taken to the woods, tied to a tree and shot. His mother was then sent for and arrived before the body was buried. Stokes is riding the horse of the poor young man, and boasts of his infamous deed of blood. Arthur Mercer, a nephew of Maj. L. D. Mercer, was recently killed in a rancounter with Col. Thomas B. Murray. My informant tells me that the entire mountain country is in a terrible partisan state, and that the return of the Confederates which is expected from week to week, will be a blessing and relief.

Writing in Front

You must not expect these letters of mine to be very carefully prepared or elaborate. If one is [unreadable], he has little time left him to be picturesque. Besides, when you have ridden for half a day over rock and hill, through the sun and the dust, and at last reach a place of shade and rest, you are not in a very rhetorical humor. I will give you facts, hints of the goings-on in these parts, stray gleams of suggestive interest. You must fill in my mere outlines with "tines of deeper hue." You must not be afraid of my skeletons. I shall not be sensational, I promise you.

The Guns

Boom! boom! boom! There they go! Just as I had written the last line above, the roll of a cannon broke upon the air. What is it? A general engagement? I don't know. An attack? Perhaps so. I will go and see.

WAVERLY.

WAVERLY: STATE OF MORALE IN ATLANTA

Atlanta was hunkering down for the coming fight. Whitehall, one of the main streets in the town, was a shadow of its former self, Waverly reported after a quick visit. Where flags and ladies used to grace the street, now ordinance jammed the thoroughfare. The ladies were all home packing in case they had to flee. The change in public confidence from two weeks previous was dramatic, the reporter wrote. Waverly used his letter to assure his readers that they were safe and that the Army of Tennessee would carry the day.

Memphis Appeal, 25 May 1864

OUR ARMY CORRESPONDENCE

Letter from "Waverly."]
All Quiet in Front—A Run to Atlanta—The Perturbation of its Inhabitants—A Causeless Alarm—the Prospects upon the Outer Wall—Chattahoochee or Etowah—Reveille, etc., etc.
ATLANTA, Wednesday, May 23.

Everything is very quiet along the line in front, and your correspondent has sought the gay metropolis for a bit of recreation.

Gay, did I say? Pardon me, I would scarce recognize its changed, tumultuous aspect. The sunny side of Whitehall, which erst did gliston [sic] with stars and bars, and petticoats, seems to be in a peripatetic condition, blockaded with guards and jammed with bales and boxes of merchandize. Surely you are not expecting a visit from Sherman, or any other distinguished foreigner? Why, I found half a dozen ladies of my acquaintance packing their preserves in bandboxes and their bonnets in butter kegs, out of down-right confusion, they said; four old gentlemen locked themselves in their patent safes, (for safe keeping, I suppose) where they will have to be dug out with pike and mattock, as they drew the keys and keyholes in after them; and even one of my canine friends, partaking of the general disquiet, and having perused the ferocious proclamation of Marshal Jones, had found a dry well and was stocking it with provisions for a siege, when I assured him with tears in my eyes that there is not the least danger in the world! Odds, tremors and quakes, are ye going insane!

But let's be serious. I frankly confess my surprise. To a cool, unagitated mind the scenes transpiring from hour to hour in the streets of Atlanta are very diverting. Why what a panic you have wrought here in this vestibule of the Empire State. I have passed the morning upon Whitehall street watching the ebb and flow of popular feeling and taking notes upon the versatile physiognomy of the town. It is magical, the change. But two weeks are gone, and confidence stood like a pillar of fire before every shop and at every corner; now the very signs are creeping in doors and the street crossings disclose the most eager multitudes of tradesmen, dealing exclusively in rumors, speculations upon reports, extortioners of mischief out of each idle story that flies on the great, national, antigalvanin, non-conductive grape-vine battery! The operators thereof, to my thinking, would find a deal better work behind a dozen batters of a different description that I know of, and as for those who betray so much simplicity as to believe all they hear, they would be happier, and just as healthy, at the front!

Aye, the front. It is not such a very ugly place as you might suppose. There are lads as cheerful as crickets and sing along from morning till night, even though they be rivalled by the shells. The front is a jolly place, and cooler than Atlanta. Come, let us seek its shades of green, its pleasant nooks and coves, its river views, its drums and fifes and flags! The blue sky above us, the blue coats before us, around us the blue fields of grass and grain, we have only to prime our piece and prove our self one, two, or three of a hundred thousand patriots. Listen! Do you not hear the shrill whistle of the iron horse? He scaneth the battle from afar and snorteth for the fray. But hark, there is another sound! It is the cheer of the troops who are going to the front. They too are eager for the fight. Will you join them? Will you step forth from your very shrine to the field which is to decide whether it shall be yours forever or that of an alien master! To the front, to the front! At least to the trenches with musket, with bayonet, with conscious right and resolution! We shall carry the day, never fear it. We shall whip back the foe. There is a handful of us who have undertaken the job, and we are bound to finish it. General Johnston says so, and also that inner spirit which prompts men to do, defy and dare. Hurrah for the front! Hurrah for the line, be it Etowah or Chattahoochee! And three times three hurrahs for the victory we are going to win! We shall make the old, dry woodlands ring with rifle and cannon and we shall strew the sands with Yankee bones. Of all these races since John Gilpin, not excepting the "Camp town Races," the race back to Middle Tennessee will be the hottest, the speediest, aye, and the bloodiest!

WAVERLY.

SPECIAL: CONFEDERATE PREPARATIONS AT KENNESAW MOUNTAIN

Nearly six weeks into the spring offensive in north Georgia, the scene of action began to settle on Kennesaw Mountain, near Marietta. This was the largest engagement fought north of Atlanta, and it was a tactical success for the Confederates, though the Union forces were not stopped for long. This story described the preparations and expectations for the battle. The author, Special, regularly submitted articles to the Appeal.

Memphis Appeal, 21 June 1864

FROM THE FRONT

MARIETTA, JUNE 20, 1864.

I have just returned from a circuit of our lines, and have only time to write you a hurried letter.

Last night our lines were withdrawn to Kennesaw mountain, for reasons which have not, as yet, transpired; and heavy skirmishing has been going on since 8 o'clock this morning along the entire line.

CAPTAIN MATTHEWS: ACCOUNT OF TRUCE TO BURY DEAD AT KENNESAW MOUNTAIN

Periodically, the fighting would be stopped so that the dead could be buried. Here, Harvey, another of the Memphis Appeal's *correspondents with Johnston's army, wrote about such a truce that was arranged three days after the Battle of Kennesaw Mountain. The burial parties turned the lull in battle into a social meeting of the Union and Confederate soldiers. Harvey was a soldier correspondent for the newspaper. All that is known about his identity is that he was a Captain Matthews, though the* Athens Southern Watchman *of 10 August 1864 reported that Captain Matthews lost a leg in the Battle of Atlanta on 22 July.*

Memphis Appeal, 1 July 1864

FROM THE FRONT

Special Correspondence of the Memphis Appeal.]
IN THE FIELD, NEAR MARIETTA,
June 30, 1864.

The last of the Yankee dead in front of Cleburn and Cheatham were buried yesterday under flag of truce. I visited those divisions this morning and endeavored from the different statements and opinions expressed by officers and men, to form an estimate of the Yankee loss. In front of Gen. Cheatham, the lowest calculation I heard made was one thousand Yankees killed, while Cleburne's command claims to have slain fifteen hundred. The killed then may be safely put down at two thousand. Owing to the short range and unerring aim of our men, the proportion of the wounded cannot be so great as usual. Some think it amounted to six or eight thousand, but I will offer no guess.

During the truce a number of officers and men from both sides met midway and mingled freely in friendly conversation. Among others Generals Hindman and Cheatham, the latter in his shirt sleeves. His easy pleasant manner pleasing the Yanks, one of them familiarly elbowed the general in the side, saying, "I think you are a good reb. Give me a drink old fel." Where upon the general politely passed over his canteen of water. "Do you know who you are talking to," inquired one of our men. "No," said the Yank, "but he is a good rebel I am certain." "Well, that is General Cheatham." Blue coat looked profound astonishment, but in a few minutes a crowd of Yankees, surrounded the two generals, gazing eagerly and presenting their pocket books for autographs, which were given.

The Yankees manifested one of their leading characteristics on every available occasion, their propensity to trade. They would sell watches, knives, stirrups, canteens, or anything they had. Tobacco was their great object, they complained of great scarcity of the article. When we sent out the flag of truce, a Yank called out, "What do you want, are you coming over to trade?" "No," replied the colonel, "I am coming to make some arrangements about burying your dead." D—m the dead, I thought you wanted to sell some tobacco for coffee.

About three o'clock this morning, the enemy believing, it is supposed, that we were evacuating our works, came out of their works and advanced cautiously upon ours, our boys though fatigued by constant vigilance, were wide awake and opened a terrible fire upon the enemy, who hastily discharged a volley or two without effect, and hastened under cover of their works. A heavy fire of musketry was kept up by both sides from their works near half an hour. One of our batteries also fired regularly. The light afforded by the flash of the guns and bursting of shells, enabled our men to see the enemy's lines distinctly until they fell back. Our loss was only one or two wounded as far as known. The enemy's unknown, as in the thick darkness that succeeded the firing, they were enabled to carry off all their dead and wounded.

Colonel Jones, of the 33d Tennessee, was killed this morning behind the works. A minie struck a limb of a tree several feet above and outside the works, glancing downwards it passed through the colonel's head, killing him instantly.

Quite a pleasant shower fell this evening, which was much needed and very refreshing.

There is a rumor afloat that Major General Stewart is to be the commander of Polk's corps. Among the numerous distinguished officers suggested for that high command, few, perhaps, combine more eminent qualifications, than this modest, unassuming Christian general.

HARVEY.

TELEGRAPH AND FELIX G. DE FONTAINE: REPORTS OF FIGHTING AROUND ATLANTA

For 2.5 months, Joseph E. Johnston waged a remarkably effective defensive and delaying campaign through north Georgia against a vastly larger Union army. On 17 July, after crossing the Chattahoochee River, an ungrateful President Davis summarily removed Johnston from the command of the Army of Tennessee. He replaced him with the impulsive, perhaps even reckless, John Bell Hood. Hood was the youngest man to achieve a four-star generalship on either side in the Civil War. A Kentucky native, Hood had been Johnston's key corps commander during the campaign for Atlanta, but he had a different strategy for dealing with the larger Union army: head-on assaults. The more aggressive approach won the approval of the Mobile Advertiser and Register, *but it lost Atlanta for the Confederacy. Once General Hood took over command of the Army of Tennessee, the nature of the campaign for Atlanta changed tremendously. As so many Southerners had hoped, he went on the offensive. The following is a telegraphic account of fighting near Griffin, which is south of Atlanta. The companion article to this telegraphic dispatch was written by Felix G. de Fontaine. In the early part of the war, de Fontaine was a correspondent, mostly in Virginia, for the* Charleston Courier. *Earlier in 1864, he had purchased the* South Carolinian *in Columbia from Dr. Robert W. Gibbes, but he left his editorial duties to his trustworthy second, Henry Timrod, and returned to the field as a correspondent for the Atlanta Campaign.*

Mobile Advertiser and Register, 31 July 1864

FURTHER OF THE FIGHT AT ATLANTA
GENS. STUART AND LORING SLIGHTLY WOUNDED
OUR OTHER GENERALS UNHURT

The Raid upon the Railroad

Punishment of the Raiders

Yankee Foragers Come to Grief
Two Negro Regiments Wh'pped
Two White Regiments to be Heard From

GRIFFIN, July 30—A citizen who arrived here late last night, from Atlanta, states that the fight on Friday was fierce and sanguinary. Our troops fought with great gallantry, carrying two lines of the enemy's entrenchments, but now hold their original position.

General Stewart and General Loring are both slightly wounded. Generals Waithall and [unreadable] reported killed, were not hurt. Stewart's is a flesh wound in the head. Loring's a ball that passed round his ribs, not entering the cavity.

Gens. Stewart and Loring started down the road on the morning train yesterday, but hearing of the enemy on the road the train turned back and escaped.

The raid, supposed to be under Col. Brownlow, captured Fayetteville yesterday morning, and burnt a lot of wagons. They are supposed to be about seventy-five.

They struck the railroad near Lovejoy's and tore up about a mile and a half of the track, at intervals extending five miles, turned the depot, and destroyed and carried off four miles of telegraph wire.

Before the arrival of their tools for the more effective destruction of the road, our cavalry under Gen. Jackson attacked and drove them off, killing eleven and wounding seventeen. The raiders fled towards Atlanta. The road is being repaired.

A small body of raiders is reported at Jackson, Bolts county this morning, making in the direction of the railroad. Our forces are after them.

Severe Fighting around Atlanta

[Correspondence of the Savannah Republican]
BEHIND THE CHATTAHOOCHEE
July 20, 1860

The movements of this morning have been in a measure significant of the events bout to follow. At daylight the enemy commenced pressing our cavalry on the right, now covering the Augusta and Atlanta railroad, several miles of which they destroyed. Heavy skirmishing ensued, during which the enemy planted a battery within range of the city and three shells in the vicinity of one of our hospitals, no more than 500 yards from the heart of the town. Gen. Wheeler, observing this diabolic act, promptly ran a battery into position, and after half a dozen well directed shells, drove the Yankees from their temporary foothold.

At just twelve o'clock a gathering of Gen. Hood's own military household in front of headquarters announced still another in the chain of mysterious events. But I had not long to wait for the unraveling of the web. The noble Texan, arrayed in full uniform, leaning on his crutch and stick, was standing in the doorway, his manner calm, his eyes flashing, with a strange indescribable light, which gleams in them only in the hour of battle. His first observation as he took my hand was, "Mr. ———, at one I attack the enemy. He has pressed our lines until he is within a short distance of Atlanta, and I must fight or evacuate. I am going to fight. The odds are against us, but I have the issue with the God of battles." We parted, and Gen. Hood, with his staff, Gen. Lovell, Gen. Mackail and escort then proceeded to the lines. I have remained at headquarters to write these hurried words anticipatory of the battle.

The moments are slipping by, as anxious moments always do, tediously and yet not without a sensation of heart agony that is utterly depressing. One hour more and the mettle of an army opposed by double its numbers, fighting behind breastworks, with diabolic incentive, the spires of Atlanta in view, and its booty in prospect, will be undergoing an ordeal by fire. One hour more and hundreds of dead friends, whose merry laugh you have answered around their camp fires, may be wallering in their blood at these strange hillsides or gone forever to their hong homes. One hour more and thousands will become widows and orphans, and weary heart cries will ascend to Heaven over the new sacrifice which the [unreadable] struggle demands; while brave men, borne together, will linger for a time under the knife and saw of the surgeons, and then perhaps return to their homes maimed for life.

We read of war and its glories, and enthusiasm pervades our nature at every recital of a heroic act, but when this dreadful reality confronts us, bounded only by the space of an hour or a moment, there is something within us which involuntarily recoils at the repetition of those scores of suffering and death which, however beneficial in their results to the country, such a fearful price for the good attained, that we remember them only with a shudder. How much more so under circumstances like the present, when the very existence of an army hangs in the balance.

Night, July 20.—A [unreadable], or rather an engagement has taken place, and the fitful splashes of musketry along the line denote that it has ended without [unreadable] results. I am too weary to enter much into details, and probably it would not be prudent to do so first, because of the incompleteness of the affair, and secondly, the liability of capture while the letter is *en route* to Macon, being fear that the enemy will strike our only remaining line of communication tonight. The following, therefore, is only a simple outline of the afternoon's work.

The object of Gen. Hood in planning the attack was of two fold, namely to withdraw if possible from the enemy's left to centre and right a portion of the forces with which he had been so persistently pressing our right, and to defeat and cut up one of its wings.

By examining the map and recalling the preceding description of the situation of Sherman's forces, you will observe that a portion of the latter extended from near the junction of the Chattahoochee and Peachtree Creek in an easterly direction. Into the [unreadable] it was believed that by a proper combination of our forces, we could drive the right of Sherman's army, and affect the object in view. Stewart's corps held our left, Hardee the centre. The attack by these two bodies was nearly simultaneous. The advance commenced about 2 o'clock. Leaving the breastworks, our men slowly but confidently pushed their way towards the front. Skirmishing began almost immediately. Strange to say, a part of the enemy's line was discovered to be also advancing. Our army charged with [unreadable], and drove it back in disorder.

One, two, and in some instances three lines of incipient or temporary breastworks were mounted and left behind, and the battle in our favor appeared to go on swimmingly. Suddenly Stewart was brought to a stand still. In his front was the main line of Yankee entrenchments and a redoubt manned by a battery. Gathering fresh strength, however, one of his brigades plunged against this work and it yielded. A heavy enfilading fire from a park of artillery on the right drove them back. The Federals reoccupied the redoubt. Our men advanced a second time and again captured it, but by the same terrible fire poured upon them from the distant artillery, were compelled to abandon the prise. Meanwhile Hardee had also reached the continuation of the same line. His men fighting bravely had overcome every obstacle thus far and were prepared to dash yet further out and drive the enemy into the creek. But here, the judgment of the commander and the gallantry of the troops were at variance. Gen. Hardee deemed it imprudent to risk the lives of his men in achieving an object which threatened to cost so much. A halt was ordered, and in brief, no further efforts were made to accomplish the end of the expedition.

Of course disappointment prevails throughout the army at the result, for the troops engaged—each one [unreadable] the dash and gallantry of the other—were satisfied of their ability to go on. No blame can, therefore, attach to any one for the negative victory plainly won, and the only regret expressed among the men is that the officers in command were, as they believe, in the present instance, over prudent in putting probabilities against what seemed a certainty.

Our losses in the affair will doubtless not fall short of a thousand [unreadable] in the corps of Gen. Steward [unreadable] captured are two or three stands or colors, and some two or three hundred prisoners. Hooker's corps is represented by [unreadable] badly crippled.

The death of Maj. W. Preston, son of Brig. Gen. John S. Preston, of Columbia, and the dangerous wound of Brig. Gen. C. B. Stevens, of S.C., commanding a Georgia brigade of Walker's division, have been reported by telegraph. The former was one of the most prominent officers in the army, and a universal favorite having filled offices of the highest trust and, in the mall, demonstrated himself with honor and courage. He was killed by a shell while giving orders to his men.

Gen. Stevens has likewise won for himself an enviable reputation for gallantry on every field of battle in which he has been engaged. He was shot while leading his men, the ball entering behind the right ear and lodging in the brain, from which it has not up to this writing been removed. His horse was killed at the same moment, and two men who went to his relief were wounded. One may judge the severity of the enemy's fire from these statements. Gen. S. will probably be sent to Macon to-morrow, and if possible from that point homewards.

While the fight I have recorded was in progress on the left, Wheeler's cavalry successfully held the enemy's infantry in check on our right. With—small brigades he contested the ground with two corps—Dodge's and Logan's—and after twelve or fourteen hours' hard fighting has prevented them from obtaining any advantage. Cannonading has been constant along the lines all day.

The enemy are evidently endeavoring to maneuver Hood out of Atlanta, but there is quite as much probability that within thirty-six hours, Sherman will be maneuvering to get away from him.

F. G. de F.

CONFEDERATE: REPORT ON THE DEFENSE OF ATLANTA

The Columbus Sun's *correspondent,* Confederate, *sent back a letter that described firsthand the fighting around Atlanta as Sherman's forces desperately tried to cut the rail lines into the city. The story makes it clear that not only are the city's military installations the targets of Sherman's artillery barrage, so is the civilian population. In the face of the Union onslaught, the writer's defiant spirit was remarkable, opening the question as to whether the letter was consciously written to boost morale or whether the writer truly believed the Confederate army might actually be able to keep up the defense of Atlanta and perhaps eventually drive off Sherman.* Confederate's *comment about the Georgia militia hinted at a long-standing argument between President Davis and Governor Joseph E. Brown over who contolled state troops and how they should be used.*

Columbus Sun, 9 August 1864 (Columbus, Ga.)

CORRESPONDENCE OF THE DAILY SUN
LETTER FROM "CONFEDERATE"

ATLANTA, Aug. 5th, 1864.

The enemy for two days have been constantly shelling the city, from the battery on the Marietta road. Three persons were killed [*unreadable*] before last. Mr. Warner and daughter ten years old killed in bed, the latter being cut in two and died instantly; the former had both his legs cut from his body, lived some hours.—The third person killed was a young lady whose name I have been unable to learn.

Such disposition has been made of our forces, as is believed will in future, prevent the recurrence of the raids which have lately disgraced the country and army and done much serious damage to our lines of communication. Squads of the raiders continue to be picked up through the country and brought in. The capture of the great raider, Stoneman, is a serious loss to the enemy.

The militia continue to arrive by every train. Let them come. They should have been at the front long ago. Among other familiar faces, I notice that of your Mr. DeWolf. He commands a squad of the unterrified. Gen. Toombs appears very active in the discharge of his duties with the militia. Gen. Smith told me yesterday that he believed they would fight as well as any other troops we have. I hope so.

The enemy continues to try and make headway to his right, towards the Atlanta and West Point Railroad. East Point, where the A & W. P. Railroad intersects the Macon Road, is no doubt the point they aim at. A bloody battle will come off before they reach it.

I was pained to notice, while passing through the soldiers cemetery in this place a few days since, the little pains taken in burying the soldiers who have died in the hospitals and been killed in the engagements near here, and the neglect in not having the graves properly marked. I noticed many that had only a rough piece of board, that will decay or fall down in a few months, with the name of the deceased, written on it with a pencil, or a small piece of paper, and in many instances has already been washed off by the rain and gone.— There is no excuse for this and it should not be. At Marietta, the grave of every soldier is plainly marked.

The mails are now sent to us from Griffin.

CONFEDERATE.

AN ANONYMOUS REPORT: FALL OF ATLANTA

Even the journalists still at Atlanta were cut off once the city fell. No information was getting in, and little was getting out. Rumors were circulating in Macon that Hood had evacuated Atlanta the previous day, as indeed he had, but there was no way at the time to verify the information since the rail lines into the city had been cut. The information about the fall of Atlanta is buried in the story, not because the Mercury's *editors did not recognize the important part of the story but because news practice of the day was to add dispatches to the bottom of the telegraphic news already typeset.*

Charleston Mercury, 5 September 1864

TELEGRAPHIC
FALL OF ATLANTA

MACON, September 3.—Parties from the front report that our losses on Wednesday did not exceed six hundred.

On Thursday the enemy made four assaults on our lines in heavy column. They were each time repulsed with great slaughter. They then concentrated their strength on GOWAN'S front, and, breaking our lines there, the retreat of our forces became necessary—which was effected on Thursday night.

Prisoners report only four Yankee corps engaged—three menacing Atlanta and guarding communications. No reliable information has been received regarding yesterday's operations or the position of HOOD.

During the last two days the city has been full of the wildest rumors, and owing to operations on the line of railroad the communication with the press reported at Atlanta is impracticable. The result of the action on Thursday was that our forces, oppressed with overwhelming numbers, fell back to Lovejoy Station, and S. D. LEE, by orders of HOOD, fell back towards Atlanta, leaving the railroad in possession of the enemy. It is now ascertained that six corps of SHERMAN'S troops were thrown upon the railroad. Only HARDEE'S and LEE'S corps confronted them.

The loss on both sides is large, but as the Yankees on Thursday attacked our entrenchments, it is supposed they suffered much heavier than we. No reliable details can be obtained.

The report is current in this city, that HOOD evacuated Atlanta yesterday morning, but there is no positive information of his movements. A collision occurred yesterday on the Macon road near Barnesville, killing twenty persons and smashing up the train badly.

EVACUATION OF ATLANTA

MACON, September 4.—All doubts about the fall of Atlanta are ended. It was evacuated by our forces on Thursday night, and occupied by the enemy at 11 o'clock on Friday morning. General HOOD blew up his supplies of ordnance, burned his commissary stores, and drew off on the McDonough Road, leaving nothing in Atlanta but bloodstained ruins.

Yesterday our whole army was concentrated at Lovejoy's Station, on the Macon and Western Railroad. The enemy is reported to be retreating from that point towards Atlanta.

In the fight at Jonesboro on Thursday, Gen. GOWAN, together with the 6th and part of the 2d Arkansas Regiments, were captured. We lost six pieces of artillery, and captured six.

GEN. HOOD'S OFFICIAL ACCOUNT

RICHMOND, September 4.—The following official despatch from Gen. HOOD, dated September 3, has been received at the War Office:

"On the evening of the 30th ult., the enemy made a lodgment across Flint River, near Jonesboro'. We attacked them there on the evening of the 31st, with two corps, but failed to dislodge them. This made it necessary to abandon Atlanta, which was done on the night of the 1st instant. On the evening of the 1st that portion of our lines held by HARDEE'S corps, near Jonesboro', was assaulted by a superior force of the enemy and, being outflanked, was compelled to withdraw during the night, with the loss of eight pieces of artillery. Prisoners taken report the enemy's loss to have been very severe."

AN ANONYMOUS REPORT: EVACUATION OF ATLANTA

The Charleston Mercury *picked up an article from the* Augusta Chronicle and Sentinel's *Atlanta correspondent that described the situation there. The correspondent, writing from Decatur, another railroad town to the east of Atlanta, was able to confirm Hood's evacuation of Atlanta and how supplies there were destroyed so as not to fall into the hands of the Yankees. The correspondent described in the following story the rush to get anything of military value out of the city or distributed to citizens or destroyed, before Hood's army moved out south to McDonough. As bad for the Confederate cause as the loss of Atlanta was, the conclusion of the story hints at an even more pressing problem: desertions and dissatisfaction among the South's soldiers.*

Charleston Mercury, 7 September 1864

THE EVACUATION OF ATLANTA

(Correspondence Augusta Chronicle.)

NEAR DECATUR, FRIDAY MORNING, Sept. 2.

The occurrences of Wednesday last have ended in what I intimated in my last might be the fortunes of the day—the evacuation of the Gate City, and the removal of the forces left in its trenches to a point where they could be united with those who have been acting independently under Gen. Hardee, for the last few days.

Early on the morning of the 1st it was officially ascertained that the disaster on Wednesday evening was fully as serious as first reported and that the forces of the enemy on the Macon road consisted of five full corps of infantry, with a large force of cavalry. It was also known that a large force was south of the Chattahoochee, in the vicinity of the railroad bridge. Both of these were threatening the city, and as it would have been folly to attempt to resist both, an evacuation was promptly determined upon, while the forces of Generals Hardee and Lee should make an attempt to reach a point where they would be joined by those that might be withdrawn from the city.

The removal of all the supplies and ammunition that the transportation facilities of the army would permit, commenced early Thursday, and was continued throughout the day. Large quantities of provisions were also distributed to the people, and at nightfall all on hand stored in the Georgia railroad warehouse, and cars on the track. Throughout the day, also, the several bodies of troops, as they were withdrawn from the defences and filed through the city, were permitted access to the public stores.

The rolling stock of the railroads, consisting of about one hundred cars and six engines, was concentrated near the rolling mill before dark, and by that hour all the troops had passed through, with the exception of the rear guard, left to prevent straggling. And here I would mention a fact creditable to the State troops. Their withdrawal was accomplished in good order, and without confusion or straggling. The regulars acted differently. The order was for the troops to mass in the vicinity of McDonough, and the wagon trains and all moved out in that direction. Previous to my leaving the telegraph office was also closed, and at dark the evacuation was completed, with the exception of the detailed guard before mentioned.

Of course great excitement prevailed throughout the day, but a moderate degree of good order obtained. A few licentious citizens and soldiers embraced the occasion to display the wickedness of their natures, but the great mass of both classes acted with the greatest decorum. The citizens who had suffered from the malice of the enemy during the bombardments, looked on sorrowingly, and indulged in conjectures as to what would be their fate when once in the enemy's power; while the troops filed through the streets, with a steady tread it is true, but nevertheless with sorrow depicted on their weather beaten countenances.

As to the scenes that followed through the night I can only report second handed. The order was to burn only government property left behind, but this would necessarily involve the destruction of the Georgia depot, the rolling stock in the city, and the rolling mill. A gentleman who left the city early this morning informs me the depot was fired about 11 o'clock, and the cars, &c., an hour or two later. The explosion consequent upon the firing of the ordnance train took place about two o'clock this morning, and was heard and felt to a great distance. There are various reports as to the burning of other property, but from the best information I can gather, no instance of great outlawry occurred.

Whether the Yankees yet occupy Atlanta I cannot say, but presume the telegraph will inform you ere this reaches you. I only know that there was nothing to prevent their making an entry, as the evacuation was complete. Many citizens came out, but thousands remained—some because they could not get away, but many from choice. At daybreak this morning the enemy had not made their appearance in the city, but there was nothing to prevent their doing it at any moment.

I hear many reports of desertions by wholesale, and of dissatisfaction and straggling. Some of this is inevitable, but it is to be hoped it has not prevailed to the extent reported. It must be admitted that the discipline of the army has not been so favorable during the last thirty days as previously; why it has been so is palpable. The police regulations of the camp have been much less stringently enforced and it is to be feared that the undue license allowed has resulted deplorably in this emergency.

DR. GEORGE W. BAGBY: GENERAL HOOD MARCHES NORTH FROM ATLANTA

After the fall of Atlanta, Hood retired to western Georgia and eastern Alabama to threaten Sherman's communications lines. His objective was to force Sherman to withdraw from Atlanta, and at first, Sherman did give chase to the Confederate troops. But then the Union general abandoned the pursuit. With Hood continuing on into Tennessee, and anticipating that Sherman was fast behind him, opportunities were opening up in Georgia for a grand movement that would demonstrate just how vulnerable the Confederacy's few remaining states were. Sherman returned to Atlanta to concentrate on planning his march through Georgia. The fact that Hood's army had moved away from Atlanta came as a surprise to many Confederates, including the Charleston paper.

Charleston Mercury, 6 October 1864

LETTER FROM RICHMOND

(CORRESPONDENCE OF THE MERCURY.)

RICHMOND, Wednesday, September 28.

Yesterday we were startled to hear that HOOD'S whole army was at Rome. Some said only two corps were there— others that 16,000 men had been sent to East Tennessee, etc., but it is generally agreed that the army has changed its base square around SHERMAN's rear. All concede that it is a "make or break" movement, and yet all like it; for, say they, "we are tired of fooling."

The fight between Early's and Sheridan's cavalry, at Brown's Gap, has been magnified into a general engagement. Not so. The Gap is a powerful position, and Early (or Longstreet) is in better condition to hold it than Fisher's Hill. People from Staunton say our cavalry ran through the town as if the devil were at their heels. Signs are brighter in the valley, and we are more cheerful.

Last night it was confidently predicted that the Secretary of War had revoked all details, and that the order would be published this morning but it does not appear in the papers. It will come, though. Of course there will be revisions of the revocations, for many men must remain detailed. Nothing more has been said within the past day or two about calling out the Virginia reserves.

Persons who were around the War Department say nothing is known there about Lieut. Gen. Forrest, or Beauregard, as commander of the Army of Tennessee, or Longstreet as commander of the Valley army. Fact is, we in Richmond are behind the times.

Mr. Benjamin, in reply to a letter of a returned prisoner, states that arrangements have been made to furnish our prisoners at the North with clothing and rations.—They need both surely. Even the officers on Johnson's Island are half starved of late, as I learn from one lately released.

Butler, the absconding clerk, got nothing from the Treasury except what he drew on Knox's checks. So far, the examination of the Treasurer (Elmore's) accounts reveal nothing wrong. This comes from trustworthy officials in that Department. Hot weather has set in again.

HERMES.

March to the Sea

Union General William T. Sherman had an abiding affection for the South, and that was why he decided he had to devastate it. His successful campaign to take the rail center at Atlanta had already accomplished two of his and Grant's goals: one, to cut off Lee's supplies from the South, and two, to ensure Lincoln's reelection. The next objective was to win the war, and that meant destroying the seemingly unflagging Confederate will to win. Accomplishing that objective meant waging war not only against the Confederate military but also against the South's civilians, a concept known among military historians as "total war." Sherman knew that the only way to get the South to stop fighting a war that, in large measure, had been lost since 1863 was to bring the region to its knees. That meant fire and devastation.

Bringing Georgia to its knees, and with it the rest of the Confederacy, had certain risks. Sherman's supply line ran 400 miles back to Nashville, and stringing it out even further was impossible. However, in late September, Jefferson Davis unknowingly handed Sherman the answer to his problem. Davis traveled to Macon, Georgia, to console the evacuees there from Atlanta. He assured the assembled crowd that the Confederacy could be saved if all the deserters from the army returned and if those not serving stepped up to defend their country. If the Confederacy's manpower problem could be solved, then there was still a chance to attain Southern independence, the president assured the evacuees. Davis's remarks were widely reported in newspapers.

In mid-November, Sherman sent Thomas and his Army of the Cumberland back to Nashville and Chattanooga before cutting his supply lines and marching east from Atlanta toward the sea with 60,000 men, 2,500 wagons, and 600 ambulances laden with supplies. His men would be living off the land. Whatever they could take would be what they would eat. With virtually no opposition, Sherman sent two columns of men, one northwest and one southwest, to cut a 50-mile-wide by 300-mile-long swath of scorched earth to Savannah. His intent was "to make Georgia howl," and that is exactly what he accomplished. His men devastated crops and burned government property; but, in fairness to the general, it must be admitted that so long as civilians stayed with their property, his men might take all their food and valuables, but their houses were not put to the torch. Sherman scrupulously ignored Hood's efforts to distract him with his invasion of Tennessee, which was effectively put to an end in the Battles of Franklin and Nashville.

Confederate Generals Beauregard and Hardee worked feverishly to prepare defenses for Savannah and Charleston. Hardee's 1,500 men abandoned Savannah after the fall of Fort McAllister at the mouth of the Ogeechee River, some 15 miles from Savannah, on 13 December. Savannah fell to Sherman on 21 December without a shot being fired. He would take formal possession of the city on 22 December.

OBSERVER: ACCOUNT OF BATTLE OF GRISWOLDVILLE

The Constitutionalist's *regular correspondent filed a story about the Battle of Griswoldville. As was common, the reporter filed a story that included the best information available at the time but that was not entirely accurate. For example, he estimated Sherman's force to be 25,000 to 30,000. That was true, so far as the number of Union infantry men moving toward Macon was concerned. But there were another 30,000 taking a more northerly path through Madison, Georgia, also moving relentlessly toward the sea. The writer was correct in his assessment that Sherman had to be stopped in Georgia if there was to be any chance of stopping the Union war machine.*

Augusta Constitutionalist, 30 November 1864 (Augusta, Ga.)

SPECIAL CORRESPONDENCE OF THE CONSTITUTIONALIST

From the Front

Battle of Griswoldville—Sherman's course and forces—Depredations of the enemy—Occupation of Sandersville—Conway's men—A gallant scout

SPARTA, Nov. 27th, 9 P.M.

Mr. Editor: We have information from men belonging to Furguson's division of cavalry of the fight at Griswoldville on Tuesday. A feint was made on Macon on Sunday afternoon by some of Kilpatrick's cavalry, but Wheeler's forces were put in line of battle up and down Walnut creek, and after some heavy skirmishing, the enemy fell back to Griswoldville, where he constructed breastworks of fence rails. On Tuesday Wheeler attacked them again, but failed to drive them until our infantry came up (composed mainly of militia.) The enemy gave way, and we followed them about three miles.— Our loss was about four hundred in killed, wounded and missing. The enemy's much heavier.—Our informant, who was in the fight, says we took two hundred and fifty prisoners in one batch, and others were taken, he knows not how many. The enemy fell back towards Gordon and Milledgeville, and destroyed the road as he went. A man who was taken prisoner while helping to repair the road, on Wednesday, says he counted fifty-one dead Confederates on the field, among whom was the brave Col. Redding, of the militia. The Yankees, as usual, tried to claim the victory.

From statements made to this prisoner, we had a fight with them at Bear creek, above Griffin, where they diverged and went down through Butts, Jasper and Jones. The central forces probably passed through Monticello, Willsboro, and on to Milledgeville. They occupied that place from Sunday evening till Friday morning. Their infantry and artillery made but little stay. They left Thursday morning, and General Furguson's cavalry drove out the rear guard of cavalry on Friday morning. Is it possible that forty thousand troops, cavalry and infantry, with a wagon train of eight miles long, could have passed through a narrow bridge in twenty-four hours? We think not; but our military men must decide. Prisoners brought to this place claim sixty thousand, but admit

only four corps. We think the evidence thickens, that Sherman's army does not exceed twenty-five or thirty thousand. Shall we let them escape and make a base at Savannah or Hilton Head? If we do, Charleston and Wilmington falls, and Grant and Sherman's forces united, will necessitate the evacuation of Richmond.

While in Milledgeville, Sherman made his headquarters in the Executive mansion. Our informant saw, and was catechised by Gen. Jeff. Davis and Kilpatrick. The State House was not burned, but much mutilated. The Penitentiary, Arsenal, &c., were burned. The magazine was blown up by the rear guard as they left the city Friday 10, A.M. We heard the double report, and thought them signal guns. The bridge was also burned, but Gen. Furguson had constructed pontoons for his wagons to cross.

From the best authority, General Kilpatrick commanded the left wing of the enemy, which passed along the county line road, from Milledgeville to Shoals of Ogeechee, where they camped on Friday night. They spread out some six or eight miles on either hand, pilfering and burning as they went. Seven miles below this place a ruffian presented a pistol to the breast of a lady, demanding her gold and silver. She told him she had none and called upon an officer in the crowd for protection. Without specially granting it, he informed her rather egotistically that he was General Kilpatrick and permitted his men to go on and pilfer and abuse as much as they pleased. They burned the gin houses of a number of our largest planters, with hundreds of bales of cotton. Among them, Judge Thomas', Col. Turner's, the Sasnetts, Dr. Green's, the Dickinson's &c. They burned no cribs or dwelling houses, and we have no reliable information of the destruction of a single mill or factory in the country, though they passed by a number.—They took nearly all the horses and mules in the country, whether hid or not, for they scoured the swamps, killed some hogs and most of the poultry. The productive interest of the country has suffered seriously— irreparably, we fear. All the young negro men and some women they captured where they were not run off. Many of these have returned, and are still coming back as they can escape.

Our escaped prisoners said that Gen. Howard's corps went down the river from Milledgeville to take the Oconee bridge. It was he, probably, that Gen. Wayne repulsed. Whether he returned to Milledgeville or crossed on pontoons below, we are not apprised. Gen. Sherman, with artillery and infantry, went to Sandersville. His van arrived there Saturday at noon, being on the road two days and a half from Milledgeville, according to escaped negroes. At this rate it will take him about seven days to reach Millen from Sandersville, and seventeen days to reach Savannah—plenty of time for all the forces of the Carolinas and Georgia, with Dick Taylor from the West, to surround, flank and destroy him. I believe it to be of more importance to accomplish this than to hold Richmond. But I have every confidence in our authorities.

Several of our scouts overtook twenty wagons guarded by only twenty-five men. With a small reinforcement they could have captured the whole party. Now is the time for our boys to strike, if they wish to win glory and serve their country.—The enemy must be greatly demoralized; they are living on the fat of land, having plenty of liquor to drink, and many of them carrying their concubines with them. How can such an army fight? Besides, a few heavy battles would expend all their ammunition. Oh, for Wade Hampton's bugle blast to strike them with consternation on their left wing, and wrest from them the plunder of more that a dozen counties.

One good, quick stroke would retard and demoralize them.
Charge! Hampton, charge!

On! Taylor, on!
And strike with all thy cavalry.

But we must come down to prose again—painful prose—and bring to the bar of public opinion some recreant scouts, commanded by one Conway. We could not get the Captain to the front when the enemy threatened our town. He sent several of his men with Captain Culver, of this county, and he retired with his company three miles on the safe side to camp. A gallant Kentuckian—Charles Manier—who was cut off from his regiment, the Fourth Kentucky Cavalry, went with him, and they were met by a large force and had to fly. Manier's horse gave out, but he would not surrender. He fired his rifle and repeater, killed one of their horses, and then drew the butt of his gun on his approaching antagonist, who shot him dead, took a Bible from his pocket, containing his name and regiment, and laid it over his heart. He told the lady at whose gate he fell to bury him decently; he was sorry he had to kill him, for he was a brave fellow. Not so, Conway. That night some of his men broke open Purvent's store and stole several hundred dollars worth of goods. They robbed a merchant in Linton of a large sum of money, flourished their five hundred dollar bills, and left Sparta without paying their tavern bill. We are informed that this has been their history during the war. We cannot vouch for this, but we state facts, and hope our authorities will arrest and punish them as they deserve.

OBSERVER.

AN ANONYMOUS REPORT: EFFECTS OF SHERMAN'S MARCH THROUGH GEORGIA

The Mississippian, of Jackson, was another of the Confederacy's displaced newspapers. It had fled to Selma, Alabama, after the fall of its home city in the summer of 1863. Like most Southern newspapers, it watched in appalled amazement as Sherman burned his way through Georgia, but the paper noted that Sherman's raid had one powerful, important, and useful effect: Its cruelty had stamped out any latent "Reconstructionism" that Southerners might have been harboring in their hearts. Antiwar Southerners had been referred to as "Reconstructionists" from the beginning of the war, and while the cruelty of Sherman's raid through Georgia, and later South Carolina, steeled many for continued resistance, other Southerners saw the destruction as evidence to back up their argument that the Confederacy should sue for peace on just about any terms.

The Mississippian, 11 December 1864

THE EFFECT OF SHERMAN'S MARCH

Sherman in his march through Georgia destroyed many things—dwellings, corncribs, agricultural implements, gin houses, clothing of women and children, and in short all that tends to make life comfortable was ruthlessly given to the flames. Cattle, horses, hogs, sheep and goats were destroyed. Nothing was spared but life. Thank God, amidst the universal ruin, one thing was extirpated, root and branch, which amply compensates for all other loss. A thing noxious, rank and un-clean. A thing that like a foul and venomous toad, leered on the graves of our slain and made light of their blood. A thing that spat on the hallowed mound of the dead and croaked dishonor to the living. This foul abortion—this political Caliban—this spawn of cowardice and treason, was Reconstruction.

Wherever the hostile tread of Sherman's legions passed, all hopes and desires of reconstruction were trampled out of existence. The logic of the bayonet and the rhetoric of the incendiary convinced the most "conservative" that nothing remained to the people of the South but triumph or degradation which would make life intolerable. But the light of his burning dwelling reflected on the pale and frightened faces of his wife and children, and the "conservative" saw the true object of the war, and the real points of the issue. The flame which consumed the labor of a lifetime purified the political atmosphere and kindled in the heart of the sufferer the fires of patriotism. There lives no man who can see his rooftree burned, his lands devastated, his property stolen, his wife and children turned penniless on the world, without resolving on revenge.

But a greater wrong than those enumerated has been perpetrated by the hounds that follow the footsteps of Sherman. Women, pure and spotless, have been violated. The people of Georgia have had the bitterest cup of misery placed to their lips, and been made to drain it to the dregs. They have felt

—the [unreadable] wrong,
    The unutterable shame
That turns the coward's heart to steel,
    The sluggard's blood to flame.

They have suffered what can never be forgotten or forgiven. To affiliate with those who have perpetrated these enormities would be worse than dishonorable—it would be base and infamous. It would not only be an acknowledgment that the heroic dead who have fallen upon an hundred battlefields in defence of their country's independence were rebels and traitors, but it would be giving assent to the violation of our household goods.

But we have no fear of this thing. As we said before, Sherman has effectually crushed out any desire for reconstruction which may have been lurking in the heart of some of our people, who have never before been scarred with the fire of Yankee invasion. It has been the experience of this war that wherever the foot of the invader pollutes the soil, such outrages upon civilization and humanity have been committed, and that an undying and unquenchable hate is born in the hearts of the people. The ashes of desolated homesteads are "vocal without noise," and plead with an irresistible, though silent eloquence, for revenge.

From the blackened track which marks the route of Sherman, there comes no cry for reconstruction and submission, but rather a shout, like the sound of many waters, for independence and revenge. And so, with a full appreciation of the ruin which has overtaken some of our worthiest and best, and with the warmest sympathy for their desolation, we cannot, in view of the purification of the State from all taint of reconstruction, help ejaculating, thank God! We have experienced the baptism of fire, and have come for the purified. Thank God!

RICHARD ORME, JR. OR SR.: MILLEDGEVILLE AFTER SHERMAN'S OCCUPATION

Two weeks after Sherman's troops swept through the Georgia capital, life there was returning to normal. Refugees from the city were returning, often to find their homes destroyed or property stolen. Those who stayed with their property were less likely to suffer at the hands of the federals. Perhaps the greatest offense perpetrated by the Union troops was the trashing of the Georgia state house. Sherman's soldiers scattered state papers all around the capitol and held a mock legislative session at which they repealed Georgia's ordinance of secession.

Milledgeville Confederate Union, 12 December 1864 (Milledgeville, Ga.)

OUR CITY

It has been two weeks since the Yankee Army left us, (today Friday) but the mournful relics of their presence are fresh as when they swarmed in our streets, and crowded our residences and public squares. Many of our citizens who left the city at the approach of the enemy have returned, and familiar faces meet us at every step; but a stillness almost Sabbath like pervades our business streets, and the blackened, sightless walls of the Penitentiary, Arsenal Magazine and Depot remind us constantly of the presence of the vandal hordes of Sherman. It is due to Sherman to say that most of the outrages committed by his men were perpetrated in private residences where the owners, both male and female, had left the premises. Where our citizens remained in their houses night and day, we hear of but few acts of diabolism such as were committed in unoccupied buildings. The attention of the enemy was principal directed to poultry, stock, provisions of all kinds, hogs, harness, money and valuables. Negroes were treated very bad by their professed friends and liberators. They were robbed of money, clothing, blankets—everything stealable. Indeed our negroes have cause to remember the enemy quite as feelingly as their masters and mistresses. Many left us and followed the Yankee army. Some have returned and more will follow in the same direction; but the loss of negroes in the section overrun by Sherman must be very great. It is a little remarkable that those negroes left who were least expected to leave, and in most cases they were idle and vicious characters. It is a little singular, too, that those negroes who took up with the Yankees were universally known to be most free, before the Yankees came. Negroes who had been managed as they should be, were content to stay with their masters, but those who had been permitted to do as they pleased were the first to run away. Our streets and public squares are filled with private papers and public documents. Even private correspondence of a nature the most sacred, is blown to and fro by the wind and subject to the rude criticism of the most vulgar and illiterate. The State House for many days has been knee deep in papers. The building is much defaced. The windows on the side towards the magazine are all broken, and the plastering injured. The fencing around the square is broken down and many of the young

trees in the square ruined, the bark being bit off by the horses tied to them. Our churches were not respected. They, too, bear the impress of the unhallowed footstep of the foul invader. But bad as it is with us, we are truly thankful it is no worse. But few ladies or children were insulted or even molested in their houses. It might have been expected to be much worse, from the known character of Sherman's Army. No occupied residences were destroyed. Many feared that the city would be burnt and were greatly relieved when assured that it would not be.—In a few weeks our public offices will be put in repair and the business appertaining to them be progressing as though Sherman had never been in a thousand miles of Milledgeville.

HENRY LYNDEN FLASH: SHERMAN'S CAMPAIGN AGAINST SAVANNAH

The key to Savannah was the earthworks fortification on the Ogeechee River to its south, Fort McAllister. Though the garrison at the fort put up a fight, its worn-out cannons and men were no match for Sherman's army. The fort fell easily, and the gates to Savannah were opened. The federal fleet waited off the coast to support Sherman's efforts to capture the town. The Telegraph *editor still held out hope, but it was a clearly unrealistic hope. Once Sherman captured Savannah, he had accomplished more than the capture of "a very pleasant city." He had proven the Union army's ability to force its will upon the people of the Confederacy. He had proven Union domination.*

Macon Telegraph and Confederate, 20 December 1864

SHERMAN'S CAMPAIGN DEVELOPING

The fall of Fort McAllister, at the mouth of the Ogeechee, is certainly a very serious loss, for thereby Sherman's army can be co-operated with by the fleet in any attempt that General may make to capture the city. Without that co-operation his chances of success are very small; with it the chances are that he will succeed, and the principal seaport of Georgia will be in the enemy's possession.

But should Sherman, contrary to our hopes and belief capture the city, what then? He simply captures a very pleasant city, but one which has been of but little value to us in a maritime point of view. By its possession he may be enabled to send raiding parties into the interior, but by no means to a sufficient extent to do any great deal of harm. The danger most to be apprehended is, that he will make it the base for inland operations against Charleston, and a campaign against Augusta.

Sherman's necessities compelled him to make a rapid march through Georgia, and the policy of his government demanded that it should be marked by wide-spread desolation. Our people laughed at the idea of his marching through Georgia—but he has done it. It was predicted he would be fought, delayed, whipped and starved before he reached the coast. But he wisely avoided battle, and has reached the coast without serious hindrance or loss. The capture of Fort McAllister with its garrison, forming a very important part of the defences of the

city, more than compensates for his losses, while it diminishes the chances of failure in his operations against it.

We regard it as impolitic and unwise to lull our people into a false security in reference to the safety of Savannah. We have believed all along that Sherman could take the city if co-operated with by the fleet. We now believe it to be in his power to take it, and that the minds of the public should be prepared for the disaster, and to meet the consequences.

Having secured Savannah what will he do? Will he remain idle? He will in all probability commence operations against Charleston on the land side, or proceed against Augusta. The defenses of the former city we doubt not are fully equal to any demands that may be made upon them, for that city has been regarded as much coveted by the Federals, and has always been looked upon as in more danger than Savannah or Augusta—hence her defences have been made more complete and substantial.

Augusta is in our opinion, too far inland, to be successfully approached. It could hardly be reduced without a cooperating gunboat fleet—and the shallowness of the river, together with the frequent bluffs on its sides, affording the best situations for batteries, will probably prevent that cooperation. Besides this Sherman would be compelled to leave a large garrison at Savannah while ours would be released; thus he would be weakened while we would be strengthened.

But suppose he should capture Augusta also and thus sever the Confederacy on this line—cutting communications between the States north of the Savannah river and those South of it. What then?

We are by no means ruined, while the more he divides and scatters his forces, the more liable he is to be whipped in detail. It is impossible for the enemy to garrison every place he captures, and as soon as he evacuates, we re-enter and repossess them. This was illustrated by Sherman being compelled to withdraw all his garrisons from Atlanta to Chattanooga, to make up an army for this expedition, whereby he lost thirty days, territory it had taken months of time, millions of money, and tens of thousands of lives to gain. As it was with Northern Georgia, so it will be with Eastern Georgia, except where the enemy has the support of his gunboats.

As with Northern Georgia, so it is now quite clear it will be with East Tennessee. That country is fast slipping from Federal clutches. We may soon expect to hear of the evacuation of both Chattanooga and Knoxville for with Hood and Breckinridge where they are, the enemy can hardly hold them.

These two points evacuated, the country is then ours, and in better condition for us than when we lost it, for thanks to the rapaciousness of the enemy, Southern feeling has been intensified and Union feeling materially weakened if not destroyed.

But more and better still, communication between Richmond, and the States South and West of the Savannah will be again re-established, and the darling project of the yankee President, of dividing the Confederacy east and west successfully defeated.

The enemy has the numbers and can flank us, avoid fighting as he desires, take our important cities and burn them, over run and devastate our lands, and destroy our farming implements. Yet this is neither conquest or subjugation; and so long as the people remain as firm and united as they have been and are now, there is no fear of their being either conquered or subjugated. We may be exterminated, but subjugated—never! Let Sherman, then do his worst; and let the people prepare to do, dare and suffer more than ever, and they will surely, in the end, defeat the machinations of our merciless foe and have their efforts crowned with a glorious success.

HENRY LYNDEN FLASH: FALL OF SAVANNAH

The Macon newspaper took three days off for Christmas in 1864, and when it began publication again after the holiday, the editor observed that, in the absence of real news, all sorts of crazy rumors had begun flying around the town. One piece of news, though, was not so crazy. Savannah had indeed fallen. Of course, Hood had also been whipped and a good number of his men captured, but for Georgia, the big news was Savannah.

Macon Telegraph and Confederate, 28 December 1864

THE SITUATION

Since the telegraphic lines have been down, and during the suspension of the city papers, the city has been, as we expected it would be, filled with all kinds of rumors. During this time the President has died—Hood has been whipped and killed, and most of his army captured—Richmond has been evacuated, and Hardee's force driven out of Savannah with a loss of double his force.

But the fog has cleared away somewhat now, and we are enabled to announce that the greatest misfortune we have experienced is the loss of Savannah, (an event the people has been prepared for for several days,) which was evacuated by Gen. Hardee, who is now at Hardeeville, S.C., about twenty-eight miles from Savannah on the railroad to Charleston, with his army intact and in good spirits and fighting trim. The enemy, it is presumed, occupy Savannah.

From Richmond we hear nothing, but as long as General Lee and his invincible army confronts the enemy before that city, no misgivings are felt, whether we hear from there or not.

The latest reliable news we hear from Tennessee is contained in special dispatches to the Mobile Advertiser & Register, from Senatobia, which indicate anything but a defeat or a retreat.

This dispatch states that Gen. Lyon, with 2,500 men, (the dispatch says 25,000, but that is evidently a mistake,) had crossed the Cumberland between Nashville and Clarksville, and was marching on Hopkinsville, Ky.; that Gen. Breckinridge was at Sparta, which is at the western base of the mountains, and about one hundred miles east of Nashville, and endeavoring to form a junction with Gen. Hood, and that our troops had torn up a long stretch of the road to Chattanooga.

Except the loss of Savannah, there is yet nothing positively known that should be in the least discouraging; and that is a much less serious loss than it seems to be. Our garrison is relieved, in excellent health and fighting condition, to be added to our effective force; while the enemy must detach a garrison for its defence, weakening his aggressive power to that extent.

Hood's Invasion of Tennessee

Reinforced by Forrest's cavalry, Hood's 54,000 men crossed the Tennessee River on 14 November and quickly moved toward Nashville. Thomas dispatched Major General John M. Schofield with two corps and Wheeler's cavalry, in all about 32,000 men, to meet the invasion and to delay it. The forces skirmished at Columbia, Tennessee, and at Spring Hill before meeting on 30 November in a major battle at Franklin.

Hood, though he had lost a leg and an arm at Chickamauga and Gettysburg, respectively, was young and impetuous. Despite the counsel of older generals, Hood decided on a frontal assault against the dug-in federals at Franklin. The bad decision was compounded by the fact that about a third of Hood's force was not present, including most of his artillery. Casualties were tremendous. Nearly 7,000 of the 38,000-man Confederate force were lost to the Union's 2,300 out of 32,000. The Confederates also lost twelve generals in that battle, six killed, five wounded, and one captured. More than sixty of a hundred regimental commanders were killed or wounded. There was no doubt that Hood's frontal attack was an unmitigated disaster. Having accomplished his delaying mission, Schofield returned to Nashville that night.

Although his force had been reduced to less than half the size of Thomas's, Hood proceeded toward Nashville, one of the most heavily fortified cities in the United States. Hood reached Nashville on 2 December, but Thomas, ever methodical, was in no hurry to engage him; the Union general was trying to get his army, made up largely of new recruits, trained for what lay ahead.

The Confederate line outside Nashville was stretched disastrously thin, especially after Hood sent Forrest off with most of the cavalry and two brigades of infantry to attack Murfreesboro. That left Hood with fewer than 20,000 men to meet Thomas's attack, which began on 15 December. The Union force easily shattered Hood's exposed left flank. The next day, Hood tried to continue the fight, but Thomas enveloped both his flanks. Wilson's cavalry managed to get behind the Confederate lines and deliver the final blow. The Union managed to inflict losses of around 6,000, compared with their own of just more than 3,000, and to reduce Hood's army to fleeing rabble.

HENRY LYNDEN FLASH: HOOD'S CAMPAIGN IN TENNESSEE

The Montgomery Mail *was one of the few newspapers that had a correspondent assigned to cover Hood's movements in Tennessee. As the Army of Tennessee crept closer to its first major battle on its foolhardy expedition to draw Sherman's main force away from Atlanta, the reporter was stationed in the rear, in northern Alabama in the hamlet of Tuscumbia where he could pick up what little news made its way from the front. The* Macon Telegraph and Confederate *properly attributed the story to the* Mail, *a small irony since the editor of the* Telegraph, *Henry Lynden Flash, a poet and former cavalry officer, constantly berated other Southern newspapers for taking stories from his newspaper without attribution.*

Macon Telegraph and Confederate, 18 November 1864

THE FRONT

[Special Army Correspondence of the Mail.]
TUSCUMBIA, ALA., Nov. 6, 1864

I am afraid that I will find it a very difficult matter to keep you posted in regard to the doings of this army. We are kept so much in the dark in regard to army movements that we know nothing of them until it is too late to be called news. I hardly know what to think of the prospect of going to Middle Tennessee. Sometimes it looks quite flattering, and then again becomes gloomy. I am pretty well convinced, however, that "grand movements," quite in keeping with those we have just accomplished are yet on the [*unreadable*]. Large quantities of "hard tack" and bacon are being brought to Tuscumbia, the transportation already quite limited, being again reduced—the usual precursors to a move.

Sherman was on yesterday reported with his forces lying between Decatur and Huntsville. Today I was told he was moving in the direction of Pulaski.

Well, let him move. We can move him back through Middle Tennessee as we did out of Georgia.

The Mobile Tribune has private information from Tuscumbia to the 4th inst.:

Our scouts reported that 15,000 of the enemy had arrived at Decatur, and were evidently following up our forces. On the 2nd inst. we shelled them at that place. There were then only three thousand there, and we could have captured it easily, but that was not in the programme. We captured thirty or forty prisoners, and killed and wounded from three to four hundred. Our loss in killed and wounded was about one hundred. We have Florence fortified. The Yankee cavalry is very numerous on the other side, but exhibit no desire to dispute the passage of the modern Rubicon.

Sherman's troops are scattered as follows: the 1st corps, Gen. Osterhaus, is at Atlanta, 15,000 are at Chattanooga, and 5,000 at Bridgeport. There are also some at Stevenson, but how many was not ascertained.

Gen. Hood has been quite unwell for two or three days, but is now all right again. Beauregard is here, but Hood is in command of the army.

HENRY LYNDEN FLASH: ACCOUNT OF BATTLE OF FRANKLIN

From Columbia, Hood's army moved on to Franklin, where it fought a fierce battle that cost Hood more than one-third of his force, including dozens of regimental commanders. The Macon Telegraph and Confederate *picked up this story from the* Chattanooga Rebel. *It is an interview with an officer from Hood's army. The story vastly overestimates federal losses in the battle but otherwise accurately captures the carnage of the day.*

Macon Telegraph and Confederate, 16 December 1864

THE BATTLE OF FRANKLIN

From an officer who left Hood's army on the 1st December, the Rebel gets full and intelligible accounts of the recent severe and bloody fight at Franklin, Tennessee. It appears that the enemy, after being driven out of Columbia evacuated Murfreesboro, and uniting all their forces, took up position on the high cliffs south of Franklin. Gen. Hood pursued them closely in their retreat, and when they formed line of battle on a series of hills below Franklin, he flanked them out of their position. They then fell back to their fortifications on the edge of town, where they formed a strong line of battle. Immediate dispositions were made to assault their works, which was done in front, chiefly by Cheatham's corps, with spirit and vigor, the various commanders leading their columns, the bands playing and men huzzaing.

Stewart's corps was on the right, and Cheatham, aided by some of Lee's corps, formed the centre and left. The remainder of Lee's corps had been detached to create a diversion. Forrest's cavalry defended our right and left flanks. The enemy

opened a very severe and destructive fire upon our assaulting line, and it was in this charge the heavy loss of general officers occurred. The irresistible bravery of our men carried everything before them. The lines were occupied by troops, several of our Generals, among them the heroic Cleburne, being shot on the breastworks. This attack was made at five P.M. Despite the terrible losses, the army entered the enemy's lines in the highest spirits, with bands playing and flags waving. It was then discovered that the enemy had a second line, where they had rallied. There they were quickly assaulted by our men, and a severe and close fight ensued, wherein the combatants were separated by a ditch and breastworks.

It soon became a hand to hand fight, which was continued into the night, until the enemy gave way and retired to the third line. The fight was again resumed on this line and kept up until 2 o'clock in the morning, when an escaped prisoner informed our commander that the enemy had evacuated this line and retired to Nashville. Our army then occupied this line, and early the next day pushed on towards Nashville, and on the first of December, when our informant left, the rear corps was at Brentwood, eight miles from Nashville. This would bring our front to the fortifications of Nashville. Our informant heard heavy firing in the direction of Nashville, and many rumors that the city had been taken. These we fear are premature. The enemy, it was understood, was commanded by Gen. Schofield, and he and General Wagner were reported to be among the killed.

The loss of the enemy could not be ascertained, as they had removed most of their dead. Our loss was heavy, between two and four hundred. The distressing mortality among our Generals is confirmed. There were five killed—Cleburn, Strahl, Granberry, Cist and John C. Carter. There were five Generals wounded: Quarles, not mortally as first reported. Brown, slightly, Johnston, and the names of the other two were not remembered by our informant. General Gordon was captured. A large amount of stores were captured, especially at Columbia. Recruits are joining Hood's army in numbers more than sufficient to supply all the losses, and the army is in high spirits. General Pillow arrived at his plantation in time to capture large stores.

The Clarion has private intelligence from Hood's army which represents that the fighting at Harpeth Creek, near Franklin on the 30th, was desperate in the extreme, and our losses great in proportion. A magnificent victory was won, but at great sacrifice. Our forces charged three lines of breastworks, and drove the enemy from every position they occupied; and at one place they had to cut a hedge before they could get to the enemy's works, being at the same time exposed to the fire of the batteries which were located behind it. The loss in Stewart's corps was large. Report says it was nearly decimated.

Gen. Loring's division lost 700 men; and the 15th Mississippi lost 79 out of 220 men taken into the fight. The loss in line and company officers was lamentably great, and altogether our casualties number from six to eight thousand. The enemy's loss in killed and wounded was very heavy—over four thousand—while we captured over six thousand prisoners.

JOHN BELL HOOD: COMMANDING GENERAL'S REPORT ON BATTLE OF FRANKLIN

John Bell Hood took nearly two weeks to send word to Richmond of his ignominious defeat at Nashville. His official report painted a very different picture of the results than actually occurred. He claimed to have inflicted heavy losses on the enemy while sustaining few casualties himself. He reported his troops retreated "rapidly" when, in truth, they fled in disorder.

Macon Telegraph and Confederate, 10 January 1865

OFFICIAL FROM GEN. HOOD

RICHMOND, Jan. 8.

Gen. Hood reports from Spring Hill, December 27, that on the morning of the 15th, in front of Nashville, the enemy attacked both flanks of his army. They were repulsed on the right with heavy loss, but towards evening they drove in the infantry outpost on the left flank.

Early on the morning of the 16th the enemy made a general attack on our entire line. All their assaults were repulsed with heavy loss until half-past 3 P.M., when a position of our line to the left of centre suddenly gave way, which caused our lines to give way at all points, our troops retreating rapidly. Fifty pieces of artillery and several ordnance wagons were lost by us that day. Our loss in killed and wounded heretofore was small, in prisoners not ascertained.

Major Gen. Ed. Johnson, Brigadier Generals L. E. Smith, and H. R. Jackson were captured.

EASTERN THEATER

Wilderness–Spotsylvania–Cold Harbor Campaign

Union General Ulysses S. Grant was named commander of the Union army in March 1864. His first action was to begin a campaign to destroy the Confederate army. Three years of bloody war had abundantly proven to the Yankee general that the Southerners would never give up, even though, arguably, their last chance of winning had died with the fall of Vicksburg and the defeat at Gettysburg the previous summer. Total destruction was all that would serve to end the conflict. To accomplish this scheme, Grant had sent his favorite general, William T. Sherman, to Georgia to take on the Confederacy's Army of Tennessee under the wily Joseph E. Johnston. Grant himself, in concert with George Meade's Army of the Potomac, would handle Robert E. Lee's Army of Northern Virginia.

Grant's plan for his and Meade's armies took into account the complexities of the situation in Virginia. No Union army had yet been able to force Lee away from Richmond. The Army of Northern Virginia doggedly and skillfully defended the Confederate capital. That had to change. Grant decided that he would take Lee on wherever he could find him and dislocate the Southern army from Richmond. Grant's plan called for the 105,000 infantrymen in Meade's army to march into the dense thickets of the Virginia wilderness and engage the Army of Northern Virginia wherever it was. Grant put two smaller forces in the field under Major General Franz Sigel and Major General Benjamin Butler. Sigel was to move south toward the Shenandoah Valley to cut Lee's supply lines, while Butler moved toward the James River to cut off Lee's support.

Lee faced an army nearly twice the size of his own. Including cavalry, Grant had nearly 118,000 men he could put in the field against Lee's 61,000. But Lee had some advantages, despite the overwhelming numbers. For one thing, Lee defended interior lines and familiar ground. He also had established key defenses along the Rapidan and Rappahannock Rivers that would dramatically limit Grant's freedom of movement. Grant also faced tactical disadvantages by fighting in The Wilderness. For one thing, command and control of his forces would be complicated by the lack of visibility. Further, maneuvering a large force, as well as artillery and cavalry, through the dense thicket would not be easy. Nevertheless, on 4 May, Grant's force moved out of its winter camps and crossed the Rapidan. Informed by scouts of Grant's move, Lee's troops left their encampments and headed east toward the engagement that would begin the next day.

On 5 May, the armies met in two separate and indecisive engagements between units confused by and entangled in The Wilderness's thickets. The battlefield itself erupted into a conflagration, compounding the terror and bewilderment of the troops. The battlefield became a firey, smokey nightmare. Tall pines blazed as giant pillars of fire. Dense smoke obscured visibility, and the fighting disintegrated into hand-to-hand combat by men blindly stabbing at one another with their bayonets or beating each other with the butts of their guns.

On the second day of the Battle of The Wilderness, Grant set about exploiting a gap in the Confederate lines between Ewell's and Hill's corps. Frontal assaults throughout the day achieved little, and by the end of the day, neither side had achieved a tactical victory, despite major casualties. Lee's biggest loss that day, though, was his subordinate Longstreet, who was wounded at almost the same location where Stonewall Jackson had been fatally shot by his own men the previous year.

Following the battle, Grant wired Lincoln that the offensive would continue no matter what. He dispatched a corps southeast to guard a rail junction at Spotsylvania Court House. Lee, almost smelling Grant's move, rushed a covering force to Spotsylvania that arrived before the Union advance units. The stage was set for another confrontation on a new battlefield.

The terrain around Spotsylvania was more conducive to maneuvering, and for five days, from 8 May through 12 May, the two armies struggled with a series of small engagements. Lee used the time to build up his position into a V-shape that came to be called the Bloody Angle. When Grant's grand assault came on 12 May, the Confederates were in a strong enough position to repulse the attack. In some places during the contest, the fighting would have to stop long enough to clear the dead, in some places five deep, from the trenches so the living could continue the carnage. In other places, the combatants had to fire their guns from their hips because the enemy was too close for them to put their guns to their shoulders. The fighting did not end in the horror at Spotsylvania. For six days, Grant searched for Lee's flanks but was thwarted by Lee's masterful shifting of his reserves. Confederate losses for the twelve-day period referred to as the Battle of Spotsylvania totaled 12,000. The Union losses were around 18,000. After eleven days of continuous fighting, Grant moved east toward Fredericksburg, then south toward Richmond, once again trying to find a way into the Confederate capital.

Grant probed the Confederate position but found it too strong for a major attack before sidestepping Lee's right flank and crossing the Pamunkey River. Lee rapidly shifted positions to interpose his army between the federals and the Confederate capital. Again, Grant probed to find Lee's right flank, and this time he located it near Cold Harbor, Virginia.

Cold Harbor proved to be a huge mistake for Grant. He believed Lee's lines were overextended, but he was not sure where the weakness was. The Union general ordered a frontal assault on the entrenched Confederates, figuring such an attack would find the weakness. Grant's miscalculation cost the Union army staggering casualties, for a delay in the arrival of a Union corps—it had gotten lost along the way—gave Lee the time to shore up his position with reinforcements. Grant's assault was pushed back by confident veteran soldiers in well-fortified positions, supported by a strong artillery corps. The Confederate fire was so thick, most of the advancing Union troops did not get anywhere near the Southern lines. Within half an hour, most of the Union troops had turned and were headed back to their lines. First reports of the battle were sufficiently misleading that Grant ordered the fighting to continue. His on-the-spot commanders, though, were so stunned by the carnage that those orders never got carried out. Grant lost nearly 7,000 men in less than an hour of fighting to the Confederate's loss of only about 1,500. Small skirmishes continued for several days, and on 12 July, the Army of the Potomac pulled out, headed for Petersburg.

Lee had inflicted nearly 60,000 Union casualties in just over a month and had stopped the federal advance on Richmond. Grant and his commanders were bitterly criticized for the bloody summer campaign in Virginia, and for Cold Harbor in particular, but the general argued that he was applying pressure Lee could not withstand. Grant's men were traumatized by their experiences and wary of their general's penchant for bloody assaults. At Petersburg, few attacks would be made, as both armies settled into trenches around the rail center where they would spend the next nine months.

JOHN R. THOMPSON: START OF WILDERNESS CAMPAIGN; POLITICAL NEWS FROM RICHMOND

The people of Richmond knew the spring fighting had begun in Richmond when the ambulances were summoned to the front. The action that was starting was The Wilderness Campaign. The war was not the only news, as the Richmond correspondent for the Appeal, Dixie, John R. Thompson, *also included in his letter. Politics were dragging on in Richmond as the Confederate congressmen debated monetary policy and sparred with one another over their support for Southern peace movements.*

Memphis Appeal, 10 May 1864

LETTER FROM RICHMOND

Special Correspondence of the Memphis Appeal.]
RICHMOND, MAY 5, 1864.

The ambulance committee has been ordered to the front and left town this afternoon by a special train. We all know in Richmond what this means. A sudden and violent depression of the barometer at sea does not more surely indicate a storm than the departure of the ambulance committee indicates a battle. The Yankees are in force on this side of the Rapidan and are endeavoring to turn the right flank of Gen. Lee's army. There will probably be much maneuvering for position for several days and then the great shock of arms. There is a feverish excitement here, as is natural, but no sort of apprehension as to the result. What we hear of Grant's army does not inspire apprehension. It is not the well appointed and well disciplined host that came under McClellan two years ago to "drive the revels to the wall." It is probably not so large nor so hopeful as the column that moved on to their destruction under fighting Joe Hooker at Chancellorsville. There are some disaffected brigades in it. Large reinforcements have no doubt arrived during the last week from Washington, brought from Tennessee and Charleston, or new levies, but they are composed in great part of negroes or foreigners, excellent materials for demoralization and [*unreadable*] should Grant be repulsed. But the proof of the material will be in the fighting. A week will probably show what sort of army Grant leads to the attack. Yankee gunboats are ascending James river to-day, probably for the purpose of creating a diversion in concert with the Federal force in the Peninsula. Preparations to meet and repel any hostile movement in this quarter have been fully made, and as for the river, the gunboats will probably come no higher than City Point. They have a salutary fear of torpedoes, and they have no idea at all of coming within range of Drewry's Bluff.

Northern papers as late as the 3rd have been received here. The news is unimportant. The military critics are still demonstrating the inevitable capture of Richmond with mathematical certainty. The committee charged with investigating the Fort Pillow "Massacer" [*sic*] have returned to Washington and made their report. It is a very lively report. The half had not been told of the "rebel" barbarities. Gen. Forrest, according to this committee, is such a man as might be the result of a combination of all the Yankee ruffians, Butler, Turchin, McNiell, Mitroy, Spears, [*unreadable*] and the lamented Ulric Dahlgren in one person. Men were not merely murdered in Fort Pillow in cold blood. They were nailed to boards. They were roasted. They were buried alive. Fortunately, Europeans will know exactly how much of this to believe—that is to say, they will believe nothing of it.

The Emperor Maximillian sailed from Civita Vecchia for Havana on the 20th of April, and if he had a favorable voyage he should be in Havana at this moment. News had not been received from the other side of the Atlantic of the passage of Winter Davis' resolutions on the Monroe doctrine. Of course, Maximillian will hear nothing of the recent successes of the Juarez party and of the flight of Vidaturri from Montgomery until he reaches Cuba. He will hear at the same time of the cordial fraternization of the Yankees and the adherents of Juarez at Matamoros, of Cortina's reception in Brownsville, etc., etc., all of which we may reasonably suppose, will not prove disadvantageous to the success of General Preston, who will repair to Mexico immediately after the new Emperor shall have arrived at the capital.

Congress has done very little yet. Both houses have changed their places of session to the halls of the Virginia Senate and House of Representatives, respectively, where they have more light and space. In the House, yesterday, on motion of Col. Swann, of Tennessee, the matter of placing the five dollar bills on the footing of the new currency, received its quietus by an overwhelming vote. Some sensation was created when Mr. J. F. Leach, of North Carolina, in making a personal explanation of his political status—what the French call a *profession du foi*—acknowledged, in reply to a question addressed to him by Mr. Staples, of Virginia, that he was for peace on any terms short of subjugation. This Mr. Leach must not be confounded with Mr. J. M. Leach, his colleague, who was said in advance of his arrival here, to be a Union man, but who declared that he stood exactly on the same platform as did Vice-President Stephens, Gov. Brown of Georgia, and Gov. Vance, of his own State. The House to-day drew for seats, and having accomplished this, a spirited debate arose between Messrs. Foote and Conrad upon the subject of secret sessions. Mr. Foot moving so to amend the old rule as to make a majority of two thirds necessary to keep the doors closed.

In the Senate a discussion took place on the matter of an early adjournment in which Messrs. Johnson of Arkansas, Orr of South Carolina, and Wigfall parted pale. The latter gentleman spoke somewhat at length on what he conceived Congress had to do—he depreciated hastily legislation—believed in the doctrine of "Festiua Lente"—alluded to the bill, laid over from the last session, for limiting the term of office of members of the Cabinet—and declared himself ready to defend the privilege of the writ of habeas corpus, avowing that when the matter came up he would be prepared to show that Vice-President Stephens did not understand the Constitution he had sworn to support. The Senate passed a bill to prevent the detention of members of Congress while traveling by provost marshals, requiring passports to be furnished them which all Confederate officers should be bound to respect. Messrs. Orr and Wigfall spoke from opposite points of view on this bill, Mr. Orr giving it as his opinion that

there was no power whatever in the Executive to authorize the military commandants to enforce military law anywhere in the Confederate States outside of the camps and military posts, while Mr. Wigfall sustained the enforcement of the most stringent regulations, and said the public had no business to travel in times like these. There was also a rambling debate on the Senate on the question of reference to the military committee of a vote of thanks to Gen. Forrest, before voting on which the Senate went into executive session.

The ink was hardly dry on my last letter, in which I spoke of the clouds giving us no rain, when a storm of great violence burn over the city, blowing down chimneys, unroofing houses, carrying off a considerable portion of the Petersburg railroad bridge, and doing other damage. There was heavy lightning and a vivid fall of rain. Since this storm the weather has been bright and cool.

DIXIE.

BENJAMIN F. DILL OR JOHN McCLANAHAN: THE WAR CAN BE WON

By the spring of 1864, the Confederate military position was dire in both the Eastern and Western fronts. Through the coming summer, Sherman would begin to push Johnston's Army of the Tennessee south toward Atlanta. Johnston had been given command of the Army of Tennessee after Bragg was forced to resign following his abysmal performance the previous fall at Chattanooga. In Virginia that May, Lee's army was driven back in The Wilderness Campaign and defeated at Spotsylvania. Civilian morale was beginning to plummet, but newspapers were striving to put a good face on the Confederate situation. Indeed, many Confederates, journalists and otherwise, believed—and some historians would agree with them—that it was still possible in the spring of 1864 for the South to defeat the North and win its independence.

Memphis Appeal, 14 May 1864

THE DAY AND THE HOUR

In the two great struggles now going on at Richmond and Dalton, all must feel that we are now in the most critical period we have passed through since the commencement of the war. In every respect except numbers, we certainly have the enemy at a disadvantage, we being the resisting and they the assaulting. We are moreover, doing battle on our own soil and in defense of our homes and property and family altars, while our foe is fighting only for plunder and his monthly pay. It is true the pride of character of the Northern people, as well as their future welfare, is involved in the issue of this great contest, and hence the gigantic efforts now being made by them to overcome and wear out the armies of Generals LEE and JOHNSTON. Success will give them a temporary respite or exemption from the calamities and disasters which defeat would speedily precipitate upon them. To postpone this evil day they are now mastering all their forces and concentrating all their energies, and to resist them successfully, will require

all the resources that we can bring to bear. If necessary, it is the duty of the States, with their militia and reserved forces, to come to the help of the Confederacy. Now is the day and now the hour to make short work of the war. By partial success over the enemy at Dalton, it may be prolonged indefinitely, whereas, by a decisive triumph, it will be brought to a speedy termination. From GRANT'S tactics, it would seem that he is disposed to carry out the original policy of the Federal authorities, and is determined to make the contest short and sharp. But this is a game which we can play at more successfully than he, if we will but summon all our energies and throw them into the contest. We can stand defeat and live to fight again, but he cannot. In this we have an immense advantage over the foe, but we hope such a thing as defeat will be thought of neither by the people nor the troops in the field. Every consideration of weal to the country should prompt us to adopt the policy of the enemy and make the contest short and sharp, by a triumphant victory over him.

With the success that has crowned our arms in the West, we now have it in our power, by similar success in the pending conflict, to put an end to the war, and once more bless the country with peace and prosperity. The Confederate authorities, we know are straining all their energies to effect this desirable result; and we trust the States will be equally as resolute and energetic in their co-operation with the Confederate Government. Now is the accepted time for us to finish up our work. We have the enemy away from his gunboats and a long distance from his base of supplies, where we have always wanted to get him, in order that we might strike him a fatal and decisive blow. Let us all then, both people and army, both Confederate and State authorities, summon all our energies, muster all our resources, and crown the triumphs of the spring campaign with victories at Richmond and Dalton, and the war is at an end.

PETER W. ALEXANDER: BATTLE OF THE WILDERNESS

This exchange story by the Savannah Republican's *Peter W. Alexander chronicled the early May Battle of The Wilderness as a victory for the Confederates. Alexander was showing his Confederate partisanism; the outcome of the two-day battle was more indecisive than Alexander indicated. However, the Confederate army's spirits were high at the end of the battle and fully expected to have the Army of the Potomac on the run back to Washington before long.*

Selma Reporter, 1 June 1864 (Selma, Ala.)

BATTLE OF THE WILDERNESS
LETTER FROM P.W.A.

ARMY OF NORTHERN VIRGINIA, Battlefield, May 7, 1864.

Again it becomes my grateful task to chronicle another victory. While it can not be regarded in its military aspects as a decisive battle, since the enemy was neither routed nor driven back across the Rapidan; yet, when we consider the circumstances under which it was fought, the elaborate preparation made by the enemy, the large arm of veteran troops with which he advanced, and the common consent with which both sides had come to regard the present campaign as probably the last act of the bloody drama which has convulsed the North American continent for the last three years, we cannot but look upon it as one of the most important battles of the whole war. The boasted leader of the Federal army chose his own time and place to deliver battle; he made the attack and was repulsed with heavy [*unreadable*]; his combinations were penetrated and defeated, and his whole movement checkmated, at least for present. These are results of great consequence, and for them the country should be grateful to the Giver of all victory, and to the brave army by whose valor they have been achieved. But let us take up the narrative at the beginning and bring it down to the present time, and thus see what was done and how it was done.

Arriving at Gordonsville Wednesday, the 4th instant, at 1 o'clock and learning that Grant had crossed the Rapidan below at Germana and Ely's Fords, and was endeavoring to turn Lee's right flank, I took horse and pushed on to the point to which both armies seemed to be approaching. The moment Gen. Lee ascertained that Grant had really cut loose from his base at Culpepper, Hill's and Ewell's corps were withdrawn from their positions on the Rapidan and ordered to advance upon the enemy's line of march, the former taking the plank road and the latter the turnpike, both leading from Orange Courthouse [*sic*] to Fredericksburg. Longstreet, who was in the vicinity of Gordonsville, ready to move upon any point, was ordered to march down the Carthaplu road. The main body of Grant's army crossed at Germana Ford, and took the road loading from thence in the direction of Bowling Green and Richmond, and known in the neighborhood as Brock's Road, by which name I shall speak of it hereafter. The first object at which he aimed, doubtless, was to reach the point where that road intersects with the Orange and Fredericksburg plank road and turnpike. These highways run nearly parallel to each other, the distance between them varying from one to three miles and more. There is an unfinished railroad which also runs nearly parallel to the other two roads, and extends from Orange Court house [*sic*] to Fredericksburg. The turnpike lies on the north side or next to the river, the railroad on the south side, and the plank road between the two. These roads do not cross Brock's Road, along which Grant was moving, at right angles, but diagonally, the distance between the points where they cut Brock's Road being as follows: between the railway bed and the plank road about five hundred yards, and between the plank road and turnpike nearly four miles. The enemy's line of battle extended along Brock's road from the unfinished railroad across the plank road to the turnpike, and was consequently about four miles in length. Chancellorsville is four miles below, on the plank road, and Fredericksburg about fifteen miles. The surrounding country is very appropriately called the Wilderness, the people being ignorant, the soil destitute of fertility, the supply of water scant, the ground broken and covered with dense and almost impenetrable growth of stunted bushes, pines and blackjacks. It is a blighted region adjoining the district known as the "poisoned fields of Orange," and producing but little for the subsistence of either man or beast. So thick are the woods in some places that it is impossible to distinguish a man, even in the absence of verdure, at a distance of fifty paces. The reader can readily imagine that it would be difficult to select more unfavorable ground for a battle between two great armies. It only remains to be added that the battle was fought near the western boundary of Spotsylvania county, the line of battle being nearly at right angles to a straight line drawn from Fredericksburg through Chancellorsville to Orange Courthouse.

If the reader will keep these points clearly in his mind, and will place a good map before him, he will find but little difficulty in forming a satisfactory conception of the battle.

As has already been stated, Ewell moved down the turnpike, which is on the left and nearest to the river, and Hill down the plank road. Stuart passed still further to the South, and marched down the Catherpin road, so as to throw his cavalry in front of the head of Grant's army and retard its march. His troopers did their duty well, especially Rosser's brigade of Hampton's division, and forced the Federal cavalry, which was marching up the road by which he was advancing, back, into Brock's Road with considerable loss in men and horses, indeed, Grant had thrown his cavalry on the turnpike, plank road and Catherpin road, in the vain hope that he might be able to interpose a screen between himself and the Confederates, and thus both protect and conceal his movements. But Lee was not slow to penetrate his designs, and immediately sprung upon his flank like a tiger upon the side of an ox. Ewell and Hill pushed rapidly down the turnpike and plank roads, encountered and drove in the cavalry and infantry supports, which had been thrown forward to block up those highways and compelled the whole army to halt and defend itself. Stuart in the meantime had reached Brock's road, in front of the enemy, and thus opposed another obstacle to his further advance. It is not known that Grant especially directed to give battle here, but he saw the danger of his position and immediately formed into line of battle and advanced nearly two miles to meet the threatened attack. This, it will be seen hereafter, was all that saved him from a most disastrous defeat, since it gave him time to send his trains to the rear and throw up strong entrenchments parallel with and in front of the road by which he had been marching, and behind which he might rally his troops in the event they were beaten back. This was Thursday, the 5th, one year and one day after the great battle of Chancellorsville.

It was about 4 in the afternoon when the two armies encountered each other. Grant attacked heavily and repeatedly along the whole line, and especially on our right, which he showed a disposition to turn, and thus place him between Lee's army and Richmond; but in every instance he was repulsed with heavy loss. He was persistent, however, in his efforts to break our lines, and continued his assaults until night. His last advance against Hill's front was made just before dark, and was handsomely repulsed by Wilcox's and Heath's division. His final attack upon Ewell was made after night, against that part of the line held by Edward Johnson's division. Here, too, he was beaten back, leaving many dead and wounded on the ground. During these operations, Ewell captured 2,000 prisoners, nearly all of whom were taken by Gordon's Georgia brigade and Hays' Louisiana, both of whom behaved with distinguished gallantry.

Longstreet had not yet reached the ground. Leaving Gordonsville at 4 o'clock Wednesday afternoon, he marched fifteen miles that night. The next day he drove the Catharpin (this is correct spelling) road (so called from a run which it crosses) seventeen miles, his orders being to strike Brock's road at a point south of the unfinished railroad. He halted during the afternoon within eight miles of the battle-field; but owing to the peculiar condition of the atmosphere and the density of the forest, he could not hear the guns of Hill and Ewell, and was not aware the battle had commenced until the receipt of a dispatch from Gen. Lee, at midnight, ordering him to come over to the plank road to the [unreadable] of Hill. Hill's corps was put in motion immediately, and reached the field Friday morning soon after sunrise. Hill's troops were aware of the approach of Longstreet's corps, and that it would take their place in the line. They had had a hard fight the previous evening and rested but little that night, and when the head of McLaws' division (now commanded by that medal soldier, Brig. Gen. Kershaw,) came in sight, they relaxed somewhat their vigilance, and were preparing to withdraw, when they were attacked in front with great fury by a very heavy force. Under these untoward circumstances, Wilcox's and Heath's divisions, which had done so well the evening before, were thrown into confusion and gave way, just as Kershaw double quicked it to the front in columns. The latter succeeded in throwing three regiments of his old brigade, commanded by Col. Hinnegan, into line, while Wilcox's and Heath's men were falling back over his troops, and with this small but heroic band, he confronted the heavy masses of the enemy; now flushed with the hope of an easy victory and pressing rapidly forward. These regiments suffered severely, but they maintained their ground until the remainder of the division could be got into some sort of line under the terrible fire to which it was exposed. Gen. Lee witnessed the unfortunate and [unreadable] confusion and withdrawal of the divisions of Wilcox and Heath, in both of which he had reposed so much confidence, and which had behaved so handsomely on former occasions, and tears rushed to his eyes. He at once placed himself at the head of Gregg's Texas brigade, Field's division, formerly Hood's, and prepared to lead in person. The heroes of the Lone Star, who had made the circuit of the Confederacy under Longstreet, remonstrated against such an unnecessary exposure of his life—a life so important and precious to the Confederacy and to all friends of liberty throughout the world. He replied that he must win this battle at every hazard—that he must whip the fight. The Texans, who had not yet moved from their tracks, answered that they could whip the fight without his leading them, and would do it. In the meantime, appeals were made by several officers to Longstreet, as the only person who could probably dissuade Gen. Lee from taking so rash a proceeding. He went immediately to Gen. Lee and begged him to restrain himself, and not to think of exposing himself and the cause which he held so much at heart to such terrible chances. The Texans, too, finally gave him [unreadable] and, in the most respectful and affectionate manner, that they would obey any order he might give, provided he remained behind, but that they would not budge an inch if he led them. Gen. Lee was at length prevailed upon to desist from, the hazardous undertaking, and right glorious did the heroic Texans redeem their pledge.

Kershaw has, by the unanimous voice of the army, won his spurs and Major General's commission. He has ever proved himself equal to the occasion, however critical, but yesterday he displayed a degree of skill, energy and intrepidity that elicited the admiration of all who witnessed or have heard of his performances. When he and Fields, another officer who behaved with great judgment and gallantry, at length got into position under these difficult circumstances, with their old leader, Longstreet, to guide and direct them, it would have done you good to have seen how they and their officers and men pressed forward with shouts that rent the skies, and finally repulsed the immense numbers that crowded upon them with terrible slaughter. They saved the day, which for nearly two hours trembled in doubt, and were at length enabled to assume the offensive. It was evidently Grant's object to turn our right wing, and if he had succeeded, it is impossible to say what might not have been the results.

On the left we were equally successful. An attempt was made to pierce that part of Ewell's line which was held by Pegram's brigade, but it was signally defeated. You will regret to hear that Gen. Pegram was severely wounded, and that Brig. Gen. Jones of Virginia and Stafford of Louisiana, were killed the evening before. With this exception, the left wing was not required to take any further part in the heavy fighting of the day, the enemy's almost exclusive attention being given to our right.

About 11 o'clock Longstreet was ordered to move upon the enemy's left flank, and if possible dislodge him from the railroad cut and the plank road, and drive him back upon Brock's Road. The brigades selected for this movement were G. T. Anderson's and Jenkins', of Fields' division; Mahone's and Davis' of R. H. Anderson's division, and Wofford's and perhaps two other, of Kershaw's divisions. Anderson's division, but lately arrived, having been left at Orange Courthouse to guard against any demonstration upon our rear. The flank movement was completely successful; the enemy was taken by surprise and driven back from the railroad cut across the plank road with heavy loss, a portion of his troops

retreating rapidly down the plankroad to Brock's road. Mahone's Virginia brigade, of Anderson's division, ran over the 4th United States infantry, a regiment which boasted that it had never been broken before. The plank road being clear, Longstreet advanced down it at the head of Jenkins' brigade, and had hardly gone a half of a mile when he was fired upon by Mahone's brigade, which was drawn up in the dense woods parallel to the road, and not more than seventy-five paces from it. Mahone was waiting there to catch such of the enemy as might have been cut off up the road, and when Jenkins' brigade arrived opposite him, his men, being unable to distinguish one man from another through the woods, very naturally concluded it was a body of the enemy retiring, and opened fire upon their friends, killing eight or ten and wounding several others. Capt. Daby, of Kershaw's staff, was killed instantly; the intrepid Gen. Jenkins, of South Carolina, received a mortal wound on the head, from which he died in a few hours afterwards, and Gen. Longstreet was shot in the neck. The ball struck him in front of the right of the larynx, passing under the skin and carrying away a part of the spine of the scapula and coming out behind the right shoulder. The wound is severe, but is not considered mortal. The only damage apprehended being from secondary hemorrhage. Should he survive ten or twelve days and the [unreadable] artery not become involved, it is the opinion of Dr. Cullen, his medical director, that he will be able to return to the field in a few weeks. He has lost temporary use of his right arm—what surgeons call the conical plexus of nerves being injured. He was carried to the rear this morning, and was doing remarkably well when he left. Gen. Lee called to see him just before he was moved, and when he bade him farewell and came out of the tent where his great lieutenant lay, his eyes were filled with tears. It is a remarkable co-incidence that Jackson received his death wound just twelve months ago, only four miles from the spot where his companion in arms fell, and just after he had completed a successful flank movement, and under almost precisely the same circumstances. Heaven grant that Lee may not lose his left arm now, as he lost his right arm then!

Gen. Longstreet had just been congratulated by Gen. Lee, Gen. Kershaw and others, upon the complete success of his attack upon the flank of the enemy, and he was sweeping down the plank road to pluck the rich fruits of his victory, then almost within his grasp, when he was struck down by his own friends. The delay of an hour which ensued gave the enemy time to escape back behind his entrenchments on the Brock's Road. The commander of the corps then devolved upon Maj. Gen. Fields, and today it was turned over to Maj. Gen. Anderson, of Hill's corps, who has been reporting to Longstreet after his arrival, and who formerly belonged to the corps.

The enemy had thus been repulsed along our whole line, and left many dead and wounded in our hands. In many places, his dead appeared to be five or six times as multitudinous as our own. Our loss was not so heavy as at first reported, and will not exceed 5,000, of whom not more than 600 were killed. Most of the wounds were comparatively slight, owing to the protection afforded by the trees and brushes. The enemy's loss cannot be much less than 15,000 inclusive of prisoners. The unfavorable character of the ground and the thick chaparral prevented both sides from using artillery, only a few guns being put in position. Among all the killed, no [*unreadable*] or braver knight ever fell to defense of the liberties of his country than the gallant and accomplished Col. Nance, of South Carolina; and no harder fighter or more perfect gentleman ever received a wound on the field of battle than General Benning of Georgia. The one has gone to the rest of the true soldier—let us pray that the other may long be spared to the country he has served with so much modesty and courage.

At half past four o'clock, General Lee determined to feel the enemy and ascertain his position on Brock's road. On the right, where I had my position, the brigades of Kershaw, Humphreys and Wofford, of Kershaw's division, Anderson, Jenkins, Gregg and Law of Field's division, and Mahone's, of Anderson's division, moved forward in the form of the letter V, with the sharp point towards the enemy. G. T. Anderson, known in the corps as "Tiger Anderson," formed the apex of the line, and succeeded in reaching the enemy's entrenchments, two of his men falling within the work. On the left, Ewell was equally successful. The result of the attack or reconnaissance was the discovery that Grant had been driven back a mile and a half; that he had thrown up a strong line of entrenchment in front of Brock's road, and that his left wing rested upon a deep cut in the railroad, along which he had posted a force that effectually protected it. His position is, therefore, a strong one, being rendered the more so by the dense woods through which his line runs. Lee's position is equally satisfactory.

Last night, Gordon, of Early's division, threw his brigade around an exposed point in the enemy's lines and took Brig. Gens. Seymore, of Ocean Pond memory, and Shaler, and about 500 prisoner. Seymore admits that Grant has been whipped and that the Federal army will continue to be whipped until their ports are closed and the troops reduced to "parched corn and beans like the rebels." He says Grant drinks too much liquor, and that the war, on the part of the North, is conducted as if it were a matter of frolic and contract.

Our lines were withdrawn a few hundred yards last night and from the enemy's immediate front, for the purpose of improving their position. Not understanding exactly what the movement meant, Grant advanced with heavy force this morning, at half past 10 o'clock, but so soon discovered where the Confederate troops were. He was driven back with ease, and now, at sunset, is cowering behind his entrenchments in the Wilderness. His troops have not done as well as they did under McClellan, Burnside or even Hooker. The Confederates, on the contrary, never fought better. Gen. Lee had caused it to be circulated among them some days ago

that they must not think of defeat as possible—it was a thing not to be even dreamed of. Nobly have his invincible legions responded to the call of their great chief. Oh, that we may ever have such a leader and such an army!

P.W.A.

ARMY OF NORTHERN VIRGINIA, Spotsylvania C.H., MAY 10, 1864.

We have had more bloody work to-day, and again, as at the Wilderness, our losses are miraculously small. It has been a singular battle, not only in its results, but especially in regard to the manner in which it was delivered by the Federal commander. The greater part of the forenoon was consumed by him in an attempt to make Gen. Lee develope [*sic*] his plans and positions. Artillery was used freely, and skirmishers and sharpshooters were pushed forward along the lines, and vigorous efforts made to provoke Lee to unmask his batteries and show his hand. At length Grant seemed to grow weary of this kind of work, and ordered an assault to be made. The infantry came up to the work in handsome style, and yet they seemed to have no stomach for the fight; for three separate assaults upon Anderson's corps (late Longstreet's) they were repulsed by his skirmishers and sharpshooters alone. The result was not dissimilar in front of Ewell. The heavy masses of the enemy were pushed back with the ease with which one puts a drunken man away from him. The Confederates fought behind field work thrown up hurriedly, and they appear to relish the fun amazingly. The last assault made upon Anderson's position was late in the afternoon, and was headed by a regiment of the old United States army. The enemy succeeded, after a hard struggle, in gaining a salient angle, occupied, I am told, by Gregg's Texan brigade; but of all who cleared the entrenchments, not one lived to return—they were either killed or taken. They met with a temporary success also in front of Rhodes' division, Ewell's corps, where they captured a portion, if not all, of the guns belonging to the 3d Company, Richmond Howitzers, of Gen. Alexander's artillery command. The guns were soon recovered, however, and the assailants beaten off with heavy loss. Toward noon, it was ascertained that the enemy were moving upon our left and center with cavalry and infantry. Early was sent off with Heth's division to drive them off and repossess us of the bridge over the Po, one of the branches of the Mattapony. He accomplished the object of his mission in his own gallant manner. Heath's men were glad of an opportunity to prove to all that the temporary confusion into which they were thrown at the Wilderness was the result of accident rather than a lack of spirit. The enemy were well punished, and driven entirely from that part of the field. I have spoken of our casualties to-day as miraculously small. They are less than 1,000; and including the loss resulting from the heavy skirmishing yesterday, they will not exceed 1,200. The enemy's loss, on the contrary, since our arrival here, is estimated as high as 15,000, and at the Wilderness, as high as 30,000, including prisoners. These figures are probably too large, though they reflect the opinion which obtains in high official circles here. The calculation rests upon the number of the enemy whom we have buried—2,700—and the 4,000 prisoners who fell into our hands. It is proper to add that papers have been captured since the battle of the Wilderness which admit the loss there of 20,000. These papers contain a confession also that Grant was beaten badly on his right, (our left,) where Ewell commanded, and that Gorman, in his night attack, inflicted heavy losses, but they claim he was successful on his left, (our right). The first is true, but the latter is not. Our victory was complete on every part of he field.

It is reported that Grant, just before opening the battle this morning, issued an order in which he announced to his troops that Butler had taken Petersburg, and was then investing Richmond, with every prospect of reducing it at an early day; also, that Johnston had been defeated at Dalton, leaving his dead and wounded in the hands of Sherman. We have not heard from Dalton for some days, but we know that the order utters a falsehood when it claims that Butler has occupied Petersburg and invested Richmond. The courage of Grant's army, however, like that of the man in the play, is oozing out at their fingers' ends, and it requires to be stimulated.

PETER W. ALEXANDER: ACCOUNT OF BATTLE OF COLD HARBOR

With 100,000 men, Grant was confident he could split Lee's overextended lines with little difficulty. Grant miscalculated, though. The frontal attack the Union general ordered at Cold Harbor ended up being one of the biggest mistakes of his career. Grant's army faced staggering casualties in the nine-day battle—more than 13,000 total, including more than 7,000 in less than an hour on 3 June. Grant's mistake gave Lee his last clear victory of the war. In this pair of dispatches that ran together, the Mobile paper's correspondent, A., better known as the Savannah Republican's *correspondent P.W.A., described the fighting and also a trick Grant tried to use to keep from admitting defeat.*

Mobile Advertiser and Register, 16 June 1864

OUR ARMY CORRESPONDENCE
LETTER FROM GENERAL LEE'S ARMY
[FROM OUR SPECIAL CORRESPONDENT.]
ARMY OF NORTHERN VIRGINIA.
Battlefield of Cold Harbor, June 6, 1864.

My last letter [*unreadable*] the 3d. Inst., 4 P.M., and concluded with an intimation that the enemy, though badly beaten in the bloody battle of that morning, was probably preparing to make an assault at night. The assault was made that night, soon after dark, against that part of the line held by Gens. Breckinridge and Finnegan, as they were preparing to establish their skirmish lines. The enemy was soon repulsed with heavy loss. Immediately afterwards an attack was made upon Gen. [*unreadable*] front, with like result.— These assaults were repeated on the nights of the 4th and 5th, and repulsed as often as made.

The assault last night was intended to cover another movement to the right, in the direction of James river. It was suggested to this correspondent some days ago, Gen. Grant was aiming for James river, and probably the south side of it, his object being to throw his army between Richmond and the South. This is now the prevailing opinion in the army of Northern Virginia, and in high official quarters in the capital. Should he stop on the north side of the river, near City Point, he might easily throw a number of pontoon bridges across at that point, (which you will see by an inspection of the map, is on the north side of the mouth of the Appomattox) or across to

Bermuda Hundreds, which is between the two rivers, and at the point of their confluences. With his army strongly intrenched on the north side of the James, his bridges protected by his monitors, and a foothold already gained by Butler between the rivers, he would be able to rush a raiding party across the river any dark night, and out the Petersburg and Weldon railroad, and probably the Richmond and Danville road also. Should he throw his army behind the Appomattox and across the Petersburg and Weldon road, with his left extending well up towards the Danville road, he might annoy us a great deal if he did nothing more, while Gen. Lee would find it exceedingly difficult, if not impossible, to dislodge him. The chief objection to this late course is the danger to which his communications would be exposed by our artillerists and sharpshooters posted along the north bank of the James. Possibly he would endeavor to guard against this danger by drawing a portion of his supplies from Norfolk by the Petersburg and Norfolk railway.

But will he be able to reach James river? If he continues to move down the north side of the Chickahominy, he probably will be; but should he attempt to cross the stream, and march directly across to the James, he will never reach his destination. But suppose he does reach the James, and establish himself on the banks of the stream or the Appomattox, what then—will he be able to carry Richmond by assault? He will not; his object will be to starve us out. Will he be able to do this? The future alone can give a satisfactory answer to this inquiry. If, however, one may be permitted to venture an opinion so far in advance, I should say that under the leadership of Lee and Beauregard, with the guidance of Heaven, which has never forsaken us except for our own good, the enemy will be able to reduce the capital neither by battle nor starvation.

As already stated, the enemy commenced to move last night. It was observed this morning that he had disappeared in front of our left wing, and the probability is that he is repeating the movement by which, like the crab, he has been advancing sideways since he left the Wilderness. In addition to the assault last night, Grant made a further effort to conceal this movement by sending a communication to Gen. Lee proposing that hereafter, when the enemies are not actually engaged, either side may send out parties to bury its dead and remove its wounded. Gen Lee replied in [unreadable] terms, stating, however, that he preferred the custom common among military men, viz: when the commander of either side desired to succor his wounded and bury his dead, he should send in a flag of truce and ask permission to do so, and that the party sent upon the field to attend to the human duty, should carry white flags. To this Grant sent a rejoinder this morning, affecting to understand that Gen. Lee had agreed to his proposition, and adding that he would send out a force to look after his wounded and dead to-day between 12 and 3 o'clock, and that they should be accompanied by flags of the kind suggested by Gen. Lee. To this *smart* attempt Gen. Lee replied, informing him that he had misunderstood

his former communication—that he meant to indicate the usual custom of a flag of truce as the proper mode of accomplishing his object as stated in his first dispatch, and notifying him that if he sent forward a burial party without conforming to the usage and first obtaining permission to do so, he would cause it to be warned off.

I am not informed whether any further communication has been received from Gen. Grant. His object was transparent enough. He desired to conceal his movement last night, to bury his dead and succor his wounded before leaving, and to avoid the confession of defeat implied by his asking permission to perform this human duty.—His dead and wounded still remain in front of our entrenchments, exposed to the rain and sun, the one poisoning the air by their stench, the other vexing it by their cries for help. The poor creatures—the wounded—may be seen appealing to their friends by waving their handkerchiefs or beckoning them with their pale hands. Grant left many of his dead and wounded uncared for at the Wilderness and Spotsylvania Courthouse, and he will be guilty of the same barbarity here, unless he smother his pride and obtain Gen. Lee's leave to attend to them. I endeavored today to obtain an official statement of our casualties on the 3d, but did not succeed. I learned enough, however, to venture to say that they do not exceed 1,000, and that in all the engagements, skirmishes and picketing that have occurred since we left Hanover Junction, they do not exceed 2,000. The loss of the enemy is probably ten times as great—say 20,000.

A.

Siege of Petersburg

After Cold Harbor, Grant immediately moved against the railroads south of Petersburg. He hoped to isolate Lee from his southern supply route. Grant's men dug in around Petersburg and conducted a number of spectacular sorties in the many months of the siege as they tried to encircle Richmond and Petersburg. The operation lasted much of 1864 and on almost to the surrender at Appomattox in April 1865.

Petersburg was a valuable Confederate asset not only because it was a rail center but also because it was home to a bullet manufacturer. The Confederates had fortified the city in 1862 as a precaution, but it was never really threatened until the spring of 1864. Twice that spring, the city nearly fell, but the resolute and outnumbered Confederates managed to hold on. The danger increased after mid-June when Grant shifted the Army of the Potomac across the James River to attack Petersburg.

P.G.T. Beauregard, commander of the Confederate forces at Petersburg, worked diligently to obtain reinforcements for the two brigades he had at Petersburg and to dig trenches to repel the federal attack in mid-June. Beauregard managed to repulse that early assault, though he lost some of the city's permanent defenses and was pushed back to a second line of trenches. On 18 June, Grant made almost his last head-on attack on a Confederate position in Virginia but was again denied Petersburg. The remainder of the campaign, he relied on grand flanking maneuvers, and the first one came on 22 June at Ream's Station. The Union infantry under Generals

D. B. Birney and H. G. Wright attacked from the Jerusalem Plank Road toward Globe Tavern on the Weldon Railroad. They were supported by a cavalry raid on Burke's station 15 miles to the west. The Union infantry was thrown back by Confederate General A. P. Hill's counterattack, and their colleagues on horseback were very nearly captured.

To distract Lee's attention from his army's attempt to cross the James, Grant sent Sheridan to threaten Lynchburg in mid-June. Lee responded by ordering cavalry commander Jubal Early to engage Sheridan's forces. Early's operation would transmogrify into a raid across the Potomac and into Maryland and Pennsylvania. Sweeping Major General Lew Wallace's 6,000 out of his way at the Monocacy, Early reached the outskirts of a terrified Washington, D.C., on 11 July. In August, Grant would send Sheridan back to the Shenandoah Valley to deal with Early and to lay waste to Virginia. Sheridan's men carried out their orders with alacrity. Through the fall, Sheridan systematically desolated the beautiful valley, and neither Early nor Confederate guerrillas could do anything to stop him.

While Sheridan and Early were pursuing one another through the Shenandoah Valley, Grant and Lee squared off at Petersburg and Richmond. Lee, a master at maneuver, was tied down defending Richmond and its communications center at Petersburg. He had been able to protect Richmond through the war by keeping the enemy far away from the Confederate capital, but Grant denied Lee the opportunity to play to his strength by constricting his position with a tactical, rather than a physical, siege. Petersburg was never surrounded by the enemy, but Grant's defensive positions at Bermuda Hundred, along the lower Appomattox and east of Petersburg, made up essentially a dug-in camp from which he could launch operations against Richmond or Petersburg. Lee had enough freedom of movement to assault Grant's communications and to counterattack Grant's offensives. Essentially, though, the two armies were spinning their wheels in place.

One of the great tragedies of the war occurred during the siege at Petersburg when Grant ordered a massive trench dug under the Confederate works. The trench was to be filled with explosives that would be set off in order to blow a hole, literally, in the Confederate defensive lines. When the 4 tons of gunpowder exploded on 30 July, the attackers were almost as surprised as the defenders. Burnside's corps was supposed to attack through the crater, but they stalled there due to a lack of clear orders from their leaders. They became sitting ducks for Confederate artillery and small arms fire that succeeded in sealing the breach in the Petersburg defenses. The Union lost nearly 4,000 men in the fiasco. Total Union casualties for the siege, including the eight offensives Grant launched during it, reached more than 61,000, not quite double the Confederacy's estimated loss of some 38,000 men.

AN ANONYMOUS REPORT: BATTLE OF THE CRATER

The Battle of the Crater was the most spectacular engagement that occurred during the long siege of Petersburg. Grant's idea was to blow a hole in the Confederate line and then spring forward in an assault. Once the mine blew, though, confusion reigned, and thousands of Union soldiers were killed in the relentless Confederate fire.

Macon Telegraph, 3 August 1864

FROM PETERSBURG

Fighting on Saturday
Our Casualties
1100 Prisoners Captured
20 Colors Taken

PETERSBURG, August 2.—Our loss in Saturday's affair foot up twelve hundred. Three hundred were killed and wounded and three hundred prisoners from Elliot's South Carolina brigade. Mahone losses 450 killed and wounded. The mine was spring on Bashrod Johnson's front.

On yesterday evening Burnside sent in a flag of truce asking permission to bury his dead. The communication was returned with the endorsement that an application from the commanding general of the army would be entertained. Meade then sent in a flag and permission was granted and the hours from five to nine named. This period was diligently occupied and over 700 were buried.

The Yankee officers said their loss in wounded was three thousand.

There is great complaint against Burnside for his failure.

Our captures of battle flags reached 20 and prisoners 1100.

Yankee prisoners say that Grant is organizing a grand raid on the Weldon railroad.

General Elliott is improving. Nothing of importance to day.

DR. GEORGE W. BAGBY: NEWS FROM PETERSBURG

In mid-September, Hermes traveled to Petersburg to see firsthand how the siege there was progressing. George W. Bagby, Hermes's real name, was clearly irritated to find so many men detailed as teamsters rather than serving as soldiers. It was one more piece of evidence, he believed, that proved the Richmond government was doing a bad job of running the country and the military. By this point, for many Confederates, it took little evidence to support accusations of incompetence on behalf of the Richmond government. Discontent and distrust of the Davis administration, and the president himself, were growing throughout the Confederacy. The recent loss of Atlanta and the inaction in Virginia were exasperating the situation.

Charleston Mercury, 16 September 1864

LETTER FROM RICHMOND

(CORRESPONDENCE OF THE MERCURY.)
RICHMOND, Monday, September 12.

On my return from Petersburg yesterday, everybody wanted to know if the city had been, or was going to be evacuated. Whether General LEE and staff had been captured, etc. In Petersburg, everybody wanted to know if Mobile had been captured. The Yankee pickets had said so, etc. So we go with our Sunday rumors.

I saw enough of the enemy's works, and talked enough with our officers, to be thoroughly convinced of the importance of filling up the ranks at once. At the same time I saw white teamsters enough to make a division. Why do not Messrs. Davis, Seddon and Lee enforce the laws, instead of complaining and appealing to the people? And why will the people continually bedevil the authorities, civil and military, until they are fairly worried into granting details which they know to be wrong?

I am glad to hear that General Butler, of your State, has been made Major General of cavalry. Unacquainted personally, I have, nevertheless, ample testimony from men in his army of the service to assure me of his competency for the important post he now fills. Perhaps, if he were in place of Lomax, we should get better accounts from the Valley.

Beast Butler's letter to Ould puts a quietus on the question of exchange. There will be none until we acknowledge the equality of the negro, or win fresh victories. The Beast is ingenious in his sophistry; but the world knows the North is afraid to let us have back our 30,000 veterans. That is the whole secret.

The official organ is rather complimentary this morning on the Chicago Convention, which it professes to regard as the inauguration of a States Rights Conservative party. A good General sent two months ago to Atlanta would have saved this useless bit of flattery. McClellan is defunct—his Convention a farce.

Gilman & Co., of Scotland, had £35,000 worth of tobacco burnt in Manchester last Friday night. It was carried there to be out of the way of the general tobacco conflagration which the citizens threaten in case the Yankees ever get to this place.

Seward's "right of succession" doctrine, promulgated in his late Auburn speech, lets the Republican cat out of the bag. It is a monarchy they are aiming at, as we long ago suspected. Seward is a little too hasty in his announcement; it will recoil heavily on his party—after the next Confederate victory—not till then.

Much cooler; fall like.

HERMES

DR. GEORGE W. BAGBY: ACCOUNT OF FIGHTING IN SHENANDOAH VALLEY

Early had sent back word of his operations in the Shenandoah Valley to the Confederate War Department, but facts were sketchy about the recent engagement with Sheridan. While the story did not name the battle described, it was most likely the Third Battle of Winchester (Battle of Opequon). Early, with 19,000 men, met Sheridan's 41,000 head-on near Winchester. Initially, it appeared that the Confederates were making headway, but the Union cavalry, personally led by Sheridan, turned Early's left and threw the Confederate force back to Fisher's Hill. Union and Confederate losses for the day were both around 5,000.

Charleston Mercury, 27 September 1864

LETTER FROM RICHMOND

(CORRESPONDENCE OF THE MERCURY.)
RICHMOND, Wednesday, September 21.

General EARLY'S despatch throws little light on our late reverse in the Valley. It is probable the enemy, taking advantage of the departure of a division, succeeded in getting in his rear—our inferior force of not too well commanded cavalry offering scarcely any opposition.

Rhodes is a great loss to the service. His fall will be deplored by the whole country. He was the brightest ornament of Alabama, and the pride of his native State, Virginia.

The President left this city yesterday on the Southern train, and the "Reliable Gentlemen" is much excited in consequence. One version is, that the President has gone to Macon, in order to foil Sherman's efforts to inveigle Governor Brown and others into a peace conference at Atlanta. Most likely his visit has reference solely to army matters.

We have pleasant rumors about events forthcoming in a certain vicinity, but do not place much faith in them. We have heard such rumors too often.

Today everybody is required to go up and register name, occupation, etc., for the benefit of the Conscript officers, who are beginning to show new energy. A very material increase of the army is expected.

How it happens that the exchange of officers and of sick and wounded (at odd and uncertain times) is allowed by the enemy, is quite a puzzle to us all; in fact the freaks of the foe in this matter are entirely unaccountable. It is to be hoped that most of the prisoners who arrived today came from Fort Delaware, the horrors of which, as detailed to me by persons lately released from there, beggar all description. Our men suffer from hunger so intensely that they actually fish up the kitchen garbage thrown into the sink, and eat it.

Dark and cloudy—the equinoctial gales coming on.

HERMES.

JOHN M. DANIEL: FALL CAMPAIGN IN RICHMOND

An exchange editorial from the Richmond Examiner *looked at the situation facing the Confederacy in late September. Its editors were confident that the South would win its independence. Somehow the editors had convinced themselves that the Union would never again be as careless with the lives of its troops as its commanding general had been in the previous year. Richmond was the key, the paper argued, and one that Grant would never attain. In fact, the* Mercury's *editors were confident Grant's reputation would sink into insignificance compared with Sherman's. This article was typical of the sorts of morale-building content most of the South's remaining newspapers were running in the fall of 1864. There is little doubt that editors had convinced themselves of the veracity of their words, though in truth the* Mercury *was more accurate than its editors knew when it predicted that the war was drawing to a close, though with a much different outcome than it predicted.*

Richmond Examiner, reprinted in the Charleston Mercury, 28 September 1864

THE FALL CAMPAIGN IN VIRGINIA

(From the Richmond Examiner.)

The final struggle for the possession of Richmond and of Virginia is now near. This war draws to a close. If Richmond is held by the South till the first of November, it will be ours forevermore; for the North will never throw another huge army into the abyss where so many lie; and the war will conclude, beyond a doubt, with the independence of the Southern States. Events have made this city—in itself insignificant—the keystone of the arch. Probably the last immense effort for its destruction which the enemy is now about to make would not be attempted had not Atlanta fallen from the hands of Hood. But Sherman's triumph compels Grant to match it, or sink into insignificance.

According to their well settled custom, the enemy proclaims the intention. Grant himself, in a public speech made during his late journey, has notified his country that whereas "Sherman had scotched the tail in Georgia, he was on his way to crush the head of the rebellion in Virginia." What is of more importance, he has brought up the James fifty-five thousand new troops. It is true that they will hardly do more than make up the depletion of the last two months. It is also true that they are troops of the very meanest descriptions—the substitutes, the crimped levies, the refuse of the Yankee army. But they are not brought here now, in mass, except to be employed immediately. The blow must be struck within the next three weeks, or it cannot be struck at all. Even success would be useless for the election, unless obtained in the coming month.

But it is useless to enumerate the proofs of the proposition which no intelligent observer can treat as doubtful, that the final struggle for Virginia is about to be made below Petersburg; and perhaps, too, in the Valley. Only one fear clouds the reflecting mind. It is not the fear that our generals will be found unequal to their duty, or that our armies are insufficient. It is a fear arising from memories of the past conduct of our central military authority on every crisis. Just when the scale trembles, just when the tiger is about to spring, just when the enemy's columns are about to emerge from the mist, that has hitherto been found their chosen moment to disintegrate our own force, and to attempt insignificant conquest a hundred miles away. Longstreet was sent to threaten Knoxville, while Grant was about to bound on Lookout Mountain; an army was distinguishing itself before "Little Washington" while Butler was landing at Bermuda Hundred; Breckinridge was ordered out of the Valley, while Hunter was entering it. Recollections like these crowd upon the mind and painfully oppress it now. This species of strategy, so often occurring, is the sole fear of the army and the country at this moment. But surely at this time at least, we tremble before shadows. Some personages in history have been styled worse than the untaught, because they were unteachable, but their existence may be doubted. By such stern lessons as the Confederate authorities have received, they must have learned at least this much—that troops must be concentrated in a country at stake, not sent out of it.

FURTHER READINGS

Cavanaugh, Michael Arthur. *The Petersburg Campaign: The Battle of the Crater "The Horrid Pit," June 25–August 6, 1864.* Lynchburg, Va.: H. E. Howard, 1989.

Davis, Stephen. *Atlanta Will Fall: Sherman, Joe Johnston, and the Yankee Heavy Battalions.* Wilmington, Del.: Scholarly Resources, 2001.

Frassanito, William A. *Grant and Lee: The Virginia Campaigns, 1864–1865.* New York: Scribner, 1983.

Glatthaar, Joseph T. *The March to the Sea and Beyond: Sherman's Troops in the Savannah and Carolinas Campaigns.* New York: New York University Press, 1985.

Grimsley, Mark. *And Keep Moving On: The Virginia Campaign, May–June 1864.* Lincoln: University of Nebraska Press, 2002.

Groom, Winston. *Shrouds of Glory: From Atlanta to Nashville—the Last Great Campaign of the Civil War.* New York: Atlantic Monthly Press, 1995.

McDonough, James L. *"War So Terrible": Sherman and Atlanta.* New York: Norton, 1987.

Miles, Jim. *Fields of Glory: A History and Tour Guide of the Atlanta Campaign.* Nashville, Tenn.: Rutledge Hill Press, 1989.

Pleasants, Henry. *Inferno at Petersburg.* Philadelphia: Chilton Book Co., Book Division, 1961.

Reasoner, James. *Shenandoah.* Nashville, Tenn.: Cumberland House, 2002.

Rhea, Gordon C. *To the North Anna River: Grant and Lee, May 13–25, 1864.* Baton Rouge: Louisiana State University Press, 2000.

Scaife, William R. *Hood's Campaign for Tennessee.* Atlanta, Ga.: W. R. Scaife, 1986.

Sommers, Richard J. *Richmond Redeemed: The Siege at Petersburg.* Garden City, N.Y.: Doubleday, 1981.

Wheeler, Richard. *On Fields of Fury: From the Wilderness to the Crater, an Eyewitness History.* New York: HarperCollins, 1991.

6

REPORTING THE WAR, 1865

In a conventional warfare sense, the Confederacy was doomed. Its Army of Northern Virginia was waging a protracted defense of Petersburg, and its resources were dwindling. Far more important, however, was the fact that the southern end of the Confederacy had no defense left. No significant force existed to even slow down William T. Sherman's marauding army. Small forces under Joseph Wheeler and Joseph Johnston could do little more than harass and shadow Sherman's immense force. The Confederate army's manpower situation was so dire in 1865 that Congress debated and passed a bill that would allow slaves to serve in combat positions in return for their freedom at the end of their service. This was an extraordinary step for the Confederacy, one that spoke to the basic premise of its revolution against the American government.

The Confederacy could have waged war in an irregular style, and the capacity for such warfare existed. Cavalry raiders such as the plumed and red-caped Colonel John S. Mosby, paramilitary cutthroats such as William Quantrill, and the formation of the Ku Klux Klan after the war demonstrated that there were white Southerners capable of guerrilla actions. Such tactics on a large scale were somewhat futile, however. Guerrilla war could not protect Southern society. As Sherman rolled through the Deep South, the slave system unraveled as he went. The war against the Union could be continued through unconventional means; the war for the Confederacy could not. Nor could such a war be fought according to the ideals and self-image of the leading Confederates, who saw themselves as gentlemen planters. Sherman's methods were also motivated by a desire to discourage any thought of continuing the war by other means.

Casualties and desertion inspired the belated decision to enlist slaves. There were no illusions about what this meant: Emancipation, for those who fought, and a widely altered social conception of the capabilities of black men. So in the closing months of the war the Confederacy offered to sacrifice part of the labor system it was defending on the altar of military victory. However, the congressional action authorizing the recruitment of slaves into combat units did not occur until March, too late to allow blacks to actually take up arms in defense of the Confederacy and in order to win their freedom.

The Confederacy also appointed Robert E. Lee its supreme military commander in February. Until then, the Confederate army had only theater military commanders who reported to the War Department and Jefferson Davis. Coordinated military command had always been difficult due to the Confederacy's poor communications and logistics. By 1865, the appointment of Lee as supreme commander was mostly a gesture since only one command retained enough troops to make a difference, but it was a decision that had a powerful and positive effect on lagging civilian morale. Lee did attempt to use his power as chief military leader to order a link with Johnston in North Carolina, but it was too late.

After months of engagements along the siege lines at Petersburg, the Confederate army was forced to withdraw from the city in early April. Richmond fell almost immediately. The Union army mercilessly pursued Lee until his remaining 30,000 men were forced to surrender at Appomattox on 9 April. Five days later, Joe Johnston surrendered near Durham Station, North Carolina. Sherman and Johnston arranged such lenient surrender terms for Johnston's that charges of treason were leveled against the Union general. In the flush of victory, these accusations were soon forgotten (not by the fiery-tempered Sherman, however).

There were no more major actions after Appomattox, although minor skirmishes continued. The last fight, a Confederate victory, occurred in Texas. Jefferson Davis was captured near Washington, Georgia, following an arduous flight from Richmond through the Carolinas. The Confederate archives and treasury were traveling with him, and the fact that the treasury gold has never been found has led many to speculate that it is buried somewhere in or near the picturesque little town. Davis was imprisoned at Fort Monroe, Virginia, where, early in his incarceration, he was forced to endure shackles and forbidden to communicate with anyone or to have visitors. His fate, though, was less final than Abraham Lincoln's. The Union president was assassinated on 14 April. This would make the postwar era far more contentious and inconclusive than it might otherwise have been.

WESTERN THEATER

Carolinas Campaign

Sherman's army spent Christmas and New Year's in Savannah, then rested there for about a month before moving out on the final stage of its march of terror through the South. Sherman knew, and had told at least one Georgia woman, that the restraint his men had shown in Georgia would evaporate when they hit the South Carolina state line. He indicated there would be little he could do to control the men once they arrived in the state that was the first to secede, but he also showed little inclination to do so. Sherman had set out on his March to the Sea to "make Georgia howl," but he knew his men intended to bring arrogant South Carolina to its knees.

Sherman's plan was to sweep through the two Carolinas, inflicting as much devastation as possible along the way, and then meet up with Grant in Virginia for the final and total destruction of Lee's Army of Northern Virginia. Lee surrendered before Sherman could reach Grant, but that was the only part of the plan that Sherman's army did not complete. South Carolinians and North Carolinians alike were terrified by the news that Sherman's men were on the move again.

When Sherman's force headed out on 1 February, all eyes were on Charleston. South Carolina Governor Andrew Magrath was frantic to protect his beloved home city. His repeated shrill demands to Richmond for additional troops to repel the invaders asked for far more than the Confederacy had to give. Magrath became so desperate that he negotiated with Governor Zebulon Vance of North Carolina and Governor Joseph E. Brown of Georgia for a "mutual protection pact" that sounded to some like an attempt to repudiate the Confederate government.

Sherman's first target was not Charleston, as Magrath had expected. It was the state capital, Columbia. Johnston, commanding a tiny force at that point, had also expected Sherman to march on Charleston and perhaps Augusta, the site of the Confederacy's only gunpowder manufacturing plant. Each of those cities had been garrisoned with about 10,000 troops. Columbia, though, was essentially undefended and would be "easy pickin's" for the Union army.

The march from Savannah to Columbia was punctuated with small cavalry raids by Major General Hugh Judson Kilpatrick's horsemen. Sherman's cavalry struck at the small towns of Aiken and Lexington and specifically targeted the home of South Carolina writer and journalist William Gilmore Simms. They destroyed his home in order to destroy his library, one of the largest and finest collections of books in the state of South Carolina.

Sherman's men arrived at Columbia on 17 February and before he left, the city had been essentially destroyed. Nearly a third of the city burned to the ground, including the new statehouse. The fire started when locals set bales of cotton on fire to keep them from falling into enemy hands, but it quickly raged out of control with the aid of Sherman's men and gale-force winds. An investigation of the fire after the war found that Sherman himself had not ordered the conflagration and had taken steps to bring it under control, but his enthusiastic soldiers were slow to obey their officers' orders to cease and desist. The ruin of Columbia significantly contributed to Sherman's reputation for ruthlessness toward Southern civilians. The day Sherman captured Columbia, Hardee abandoned Charleston and set out toward North Carolina, where he was to combine forces with Johnston. Sherman rushed to cut off the concentration of the Confederate troops.

Union General John A. Schofield was already operating in North Carolina with the objective of combining his army with Sherman's. Along the way, his army captured Wilmington, North Carolina, on 22 February, the Confederacy's last open port. The Confederate garrisons from Augusta and Charleston abandoned those positions and headed toward North Carolina, too, so as to block Sherman's route toward Grant.

On 15 March, Sherman reached the vicinity of Fayetteville, North Carolina, just south of Raleigh, his next target. Johnston was in a desperate situation. He had too few men to contend with Sherman's 60,000-man legion, but he hoped to defeat at least a portion of the Union army before it could concentrate with Schofield's. Johnston attacked Sherman's advance units near Bentonville on 19 March and was initially successful, but he was unable to hold on to his gains. Sherman's force smashed

Johnston's left, and on 23 March, the Confederates withdrew to Goldsboro where the troops from Augusta and Charleston were rendezvousing.

A by-product of Sherman's march through Georgia and the Carolinas was a much smaller and weaker Confederate press. During his occupation of Atlanta, the newspapers there all either fled or shut down permanently. Several were back in operation within a few weeks but not all. Of the two Savannah newspapers, one closed down and the other was taken over by a Yankee journalist traveling with Sherman's army. The Southern press's voice was becoming fainter.

AN ANONYMOUS REPORT: OPPOSING SHERMAN IN SOUTH CAROLINA

Sherman had been on his move through South Carolina for slightly more than two weeks when an Augusta newspaper picked up this piece from the Edgefield Advertiser, *a newspaper located in a community just across the Savannah River in South Carolina. News was slow to come in about Sherman's movements, though that did not stop newspapers from speculating about the Union army's whereabouts. This story described the feint Kilpatrick's cavalry made on the Edgefield County town of Aiken. Though the fighting there has been referred to as the Battle of Aiken, it was a relatively minor engagement. However, any news of Sherman's whereabouts and doings was welcomed by readers. The* Advertiser *made an important point in its editorial. Up to that point in the war, the people of the South Carolina homefront, beyond Charleston, had been relatively unscathed by the fighting.*

Augusta Constitutionalist, 18 February 1865 (Augusta, Ga.)

FROM THE ADVERTISER
TROUBLOUS TIMES IN EDGEFIELD

During the war, we people of Edgefield have had, compared to the hundreds of other places in the Confederacy, a very calm and pleasant walk on the highway of life. And our walk is still comparatively calm and pleasant. How long will it remain so, God only knows? Lately however, we have been wandering in wet and slippery roads, in bad times and wintry weather. For four days, our whole population was in hourly expectation of being pounced upon by a pack of howling, ravenous, blood thirsty wolves—of being at any moment, night or day, gnashed, gnawed, crashed and gobbled up, in the most merciless and ferocious manner. Women imagined all sorts of battle, murder and sudden death. Children had "Raw Head and Bloody bones" ever before their eyes. Men of large property were green and yellow and grinned with horrible agony. But let us narrate facts. Early on Thursday morning last, it was announced among us that a large and formidable body of Yankee cavalry, under Kilpatrick, had entered Aiken during the previous night. Refugees and straggling soldiers, passing through from below, confirmed this rumor, and added that Kilpatrick was passing on to Graniteville and Vaucluse and would no doubt devastate the whole country. The supporting force of Edgefield district being in camp near the village, our vigilant and energetic enrolling officer, Lieutenant Moses, immediately chose from that body a number of brave

and well mounted men and departed with them towards Aiken, intending to establish a line of couriers between that place and Edgefield; this he did, and to him and them the community is not a little indebted.

About noon on Thursday, some half dozen soldiers from Wheeler's command, in charge of 150 or 200 broken down cavalry horses, entered our town—horses and all. On the approach of the Yankees, they had quitted a recruiting camp on the South Carolina Railroad, and were taking their horses up the country. They reported no Yankees in Aiken, but a large force twelve miles below. These bare and bony *chevaux de battle* were the Yankees that had entered Aiken the night before!

By nightfall on Thursday, our courier brought us reliable intelligence that none of the enemy had entered Aiken; and that a considerable body of Wheeler's cavalry was between that point and the enemy. In the meantime, our people, though for the most part calm and collected, were busy setting their houses in order for the reception of the foe; or rather in turning them topsy turvy. Provisions, furniture, clothing, were sent off and lodged in safe places; silver, jewelry, glass, china &.,&., were consigned to the safe and silent bosom of earth. Oh that we possessed half the gold and silver now hid in Edgefield soil! We would snap our fingers scornfully at Potosi, Golconda, and Ophir.

Friday was comparatively a quiet day, the couriers bringing

news from time to time that Wheeler was successfully holding the enemy at bay some miles below Aiken. In the course of Friday night, however, a courier brought tidings that the Yankees had entered Aiken and burned it. Refugees and stragglers again confirmed the report, and many strange and horrible items of information. This report was premature; the enemy did not enter Aiken until Saturday. Nor did they burn it, or any part of it.

Excitement in Edgefield was now high and wild, and continued so until Saturday night, when it was ascertained for certainty that the enemy had been driven out of Aiken and pushed back some miles down the railroad. During the day the enemy had dashed into Aiken, and Wheeler's cavalry had engaged them fiercely in the very streets of the town, whipped them back and finally compelled them to retire discomfited. On this day, Sunday, Wheeler shipped them in three or four different fights in and around Aiken. General Wheeler may have a great many worthless men in his command, evidently has, but after this, let us cease to talk about his troops not fighting.

On Sunday, according to the report of our couriers, the enemy retired from the railroad and made off eastwardly towards Orangeburg. Gen. Wheeler had followed them, going to Merritt's bridge, which leads across the Edisto from Barnwell into Lexington. This bridge is thirteen miles from Aiken, and twenty-three from Edgefield.—The Yankee force operating lately below Aiken was a part of Kilpatrick's cavalry; it is said they have a large infantry support. For two days past, we have been tranquil and free from war's wild alarms. We know not how long this tranquillity will last. Perhaps but few days. God grant it forever. Wonder if the earth is giving up its treasures!

DR. NAGLE: SHERMAN'S ADVANCE INTO NORTH CAROLINA

Sherman was on the move. He had passed through Columbia, and all eyes were turning to Charlotte, North Carolina, anticipated to be his target. Once again, though, Sherman surprised the Southerners and moved out instead toward the North Carolina capital. He would meet light, ineffectual resistance. The Dr. Nagle mentioned in the following story was a reporter for the Confederate Press Association.

Augusta Constitutionalist, 23 February 1865 (Augusta, Ga.)

[Dr. Nagle, of the Press Association, has favored us with the following interesting items:

Sherman's force consists of about 50,000 men of all arms. He is evidently advancing on Charlotte, effectually destroying the Railroad and everything else, along a wide track. Apparently, his intention is to reach Greenesboro, and destroy the Danville Road, avoiding castles and fortified places.

Columbia was occupied by the enemy for a short time.

Troops are being well armed and equipped as they arrive here.

The wagon train of the Army of Tennessee is arriving and will rendezvous at Washington, Ga. Parties going to Columbia and Richmond pass through Augusta.

General D. H. Hill has been relieved from the command of this military district. Gen. B. D. Fry succeeds to the command of the District of Georgia, in addition to his present duty as Commandant of Post. Much satisfaction is expressed by the people at the appointment.

The most extravagant prices ever paid in this country for goods occurred at auction yesterday in this city.

AN ANONYMOUS REPORT: EVACUATION OF CHARLESTON

With all the usual means of disseminating news breaking down, Southern newspapers in 1865 were much slower than usual in reporting important events. This story, written as the result of an interview with a railroad employee, was the first news in Augusta of the fall of Charleston. Without the usual sources available, it was impossible to verify the story, but any news, by this point, was better than no news.

Augusta Constitutionalist, 25 February 1865 (Augusta, Ga.)

AUTHENTIC FROM CHARLESTON
THE EVACUATION—TERRIBLE CALAMITY
THREE HUNDRED WOMEN AND CHILDREN
KILLED

We have at length what we conceive to be authentic intelligence of the fall of Charleston. It were worse than useless to bemoan over this event, though it will cause poignant sorrow in the hearts of thousands. Not only those whose homes were in the beautiful "city by the sea," will lament the giving up of the place to the enemy; who for four years have vainly thundered at its portals; but there are myriads of sympathizing hearts throughout Christendom who must mourn the military necessity that has yielded to our vandal foe the seat of so much elegance, refinement, hospitality and true chivalry. Fallen though Charleston be, her name will live in history, and her heroic defence be chronicled on the brightest pages of that record which transmits to posterity the matchless deeds of this revolution.

The evacuation was successfully completed on Thursday, the 16th of February, between the hours of twelve and one o'clock. Our troops left on the cars of the North Eastern railway going in the direction of Kingstree.

In addition to the fall of the city, of itself sorrowful in the extreme, we have to record one of the most horrible calamities that ever befell any population. The Depot of the South Carolina Railroad company between Mary and Ann streets was filled with stores of the Commissary, Quartermaster and Ordnance Department. Upon the departure of our forces such supplies as could not be removed were allowed to the indigent citizens, and the building was thrown open for them. While crowded with women and children some fixed ammunition was exploded, destroying the house and causing the death of three hundred persons. The sight was a most pitiable one an beggars description.

The flames immediately spread with the greatest rapidity, and it is feared that a large portion of the city must have been destroyed. The fire was in progress when the Federal troops landed, and they immediately tendered assistance and protection to the firemen engaged in staying the conflagration.

The explosion is supposed to have been purely accidental, some boys having been seen engaged in amusing themselves with shells. It was certainly not caused by any military order.

There is now no enemy between this city and Charleston, the line of the South Carolina Railroad being occupied at no point.

We are indebted to Captain Disher of the South Carolina Railroad for the above interesting items. He left Johnson's Turn Out yesterday, where he conversed with one of General Young's scouts who had just arrived from Ridgeville.

The story circulated of an alleged Yankee Indignity to the British Consul and flag, is without foundation. England has no commercial representative in Savannah at present. Mr. Molyneux, the Consul, died in Paris some months ago, and Mr. Fullerton, the Vice Consul, was ordered out of the country by the President about a year ago, for insolent interference with the conscript law.

Fifty three officers, including Gen. G. P. Harrison, a private citizen of much worth, captured by Sherman, have arrived at Washington from Savannah, and were committed to the Old Capitol.

J. W. Morrel and Isaac Cohen, leading merchants of the city, have died.

No order for the banishment of the families of Confederate officers had been executed at last accounts, though the policy was still under discussion.

WILLIAM W. HOLDEN: UNION ADVANCE ON WILMINGTON

The next important Southern city to fall after Charleston was Wilmington, the Confederacy's last open port. Lee had earlier predicted that if Wilmington fell, he would not be able to maintain his army, and after the fall of Fort Fisher in January, it would only be a matter of time before the vastly stronger Union combined naval and land force would capture the coastal city. The loss of the city received little coverage throughout the Confederacy because virtually no newspaper had a correspondent on the scene. All relied on telegraphic or exchange coverage, which was constructed from interviews with people who had escaped from the city. Even then, few details were available.

Raleigh Weekly Standard, 1 March 1865

FROM WILMINGTON

The Goldsborough *Journal* of the 24th contains some information from Wilmington, most probably furnished by the Editor of the Wilmington *Journal* who was in that town. We shall get no more papers from Wilmington soon. It is believed that Hagood's brigade, with the exception of the 7th battalion, was captured by the enemy. Our troops retreated across the northeast branch of the Cape Fear, at what is known as Big Bridge Ferry. They were pursued by the enemy, and some skirmishing took place. The *Journal* complains that the authorities were too silent in relation to the approach of the enemy and the probabilities of the capture of the town. "About the sacking of the town of Wilmington," says that paper, "we believe very little of it, indeed almost nothing. All citizens were out as a guard for private residences, especially those in which ladies resided. Of course there will be suffering, but all those who are compelled to stay in Wilmington ought not to be denounced. They are there, and physically and pecuniarily they are unable to leave. There are good and true men and women among them.

Gen. Schofield is probably in force no further north of Wilmington than Northeast River, some fifteen miles, at which point the exchange of prisoners is going on. We fear that a considerable portion of our forces fell into the hands of the enemy. We have no idea of the number of our troops in that quarter. Those mainly engaged with the enemy were of Hoke's division. We notice a conjecture in the *Confederate* of Monday morning, that Schofield "will try next the Fayetteville route, or attempt to effect a junction with Sherman."

DR. NAGLE: GENERAL JOHNSTON'S BATTLE NEAR BENTONVILLE: OCCUPIED SAVANNAH

One of the last major battles in the Western Theater occurred near Bentonville, North Carolina. It was the largest battle ever fought in North Carolina and the only serious attempt General Joseph E. Johnston's men would mount to stem Sherman's march through the Carolinas. Johnston's 20,000 men did their best to halt Sherman's advance toward Goldsboro but were forced to evacuate by torch light on 21 March. The great slaughter of 5,000 enemy soldiers referred to in the story actually equaled 1,500 killed, wounded, and missing Union soldiers over the two-day battle. The Confederate army, on the other hand, lost nearly 2,500 men in the Battle of Bentonville. With news about the battle so scarce, the author of this story, a reporter for the Confederate Press Association, turned to a second topic: the state of affairs in occupied Savannah.

Augusta Constitutionalist, 23 March 1865 (Augusta, Ga.)

GEN. JOHNSTONS' BATTLE

[DR. NAGLE'S DISPATCH.]

AUGUSTA, March 23.

General Johnston attacked the army under the immediate command of Sherman near Bentonville, Sunday morning, the 19th, and at nightfall had killed, wounded and captured five thousand. Our loss about five hundred. The battle was renewed on Monday morning and was progressing at 4 P.M., Monday. Results not known but good.

By special request of General Joseph E. Johnston, Surgeon A. J. Foard is placed on his staff as Medical Director of the Army. By orders received from the War Department on the 20th instant, he is relieved from duty as Medical Inspector of the hospitals and armies in Georgia, Alabama and Mississippi and assigned to duty with General Johnston in the field.

General S. D. Lee left Augusta on the 17th, Address Army of Tennessee.

Ladies who left Savannah on the 16th instant, report that the city is garrisoned entirely by negro troops, officered by white fellows. Their pickets are very insolent and strict.

The Yankees were very anxious to learn the result of Sherman's operations. Many fears were entertained that he had received serious opposition from General Johnston. They eagerly seek news from Augusta and other points in the Confederacy, but do not permit anything to be brought out.

Scouting parties, composed of negroes, hunt our scouts in the vicinity of that city with dogs. They capture all the able bodied negroes they find on the plantations in their route, and place them in the Yankee army.

Northern journals declare that Andy Johnston was immured in the asylum for insanity near Silver Springs by a cabal with Preston King and Blair to manage the matter.

They look on his accession to the second position in the Executive Administration of National affairs as disgraceful and an insult to the people.

A competent board of medical examiners pronounced him to be laboring under temporary aberration of mind—insanity caused by beastly intoxications, requiring his confinement.

It is expected the opposition faction will manage his overthrow, despite the influence and interference of his friends with his patron Seward at the head.

On Sunday evening the 19th, scouts from Chalk Bluff, twenty miles down the river from this city, reported to General Fry that they heard heavy and rapid discharges of artillery during the evening as though a hard battle was occurring somewhere northeast. On Monday noon the telegraph announced the battle of Bentonville.

The firing was heard a distance of more than two hundred miles.

Yankees are concentrating a force at Corinth, Miss., and Pittsburg Landing on Tennessee River.

REFUGEE: EVACUATION OF FAYETTEVILLE

As Sherman's invading troops neared Fayetteville, North Carolina, the town's newspaper, the Observer, *continued to publish. The* Observer's *legendary editor, E. J. Hale, had been one of North Carolina's political king-makers for decades, and he showed his characteristic aplomb by continuing to print and distribute copies of his paper—free to Confederate soldiers—even as the enemy threat loomed nearer and nearer. Eventually, though, Hale was forced to flee, along with the rest of the Fayetteville citizens, and his newspaper office was wrecked by the conquering Union army. The source of the information, the* Biblical Recorder, *was the state's Southern Baptist newspaper.*

Charlotte Western Democrat, 28 March 1865

THE EVACUATION OF FAYETTEVILLE

The following interesting account of the evacuation of Fayetteville is taken from the Biblical Recorder:

When Gen. Sherman started on his raid from Savannah, it was generally believed in military circles that he would follow the course of the railroad from Columbia to Charlotte. Preparations were made to check him before he reached the latter place. On arriving at Chester he turned his column to the right, captured Camden, and moved on the main road to Cheraw. Gen. Hardee was compelled to evacuate the town and retreat to Rockingham. He was then ordered by General Johnston to fall back upon Fayetteville. On reaching the vicinity, on Wednesday the 8th, he took a position six miles from town, where he was reinforced by the command of Lieut. General Hampton. It was believed that a stand would be made and the place defended. It did seem that the splendid arsenal, the seven cotton and three oil factories, &c., made it a place of sufficient importance to the government to make a more determined defence. On Thursday the artillery and trains began to cross the river. Then it was announced that Gen. Johnston had left, and all hope of defence abandoned. Thursday was a gloomy day. The weather was inclement; the people sad; the soldiers disappointed. The citizens began to secrete their provisions, plate, jewelry, &c. The ladies had provisions cooked for the soldiers, and the citizens who were likely to be molested began to prepare to leave.

Friday was fast day. In the morning it rained heavily. The church bells called the people to the house of prayer, but few obeyed the call. About noon the clouds passed away, and the sun shone as brightly and the evening was as calm as if the sound of war had never been heard in the land. Late in the afternoon it was announced that the infantry were entrenching, and this led many to believe that the town was not lost. The wish was father to the thought. To those conversant with military movements it indicated an immediate retreat. About sunset nearly five hundred prisoners, captured in the morning, were brought in and hurried to the front. As the shades of darkness began to cover the old town, the quartermaster and ordnance wagons moved towards the river and the infantry began to pass to the front. Those of us who intended leaving

were assured that we could not remain till morning; and we retired to our homes and partook of our evening repast with feelings that are not easily described. Loved ones separated; fathers embraced their children; husbands and wives parted—but I must stop. The grief of such partings is too sacred for the public eye. On hurrying to the streets, I found them thronged with soldiers. It took me three hours to cross the bridge, just one mile from my residence. On crossing we repaired to the house of a friend, and sought a few hour's repose.

Saturday morning, we returned to the river. Soldiers and citizens were hurrying across. The enemy had entered the town, and been driven back in confusion. The cavalry on the outposts were drawn in and a line formed for the defence of the bridge. The troops crossed in a very orderly, quiet manner. Just before the last detachment of cavalry crossed, the steamers and flats in the river were fired. These well known favorites floated from their moorings as the flames shot up towards the heavens. The enemy, in force, entered the town and commenced firing upon the rear of our retreating column.

The confusion among the citizens was, of course, intense. In a few moments the streets were cleared, and the troops engaged in a spirited fight at long range. Just as soon as the last detachment crossed, the bridge was fired. In a few moments it was enveloped in flames and fell with a crash that resembled the roar of artillery. A 32-pounder was posted in front of the bridge, so as to command a portion of Hay street, and all that portion of it which passes through what is called Campbellton. The street was in a few moments crowded with mounted men. The roar of the flames that were consuming the bridge, boats and old ware houses, the exultant cheers of the invaders, the screams of excited females, the hallooing of thoughtless boys, all broke upon the stillness of a lovely morning. The enemy rush in triumph towards the bridge, heedless of danger, when a solid shot, from a 32-pounder, strikes the head of their column and passes through it. Then, after a momentary pause, the column closes, and on they come. The next moment a shell is thrown into their midst; the shell explodes; there is confusion; another and another, and the street is deserted. Gen. Hampton then discovered that they were endeavoring to reach a [*unreadable*] to the left of the bridge. To do this they had to pass over an open field. The gun was moved to a point which commanded the field, and a few well directed shots completed the evacuation. Scarcely a man was cut off, and no stores were lost.

E. J. Hale, the *veteran* editor of the Observer, had just finished working off the usual issue of his paper on Thursday. Having a good supply of paper on hand, he put his press to work on Friday and supplied the troops with the Observer gratis.

The citizens, up to the night of the evacuation, continued to receive Confederate money. The ladies were as indefatigable as ever in ministering to the wants of the soldiers. They have the proud satisfaction of knowing that the troops will never forget them. They are a noble people.

REFUGEE.

EASTERN THEATER

Petersburg to Appomattox

While Union forces were finishing off the Confederacy in the Deep South, in Virginia, Grant concentrated on keeping Lee pinned down between Petersburg and Richmond. Through the winter and early spring 1865, Grant tightened his grasp on Petersburg by driving deeper and deeper into Dinwiddie County. Grant was able to accomplish this in spite of diverting several brigades to North Carolina to assist with the assaults on Fort Fisher and Wilmington. Lee put up the best fight he could. In late March, Confederate troops under John B. Gordon launched a surprise attack. Lee hoped the attack would allow his army to slip out of Grant's grasp, but it only succeeded in making matters worse for the Confederates. The Southerners were able to conquer the position they were attacking, but they were pushed back again in a four-hour battle.

Grant began his final offensive on 29 March with an attack near the Dinwiddie county seat. He caught Lee by surprise and was able to mass sixteen divisions against the seven Southern divisions protecting Lee's communications line into Petersburg. The Southerners, under George Pickett and Fitzhugh Lee, counterattacked and drove the Union cavalry back to Dinwiddie Courthouse, but the Confederate forces were routed the next day near Five Forks.

On 2 April Grant achieved a decisive victory at Petersburg. Union infantry spearheads broke through Lee's thin lines. Only Gordon's force at Petersburg was able to hold its position, but he was virtually encircled by Union troops. Lee had only one choice: Evacuate Petersburg and Richmond and get his army to North Carolina, where he could join forces with Johnston. Lee sent Longstreet to Petersburg to reinforce Gordon long enough to buy additional time to evacuate Richmond, and he sent word to Davis that it was time to flee.

Davis was at church that Sunday morning when Lee's telegraph arrived. He rose and quietly left to go to his office. Davis had been expecting Lee to abandon Petersburg, had known the general could not hold out forever, but the speed with which the city had fallen caught him by surprise. Davis telegraphed Lee, asking if it was possible for the general to stall the Union army longer, so as to facilitate the evacuation of Richmond. Lee's answer was a terse no. He had given Davis all the time he could. That night, Davis and his cabinet were on a train to Danville, a town to the southwest of Richmond and right on the Virginia/North Carolina border. Davis paused in Danville, fully expecting Lee to arrive to protect the town and the government.

Lee had no hope of making it to Danville, though. The better supplied, equipped, and fed Union army was moving faster than Lee could, which made it impossible for him to make for North Carolina and join up with Johnston south of Danville. Instead, Grant was pushing Lee due west, toward a river and a small place that shared a name: Appomattox. By 8 April, the Union army blocked Lee's way west as well. Breckinridge, by then the Confederate secretary of war, reported to Davis that Lee's situation was close to hopeless. That night, a young officer who had slipped through the Union lines made it to Danville and reported to Davis and his cabinet that surrender was imminent. On 9 April, Lee and Grant met around midday at Appomattox in the home of Wilmer McLean, who had fled Manassas in 1861 to get away from the fighting.

The surrender of Lee has been the inspiration for many myths, including the one about the great Confederate general proffering his sword to Grant, and the Union general's refusal. That myth sprang up almost spontaneously at the moment, for it was reported as truth in Confederate newspapers. The surrender was not without its poignant moments, though. On 12 April, Gordon was leading the Confederate soldiers to surrender their arms when a Union general, Joshua Chamberlain, ordered his men to salute the ragtag, exhausted Southerners. Gordon, touched by the gesture, had his men return the honor.

The surrender at Appomattox was, for all intents and purposes, the end of the Civil War. It would be many weeks before word spread to the far reaches of the Confederacy that the war was over, and it would be a year before Andrew Johnson issued a proclamation declaring the hostilities over. In that year, much happened to reconcile the sections and much happened to push them further apart, particularly Lincoln's assassination on 14 April. Three days later, Johnston and Sherman began negotiating an armistice in North Carolina, but the terms were considered too generous, and the U.S. Congress rejected the arrangement. Johnston finally surrendered on 26 April.

LARKIN: LETTER FROM RICHMOND

Robert E. Lee was among the supporters of the bill to draft slaves into the Confederate army. His support was imminently practical. Lee, somehow, was supposed to keep Richmond out of the hands of the Union army and take back all the territory captured elsewhere in the South. But Lee was hemmed in at Petersburg, and he did not have enough men in the field to break his way through, just as there had not been enough men in Georgia and the Carolinas to subdue Sherman. To compound Lee's problems, citizen morale was flagging in the wake of all the many reverses of the Confederate cause in 1864. Further, a Tennessee representative, Henry S. Foote, had thrown up his hands in frustration with the Davis government's willingness to stomp on individual rights or to end the war. Foote left Congress and traveled to the North, hoping to work out peace terms himself. The Union secretary of state rebuffed Foote's advances.

Augusta Constitutionalist, 5 January 1865 (Augusta, Ga.)

Letter from Richmond.
RICHMOND, Dec. 29th, 1864.

"Sherman's army will be decimated;" and "Savannah will be held to the last extremity," had deluded our people to a full confidence in the false assurances of (what now appears) almost a shameless military censor. The fall of Savannah was totally unexpected, and created a gloom and despondency I have never before witnessed in the Capitol. Hardeville will never claim her own until she has a full receipt for all the military leaders who amuse themselves by feeding our people with false hopes only to be crushed, and grind their heroic spirits to dust. This may be military "strategy," or "secrecy," or "necessity," but it is not what is due to, or expected by, a brave people.

The heavy raiding column of the enemy in Southwestern Virginia seems to have accomplished all it was sent out for, and has returned to East Tennessee. They succeeded in destroying a large amount of the rolling stock, and some fifty miles of the Virginia & Tennessee railroad, the Wythe county lead mines and the [unreadable] works—the latter, I hear was almost totally destroyed. Many and horrible were outrages perpetrated upon the citizens of the county through which they massed. Neither age nor sex could claim immunity at the hands of the dastardly scoundrels.

The currency bill has passed the House by a decided vote, and is now under discussion in the Senate, where it will, it is thought, be passed without much opposition, after going through the "regular channels."

We are again assured that Wilmington is "safe." The attack on Fort Fisher has commenced in dead earnest, and all eyes are turned in that direction. We hope the great efforts, we know the Government is making to hold this important seaport, may be successful. Great confidence is felt here of the result.

The gallant partizan, Colonel John Singleton Mosby, has again been badly wounded, though it is reported not to be dangerous.

True to his threat, Hon. H. S. Foote, of Tennessee, has not been in his seat since Monday.

LARKIN.

AN ANONYMOUS REPORT: BATTLE IN FRONT OF PETERSBURG

For months, both the Union and the Confederate armies had been entrenched around Petersburg. Both sides were expecting decisive results in 1865, and in late March, both sides began making the initial moves in a short-lived campaign that did indeed lead to a decisive result—Lee's surrender on 9 April at Appomattox.

Augusta Constitutionalist, 28 March 1865 (Augusta, Ga.)

BATTLE IN FRONT OF PETERSBURG

PETERSBURG, March 26.

About 4 o'clock this morning General Lee attacked the enemy on our left in the vicinity of the Appomattox, assaulting and capturing two lines of works, and one or more heavy forts.

Our men advanced well into action, but the enemy massed his artillery so heavily in the neighborhood of the forts, and was enabled to pour such a terrible enfilading fire through our ranks that it was deemed best to withdraw.

The captured works were therefore abandoned, and our troops reoccupied their original position.

Gens. Gordon's and Bushrod Johnson's divisions were the troops engaged on our side.

Our loss was several hundred. Five hundred prisoners were captured from the enemy, among them Gen. McLaughlin, and a number of officers.

The Yankee General Warren is reported killed.

On our side Brigadier General Terry was wounded. Many pieces of artillery and mortars are captured. The latter were abandoned, and some of the former brought off.

The attack was a surprise to the enemy.

Their lines were swept for a distance of five hundred yards right and left. The enemy made two efforts to recover the captured works which were handsomely repulsed. It was found, however, that enclosed works in the rear, commanding the enemies main line could only be taken at a great sacrifice, and the troops were withdrawn to their original position.

AN ANONYMOUS REPORT: SHERIDAN'S RAID IN SHENANDOAH VALLEY

The following story, reprinted from the Richmond Sentinel, *detailed Sheridan's operations in the Shenandoah Valley. In his raids, Sheridan destroyed all railroads and rolling stock he could find, while occasionally fighting small engagements with Confederate troops. The engagement at Waynesboro described in this story allowed Sheridan to crush what was left of Early's army.*

Augusta Constitutionalist, 31 March 1865 (Augusta, Ga.)

[From the Richmond Sentinel.]
SHERIDAN'S RAID

From the reports published by the enemy and the accounts which have gained publicity in our own papers, we make up the following memorandum of Sheridan's cavalry expedition:

Sheridan's force consists of the 1st cavalry division, General Merritt; the 3d cavalry division, General Custar, and one brigade of the 2d cavalry division, commanded by Colonel Caphart. Four pieces of artillery accompanied the expedition. The whole numbered five to six thousand men.

General Sheridan broke camp on the 27th. He moved very rapidly, reaching Staunton, as is alleged, on the third day.

The next morning, (March 2d,) Sheridan pushed for Waynesboro, Custar's division in the advance. Near Waynesboro, Custar encountered Early's small force, and speedily dispersed it. The Yankee accounts claim the capture of eighty-seven officers and one thousand one hundred and sixty-five privates, seven cannon and one hundred wagons, ambulances, &c. General Early escaped. The Yankees claim to have captured his staff; also a railroad train, laden with stores, artillery, &c.

The next day (Friday, the 3d inst.,) Sheridan entered Charlottesville about two p.m., without opposition. The mayor and civil authorities met him outside and surrendered the town, receiving a promise of protection. General Merritt's headquarters were at Mrs. B. H. Shackleford's; General Sheridan's at Mrs. E. Cole's. The supplies of citizens were seized, and the thieving around town was universal. The factories in reach were destroyed. On Monday morning, the 5th, they evacuated Charlottesville, leaving in four columns, carrying off many negroes with them. A detail of their subsequent operations is, for the present, contraband.

AN ANONYMOUS REPORT: REPORT OF FIGHTING AROUND PETERSBURG

The Appomattox Campaign, Lee's last, officially began on 29 March when Grant's army moved to cut the Southside Railroad, Petersburg's major supply line. The following story describes some of the early action in the campaign that led up to the first decisive battle of the campaign at Five Forks on 1 April.

Augusta Constitutionalist, 1 April 1865 (Augusta, Ga.)

FROM PETERSBURG

RICHMOND, March 30.

The Petersburg Express of this morning says:

Last night at 11 o'clock the enemy opened on our lines near the Appomattox with a fearful artillery fire, while a simultaneous movement made on the part of their infantry.

The troops of Gen. Gordon repulsed the troops with coolness.

Up to 12 o'clock the fighting was continued with great rigor and fierceness.

The enemy in all made five separate assaults—all of them being repulsed.

The enemy's loss must have been immense.—They came in swarms, supposed to be several lines, and we are informed that the slaughter was fearful.

The gallantry of our troops was displayed in the most gratifying manner. Their conduct is the theme of universal praise. During the entire fight, which lasted two hours, not a man was seen coming to the rear.

P.S.—An officer just from the front says the enemy charged up within ten feet of the muzzles of our guns, and were literally mowed down. Our loss unprecedentedly small.

LATER FROM PETERSBURG

RICHMOND, March 30.

Passengers from Petersburg say that the reports of the fight last night are greatly exaggerated. The enemy made demonstrations on a portion of General Gordon's lines, and were repulsed.

The cannonading was very heavy, and distinctly heard here.

AN ANONYMOUS REPORT: NEWS OF UNION BREAKTHROUGH AT PETERSBURG

Grant's army had begun moving in late March, and by 1 April, it was poised for the final assault on the beleaguered Petersburg. The attack came on 2 April. Lee was able to hold off Grant all through the day, but that night he began the evacuation of his forces from Richmond and Petersburg toward Amelia Courthouse.

Richmond Examiner, 3 April 1865

THE WAR NEWS

The decisive battle of the war in Virginia, as far as concerns the fate of Richmond, is believed to have been fought yesterday. On Friday and Saturday there had been preliminary skirmishing of a determined character on the Petersburg lines, but not until daylight yesterday morning did the storm of battle burst with all its fury. At that hour General Grant made a general attack upon General Lee. The front of battle was many miles in extent, stretching from Appomattox east of Petersburg, south of that city, and thence westward to the Southside railroad. General Lee's lines were penetrated in several places, and all attempts to recover the lost ground were unsuccessful.

This is believed to decide the fate of Richmond. It is not for us to write any particulars as to the future.

AN ANONYMOUS REPORT: LATEST FROM LEE'S ARMY

Readers were anxious for the latest news from Virginia, and miraculously, the telegraph lines continued to reach the lower South. The news, though, was not encouraging, despite this writer's feeble attempt to offer some ray of hope by mentioning Northern casualties and the supposed fear in the North about the prospects of war with a foreign nation. Nevertheless, Lee was still on the run, fighting was heavy, and prospects for the South were growing dimmer daily.

Augusta Constitutionalist, 11 April 1865 (Augusta, Ga.)

LATEST FROM LEE'S ARMY
HEAVY FIGHTING

DANVILLE, April 9.

General Lee has moved to the vicinity of Farmville, followed by Grant, fighting daily.

There was heavy fighting on Thursday. No particulars.

The enemy have established hospitals at the Junction, where there is a large number of their wounded. Their loss was very heavy in the late fights.

They are not approaching this way on the line of the Richmond and Danville Railroad.

Communication being still open to Keysville.

A wounded soldier who escaped from the enemy says they are very uneasy about a foreign war.

It is reported that a courier from the army brings a New York Herald which says, the Emperor Napoleon recognized this Government on the 5th of March.

LATER FROM DANVILLE

DANVILLE, 9th.

A column of cavalry is reported at Henry C.H. Thirty eight miles from here, probably Stoneman's.

A slight skirmish took place near there Saturday without results.

A column of the enemy is reported near Lynchburg.

Persons coming out from Richmond confirm the burning and say the enemy treated the blacks very harshly.

AN ANONYMOUS REPORT: EVACUATION OF RICHMOND

Lee's army was no longer able to protect Richmond. His soldiers evacuated, the Confederate government fled, and citizens were left to fend for themselves as best they could. Davis and his government evacuated on 2 April, hoping to reestablish the Confederate cause in the trans-Mississippi. They took with them the treasury and as many government papers as they could carry. Many citizens did not have the luxury of escape; they had nowhere to go. The Richmond mayor and his staff met a small party of Union officers around 5:30 A.M. on 3 April with a flag of truce. Later that morning, U.S. flags were raised over city hall

*and the state capitol. The fleeing Confederate army had set fires that decimated a huge section of
the city.*

Augusta Constitutionalist, 14 April 1865 (Augusta, Ga.)

THE EVACUATION OF RICHMOND

The Danville (Va.) Register of Wednesday, April 6th,
states that persons who left the capital Sunday night and
Monday morning, represent that the scene which followed
the evacuation of the city by our troops, beggars all description. To preserve order and protect the property of the citizens who unavoidably remained there, as far as could be
done, the 19th Virginia militia under Colonel Evans, was
placed on police duty in the city, to await the coming of the
enemy; but accounts state they failed to render any aid or
protection to the people whatever. On Sunday night a mob of
the lower classes of the city, composed, it is said, mostly of
the foreign element, visited a number of the largest store
houses of the city and robbed them of their contents.

It is affirmed that Main street was pillaged and then
burned, and that some of the milling establishments were
also committed to the flames. We have no doubt that a considerable portion of that brave city has been laid in ashes,
and a number of its people insulted, outraged, robbed and
massacred. How painful the thought that the place should be
given over to rapine and plunder even before the public enemy entered its limits! But the fact only proves that the people of Richmond have had secret enemies in their own midst
scarcely less savage and even more treacherous and vindic-
tive than the open foe.

We are told that the people banded together, during the violent proceeding of the mob, and resisted them with force, a
street fight ensuing in which several persons were killed.

No intelligence has reached us of the enemy's troops occupying the city. The last trains on the Danville railroad which
came out of the place left Monday morning, and passengers
upon them had heard nothing from the enemy. The greater
portion of Grant's army was transferred to the southside of
James river some days ago, only the command of Gen Ord,
which is composed mostly if not entirely of negro troops, being left on the north side. This command will enter and occupy the city. Some of our people who are acquainted with

the character of Gen. Ord, think they have reason to hope
that his treatment of the unfortunate people of Richmond will
not be so hard and cruel and inhuman, as that which has
fallen upon the heads of our fellow citizens in some other
captured cities.

All the specie and other valuables belonging to the banks
in Richmond was removed from the city on Sunday, and have
been carried to places of safety.

A considerable amount of goods purchased by the State,
for distribution to the people, we regret to learn, had to be left
behind. Also the archives remained in the city, but we perceive no motive the enemy can have in destroying them, as
they will, no doubt, endeavor to occupy the city permanently
and establish a State Government at Richmond under the
Federal Union.

The newspapers of Richmond, we suppose, all fell into the
hands of the enemy. The evacuation of the city was so sudden
and unexpected—scarcely any one being prepared for it—
that no time was left for the removal of so cumbrous an establishment as a city newspaper office. In a few days we may
expect to hear that the Enquirer or the Whig or the Examiner
is issued as a Yankee paper.

All the rolling stock of the Richmond and Danville railroad, in running order was saved, on the retreat from Richmond. A few old cars, not in a movable condition were left at
Manchester. No trains were captured by the enemy near the
Junction, as was at one time reported; and indeed we do not
believe that any body of Yankees had struck the road, at any
point up to yesterday evening.

The Secretary of War, the Quartermaster General, Commissary general, and a number of other officers of the Government left Richmond on horseback, and will probably
arrive at this place to-morrow.

Should General Lee establish his lines east of the June-
tion, we suppose the State Legislature will be convened at
Lynchburg.

CARTOUCHE: TERRIBLE BATTLE OF PETERSBURG

The Constitutionalist *took from its exchanges with the* Danville Register *another story of the fall of
Richmond, this one written by the Virginia newspaper's correspondent as he fled the Confederate capital
on the last train out. The writer's story was told with great excitement and sadness. The Confederacy's
hopes had all died. The cause was lost.*

Augusta Constitutionalist, 19 April 1865 (Augusta, Ga.)

FROM THE DANVILLE REGISTER
TERRIBLE BATTLE OF PETERSBURG, 2D OF APRIL

ON CARS TO DANVILLE,
April 3d, 1865.

Richmond is fallen—Petersburg captured—our noble army defeated! Sad day. Secretly and silently, Grant moved a heavy force from north of the river, on Saturday, the 1st of April, the fight commenced, but on Sunday the decisive battle was fought. The enemy's line of battle extended from the banks of the Appomattox, east of Petersburg, thence westward to the Southside railroad. The Confederate lines were penetrated at several points and the unity of the army destroyed. Loss on both sides very heavy; the precise amount not ascertained at this early date. It is said that General A. P. Hill was killed and Fitzhugh Lee mortally wounded. Lane's N.C. Brigade is cut to pieces and captured. General Longstreet came up with reinforcements, but was utterly unable to restore the order of battle. General Gordon drove the enemy back and succeeded in regaining his lost positions, except that of Rive's salient; Gordon is regarded as the hero of the day.

On the reception of this news, all Richmond was in the greatest consternation. Every truck, dray or other carriage that was in the city was placed in immediate requisition on Sunday afternoon. Main street was covered with vehicles taking out beds, chairs and other furniture from the city. People running in every direction with anxious countenances enquiring the news. Greatest activity prevailed in Government offices; heads of departments, packing up records and shipping by rail. The President and other high officials left at 8 P.M., on a special train. At night a lawless mob commenced breaking open stores, restaurants, banking houses, and this morning the sidewalks were covered with the debris of the gutted establishments. As I hurried down Main street at an early hour this morning, on my way from the hotel to the depot, I noticed particularly the houses of Powhatan Weiseger and Genet; they were turned upside down. The loss of the latter was estimated at $500,000.

A little after midnight the city was terribly concussed by the explosion of the magazines of ironclads Virginia, (Commodore Semmes' flag ship,) the Richmond, Fredericksburg and Torpedo, and of the wooden ships Raleigh, Hampton and Nansemond. After daybreak the Patrick Henry, (used as a school ship) and the Schrapnel were destroyed. The shock was so severe that the panes of glass were shivered in the Spotswood Hotel. There were no bridges burnt over James river at the hour of our leaving (8 A.M.) save that of the Petersburg and Richmond railroad. The burning of that costly structure was one of the most magnificent sights that I ever beheld.

As the cars rolled off, we were told that Mayo's bridge was burnt. The crackling flames and falling timbers of Haxall's immense buildings, other contiguous houses, reports of bursting ordnance, explosion of bombs at the Laboratory and Arsenal, the devoted city enveloped in thick wreaths of pitchy smoke; (its localities identified only by the thickest smoke of more recent explosions, or the fiery tongues of the leaping flames,) presented a sight, the like of which, may I never see again. The quartermaster's establishment at the basin, commissary's quarters, the Gallego Mills and Haxall's tobacco warehouses and lots, with whole acres of tobacco, the shipping at Rookett's, and perhaps immense amounts of other property beyond the reach of my vision, were all on fire about the hour of sunrise.

From the stand point of your correspondent, south of the James, the unfortunate metropolis seemed to be one vast funeral pyre.

At 3 P.M., on Sunday afternoon, the Legislature was called together; no quorum appearing, it adjourned to meet at some other place.

The Dispatch is the only paper on to-day that I have seen; do not know whether any other is out, as the second class militia were all out yesterday and last night.

This is written on the last train leaving Richmond. No rolling stock that can be moved is left behind. Two detached locomotives follow this train. Admiral Semmes and all the personnel of the navy have just entered the cars. We are now six miles of Burkville (junction) and hear that a body of Yankees are there pressing us. An artillery officer, our latest arrival from Richmond, crossed the James in a canoe, says the enemy entered the city, and an officer (supposed Yankee general) was addressing a crowd from the Washington monument.

I have seen the last of Richmond—poor, unhappy Richmond. Heaven save her the fate of Columbia.

CARTOUCHE.

AN ANONYMOUS REPORT: CAPITULATION OF LEE'S ARMY

A few days after announcing Lee's capitulation, the Constitutionalist *ran a full article on the surrender at Appomattox. The story is prepared from information taken from the* South Carolinian, *then in publication at Charlotte. The section of the story that dealt with Lee's proffer of his sword and Grant's refusal is, according to modern historians, merely apocryphal. Articles such as the following one were indeed the stuff of which legends were made.*

Augusta Constitutionalist, 23 April 1865 (Augusta, Ga.)

CAPITULATION OF LEE'S ARMY

General Lee a Prisoner of War
Sad Details

From the Carolinian we make a summary of the sad intelligence below. Prior to the eventful Sunday of capitulation, and from the evacuation of Richmond and Petersburg, our army suffered from retreat and disasters, and was sorely pressed from overwhelming odds, but still fought bravely, until completely surrounded:

Sunday, April 10th—A bright, clear, beautiful day, but it opened gloomily. Our army had reached Appomattox Court House, on the road to Lynchburg. Thomas, with his army, had arrived before us and effected a junction with Grant; cavalry, infantry and artillery completely surrounded our little command. We had from five to eight thousand prisoners, and only eight thousand effective men with muskets, all told. The supply of ammunition was nearly exhausted. In this emergency General Lee determined to cut his way through. Orders were given for a grand charge, and our troops massed accordingly.

General Grimes' division led the charge, followed successively by two others. The engagement commenced shortly after sunrise, and was continued until our men had broke through the Federal lines, driven them nearly a mile and a half and captured several pieces of artillery, and some hundreds of prisoners. The old spirit of fight was unsubdued. Meanwhile a heavy force of cavalry threatened our flanks. For some reason General Lee issued orders to the troops to cease firing and withdraw.

Subsequently an officer, said to be Gen. Custar of the Yankee cavalry, entered our lines with a flag of truce. Whether his appearance was in response to a request from General Lee, or he was the bearer of a formal demand for the surrender initiated by Gen'l Grant, we are not informed. At this time, our army was in line of battle on or near the Appomattox road, the skirmishers thrown out, while 250 yards from these, over an emanence, was a large body of federal cavalry.

Soon after the return of Gen. Custar to his lines, Gen. Grant, accompanied by his staff, rode to the headquarters of Gen. Lee, which were under an apple tree near the road. The interview is described as exceedingly impressive. After the salutatory formalities, which were doubtless brief and business-like, General Lee tendered his sword to Grant in token of surrender. That officer, however, with a courtesy for which we must accord him due respect, declined to receive it, or receiving it declined to retain it, and accompanied its return with substantially the following remarks:

"General Lee keep that sword. You have won it by your gallantry. You have not been whipped, but overpowered and I cannot receive it as a token of surrender from so brave a man."

The reply of Gen. Lee we do not know. But Grant and himself are said to have been deeply affected by the occasion and to have shed tears. The scene occurred between ten and eleven o'clock A.M., when the sad event became known to the army, officers and men gave way to their emotions and some among the veterans wept like children. A considerable number swore that they would never surrender and made their way to the woods. Generals Gary of South Carolina and Rosser of Virginia, with a few followers, cut their way out and escaped. But the bulk of the army, the men who for four years have done battle so nobly for the cause, together with leaders like Longstreet, Gordon, Kershaw and others whose names are forever distinguished, were obliged to accept the proffered terms.

These were—capitulation with all the honors of war—officers to retain their side arms and personal property and the men their baggage. Each one was there upon paroled and allowed to go his way.

During Sunday and Monday a large number of Federal soldiers and officers visited our camps and looked curiously on our commands, but there was nothing like exultation, no shouting for joy and no word uttered that could add to the mortification already sustained. On the contrary every symptom of respect was manifested, and the southern army was praised for the noble and brave manner in which it had defended our cause.

The force of the Yankee army is estimated at 200,000. Our own, at the time of surrender, embraced not more than 8,800 effective infantry and 2,000 cavalry, but it is said that the total number paroled was about 23,000 of all arms and conditions.

All the Federals spoke of General Lee in unbounded praise. The remark was frequently made "he would receive as many cheers in going down our lines as Gen. Grant himself."

It is understood that Gens. Lee, Longstreet and other officers are now on parole in the city of Richmond.

The following is a true copy of General Lee's address to his army, issued after the surrender to General Grant at Appomattox C.H., on Sunday April 9th, 1865.

HEADQUARTERS ARMY NORTHERN VA.
April 10, 1865.
GENERAL ORDERS,
No. 9
After four years of arduous service marked by unsurpassed

courage and fortitude, the Army of Northern Virginia has been compelled to yield to overwhelming numbers and resources.

I need not tell the brave survivors of so many hard fought battles who have remained steadfast to the last, that I have consented to this result from no distrust of them. But feeling that valor and devotion could accomplish nothing that could compensate for the loss that would have attended the continuance of the contest I determined to avoid the useless sacrifice of those whose past service have endeared them to their countrymen.

By the terms of the agreement officers and men can return to their homes and remain until exchanged. You will take with you the satisfaction that proceeds from the consciousness of duty faithfully performed, and I earnestly pray that a merciful God will extend to you his blessing and protection.

With unceasing admiration of your constancy and devotion to your country and a grateful remembrance of your kind and generous consideration for myself, I bid you an affectionate farewell.

R. E. LEE, General.

Below is a special order embracing Gen. Grant's order for the passage of paroled soldiers to their homes and also the form of pass given them.

HEADQR'S ARMY OF N.V.

April 10, 1865

Special Order

No. ————.

All officers and men of the Confederate service paroled at Appomattox C. H. Va., who, to reach their homes are compelled to pass through the lines of the Union armies, will be allowed to do so, and to pass free on all Government transports and military railroads.

By command of Lt. Gen. Grant.,
E.S. Parker,
Lt. Col. A.A.G.

By command of
R. E. LEE
C. L. Venable, A.A.G.

[Form of pass.]

APPOMATTOX, C. H., VA.,

April 10th, 1865.

The bearer ———— of Co ———— right ———— of ————, a paroled prisoner of the Army of Northern Virginia, has permission to go to his home and there remain undisturbed.

Lastly is the form of the parole of honor signed by commanding officers of divisions &c., in behalf of the men of their command. This is taken from a copy of one signed by General Fitz Hugh Lee.

I, the undersigned, commanding officer of ———— do for the within named prisoners of war belonging to the army of Northern Virginia, who have been this day surrendered by Gen. R. E. Lee, C.S.A., commanding said armies, to Lieut. Gen. U. S. Grant, commanding the armies of the United States, hereby give my solemn parole of honor that the within named shall not hereafter serve in the armies of the Confederate States or in any military capacity whatever against the United States of America, or render aid to the enemies of the latter, until properly exchanged in such manner as shall be mutually approved by the respective authorities.

Done at Appomattox Court House, Va., this 9th day of April 1865.

AN ANONYMOUS REPORT: DEATH OF LINCOLN REPORTED

The assassination of President Abraham Lincoln sent shock waves through people of both the South and the North. For the first time in the history of the nation, a chief executive's life had been taken by a disgruntled citizen. The assassination of Lincoln by a Southerner, John Wilkes Booth, further enflamed passions of Northerners who were already demanding that the South be punished for its rebellion.

Augusta Chronicle and Sentinel, 27 April 1865 (Augusta, Ga.)

THE DEATH OF LINCOLN

DeQuincy in that strange essay "Murder considered as one of the Five Arts," has collected a multitude of instances not unlike the tragedy at Ford's Theatre, which resulted in the death of the President of the United States. As we anticipated, it has aroused a tempest of indignation throughout the North, but the more sober journalists are disposed to regard it as the act of a half crazy fanatic; while none, we believe, have been so reckless as to charge the Confederate authorities with complicity in this design.

Assassination for political ends has rarely occurred amongst civilized nations. The assassination of Caesar by Brutus and his fellow-conspirators, was an ill-advised affair; and as is well known, proved the overthrow of the Senatorial party and paved the way to the Imperial rule of Augustus. The murder of Henry Fourth was prompted solely by religious fanaticism and was so far successful in its aims that next to the St. Bartholomew massacre it did more than any single event to root out the reformed religion from France. The assassination of William of Orange at Delft was likewise the offspring, in part, of religious fanaticism and it inflicted a stunning blow on the rising Dutch Republic. Fortunately, however, it came too late to be of any material service to the Spanish cause.

The assassination of Abraham Lincoln is the first example of the kind that has occurred in American history. John Wilkes Booth, the individual accused of the deed, is the third son of J. B. Booth, an actor of some celebrity in the past generation, who resided for many years in the vicinity of Baltimore, is about thirty years of age, a professional actor of reputation— and altogether, fine looking, if not prepossessing in appearance. He is represented by the Northern papers as a fierce secessionist and personally hostile to Lincoln, having frequently given vent to his feelings during the war. His trial, which we suppose will be conducted according to the form of law, will doubtless rank with the *cause celebres* of all countries.

ANDREW JOHNSON: PRESIDENT JOHNSON'S AMNESTY PROCLAMATION

The fighting in the Civil War ended with the surrender of Lee's army at Appomattox and Johnston's army in North Carolina, but the political machinations were only beginning. Many in the North favored harsh punishment for the Southern states they believed had been in rebellion for the previous four years. President Andrew Johnson, though, favored a more magnanimous ending and offered liberal terms of amnesty to the South's former combatants. This was one of his early missteps—from the perspective of the Northern Congress—that would eventually lead to an attempt to impeach Johnson.

Augusta Chronicle and Sentinel, 3 June 1865 (Augusta, Ga.)

PRESIDENT JOHNSON'S AMNESTY PROCLAMATION

Through the kindness of an official stationed at Atlanta, the Intelligencer of that city has been favored with the perusal of the Chattanooga Gazette of May 30. From it is taken the following important telegraphic report containing the President's Amnesty Proclamation. We hope soon to lay before our readers the Proclamation itself in all its details. What we present below embraces only the Oath to be administered and the exceptions prescribed in this amnesty.

THE OATH

I do solemnly swear or affirm in the presence of Almighty God that I will henceforth faithfully defend the Constitution of the United States and the union of the States, and will abide and faithfully support all laws and proclamations which have been made during the existing rebellion with references to the emancipation of slaves. So help me God.

PERSONS EXCEPTED

All who have been civil, diplomatic or otherwise, domestic or foreign agents of the pretended Confederate States.

All who left Judicial stations under the United States to aid the rebellion.

All Military and Naval Officers above the rank of Colonel in the Army, and Lieutenant in the Navy.

All who left seats in the Congress of the United States.

All who resigned or tendered the resignation of their commissions in the Army and Navy of the United States.

All engaged any way in treating otherwise than lawfully as prisoners of war persons forced (found) in the United States service.

All Military and Naval Officers who were educated in the United States.

All the pretended Governors in the insurrectionary States.

All who left their homes within the Federal lines and passed into the rebel lines to aid the rebellion.

All who have engaged in the destruction of the commerce on the high seas, and all who have made raids from Canada or engaged in destroying commerce on land and rivers.

All who at the time when they seek to obtain benefit hereof by taking the oath and remain in military, naval or civil confinement, or under bond of military or naval authorities as agents of the United States, prisoners of war, or persons detained for offenses of any kind whether before or after conviction.

FURTHER READINGS

Davis, William C. *The Last Days of the Confederate Government*. New York: Harcourt, 2001.

Fonvielle, Chris Eugene. *The Wilmington Campaign: Last Rays of Departing Hope*. Campbell, Calif.: Savas, 1997.

Hitchcock, Henry. *Marching with Sherman: Passages from the Letters and Campaign Diaries of Henry Hitchcock, Major and Assistant Adjutant General of Volunteers, November 1864–May 1865*. New Haven, Conn.: Yale University Press, 1927.

Korn, Jerry. *Pursuit to Appomattox: The Last Battles*. Alexandria, Va.: Time-Life Books, 1987.

Marvel, William. *A Place Called Appomattox*. Chapel Hill: University of North Carolina Press, 2000.

Rawl, Miriam Freeman. *From the Ashes of Ruin*. Columbia, S.C.: Summerhouse Press, 1999.

Simms, William Gilmore. *Sack and Destruction of the City of Columbia, S.C.* Columbia, S.C.: Power Press of Daily Phoenix, 1865.

Trudeau, Noah Andre. *The Last Citadel: Petersburg, Virginia, June 1864–April 1865*. Boston, Mass.: Little, Brown, 1991.

Winik, Jay. *April 1865: The Month That Saved America*. New York: HarperCollins, 2001.

7

THE CONFEDERATE HOME FRONT: WOMEN AND SLAVES, SACRIFICE AND VALOR

Women fought the Civil War, just as men did. Their battles and their battlefields were different, and their weapons were as well, but without the contributions of women, the Confederate army and the Confederate cause would have been severely disabled. Women sacrificed food, money, companionship, clothing, and leisure so as to provide for their families, both those members at home and those at the front. They raised money, sewed garments and flags, and cared for ill and injured soldiers in hospitals or even in their private homes. Some women were even forced to go so far as to take jobs outside their homes. While this was not necessarily anything new for lower-class women, it certainly was for women of the upper social echelons. Further, lower-class women, in particular, replaced men as essential labor in factories and on farms, and upper-class women, many for the first time ever, were left on their own to manage hearth, home, fields, and slaves without the support and protection of a man.

Women of all classes also faced shortages and deprivations, particularly as the war became more and more protracted. Some women, even of the middle to upper classes, were forced to buy secondhand clothing. When soldiers came through, either the enemy's or the Confederacy's, women were often left with little. Lower-class women, especially, faced tough times with food shortages, no money, and no man to do the heavy physical labor around the farm. In some Southern cities, including Richmond, Virginia, and Columbus, Georgia, women of the lower classes would become so desperate to feed their children later in the war that they resorted to rioting to call attention to their plight. In Richmond in 1863, more than 1,000 women rampaged through the streets and looted shops. Women and their children suffered especially from the South's wartime economic problems and the high prices speculators charged for necessary goods.

Many upper-class Southern women were strong supporters of secession and war, at least initially. Women of the lower classes were almost immediately forced to contend with the realities of life without a male provider or head of household. For women who had been brought up expecting male protection as their due, coping on their own was demanding.

Because of their strong support for the war and the fact that they were used to a type of rarified treatment as due their gender, women were more likely than men to challenge the Yankees with taunts and jeers. In occupied New Orleans, women were so rude and so provocative to General Benjamin Butler's troops that he was finally compelled to issue an order that proclaimed any woman arrested for her conduct toward Union soldiers would be treated as a prostitute. "Woman of the town" was the term Butler used, but his implication was clear. Southerners were so appalled by his order that they nicknamed the general "Beast Butler," an epithet that followed him throughout the war in the Southern press.

Slaves and free blacks were also denizens of the home front during the Civil War, and their experiences were documented, too, in Southern newspapers, though not to the same level as that of women. Early in the war, newspapers often carried articles about loyal slaves who stood with their white masters in their support for the war for Southern independence. Even free blacks were depicted as supporting the war effort through donations of money or flags to Confederate combat forces in which they would not have been allowed to serve, even had they wanted to. As the war progressed, though, and the availability of Southern manpower declined, blacks, usually slaves, were mustered into the army to serve as teamsters, cooks, or officers' valets. In late 1864, the shortage of men became so acute that Jefferson Davis asked, and Congress seriously considered, drafting slaves into the Confederate army with the promise of emancipation for military service.

J.C.C. FEATHERSTONE OR JAMES A. HOYT: "THE WHEEL OF LIFE"——SIX ARTICLES ON NINETEENTH-CENTURY SOCIAL THOUGHT AND VALUES

The following six articles appeared as a unit in the third column on page 1 of the 1 November 1860 edition of the Anderson Intelligencer *of Anderson, South Carolina, and are representative of the types of "improving" articles that many Southern newspapers carried during the antebellum and Confederate periods. These articles were intended primarily for female readers and, in some cases, to be used as material to assist mothers as they taught their children to read. To twenty-first-century readers, the articles provide helpful insight into the "mind" of Southerners and into nineteenth-century Southern values. The article headed "The Advantages of Necessity" is particularly useful in explaining the thinking that allowed Southerners to own slaves and to proscribe a more restrictive lifestyle for women in the region. Southerners accepted the idea that all people are born to a particular station of life, what they termed a "sphere." Women and slaves lived in the private sphere behind the fence gate because of their alleged inherent inferiorities to white men. Men were considered to live in the public sphere due to their various involvements and entanglements with the world outside the home.*

Slaves were considered family members, just like children were, though they had none of the rights and privileges of white children. Southerners believed slaves were born into bondage because that was where God decreed they should be. Such ideas are abhorrent today but were as commonplace and accepted in the nineteenth century as our more enlightened twenty-first-century notions that women should be paid the same as men for the same work and that people of all races are entitled to the same civil rights.

Anderson Intelligencer, 1 November 1860 (Anderson, S.C.)

THE WHEEL OF LIFE.—Man is the most destructive of beings. He pursues the great leviathan within the polar circle to light his home. He ransacks the sea and land in every latitude; he slays and plunders with unsparing hand. He enslaves the horse, camel, and elephant, he robs and slaughters the ox, the sheep, the swine, the bee, the beaver, and the worm; the fowls do not escape him, and he levies taxes on everything taxable. In this manner he gathers his food and his raiment, the balsam of his diseases, and the fuel that cheers his hearth. Despite the ravages of diseases, and violent and natural deaths he increases in number, every season opens to him as bountiful a supply as before. In civilized life he is often a prey to numberless accidents, to the beasts of the fields, and the monsters of the deep. If he escape these, at the last he becomes food for worms. Man eats his mutton, and the lion eats man. One law encircles, directs and confines all created beings—each within its proper sphere. The evil that befalls one, the other cannot escape—disease and death are the lot of all.

THE ADVANTAGES OF NECESSITY.—If every man were wise and virtuous, capable to discern the best use of time, and resolute to practice it, it might be granted, we think, without hesitation, that total liberty would be a blessing; and that it would be desirable to be left at large to the exercise of religious and social duties, without the interruption of importunate avocations.

But since felicity is relative, and that which is the means of happiness to one man may be to another the cause of misery, we are to consider, what state is best adapted to human nature in its present degeneracy and frailty. And, surely, to the far greater number it is highly expedient, that they should by some settled scheme of duties, be rescued from the tyranny of caprice; that they should be driven on by necessity through the paths of life, with their attention confined to a stated task, that they may be less at leisure to deviate into mischief at the call of folly.

PLEASURE OF CONTENTMENT.—I have a rich neighbor who is always so busy that he has no leisure to laugh; the whole business of his life is to get money, and more money. He is still drudging on, saying that Solomon says, "The diligent hand maketh rich." And it is true, indeed; but he considers not that it is not in the power of riches to make a man happy, for it was wisely said by a man of great observation, "that there be as many miseries beyond riches as on this side of them." We see but the outside of the rich man's happiness; few consider him to be like the silk-worm, that, when she seems to play, it is at the very same time spinning her own bowels, and consuming herself. And this many rich men do—loading themselves with corroding cares, to keep what they have already to. Let us, therefore, be thankful for health and competence, and above all, for a quiet conscience.

JUDGE NOT RASHLY.—Alas! how unreasonable as well as unjust a thing it is for any to censure the infirmities of another, when we see that even good men are not able to dive through the mystery of their own! Be assured there can be but little honesty, without thinking as well as possible of others, and there can be no safety without thinking humbly and distrustfully of ourselves.

THE BEST MEDICINE.—Good, wholesome food, and temperance, with pure, cold water to drink, and bathe in, with fresh air, plenty of exercise, and a clear conscience, are said to do more to restore or preserve health, and prolong life, than every doctor and medicine in the universe.

OUR COMMON INDEBTEDNESS.—Of those whom Providence has qualified to make any additions to human knowledge, the number is extremely small; and what can be added by each single mind, even of this superior class, is very little. The greater part of mankind must owe far the larger part of it, to the information of others.

D. A. HOBBIE OR B. H. THRASHER: EDITORIAL—THE PLACE OF WOMEN

The place of women in nineteenth-century America was the home. They lived within the fence gate, and their role was to care for the household. With this limited role, though, came a sort of veneration that is strikingly odd, compared to more modern ways of thinking. Women were vessels of purity and domesticity, and those were considered high callings, worthy of great honor. However, as this editorial from an Alabama newspaper indicated, men also well understood that women had reserves of strength that could carry them through hard times.

Troy Southern Advertiser, 4 January 1861 (Troy, Ala.)

WOMAN.—Place her among flowers, foster her as a tender plant, and she is a thing of fancy, waywardness, and sometimes folly—annoyed by a dew drop fretted by the touch of a butterfly's wing, and ready to faint at the rustle of a beetle; the zephyr are too rough, the showers too heavy, and she is overpowered by the perfume of a rosebud.—But let real calamity come—rouse her affection—enkindle the fires of her heart, and mark her then; how her heart strengthens itself—how strong is her purpose. Place her in the heat of battle—give her a child, a bird—any thing she loves or pities, to protect—and see her, as in a relative instance, raising her white arms as a shield, as her own blood crimsons her upturned forehead, praying for life to protect the helpless.

Transplant her in the dark places of earth—awaken her energies to action, and her breath becomes a healing—her presence a blessing. She disputes, inch by inch, the stride of the stacking pestilence, when men, the strong and brave, shrinks away pale and afrighted. Misfortune haunts her not; she wears away a life of silent endurance, and goes forward with less timidity than to her bridal. In prosperity she is a bud of odors, waiting but for the winds of adversity to scatter them abroad—pure gold, valuable, but untried in the furnace. In short, woman is a miracle—a [unreadable] the centre from which radiates the great charm of existence.

C. E. HAYNES: SOUTHERN WOMEN AS NURSES

Armies from throughout the new Confederate States of America began massing in Virginia after the shelling of Fort Sumter and Lincoln's immediate call for 75,000 volunteers to put down the Southern rebellion. Southerners and Northerners alike knew it was only a matter of time until their armies clashed. Nurses would be necessary once the conflict escalated to outright war, and with so many men under arms, that role would likely fall to women. Already in the North, according to the Cahaba Gazette, *women were volunteering to nurse sick and wounded soldiers, just as the most famous military nurse of the day, Florence Nightingale, had during Britain's Crimean War. The paper suspected that Southern women would be called on to fulfill the same role—and would be up to the task—despite their more delicate upbringing. This article offers an excellent view of how women were viewed in the Old South and just how much the war would change their place in that society. The reference to Pensacola at the very end of the article calls attention to the city's importance as a port and the recent confrontation there over another coastal installation, Fort Pickens.*

Cahaba Gazette, 31 May 1861 (Cahaba, Ala.)

NURSES

The ever famous FLORENCE NIGHTINGALE did much to alleviate the sufferings of her sick and wounded countrymen, and set an example to her sex which will be followed by them in all countries. We see that great numbers of Northern women have volunteered as nurses to the Northern troops. Southern women are more delicately nurtured than those of the North, and have not been at all accustomed to being brought into rude or disagreeable contact with the sterner sex. We will not say that they have more real virtue than the women of the North, but they have been taught to be more reserved in their intercourse with men.

But stern times have come upon us, and our women must prepare themselves to perform stern and disagreeable duties. Like angels of mercy, they must visit our brave defenders and nurse them in their sickness and in their wounds, and must smooth their dying pillows. It needs not prompting from us to remind them of their duty. They will perform it, God bless them, willingly.

It is with pleasure we copy the following from a late number of the Montgomery Advertiser:

Some time ago a letter was sent from Columbus, Georgia to President Davis, written by a patriotic lady, offering her services and those of several young ladies as nurses during the war. The President expressed much gratification at the offer, and spoke in commendable terms of the ladies of Columbus. It seems they are still active in good work for the soldiers. The Enquirer contains the following:

The Ladies of Columbus held meetings on Tuesday and Wednesday morning, and organized a "Soldiers' Friend Society," the object of which is to perform Woman's part in the service of their country in time of war.—The officers elected are Mrs. A. Chappell, President; Mrs. Robt. Carter, Vice President; Mrs. J. A. Urquhart, Secretary; and Mrs. Richard Patton, Treasurer.

In addition to this we will state that a letter has been received from Dr. THOMAS LENOIR (son of Maj. JAMES M. LENOIR), who belongs to Col. WITHERS' Regiment, in which he says he was left near Norfolk, with 30 or 40 sick under his charge, and that the ladies of the neighborhood—rich and poor, young and old—came to his assistance and tenderly nursed the brave men who had come from Alabama to defend Virginia from invasion.

The ladies who read our paper, we know, will be ready to go to the place where their services may be needed, and in such numbers as will be necessary. If our own friends and neighbors at Pensacola should get into a fight, or if disease should spread among them, they should first be attended to.

JOHN HARVEY: HOW SOUTHERN WOMEN SUPPORT THE CONFEDERATE WAR EFFORT

Women were prevented by their gender and by rigid social roles in the nineteenth-century South from participating directly in the Civil War. However, they played vital supporting roles, particularly as nurses and caregivers for sick and wounded soldiers, seamstresses who made clothing and knitted socks for the men at the front, and as fund-raisers who gathered money and goods for the Southern armies. This article recognizes the efforts of local women—especially those from the country—in gathering winter clothes for soldiers serving in the Virginia mountains.

Alabama Beacon, 2 August 1861 (Greensboro, Ala.)

RESPONDING TO THE CALL.—The ladies of this section are responding promptly, and in a most patriotic spirit to the call made upon them for clothing for the soldiers. Mr. Carson has already received quite a number of articles sent in from the country, which will be forwarded at an early day.

As the nights will soon be getting cool in the mountainous regions of Virginia, the soldiers should be supplied with woolen clothing—especially drawers and undershirts—as early as possible, certainly by the first of September. Flannel shirts, made to fit loosely, and good woolen socks, also made large—(no sock, or shoe, that fits closely, is suitable to march in)—are essential to the health and comfort of the soldier.

JOAN: FEMALE CORRESPONDENT DESCRIBES WOMEN'S WAR WORK

Women's contributions to the Confederate cause were often overlooked by male correspondents and editors who might be likely to publish brief articles thanking women for their contributions but who were not always aware of the work that went into knitting twelve pairs of socks or sewing uniforms. Joan, a correspondent for the Charleston Courier *in Virginia, was familiar with women's work, and in this story, she painted a clear picture for her readers that at first seems to be a color piece about life in Richmond. The article took a bend, though, to touch on the work by Richmond women to tend to the needs of the South's soldiers. One of the more interesting stories to which Joan gives only a brief mention is that of Major General John C. Frémont, commander of the Union's Western Department, which included Missouri. Frémont shocked the nation, and caused big headaches for President Lincoln, when he issued his own Emancipation Proclamation in Missouri. He also declared martial law in that state and threatened to court-martial any man found armed in the Union-controlled areas of Missouri. The article is remarkable, too, because it was written by a woman. Because Southern women lived in the private sphere, few ever wrote for publication. That Joan was willing to do so is an indication of how, even early in the war, women's roles were already changing.*

Charleston Courier, 7 September 1861

CORRESPONDENCE OF THE COURIER

Richmond, September 3, 1861.

Every interest of life in Richmond is secondary to military considerations. If you pass a cabinet warehouse, you see nothing exposed for sale but camp bedstands, camp stools, cots for hospitals and the like, while the exposition of wares at the tinners is confined almost wholly to tin cups and pans, coffee pots and canteens. Tent makers establishments are numerous. If you go to a shoe store and asked to be measured for a pair of gaiters, they will tell you they take none but Government; or to a saddler's establishment, and ask even the small favor to have a handle repaired on your traveling bag, you meet with the same reply. You cannot get a piece of goods woven at a factory in the State for private use; they are under contract to manufacture alone for the Government, while a statement of operations at the Armory at this place, together with the Military Institute at Lexington, says that since the 1st of April they have issued 61,954 arms and 186 pieces of cannon; have re-bored 200 pieces of artillery, mounted them on good carriages, and carefully prepared the accompanying caissons, and mounted 40 brass field pieces. Military trappings are exposed in about every third shop window, and signs informing you of the whereabouts of military tailors are frequent—though I should suppose they would hardly find much to do, so diligent are the ladies with their needles. Hundreds of ladies have been sewing every day since last April—many of them from eight o'clock in the morning until dark, and when the work was hurrying, have had their dinners sent to them. Some among them, unused to such toilsome service, have had their health seriously impaired by it. Very many have ignored in a great [*unreadable*] all social and domestic ties to devote themselves to this labor of love. Each church has its own organization, and officers wanting clothing made for their men no matter of what description, can always get it done by applying to the rooms. Then when you remember that almost every man's house is thrown open to the sick, and that ladies are continually passing about in their carriages laden with delicacies for the sick at the hospitals, and edibles for the haversacks of the departing soldiers, you will realize something of the all-absorbing interest felt in those who are defending our rights.

The New York Times has a very gloomy article upon the war. It says the people are giving millions of dollars and hundreds of thousands of men, but the country reaps no benefit from the gift, and they look to the War Department as being responsible for the "disheartening disappointment." The peace feeling at the North is increasing, and has so alarmed Lincoln that he has issued another royal edict, declaring that the Administration regards all Peace Conventions as in the highest degree treasonable, and all advocates of peace as traitors, and prescribing the Conventions advertised to be held in Maryland and Kentucky on the 10th inst. It is possible that before that time Maryland will be beyond his jurisdiction, and Kentucky—will she stand such dictation? Fremont's abolition proclamation may well be received by them with amazement; they can see their own doom foreshadowed in it if they stand paralyzed much longer. East Tennessee is gracefully yielding in the matter of allegiance to her State, and the loud mouthed demagogues who were so anxious to see her kneeling at Lincoln's feet are now foremost among those who oppose his rule. The protestations of those who go only with the tide are valuable to us merely as indications of which way the tide is running. Fremont has over reached himself. Had his proclamation been a little more

moderate, he might possibly have retained a party about him. If he would like to know how many will sustain him in it let him count the number of Yankee hirelings by whom he is surrounded, and he can tell to a man, for well we know that no Southerner living can ever stoop low enough to have such a yoke fastened around his neck. If he has any in his ranks who claim to be Southerners let him watch them well; they do but bide their time. It is said one company of "Fremont Body Guards," numbering eighty well mounted cavalry, deserted in a body and made tracks for Gen. Pillow's quarters, and that desertions are constantly occurring.

A New York correspondent of a Philadelphia paper is distressed at the Secession sympathy manifested in New York. He says "I am not sure that an army of Confederates invading New York would not find a good amount of their own colors waiting for them. There is a dreadful state of sentiment here; of this there is no doubt." And another states that two hundred men in Belfast, Maine, have received muskets from Boston and armed themselves, declaring they will resist any attempt made to collect war taxes, or to draft any of their men. It is the leaven of interest working which is stirring up the peace feeling. There are, too, hundreds of thousands of people who know as confidently as we do that there is no question about our ultimate success, who would be as ready perhaps as any to prosecute the war, if they thought there was any possibility of their being able to accomplish their aims, but convinced of the fruitlessness of them would fain desire ere they are driven more deeply into the vortex of ruin.

The Washington Cabinet seem very anxious to devise some plan by which they may be able to retain the benefits of the telegraph themselves, and at the same time deprive us of them. They will hardly succeed, though it seems Kentucky has consented to a censorship. Seward has made a very convenient errand to New York. We do not hear that Lincoln and Scott have followed suit, but it is more than likely they have. The atmosphere of Washington is perhaps too heavily charged with electricity to please them.

It seems the Union gun which has been held up to us as such a formidable monster, one which was to prove so efficient in our subjugation, signally fails in its execution, not only requiring a great many men but a great deal of time to load and fire it, but it cannot throw a projectile either with directness or precision, nor is the range satisfactory.

It seems the people of Quincy, Ill., are getting excited upon the subject of an attack. They may well expect retaliation from us, for their encroachments. Even Christian forbearance does not demand of us always to sit with folded hands, and tamely take their insults. We should not have submitted as quietly as we have, had we not known our power; it will not be long now before they will be made to know it. Our President, when he was a member of the Washington Congress, in his closing speech before them, exhibited to them in glowing colors the advantages we would have over them in a conflict. The day is not far distant when they will appreciate his logic.

Some fifty Yankee prisoners came in last night, many of them wounded. All we heard about their capture was, that they were taken on the Potomac, in a skirmish. The prisoners in the city have been allowed to go to market, under a guard, and purchase such supplies as they choose to pay for; but I understand orders have been given to put a stop to it. I do not know why. The guard now does the marketing for them.

JOAN.

SOUTHRON: TRIBUTE TO THE WOMEN OF THE SOUTH

As the Civil War moved into its second year, the demands on Southern women became greater. Not only did they give their husbands, sons, and fathers to the army, they also contributed their labor in sewing or nursing sick soldiers and their household supplies to keep the soldiers fed. This story, which ran in the Christmas Day edition, served as a tribute to the South's women and their contributions but also as a recognition of the power—informal though it be—of women. The mention of "Roman matrons" and of the "mothers of '76" was typical of the day. Southerners identified with the Roman republic, and they esteemed the War of Independence and its leaders as the great cause of great Americans. In reality, women were not always so patriotic nor so patient with the new roles in which they were cast as a result of the war. Many women, for example, wrote to the Confederate government to send their men home because they were having trouble accomplishing their agricultural work or supervising their slaves without a strong male presence. Still, though overly romanticized and showing little real understanding of what the life of a typical woman was like, the article is a nice tribute to those women who were making sacrifices for the war.

Troy Southern Advertiser, 25 December 1861 (Troy, Ala.)

THE WOMEN OF THE SOUTH

Woman, in all ages of the world, has been the ruling spirit; from the time when Mother Eve decoyed Adam to taste of the forbidden fruit, til the present time, woman, exerting her power over man, has wielded the destinies of the world.

Man may for a time resist her power, but woman's influence is felt throughout the whole civilized world. It is to our mothers and our sisters that we all owe what little of goodness, politeness or generosity we may possess; and peculiarly is this true of the women of the present age. The Roman matrons had justly been celebrated for their devotion to their country; and the Spartan mother, who told her son to return with his shield, or on it, will be remembered by all posterity. To the memory of Josaphine, of Madame Roland, of Charlotte Corday, and many other noble women of the perilous times of the French Revolution, be many a line inscribed.

Our mothers of '76 will always be remembered by their sons with pride, that they are the descendants of such women; but to the brave Southern women of '61, it has been reserved to excel in devotion to the cause of liberty, love of their country, and in the predominance of those virtues which should characterize a soldier's wife or mother. We read of women, who, in the revolutionary times, when our forefathers gained the liberty which we have inherited, repulsed the insolent British soldiery when they attempted to insult or plunder, and we have read of some who fought for their country, but where is an example equal to that of the brave and noble lady, who replied when asked if she really desired her husband to go to war, "I do not like to be separated from him. It will be a terrible trial; but some must go; and between submission to the North and a separation from my husband, it is easy to choose. I cannot go and fight, but I can stay and take his place on the plantation while he is gone. Let him go and do his duty, and I will stay and do mine."

And there are thousands of just such women all over the Confederacy. Their language is, "If we cannot fight, we can stay at home and take care of our husbands' crops, and take the places of our brothers." Young ladies, who a year ago, were not esteemed of any use, but to pore over embroidery or while away their time at the piano, are now engaged in knitting socks, making uniforms, or sewing on underclothing for our brave volunteers. Ladies, who not long since thought it a disgrace to work, are now engaged in teaching school, or take the places of their brothers behind the counter.

Such is the character of our Southern women; and with such mothers and sisters to encourage us in our brave work what need we fear? As I have frequently heard it observed, before the hordes of the North could conquer us, the very women and children would meet the invaders of their peaceful homes, and drive them from their hearth stones. No! the South can never be conquered. We are fighting for our homes, for our loved ones, and while one spark of Southern blood flows through the veins of the free people, submit we will never.

SOUTHRON.

AN ANONYMOUS REPORT: ACCOUNT OF SOUTHERN WOMEN OUTWITTING YANKEES

Confederate newspapers published many articles celebrating the accomplishments of Southern women during the war, particularly when those accomplishments involved outwitting Union forces. This story, taken from the Richmond Dispatch, *purports to have a Northern source and tells an amusing story about a pro-Southern woman who fled Washington, D.C., for Richmond. The story served a double purpose—it was amusing and entertaining, but also such stories about the supposedly weak and frail woman outsmarting the Union soldier served the purpose of building Confederate morale; for certainly if a Southern woman could best a Yankee soldier in repartee, it would be a small matter for a Southern man to do the same thing on the battlefield.*

Richmond Dispatch, reprinted in the *Savannah Republican*, 5 March 1863

SOUTHERN WOMEN.—On the occasion of the recent departure of women for the South, from Washington, some remarkable developments took place. A Yankee correspondent says:

One lady had seven pairs of gaiters, five pairs of boots, five pairs of morocco slippers, three pairs of dancing slippers of white kid, four pairs of India rubber overshoes, and a pair of the longest legged cavalry boots, with double soles, studded with good spikes, heels tapped with shoes of iron, and tops splendidly ornamented with an abundance of patch work of waxed ends on a ground work of patent leather.

"How about these, madam?" said the officer, as he quietly insinuated the cavalry boots into her astonished gaze. "If you

will put them on and wear them on your trip to Richmond, you can take them, but they can go with you under no other circumstances."

"Done—I'll do it," said the heroine, and grasping the heavy leather in her hands, she retired behind the friendly crinoline of a group of sympathizers, and planting her pretty feet—gaiters and all—into the depths of that monstrous foot harness, returned, and awkwardly displayed them, double-cased, to the gaping eyes of the this time astonished official. He kept his word. The boots went to somebody in the Confederate army, or they may have been an intended Christmas present for Gen. Stuart. These secesh women do such things.

Richmond Dispatch.

ANONYMOUS REPORT: USEFUL ADVICE FOR WOMEN—A SUBSTITUTE FOR BREAD

Newspapers would not add women's pages for more than half a century, but they were already carrying news of interest to women. Often during the Civil War, the stories would offer advice on how to stretch staples or what could substitute for what. This became particularly useful information as shortages and speculation on prices placed many kinds of goods out of the reach of many women. The following article on bread originally appeared in the Edgefield Advertiser *in South Carolina.*

Edgefield Advertiser, reprinted in the *Savannah Republican*, 20 March 1863

A SUBSTITUTE FOR BREAD.—Now that meat is hard to get about our villages and towns, we recommend lie-hominy as a good substitute, at least as a change. The simple plan of preparing it is follows: To a gallon of shelled corn add a half gallon of good ashes. Boil together until the husk begins to come off the corn. Then rub briskly to clear the grain completely of husk. Wash the corn clear and boil it for ten or twelve hours, adding water from time to time to keep it from

burning. It is then ready, and has only to be warmed over for use as it is needed. It is perhaps better fried. This is said to be more wholesome than big hominy, and it is as good diet as corn bread, if not better. It is easy to prepare, and saves the toll. Most housekeepers know how to make it; but a few may not be informed on this important subject; and we pen this paragraph for their benefit.—

Edgefield Advertiser.

JAMES R. SNEED: CAREER OF A FEMALE VOLUNTEER

While most women contented themselves with aiding the war effort through traditional women's work, a handful shouldered arms and took to the battlefield. Mrs. Laura J. Williams volunteered after being deserted by her Yankee husband at the beginning of the war. Other women also were documented as serving in both the Union and the Confederate armies. For lower-class women, one of the inducements for joining up was the pay. With their husbands away, and the Confederate government often unable to pay the salaries promised to soldiers, uneducated women of the under classes had few legal ways of earning money.

Savannah Republican, 29 June 1863

CAREER OF A FEMALE VOLUNTEER

Among the registered enemies of the United States government who have been recently sent across the lines from New Orleans, there is now in Jackson, Mississippi, a lady whose adventures place her in the ranks of the Molly Pitchers of the present revolution. At the breaking out of the war Mrs. Laura J. Williams was a resident of Arkansas. Like most of the women of the South, her whole soul was enlisted in the struggle for independence. Her husband was a Northern man by birth and education, and a strong Union man. After Arkansas seceded from the Union he went to Connecticut, he said, to see his relations and settle up some business. Mrs. Williams suspected his purpose and finally she received information that he had joined the Yankee army. The Jackson Mississippian gives the rest of her history:

She disguised herself in a Confederate uniform, and adopting the name of "Henry Benford," she proceeded to Texas, where she raised and equipped an independent company, and went to Virginia with it as 1st Lieutenant. She was in the battle of Leesburg and several skirmishes; but finally her sex having been discovered by the surgeon of the regiment—the 5th Texas Volunteers, to which the company had been attached—she returned to her home in Arkansas. After remaining there a short time she proceeded to Corinth, and was in the battle of Shiloh, where she displayed great coolness and courage. She saw her father on the field, but, of course, he did not recognize her and she did not make herself known to him. In the second day's fighting she was wounded in the head and was ordered to the rear. She wrote to her father, and then came on down to Grenada where she waited for some time, but never saw or heard from him.

She then visited New Orleans, was taken sick, and while sick the city was captured. On recovery she retired to the coast, where she employed herself carrying communications and assisting parties to run the blockade with drugs and cloth for uniforms. She was informed on by a negro and arrested and brought before Gen. Butler. She made her appearance before Gen. B. in a Southern homespun dress. She refused to take the oath—told him she gloried in being a rebel—had fought side by side with Southern *men* for Southern rights, and if she ever lived to see "Dixie" she would do it again. Butler denounced her as the most incorrigible she-rebel he had ever met with. By order of the Beast she was placed in confinement where she remained three months. Some time after her release, she was arrested for carrying on "contraband correspondence," and kept in a dungeon fourteen days on bread and water, at the expiration of which time she was placed in the State Prison as a dangerous enemy. Her husband, it so happened, was a Lieutenant in the 13th Conn. Regiment, and on duty as provost guard in the city. He accidentally found her out and asked if she wanted to see him. She sent word she never wanted to see him so long as he wore the Yankee uniform. But he forced himself upon her, tried to persuade her to take the oath, and get a release, when he said he would resign and take her to his relations in Connecticut. She indignantly spurned his proposition, and he left her to her fate. When Gen. Banks assumed command he released a great many prisoners, but kept her in confinement until the 17th of May last when she was sent across the lines to Meadesville with the registered enemies.

An article was recently published in the New York World in relation to the part Mrs. Williams has played in this war, but the above is, we are assured, a true account of her remarkable career. We understand she has attached herself to the medical staff of a brigade new in this city, and will render all the assistance in her power to the wounded in the approaching struggle for possession of the great Valley of the Mississippi.

JAMES R. SNEED: GEORGIA WOMEN RIOT AGAINST SHORTAGES

As prices soared, speculators preyed on civilians at home; as shortages grew worse, some Confederate women decided to take matters into their own hands. Bread riots occurred in several Southern cities, including the capital at Richmond. The women were frustrated at their inability to find food at affordable prices for their families and for the lack of government aid to the families of soldiers in the field. Large cities were not the only locales for these protests; hinterland towns were not immune to female unrest, either. The shortages could be accounted for in part by the impressment of goods for use by the military. The story below mentions the problem Georgia had had in 1861 with overpriced salt and is a reference to the shortage of salt experienced throughout the South during the war. Salt was an essential item for preserving meat, but because of the military demand for it, it was in short supply. Georgia Governor Joseph E. Brown, quite a Populist, had used state resources to acquire salt that could be distributed to poorer families at reasonable prices.

Savannah Republican, 13 April 1863

AMAZONIANS.—On Thursday and Friday last, feeble outbreaks of females armed with pistols and bowie knives, headed by a few vagabonds, were made in Augusta, Milledgeville and Columbus, in this State, for the purpose of helping themselves to merchandize at what they considered fair prices—all of which were promptly suppressed by the proper authorities.

The Columbus Sun, alluding to the affair in that city, says:

This is some of the legitimate fruits of what Gov. Brown is pleased to call "impressments" for the benefit of the *people*! It began in this state with that functionary, two years ago, in Atlanta, or other markets in Georgia, where salt was selling at ten and twelve dollars per sack, and has culminated in just such riots and lawless outbreaks as we witnessed in Columbus this morning.

AN ANONYMOUS REPORT: PATRIOTIC FEMALES MAINTAIN TELEGRAPH COMMUNICATION IN GEORGIA

Women did not limit their contributions to the war to merely nursing and sewing for the soldiers. Some undertook very practical, but very dangerous, chores, as did Mrs. Blackman and Miss Carrie Simms who did their best to ensure that the Confederate army in north Georgia did not lose its telegraphic communications, despite the efforts of Yankee raiders.

Memphis Appeal, 14 May 1864

PATRIOTIC FEMALES.—A correspondent of the AP-PEAL, a few days since, stated that when the party of Yankee raiders cut the telegraph wires between Resaca and Tilton, that two ladies, whose names he did not learn, united the wires, on the retreat of the foe. The *Intelligencer*, of yesterday, gives the following version of the occurrence, with the names of the noble women: "A portion of the enemy succeeded in getting to the railroad at Green's station, three miles above Resaca, and immediately set fire to the wood shed and cut the telegraph wire. Being apprehensive, no doubt, that they were risking their lives, they did not remain very long to enjoy the mischief they supposed they had done. As soon as they left, Mrs. Blackman and Miss Carrie Simms, daughters of Col. Henry L. Sims, who are living near, carried water and extinguished the burning wood shed, and then attempted to mend the telegraphic wire. Their strength was not sufficient to accomplish this feat; but still they continued their efforts until Capt. Clerk of our forces, came up, when, with his assistance, these patriotic ladies succeeded in drawing up and uniting the wires."

D. A. HOBBIE OR B. H. THRASHER: STORY OF YANKEES OUTWITTED BY A SLAVE

The following untitled tale is no doubt apocryphal and was probably meant as a joke on abolitionists. However, it had a second theme that was also important: the clever slave who bested a bunch of not-so-bright Yankees. Such stories were intended to play to Southern feelings of superiority over Northerners, but it is placed here because it reflects contemporary attitudes about blacks as well. After all, many Southerners believed, if a slave could outwit a Yankee, there could be no question that the Confederate army would easily whip the North's, should the Yankees be so stupid as to begin a war over secession.

Troy Southern Advertiser, 4 January 1861 (Troy, Ala.)

A short time ago, a widow lady living near the northern line of Missouri, sent her negro man with a load of wheat to a mill in Iowa, to have it manufactured into flour.—The mill was much crowded on his arrival there, and the prospect was that he would have to wait several days for "his turn."— While waiting, some of the "freedom shriekers" in that latitude got around the darkie and proposed aiding him in securing his freedom. The negro seemed to be struck with the idea but did not have any money to pay his expenses.

"Well," said they, "sell your mules."

"Dont know bout dat, missus couldn't get'long widout dem," said Cuff.

"Well, then," rejoined they, "you can sell the wagon, that will bring the money."

"Well, I believe, missus needs the wagon, too," answered the black, "but if I had de wheat ground, I could sell de flour, dat wud fetch de money."

"Oh, well," said the negro equalists, "we will swap you flour for your wheat to accommodate you."

So the trade was made. The wheat was exchanged for the proper portion of flour and the colored man was loaded all ready to drive off and sell his flower. But when he was about ready to start, he said, "Massa I's binstudyin bout freedom, but I don't believe missus can spare the flour either," and drove off with a grin, displaying two rows of ivory, much to the mortification of the negro-loving Iowains.

JAMES R. SNEED: DEDICATION OF FIRST AFRICAN BAPTIST CHURCH OF SAVANNAH

Religion was an important part of life for both Southern whites and blacks. The completion and dedication of a newly completed church for a black Baptist congregation was a significant community event that would be attended by representatives of all classes. Civic and religious activities of blacks, both free and slaves, got more coverage in the Confederate press than might be supposed.

Savannah Republican, 4 May 1861

FIRST AFRICAN BAPTIST CHURCH

The new and tasteful house of worship just finished by this congregation on Franklin Square, will be dedicated on Sabbath next, with appropriate exercises. To avoid interfering with the regular morning services of other congregations, some of whom wish to attend, the services will commence at 12 o'clock in the following order:

1st, Anthem by the Choir.

2d, prayer by Rev. D. G. Daniell.

3d, Reading Scriptures and Hymn by Rev. D. O. Tibeau.

4th, Sermon by Rev. S. Landrum.

5th, Dedicatory Prayer by Rev. S. G. Daniel, of Albany, Ga.

6th, Doxology and Benediction.

The building is of brick and contains a lecture room in the basement, and a main audience room above, with galleries on the sides and end. The audience will seat, comfortably, 700 persons. The house is neatly finished, plastered and painted. The pulpit is white and pews oaked, and the aisles covered with oil cloth. The house is provided with a good organ, which will be played on the occasion by a young lady of this city.

The cost of the building is a little over $10,000; about $1,500 still unpaid.

The Trustee, masters of the servants, citizens generally, and Baptists especially, are invited to attend the dedication, and to contribute to the payment of the debt.

JAMES R. SNEED: OUR FREE COLORED POPULATION

Free persons of color were in a difficult position when the Civil War broke out. There was considerable pressure for all Southerners, white and black, to fall in line and support the Confederate war effort. A number of free blacks did volunteer to aid the military, and it is an open question as to whether they did so out of Southern patriotism or because they believed they must in order to protect themselves and their families.

Savannah Republican, 11 June 1861

OUR FREE COLORED POPULATION

It is gratifying to witness the public spirit that rules among this class of our community. Not content to be idle spectators of the military operations progressing for the defense of the State against invasion, they have nobly come forward and offered their services, as will appear from the following written tender addressed to General Lawton:

TO BRIGADIER GEN. LAWTON,
Com. Military District.

The undersigned free men of color, residing in the city of Savannah, and county of Chatham, fully impressed with the feeling of duty we owe to the State of Georgia, as inhabitants thereof, which has for so long a period, extended to ourselves and families its protection, and has been to us the source of many benefits,

Beg leave respectfully, in this the hour of danger, to tender to yourself our services, to be employed in the defence of the State, at any place or point, at any time, or for any length of time, and in any service for which you may consider us best fitted, and in which we can contribute to the public good.

Signed by fifty-five free men of color.

The Commanding General promptly accepted their proposition, and yesterday fifty-five able bodied men embarked on board the steamer *Ida*, for the military works below the city. Their services are entirely voluntary without any stipulation for pay, and many more were ready to go, but as they constitute an important branch of our fire department, is was thought best not to spare them from the city.

Such bearing on the part of our colored population is worthy of all praise, and our authorities will doubtless see to it that they lose nothing by their devotion to their State and country.

D. A. HOBBIE OR B. H. THRASHER: MAINTAINING CONTROL OF SLAVES WHILE THE MEN ARE AWAY AT WAR

Despite the bravado about the loyalty of their slaves, there was much anxiety among Southerners regarding the bondsmen. A major concern was that so many men were away, serving in the army. That left women in charge of slaves, often large numbers of them, and the women themselves felt inadequate to meet the demands of motivating and disciplining their slaves. This editorial put those concerns into words.

Troy Southern Advertiser, 31 July 1861 (Troy, Ala.)

LOOK OUT.—It is very important at the present time for our citizens to keep a sharp watch over the slaves of the country. There is no knowing what is brewing among them. Almost every one knows something of the difficulty that is going on and has vague ideas as to the cause of it. Some no doubt suppose that old Abe is really coming South, having heard white men speaking in a jesting manner about his threatened visit to Richmond and Montgomery. And now men leaving our own part of the country and every one speaking of the battles that are being fought, the negroes may shape their dark imaginations into a belief that Lincoln is really advancing to Montgomery. There can be nothing wrong with taking care now that the country is being depopulated by men volunteering for the war. The absence of

men, will cause some negroes to feel a degree of importance, independence and restlessness, which they would not otherwise possess.—The negro who has always been obedient in the presence of his master, may in his absence become the most turbulent and disobedient. Add to this the knowledge of the negro—(for they are close observers of the movements and diligence of white men) that a careful watch of superintendence is not kept over them, and the probability of disobedience and turbulence is increased. Whereas if they discover that a sharp look out is kept over them they will be afraid to attempt or do many things they otherwise would do. We would not become alarmists but we wish to call the attention of our people to this thing so that due care may be taken of it.—A patrol, simply the knowledge of one's existence has a great influence on the slave, to keep him in his place. In some parts of the country, not even these are in existence. Every man should strictly superintend his own premises during the present time. A little neglect might be the cause of much trouble. Let our citizens then look out.

HENRY CLEVELAND: TREATMENT OF SLAVES AND FREE BLACKS—MAY DAY PARTY FOR BLACK "ELITES"

An Augusta newspaper gave considerable space to the story of a May Day party for the "elite" of the local black society. It did so not because its editors believed the story deserved such coverage in and of itself but to use the story as an illustration of how slaves and free blacks were treated in the South. The party story ran only a few months after Lincoln's Emancipation Proclamation, and the paper specifically mentioned the Union president, saying it wished the Yankee administration could only see how closely Southern slaves resembled in dress and manners the "wage slaves" of the North. There was one major difference between the South's black slaves and the "wage slaves" of the North: One was free, and the other was not.

Augusta Constitutionalist, 3 May 1863 (Augusta, Ga.)

SABLE CORONATION

The "Americans of African descent" in our city had quite a novel and *recherche* entertainment on Friday night, at which the elite portion of our "colored siety" was out in full leather. The festival consisted of the coronation of a May Queen, a supper, and a dancing party. The affair was gotten up by permission from the authorities, with city officers in attendance. Every thing was done up *a la mode*. The addresses were rehearsed, and the queen wore her honors with a degree of taste and majesty that would have illustrated the court of the Queen of Dahoumey in her palmiest days. The court costumes were unexceptional—the muslins and tarletons ethereal—the white kids immaculate—the wreaths gorgeous and of a redolence rivalling the native frangipane. The table groaned beneath a wealth of cakes and condiments that would tempt an epicure, and the wines—yes the wines—were pronounced by a testing committee of "buckra's" present, to be fragrant with the "boquet" of purity and age.

The dance was equally *au fad*; none of your Ethiopian fandangos, but such a combination of square dances and round dances, and squeezing dances, (we are ignorant of the technical names) as would have met the admiration of Professor Nimbleheels, the dancing master.

But enough, perhaps some may say, too much, of this festival of the colored people. We allude to it to show the way in which the "poor slave" wears his chains in these days of scarcity and suffering. We wish Lincoln and his Cabinet could have looked on that happy throng, that they might have compared them with the deluded beings they are dragging from happy homes to the squalid want and degradation of a quasi freedom. Aye, that he might have compared them in dress and manners, or elasticity of spirit, with the working classes who cringe and fawn beneath his despotic rule.

The admission fee to this festival was $5, and woe to the darkey whose finances were not equal to the crisis. While we regard the frequent recurrence of negro balls in our city as mischievous, we see no objection to allowing them to hold occasional holiday festivals. They have always been the favorite pastimes of the slave, from the grotesque fandangos of the Gold Coast, to the diablerie of the "Dios de Reyes" in the West Indies. They are about the only people on this continent whose spirits are not bowed down with care or suffering, and who may with propriety and taste indulge in frivolous amusement.

RUTH RAYMOND: CONVERSATIONS WITH MY FEMALE FRIENDS—THE LIKELY CONSEQUENCES OF THE WAR FOR SOUTHERN WOMEN

The following is a truly amazing article for two reasons. First, it is one of only a handful of bylined articles located in any Confederate newspaper; second, it was written by a woman. Further, Ruth Raymond, the author, accurately predicted what the outcome of the Civil War would be for Southern women: an entirely new way of life where privilege and special status due to one's gender gave way to the realities of earning a living.

Darlington Southerner, 28 October 1864 (Darlington, S.C.)

CONVERSATIONS WITH MY FEMALE FRIENDS BY RUTH RAYMOND
AN HONORABLE INDEPENDENCE

There is one fact, which sooner or later, our Southern women must look boldly in the face—and that is how they can best gain *an honorable independence.*—Hitherto, as a class, they have depended on the exertions of their male relatives, or looked to matrimony as a source of support. Many a woman sooner than exert herself in her own maintenance has married a man for whom she cared about as much as she did for the Emperor of China, nay, even whom she positively loathed. No wonder when matrimony is only a thing of convenience, and people rush into it utterly regardless of affection or congeniality, that we hear of so many unhappy matches, so much strife and selfishness, so little of the genuine sunshine of love. Better, far better is it for a woman to live a single life of honorable independence, supporting herself by her own exertions than thus to perjure herself by a loveless marriage; looking upon man not as a companion and friend, but as a disagreeable appendage to the purse strings, something which in taking the purse has to be taken with it. This is a degrading view certainly for women to take of the most sacred of all human connections.

The immense slaughter of our male population caused by this terrible war, has thrown many women on their own resources for a living. In the future, the women of the South must preponderate greatly over the males. Where will husbands be found for one third of them? The hope of marrying for a living, then, will be utterly cut off. The inroads of the enemy, too, upon our lands, and the immense destruction and capture of property, has deprived many a Southern woman of a comfortable home and support, and thrown her upon the cold charities of the world. Many a luxurious Southern girl, who dressed in velvet and diamonds, lived in a costly mansion, and was waited upon by liveried servants, now finds herself suddenly shorn of these bright possessions, and with the stern necessity of doing that from which her very soul recoils—gaining her own livelihood. But exiled royalty has had to do the same; and the struggle of the French Revolution threw the future of Queen of Holland, the beautiful Hortense into a milliners shop. With the prospect then before them of gaining their own living, the question naturally occurs how can the women of the South best meet the emergency before them? The one great idea now appears to be to rush into the "note department" in Columbia, where the work is light, and the pay good.—But as the services of *all* needy Southern women are not required in this charitable institution, many must necessarily be excluded. The times do not admit of new boarding-houses being opened, nothing then remains but teaching. The avenues of business for a woman, especially at the South, are very few. At the North they have their female physicians, a class rapidly increasing, and much patronized by their own sex; female clerks are numerous, female writers, who gain support by their literary labors, and painters, who dare to compete in this field of labor with their brother artists. The School of Design, too, has by its instructions afforded women a pleasant means of subsistence. The women of the South are greatly restricted in their means of support. Perhaps the most common and the most useful is that of teaching. This opens a wide sphere of usefulness; and though I cannot see with a friend, who has been engaged many years in this honorable employment, "the poetry of teaching," it is not, at all events, the worse prose. There was a time—and I fervently pray that this time has forever past, when we thought that unless our young ladies were sent to the North to be educated, or we obtained Northern teachers for them, that they were not properly instructed. So well aware are the Yankees themselves of this fact, a fact disgraceful to the South, that they have never ceased to exultingly remind us of it. Now, why was this? Not that as a people we have not as much brains as those of the North, not that we have not sufficient intellectual force and training to fit us for good teachers, but because our Southern women refused to come before the world in this capacity. Sooner would they be a clog on some unwilling male relative, than thus shake off the iron shackles of dependence. They would rather sell themselves to some unworthy or unloved suitor than live a true, honest life of independence.

But our people are at fault here too. Whilst they encouraged Northern adventures, whilst they freely gave up their children to be influenced by Yankee teachers, home merit, home industry, was entirely overlooked, ignored, despised.—Whilst the Yankee teacher could count her pupils by the fifties, the Southern lady counted hers by the fives. Of course, discouraged, disappointed, she retired from the field, leaving it to her exultant rival; and her example proved a beacon-light to others. I say that I earnestly pray that the time for this prejudice has forever past, and that Southern people are prepared to recognize Southern talent, and encourage Southern industry.—If not, then we must make up our minds to continue in the future what we have been in the past, mere vessels and dependents of the North, looking to them for our goods, our literature, our education. There is no reason why we should not, indeed, there is every reason why we should, educate our own children. Let our women come out nobly and independently, and educate the youth of the land. Let all who feel themselves fitted for this work, and whose circumstances require an exertion on their part, exert their talents in this useful field. Let the women of the South be so educated, that it will be needless to encourage Yankee teachers. Let every exertion be made to educate thoroughly the girls of the present day, so that we may have properly qualified female teachers of our own—women, who whilst they are occupying an honorable and useful position, can yet be gaining a respectable livelyhood, an agreeable independence.

FURTHER READINGS

Bailey, Anne J., and Joslyn, Mauriel. *Valor and Lace: The Roles of Confederate Women, 1861–1865.* Murfreesboro, Tenn.: Southern Heritage Press, 1996.

Berlin, Ira. *Free at Last: A Documentary History of Slavery, Freedom, and the Civil War.* New York: New Press, 1992.

Blair, William Alan. *Virginia's Private War: Feeding Body and Soul in the Confederacy, 1861–1865.* New York: Oxford University Press, 1998.

Campbell, Edward D. C., and Rice, Kym S. (Eds.). *A Woman's War: Southern Women, Civil War, and the Confederate Legacy.* Richmond, Charlottesville: Museum of the Confederacy, University Press of Virginia, 1996.

Durden, Robert Franklin. *The Gray and the Black: The Confederate Debate on Emancipation.* Baton Rouge: Louisiana State University Press, 1972.

Faust, Drew Gilpin. *Mothers of Invention: Women of the Slaveholding South in the American Civil War.* Chapel Hill: University of North Carolina Press, 1996.

Jordan, Winthrop D. *Tumult and Silence at Second Creek: An Inquiry into a Civil War Slave Conspiracy.* Baton Rouge: Louisiana State University Press, 1993.

Leonard, Elizabeth D. *All the Daring of the Soldier: Women of the Civil War Armies.* New York: W. W. Norton, 1999.

McCline, John. *Slavery in the Clover Bottoms: John McCline's Narrative of His Life during Slavery and the Civil War.* Knoxville: University of Tennessee Press, 1998.

Moore, John Hammond. *Southern Homefront, 1861–1865.* Columbia, S.C.: Summerhouse Press, 1998.

Ransom, Roger L. *Conflict and Compromise: The Political Economy of Slavery, Emancipation, and the American Civil War.* New York: Cambridge University Press, 1989.

Vorenberg, Michael. *Final Freedom: The Civil War, the Abolition of Slavery, and the Thirteenth Amendment.* New York: Cambridge University Press, 2001.

Whites, Lee Ann. *Civil War as a Crisis in Gender: Augusta, Georgia, 1860–1890.* Athens: University of Georgia Press, 1995.

SELECTED BIBLIOGRAPHY

BOOKS

Abbott, A. O. *Prison Life in the South: At Richmond, Macon, Savannah, Charleston, Columbia, Charlotte, Raleigh, Goldsborough, and Andersonville, during the Years 1864 and 1865.* New York: Harper & Bros., 1865.

Alexander, Edward Porter. *Fighting for the Confederacy: The Personal Recollections of General Edward Porter Alexander.* Chapel Hill: University of North Carolina Press, 1989.

Alexander, Thomas B., and Beringer, Richard E. *The Anatomy of the Confederate Congress: A Study of the Influences of Member Characteristics on Legislative Voting Behavior, 1861–1865.* Nashville, Tenn.: Vanderbilt University Press, 1972.

Andrews, J. Culter. *The South Reports the Civil War.* Princeton, N.J.: Princeton University Press, 1970.

Ash, Stephen V. *When the Yankees Came: Conflict and Chaos in the Occupied South, 1861–1865.* Chapel Hill: University of North Carolina Press, 1995.

Bailey, Anne J. *The Chessboard of War: Sherman and Hood in the Autumn Campaigns of 1864.* Lincoln: University of Nebraska Press, 2000.

———. *War and Ruin: William T. Sherman and the Savannah Campaign.* Wilmington, Del.: Scholarly Resources, 2003.

Bell, Earl L., and Crabbe, Kenneth C. *The Augusta Chronicle: Indomitable Voice of Dixie, 1785–1960.* Athens: University of Georgia Press, 1960.

Berringer, Richard E.; Hattaway, Herman; Jones, Archer; and Still, William N., Jr. *The Elements of Confederate Defeat: Nationalism, War Aims and Religion.* Athens: University of Georgia Press, 1988.

———. *Why the South Lost the Civil War.* Athens: University of Georgia Press, 1986.

Black, Robert C., III. *The Railroads of the Confederacy.* Chapel Hill: University of North Carolina Press, 1952.

Bridges, Peter. *Pen of Fire: John Moncure Daniel.* Kent, Ohio: Kent State University Press, 2002.

Cardozo, John N. *Reminiscences of Charleston.* Charleston, S.C.: Joseph Walker, Agt., Stationer and Printer, 1866.

Carpenter, Jesse T. *The South as a Conscious Minority, 1789–1861.* Columbia: University of South Carolina Press, 1990.

Carter, Hodding. *Their Words Were Bullets: The Southern Press in War, Reconstruction and Peace.* Mercer University Lamar Memorial Lectures No. 12. Athens: University of Georgia Press, 1969.

Carter, Samuel. *The Final Fortress: The Campaign for Vicksburg, 1862–1863.* New York: St. Martin's Press, 1980.

Clark, Thomas D. *The Southern Country Editor.* Columbia: University of South Carolina Press, 1991.

Cooper, William C. *Jefferson Davis: American.* New York: Knopf, 2000.

Cozzens, Peter. *The Shipwreck of Their Hopes: The Battles for Chattanooga.* Urbana: University of Illinois Press, 1994.

———. *This Terrible Sound: The Battle of Chickamauga.* Urbana: University of Illinois Press, 1992.

Daniel, Larry J. *Soldiering in the Army of Tennessee: A Portrait of Life in a Confederate Army.* Chapel Hill: University of North Carolina Press, 1991.

Davis, Stephen. *Atlanta Will Fall: Sherman, Joe Johnston, and the Yankee Heavy Battalions.* Wilmington, Del.: Scholarly Resources, 2001.

Davis, William C. *Brother against Brother: The War Begins.* Alexandria, Va.: Time-Life Books, 1983.

———. *First Blood: Fort Sumter to Bull Run.* Alexandria, Va.: Time-Life Books, 1983.

———. *"A Government of Our Own": The Making of the Confederacy.* Baton Rouge: Louisiana State University Press, 1994.

———. *An Honorable Defeat: The Last Days of the Confederate Government.* New York: Harcourt, 2001.

———. *Look Away: A History of the Confederate States of America.* New York: Free Press, 2002.

———. *The Union That Shaped the Confederacy: Robert Toombs and Alexander H. Stephens.* Lawrence: University of Kansas Press, 2001.

DeLeon, Thomas Cooper. *Four Years in Rebel Capitals.* Mobile, Ala.: Gossip Press, 1890.

Durden, Robert F. *The Self-Inflicted Wound: Southern Politics in the 19th Century.* Lexington: University of Kentucky Press, 1985.

East, Charles. *Sarah Morgan: The Civil War Diary of a Southern Woman.* New York: Simon & Schuster, 1991.

Eaton, Clement. *A History of the Southern Confederacy.* New York: Macmillan, 1956.

———. *Jefferson Davis.* New York: Free Press, 1977.

Elkins, Stanley M. *Slavery: A Problem in American Institutional Life.* 3rd ed. Chicago: University of Chicago Press, 1976.

Elliott, Robert Neal, Jr. *The Raleigh Register, 1799–1863.* Chapel Hill: University of North Carolina Press, 1955.

Escott, Paul D. *After Secession: Jefferson Davis and the Failure of Confederate Nationalism.* Baton Rouge: Louisiana State University Press, 1978.

Faust, Drew Gilpin. *The Creation of Confederate Nationalism.* Baton Rouge: Louisiana State University Press, 1989.

Gallagher, Gary. *The American Civil War: The War in the East, 1861–May 1863.* Oxford, United Kingdom: Osprey, 2001.

———. *The Confederate War: How Popular Will, Nationalism and Military Strategy Could Not Stave Off Defeat.* Cambridge: Harvard University Press, 1997.

———. *Lee and His Army in Confederate History.* Chapel Hill: University of North Carolina Press, 1997.

———. *The Myth of the Lost Cause and Civil War History.* Bloomington: Indiana University Press, 2001.

————. *The Wilderness Campaign*. Chapel Hill: University of North Carolina Press, 1997.

Genovese, Eugene D. *The Political Economy of Slavery: Studies in the Economy and Society of the Slave South*. New York: Pantheon Books, 1965.

Gibson, John M. Gibso. *Those 163 Days: A Southern Account of Sherman's March from Atlanta to Raleigh*. New York: Coward-McCann, 1961.

Greene, A. Wilson. *Breaking the Backbone of the Rebellion: The Final Battles of the Petersburg Campaign*. Mason City, Iowa: Sawas, 2000.

Griffith, Louis Turner, and Talmadge, John Erwin. *Georgia Journalism, 1763–1950*. Athens: University of Georgia Press, 1951.

Grimsley, Mark. *The Hard Hand of War: Union Military Policy toward Southern Civilians, 1861–1865*. New York: Cambridge University Press, 1995.

Grimsley, Mark, and Rogers, Clifford J. *Civilians in the Path of War*. Lincoln: University of Nebraska Press, 2002.

Grimsley, Mark, and Simpson, Brooks D. *The Collapse of the Confederacy*. Lincoln: University of Nebraska Press, 2001.

Hattaway, Herman, and Beringer, Richard E. *Jefferson Davis, Confederate President*. Lawrence: University Press of Kansas, 2002.

Hennessy, John J. *Return to Bull Run: The Campaign and Battle of Second Manassas*. New York: Simon & Schuster, 1993.

Hess, Earl J. *Banners to the Breeze: The Kentucky Campaign, Corinth, and Stones River*. Lincoln: University of Nebraska Press, 2000.

Huntzicker, William E. *The Popular Press, 1833–1865*. Westport, Conn.: Greenwood Press, 1994.

Jones, Charles Colcock. *The Siege of Savannah in December 1864, and the Confederate Operations in Georgia and the Third Military District of South Carolina during General Sherman's March from Atlanta to the Sea*. Albany, N.Y.: J. Munsell, 1874.

King, William L. *The Newspaper Press of Charleston, S.C.: A Chronological and Biographical History, Embracing a Period of One Hundred and Forty Years*. Charleston, S.C.: Edward Perry Book Press, 1872.

McDonough, James L. *Chattanooga—A Death Grip on the Confederacy*. Knoxville: University of Tennessee Press, 1984.

————. *Five Tragic Hours: The Battle of Franklin*. Knoxville: University of Tennessee Press, 1983.

————. *Shiloh, in Hell before Night*. Knoxville: University of Tennessee Press, 1977.

————. *Stones River—Bloody Winter in Tennessee*. Knoxville: University of Tennessee Press, 1980.

McPherson, James M., and Cooper, William J. *Writing the Civil War: The Quest to Understand*. Columbia: University of South Carolina Press, 1998.

Mohr, Clarence L. *On the Threshold of Freedom: Masters and Slaves in Civil War Georgia*. Athens: University of Georgia Press, 1986.

Moore, Albert B. *Conscription and Conflict in the Confederacy*. New York: Macmillan, 1924.

Moore, John Hammond. *Southern Homefront, 1861–1865*. Columbia, S.C.: Summerhouse Press, 1998.

Neely, Mark. *Southern Rights: Political Prisoners and the Myth of Confederate Constitutionalism*. Charlottesville: University of Virginia Press, 1999.

Osthaus, Carl R. *Partisans of the Southern Press: Editorial Spokesmen of the Nineteenth Century*. Lexington: University of Kentucky Press, 1994.

Putnam, Sallie Brock. *Richmond during the War: Four Years of Personal Observations*. Introduction by Virginia Scharff. Lincoln: University of Nebraska Press, 1996.

Rable, George C. *Civil Wars: Women and the Crisis of Southern Nationalism*. Urbana: University of Illinois Press, 1989.

————. *The Confederate Republic: A Revolution against Politics*. Chapel Hill: University of North Carolina Press, 1994.

Ramsdell, Charles V. *Behind the Lines in the Southern Confederacy*. Baton Rouge: Louisiana State University Press, 1944.

Reasoner, James. *Savannah*. Nashville, Tenn.: Cumberland House, 2003.

Reynolds, Donald E. *Editors Make War: Southern Newspapers in the Secession Crisis*. Nashville, Tenn.: Vanderbilt University Press, 1970.

————. *Southern Newspapers in the Secession Crisis*. Nashville, Tenn.: Vanderbilt University Press, 1966.

Rhea, Gordon C. *Cold Harbor: Grant and Lee, May 26–June 3, 1864*. Baton Rouge: Louisiana State University Press, 2002.

Ringold, Mary Spencer. *The Role of the State Legislatures in the Confederacy*. Athens: University of Georgia Press, 1966.

Robinson, William M., Jr. *Justice in Grey: A History of the Judicial System of the Confederate States of America*. Cambridge: Harvard University Press, 1968.

Sachsman, David B.; Rushing, S. Kittrell; and van Tuyll, Debra Reddin (Eds.). *The Civil War and the Press*. New Brunswick, N.J.: Transaction Publishers, 2000.

Sass, Herbert Ravenel. *Outspoken: 150 Years of the News and Courier*. Columbia: University of South Carolina Press, 1953.

Smith, Culver H. *The Press, Politics and Patronage: The American Government's Use of Newspapers, 1789–1875*. Athens: University of Georgia Press, 1977.

Soley, James Russell. *The Blockade and the Cruisers*. New York: C. Scribner's, 1883.

Spencer, Cornelia Phillips. *The Last Ninety Days of the War in North Carolina*. New York: Watchman Publishing, 1866; reprint, Wilmington, N.C.: Broadfoot Publishing, 1993.

Tatum, Georgia Lee. *Disloyalty in the Confederacy*. Chapel Hill: University of North Carolina Press, 1934.

Turner, George Edgar. *Victory Rode the Rails: The Strategic Place of Railroads in the Civil War*. Indianapolis, Ind.: Bobbs-Merrill, 1953.

Wagner, Margaret E., and Gallagher, Gary. *The Library of Congress Civil War Desk Reference*. New York: Simon & Schuster, 2002.

Wheeler, Richard. *On Fields of Fury: From the Wilderness to the Crater, an Eyewitness History*. New York: HarperCollins, 1991.

White, Laura. *Robert Barnwell Rhett: Father of Secession*. Gloucester, Mass.: Peter Smith, 1965.

Woodward, C. Vann. *Mary Chesnut's Civil War*. New Haven, Conn.: Yale University Press, 1983.

Woodworth, Steven E. *Cultures in Conflict—The American Civil War*. Westport, Conn.: Greenwood Press, 2000.

THE SOUTHERN PRESS

Abbeville Press (Abbeville, S.C.)

Alabama Beacon (Greensboro, Ala.)

Albany Patriot (Albany, Ga.)

Anderson Intelligencer (Anderson, S.C.)

Athens Southern Banner (Athens, Ga.)

Athens Southern Watchman (Athens, Ga.)

Atlanta Intelligencer

Atlanta Southern Confederacy (Atlanta, Ga.)

Augusta Chronicle and Sentinel (Augusta, Ga.)

Augusta Constitutionalist (Augusta, Ga.)

Augusta Evening Dispatch
Cahaba Gazette (Cahaba, Ala.)
Carolina Spartan
Central Georgian (Sandersville, Ga.)
Charleston Courier
Charleston Evening News
Charleston Mercury
Charlotte Western Democrat
Chattanooga Rebel
Columbia South Carolinian
Columbus Enquirer (Columbus, Ga.)
Columbus Sun (Columbus, Ga.)
Daily Morning News (Savannah, Ga.)
Darlington Southerner (Darlington, S.C.)
Edgefield Advertiser (Edgefield, S.C.)
Greensborough Patriot (Greensborough, N.C.)
Greenville Southern Enterprise (Greenville, S.C.)
Hillsborough Recorder (Hillsborough, N.C.)
Live Giraffe (Raleigh, N.C.)
Macon Telegraph and Confederate
Memphis Appeal
Milledgeville Confederate Union (Milledgeville, Ga.)
The Mississippian
Mobile Advertiser and Register
Montgomery Mail (Montgomery, Tenn.)
New Orleans Delta
New Orleans Picayune
New York Herald
New York Times
Raleigh Standard
Raleigh Weekly Standard
Richmond Dispatch
Richmond Examiner
Richmond Sentinel
Richmond Whig
Rome True Flag (Rome, Ga.)
Sandersville Central Georgian
Savannah Daily Morning News
Savannah Republican
Selma Reporter (Selma, Ala.)
Troy Southern Advertiser (Troy, Ala.)
Western Democrat (Charlotte, N.C.)

WEB SITES

The American Civil War Home Page. http://sunsite.utk.edu/civil-war. U.S. Civil War Center. http://www.cwc.lsu.edu.

The Avalon Project at Yale Law School: Confederate States of America Documents. http://www.yale.edu/lawweb/avalon/csa/csapage.htm.

The Civil War Home Page. http://www.civil-war.net.

Civil War Maps. http://memory.loc.gov/ammem/gmdhtml/cwmhtml/cwmhome.html.
Civil War Women: Primary Sources on the Internet. http://scriptorium.lib.duke.edu/women/
     cwdocs.html.
The History Place: The U.S. Civil War, 1861–1865. http://www.historyplace.com/civilwar.
Journal of the Congress of the Confederate States of America, 1861–1865. http://www.yale.edu/
     lawweb/avalon/csa/csapage.htm.
Selected Civil War Photographs. http://memory.loc.gov/ammem/cwphtml/cwphome.html.
The Valley of the Shadow. http://valley.vcdh.virginia.edu.

INDEX

About the Author

DEBRA REDDIN VAN TUYLL is Associate Professor, Department of Languages, Literature and Communications at Augusta State University, Augusta, GA. She is co-author of *The Civil War and the Press* (2000).